CHEERIO AND BEST WISHES

CHEERIO AND BEST WISHES

★ ★ ★

Letters from a World War II Hoosier Pilot

Ralph H. Schneck and Donald R. Schneck

Purdue University Press ★ West Lafayette, Indiana

Printed in the United States of America.

Library of Congress Cataloging-in-Publication Data

Schneck, Ralph H., 1919-
Cheerio and best wishes : letters from a World War II Hoosier pilot / Ralph H. Schneck and Donald R. Schneck.
p. cm.
Includes bibliographical references and index.
ISBN 978-1-55753-640-2 (pbk. : alk. paper) 1. Schneck, Ralph H., 1919---Correspondence. 2. United States. Army Air Forces--Biography. 3. World War, 1939-1945--Aerial operations, American. 4. World War, 1939-1945--Personal narratives, American. 5. Air pilots, Military--United States--Biography. 6. Posey County (Ind.)--Biography. I. Schneck, Donald R. II. Title.
D790.2.S36 2013
940.54'4973092--dc23
[B]

2012029106

To the men who served in the
8th Air Force during World War II
and especially to those who lost
their lives while doing so, this book
is dedicated.

God bless them all.

CONTENTS

PREFACE

In 2010, my ninety-year-old father, Ralph Schneck, was living at the Air Force Village in San Antonio, Texas, occupying the same house he and my mother, Norma, had moved into when he retired. It had been about ten years since she passed away, and the house had become too much for him. Ralph asked me to come down and help him select a new place in the high-rise apartment building that is part of the village. He also wanted me to take home most of the family heirlooms.

I arrived with a rental truck and spent the week looking at apartments and packing furniture, china, crystal, and some personal belongings. After two days of searching, he finally settled on the right apartment and selected a date for the big move. The village would provide the movers and a hotel-styled room for him to stay in while they moved everything and set it up.

The last two days were spent going through odds and ends and packing the truck. On the last day, as I was about to finish up, Ralph stepped out of the house and said, “Hey, don’t forget these two boxes.” I went back in to take a look. I had never seen the two boxes before, but I scooped them up and set them in the back of the truck. They were heavy-duty document boxes with separate lids. Scrolled on the side of each lid, in dark marker, was the word “genealogy.” I opened one box to find an old family Bible, a couple of photo albums, and a few framed photographs. Satisfied, I put the lid back on and didn’t give the two boxes another thought.

When I arrived back in Ohio and unpacked the truck, I set the boxes aside until I was finished. Because I was not interested in genealogy at the time, they held little interest, so I took them to the basement, found an empty shelf, and parked them.

Later in the year, my wife and I decided to take our own retirement to another level and move to West Lafayette, Indiana, my adopted hometown. Our real estate agent told us that we needed to de-clutter and get rid of some things, or at least move them out of sight. The easiest to hide were books and other items that we could pre-pack. I boxed some of these up and moved them to a storage unit not far away.

When I ran across the two genealogy boxes, I decided it would be best to repack them into standard moving boxes. With the first box repacked, I turned my attention to the second box and was totally surprised. Apparently, Ralph had repurposed a box without relabeling it, for it contained memorabilia from his military career. I carefully began unpacking the box. Some of the items I had seen before, but most were new to me. In the bottom, I found a couple of smaller boxes that contained bundles of letters, neatly tied with twine and separated by year. Upon closer inspection, I realized they were letters Ralph had written during World War II . . . one hundred and thirty-eight letters, along with numerous newspaper clippings, theater programs, and a few photographs, all bundled together. I started reading . . .

Even though I grew up in the US Air Force, my view of World War II bomber pilots was defined mostly by Hollywood and Milton Caniff’s *Steve*

Canyon comic strip: pilots wearing their leather flight jackets and a crusher[1], with their headphones perched on top of their head, barking orders and making airplanes do things they were not designed for; pilots that flew all day, every day, and partied every night; pilots who never got tired and lived a happy-go-lucky life. I never gave much thought to the training they went through or how they got to the war front. I did not know what they did in their spare time or even if they had any. What unfolded as I read the letters was a completely different view. So different, that I thought it was important to tell the story.

★★★

Some obstacles emerged while transcribing the letters. The first was that writing paper was sometimes hard for soldiers to find. As a result, some letters have only one paragraph, starting at the top of the first page and continuing to the very end of the last page. Little effort was made to set up paragraphs. This is especially true of the V-mail letters.

Another problem, perhaps more troublesome, was that almost all of the letters were written with a fountain pen. The single tap of the pen that may have formed a period or comma did not always leave any ink. Consequently, it appears there are a lot of run-on sentences.

Lastly, Ralph's spelling and use of capital letters reflects his educational background at the time. It is obvious that he did not have a lot of experience writing essays. The reason is easy to understand. Ralph and his high school classmates, all eleven of them, would have written their essays in the evenings, by the light of a kerosene lantern—an arduous task that may have been of little value at the time.

As I transcribed the letters, I did some interpretation, placing some periods where they belonged and adding paragraph indentation where Ralph obviously intended for one to appear. These places were easy to spot—a little extra space between sentences or starting a new line when there was room on the previous line. These modifications were only implemented to make the letters easier to read. Ralph sometimes highlighted his writing by underlining certain words or sentences. During the editing process, I converted the underlines to italics in keeping with modern printing practices. Beyond that, they were transcribed exactly as they were written, complete with misspelled words, bad punctuation, and colloquial grammar.

Included in this book are almost all of the surviving letters. At first, Ralph tried to write to everyone on his list. To facilitate this, he would write the exact same letter over and over, adding a little personal notation every now and then. I did not include letters that were identical to other letters as there is no reason to show the same letter again. In other instances, I included only the unique text included in the duplicate letter.

In preparing the original manuscript I sometimes found it difficult to figure out *where I was* as jumping from one chapter to another and letter to letter presented problems. I eventually put together a detailed timeline, pulling dates from Ralph's military records. This timeline is presented in Appendix C for the reader's use.

★ ★ ★

As I conducted my research, I discovered that I was asking questions that no one seemed to be able to answer. Answers that seem so obscure, yet so integral, to the war effort have long been forgotten; however, they did exist, and as I dug further and further, I became more resolute in preserving this knowledge for others. Still, I did not find all the answers for which I searched.

The end result is a personal story that is representative of the experiences of many of the sixteen million young men who went to war, as told through the letters written by one of them. It follows Ralph through all of his training, the arduous trek to the war front, and his return home. Through it all is the awe and amazement of youth accomplishing new things—a story that I thought was worth telling, and one that I hope you enjoy.

★ ★ ★

When Ralph returned from the war, he went back to see his parents. While he was there, he spent many hours putting together photo albums by the light of a kerosene lantern. Three albums, painstakingly detailed, chronicle his life to that point. After they were completed, Ralph put them away, and for many years they were only for his enjoyment. The albums were stored in the first cardboard box.

At one point in the 1990s Ralph produced a home video of his military career. *The Flier* included many of the pictures in the albums. For the most part, this was the first time any of his family had ever seen the pictures. All of the pictures in this book came from these three albums and from loose photographs found with the letters. Like the letters, some of the pictures are flawed and blurry.

The letters, newspaper clippings, theater programs, three photo albums, a copy of *The Flier*, and other papers mentioned in this book have been donated to the Purdue University Archives and Special Collections. The authors are grateful that they will be preserved for future generations to study.

★ ★ ★

NOTE

1. Pilots often removed the stretcher from the inside of their dress hat so that their headphones could be worn over it. Wearing headphones over the hat flattened it, hence the name "crusher." Due to severe cold at high altitudes, this practice was not recommended.

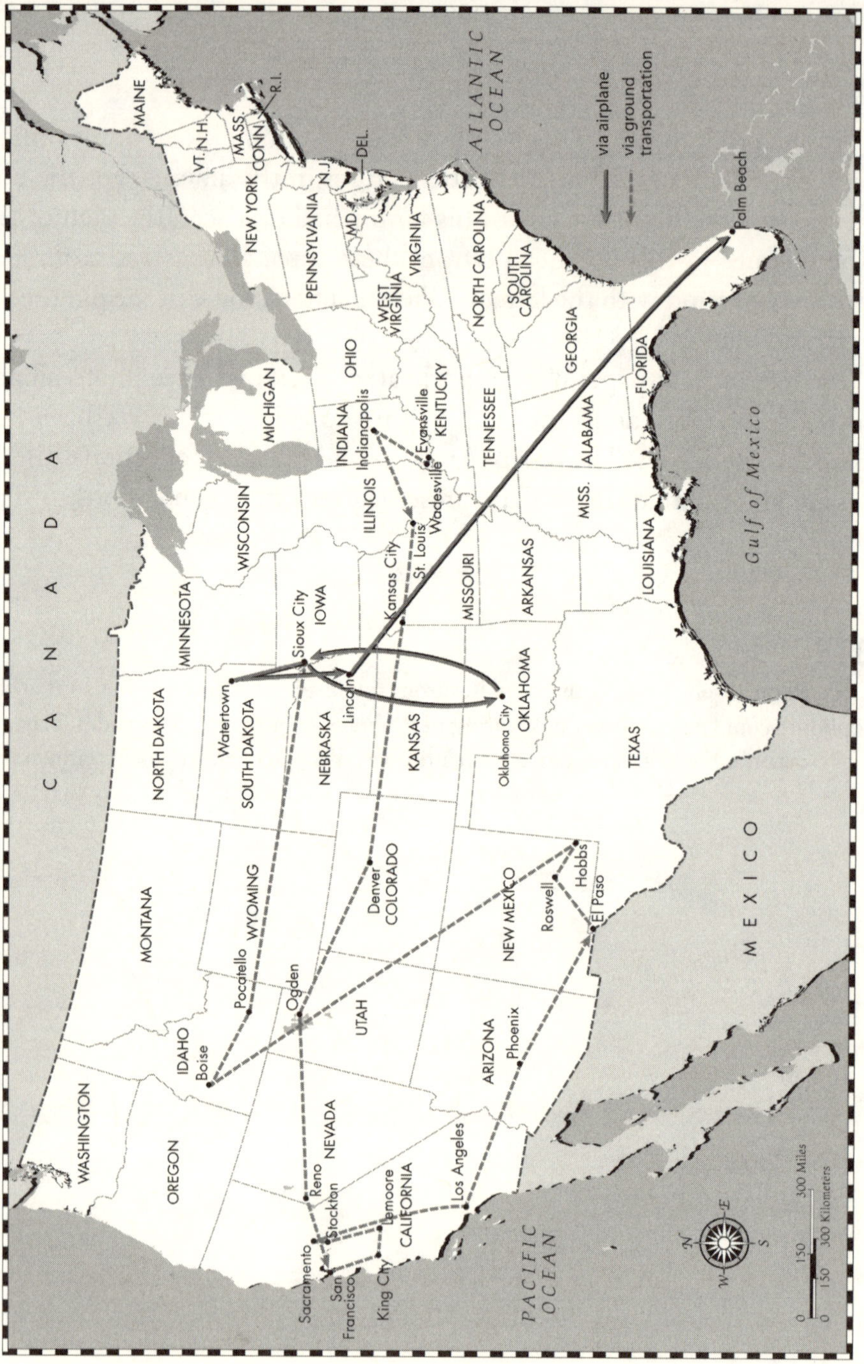

Ralph received all of his pilot training in California before heading to New Mexico as an instructor pilot. In the early summer of 1943, he was sent to Idaho and the upper Midwest to join a newly formed bombardment group that was going to England. The last stop in the United States was Palm Beach, Florida.

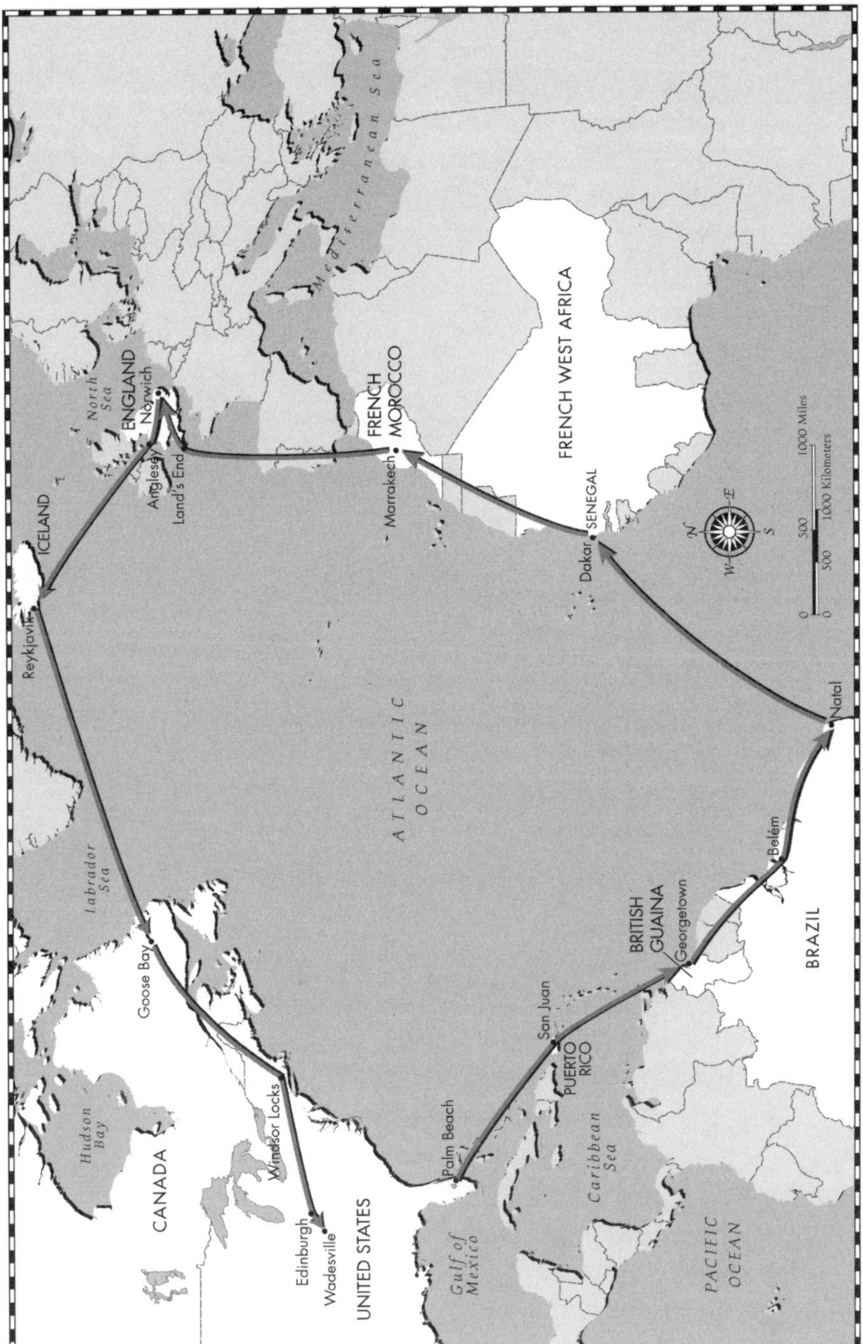

Ralph's group of B-24 Liberators followed the South Atlantic Air Route, making their way from Florida to eastern Brazil before crossing the Atlantic Ocean. They stayed in Dakar and Marrakech while they waited for good weather in England. After the war, the 93rd Bomb Group took the most direct route back to the United States. When he arrived at Windsor Locks, Ralph had been gone eighteen months to the day.

INTRODUCTION

★ ★ ★

This is the true story of a young boy from Posey County, Indiana, who had a dream to fly. The outbreak of World War II enabled him to fulfill that dream.

In the grand scheme of things, Ralph was not extra special. He was not an ace. He did not set any records or win a multitude of awards. He was just a young boy who thought going to war was the right thing to do. He was no different than the millions of others that followed in his footsteps.

★ ★ ★

For most of the boys at war, writing home was a difficult task. They could not write about where they were or where they were going, because that information was censored. And none of them wanted to write about what they had done or what they had seen. Nevertheless, sitting down with a blank piece of paper and collecting their thoughts gave them a few minutes to get their mind off the war and feel homesick for their loved ones and the life they left behind. Even if many of them put the paper away without writing a word.

Ralph was lucky in that regard. His family was very inquisitive; they wanted to know everything. So he filled the pages with whatever came to mind, knowing they would find it interesting. And to make sure he always had something to write about, he asked, in almost every letter, for them to send him questions. The more questions they asked, the easier letter writing became. In reading some of the letters, one may wonder, "Why is he telling this?" The reason is because someone asked.

At first, Ralph wrote letters to everyone who had requested he stay in touch. This was time consuming, and it was difficult to come up with enough different things to say. He solved that problem by writing the very same letter to each person. Fortunately, somewhere along the way he discovered that he only needed to write one letter with instructions to share.

Sharing created a problem that did not surface for almost seventy years. Ralph's mother wanted to save all of his letters, and she asked his oldest sister, Juana, to help in that regard. As letters arrived they were re-mailed or hand delivered to other family and friends with instructions to return them to either his mother or sister when they were finished. At the time, it probably appeared to be a good way to collect all of the letters. However, upon reading the collection during transcription, it became clear that some letters are missing.

In the 1940s, letterhead stationery was quite fashionable; hotels, trains, and buses almost always provided stationery and postcards for this purpose. Ralph was very fond of using letterhead and always tried to find the most unusual and elaborate. Some of these are highly collectable today, and some do not exist in any other collection.

★ ★ ★

Like a lot of the boys that went off to fight, the men that returned almost never discussed what they had done or what they had seen. Ralph was no exception. When I was growing up, if I asked about the war, he would just say it was his job and leave it at that. However, in his later years, he began to open up. At first he hinted around that he wanted to talk about it, but when no one followed up with questions, he produced a homemade video titled *The Flyer*. This video tells much of his story; the letters tell the rest.

Some of the stories included here have been told over and over again, to the point of becoming family lore. Other stories were new to me and raised a lot of questions. Some of these unfolded for the first time in his letters.

As my reading of the letters progressed, I developed a long list of questions that needed answers. I had the luxury of being able to ask him those questions personally. Most of the time he had an answer, but it is sometimes difficult to remember things after seventy years, no matter who you are. In those instances, I relied on a lot of research.

This was not intended to be an in-depth lesson in history or to be a definitive study of the 8th Air Force or the US Army Air Corps. However, unless readers have some knowledge of World War II nomenclature, different aircraft, and the home front, they would have a hard time completely understanding what Ralph is referring to in his letters. As a result, I have provided some very basic notes on various subjects that I hope each reader find helpful and interesting.

Some of the research came from the Internet, a vast resource that just keeps growing. Perhaps it is my old-fashioned values or an instilled distrust of all things new, but every researched element was cross-checked with multiple sources. Even then I am sure there are discrepancies.

★ ★ ★

I was unsure how to tell the story, or if I would even get it finished. I was also very concerned that my father would not be happy with my endeavor. Early on, I told him that I thought I would like to publish the letters and got a terse response, "Why on earth would you want to do that?" But, in the winter of 2011, as I was completing the first draft, he came for a visit to see our new home in Indiana. One evening, over drinks, I told him I was writing another book, but this one was kind of a history book. I mentioned that it tells the story of a young boy from southern Indiana who had a dream to fly. World War II came along, and his dream came true.

He smiled and said, "That sounds like my story."

And it is.

Chapter 1

I WANT TO BE A FLIER

★ ★ ★

"Birthplace of man's wings. America today watches her skies with grave concern, for in these skies of peace, the nation is building the upper battlements of its defense."[1]

The men who fought in World War II came from different backgrounds and from different parts of the United States. Some grew up in big cities, others grew up on farms. They dressed differently, walked differently, and talked differently. Some had money, others did not. Some were tall and athletic. Some were short and clumsy. Some were smart, others were not.

As different as these men were, they all had a lot in common. They had all survived the effects of the Great Depression, the Dust Bowl, and Prohibition. Every family knew someone who had been killed or wounded in the Great War.[2] Everyone personally knew someone who had died from tuberculosis; most people knew more than one casualty.[3] Everyone had a close family member born in the nineteenth century. Most had a family that had formed them into the men they were—a close-knit, supportive, and caring family.

Ralph Schneck was no different than the others. He was the same.

★ ★ ★

Ralph's mother and father were Jessie and Rolla[4] Schneck, hard-working farmers in the rich countryside of Posey County, Indiana.

Rolla was a second generation German American. His grandfather, John Frederick Schneck, was born in Stockheim, Germany, in 1812. He immigrated to the United States in 1839. A carpenter by trade, he met his wife, Elizabeth, in Lancaster, Pennsylvania, where they married in 1843. Elizabeth had relatives in New Harmony, Indiana, and they urged John to bring his carpentry skills to the area. So later the same year, John and Elizabeth moved west to New Harmony in Posey County.

Rolla's father, Henry, started out as a carpenter, following in his father's footsteps. After deciding that the carpentry profession was not going to work out, he switched to farming, raising sheep. He married Sarah Norris, who was a very ambitious and adventurous woman. She was not content to sit in one place and be tied down.

Sarah had heard about a land rush to be held in the unassigned territories of Oklahoma in April 1889. She convinced Henry to give her some money so she could buy land. She took Rolla, then five, and his brother, Clarence, and headed for the Oklahoma territories.

They got as far as Joplin, Missouri, where she hired an agent to find suitable land. The rules required that after you staked your land, you had to go to the local land office to file your claim in person. The agent found a tract of land near Tulsa and staked it out for her. But Sarah could not get to the land office. What she had not counted on was that there was no means of transportation beyond Joplin. If you did not bring your own buggy or a horse, you were out of luck, because everything that would normally have been available had already been sold.

Undaunted by this setback, Sarah took the boys to Fort Smith, Arkansas. Using the rest of the money, they set out for California by train. Somewhere, in what is now west Texas or eastern New Mexico, they had to leave the train and take a stage coach to California. They spent the winter near what is now Los Angeles and returned to Indiana the following spring.

Henry was extremely upset with all the travel and the absence of his children. He told Sarah that her traveling days were over and that the boys had to stay home so they could get an education. Sarah did not like that idea and decided to leave Henry one more time, for good. They divorced in September 1891.

★ ★ ★

While Rolla was a fairly good student, he dropped out of high school after only two months because he did not think he could learn Latin. There was probably more to that, since he and his elders still spoke some German around the house. With him already speaking two languages,[5] adding a third should not have been a problem. However, somewhere in the family make-up there were animosities toward Catholics. Latin was used extensively in the Catholic Church, and there were many Catholic-only communities in Rolla's part of Indiana. He may have been coached that learning Latin was the start of indoctrination. Hence, he probably thought he had good cause to skip that part of his education, even if it meant dropping out of school. Indeed, religious beliefs and feelings ran deep in all of the European immigrants, and they tended to instill their viewpoints in the minds of their children for many generations.[6]

After he quit school, Rolla helped his father around the farm. When he turned sixteen, his father gave him a horse and a buggy. From that point he was on his own. After four years, at the age of twenty, he had saved enough money to consider getting married and starting a family. On August 15, 1906, he married Jessie Johnson.

The Johnson family of Posey County was considered to be quite prosperous. They owned a lot of the choice farmland in the county, and they too were a close-knit family. When Jessie and Rolla married, the Johnsons gave them an organ imported from Germany, symbolic, perhaps, of the strong German heritage of the Schneck family.

The first farm was small. Located near New Harmony, it was the ideal homestead to start a family. They had four children. Juana Marie was the oldest, followed by Marcia Elizabeth, Charles Robert, and finally Ralph Herbert. Charles died shortly after birth.

Juana[7] was born in 1907. From the very beginning she was introspective, inquisitive, and studious. Marcia was born in 1911, and by that time, Juana was more than happy to groom a sister to take over the household chores. Even at the age of four, Juana knew what she wanted and what she did not want. As the two grew up, Marcia became the take-charge daughter. Assuming the role of the older sister and assistant homemaker, she was always ready to help around the house. On the other hand, Juana spent time helping Rolla and, at times, totally distracting him with question after question.

Ralph was born on November 11, 1919, on the first anniversary of the signing of the armistice with Germany, ending the Great War. It is ironic that he would be born on what would later become the Veteran's Day holiday, since he would end up spending most of his life serving in the military. By the time Ralph was born, Juana was twelve and Marcia was eight. The age differences meant that Ralph had the opportunity to be bossed around by everyone in the family, and he took it all in stride.

★ ★ ★

Jessie's father died in January 1919 and left her $4,000. She and Rolla found a larger farm near Wadesville and purchased it for $12,000. Using the inheritance as a down payment, they got a mortgage with a 4 percent interest rate. Rolla started out with cattle and grain crops, but soon after, the economy began to slide as the United States entered the Great Depression. Fortunately, the bank lowered their interest rate to 2 percent and told the family that as long as they could cover the interest payment, there was no chance of losing the farm. Rolla expanded his operations to include pigs and sharecropping. With the expanded operations and other income opportunities, they were always able to make ends meet.

Their farmhouse, built sometime around 1905, was situated at the end of a tree-lined lane nearly sixteen hundred feet long, on the north side of Hidbrader Road, just west of Wadesville. The house had four entrances. The main entrance was from the large, covered front porch that faced east toward the end of the lane. Guests using this door entered the house directly into the living room.

On the north side of the house was another porch that entered into the mudroom, just off the kitchen. This door was the most commonly used because it also provided access to the main well, the chicken coop, the barn, the grain storage, and the outhouse.

Just across the kitchen from this door was another porch on the south side of the house. It was built as a summer porch; enclosed on three sides, it used the overhang from the second floor as the ceiling. This entrance not only provided total shade almost all day during the summer, but it also accessed the woodpile. During the winter, firewood for heating and cooking would be stored on the summer porch.

The fourth entrance was a private entrance off the front porch that opened directly into the master bedroom.[8] This was convenient for Rolla and Jessie because they could come and go without disturbing the rest of the household.

There were two wells in the north yard. One was for the household, and the other provided water for a horse trough. The household well was a hand-dug bucket well with a wooden enclosure and a large overhead pulley.

A few feet west of the two wells was a grain-storage shed, which also doubled as tool storage. The entrance to the chicken pen was behind the storage shed. Inside the pen were both the chicken coop and the outhouse. Rolla always let the weeds grow around the outhouse to give the chickens a place to hunt crickets, grasshoppers, and June bugs. Anyone who needed to use the facility had to be brave enough to fight through the chickens, the weeds, and the bugs.

Directly north of the house, about one hundred feet on the other side of the cattle fence, was the barn, which was used to store harvested crops, farm implements, wagons, and the car. The barn was surrounded by pasture, with a small pond on the north side.

The first floor of the farmhouse consisted of the living room, dining room, kitchen, master bedroom, and mudroom. The master bedroom was next to the living room, and both rooms had doors that opened to the front porch. The kitchen was at the opposite end of the house from the living room. The dining room was situated between the kitchen and the living room. With the living room, master bedroom, and front porch facing east, there was plenty of shade to escape to during the hot summer afternoons.

A steep, narrow stairway led from the dining room to the second floor, where there were two small bedrooms. The first, at the very top of the stairs, was Ralph's. The second belonged to Marcia and Juana. The girls had to walk through Ralph's room to get to the stairs. These two bedrooms were directly over the living room, master bedroom, and part of the dining room. The rest of the area over the dining room and kitchen was all attic storage.

Typically, especially in the winter, no one ever ventured to the outhouse once they were tucked in for the night. Consequently, every room had its very own chamber pot. The rule of the house was that "he who used the pot, emptied it."

Since the entire house relied on the fireplace in the living room and the stove in the kitchen for heat, it was essential that everyone turn in at about the same. Otherwise, the fires had to be maintained for the one or two that stayed up, which was a waste of firewood. The only salvation on really cold nights was that after dinner was prepared, Rolla would put bricks on the stove to heat them. Just before bedtime, he would wrap the hot bricks in old blankets and towels and place them under the covers so everyone started out with a warm bed.

The house did not have electricity, relying instead on kerosene lanterns. In the winter months, the family relied on the lanterns during dinner. After dinner, Rolla would move one lantern to the living room, while Jessie would take another to the kitchen. Just before bedtime, Rolla would go upstairs and light a lantern so everyone could find their way to bed. That lantern was left dimly lighted all night. Every day, Rolla would check the lanterns. Those that needed refilling were taken outside as he did not want to spill any kerosene in the house.

A crank-styled telephone was mounted on the dining room wall, adjacent to the stairway. They shared a party line with five other families. To make a call, they would lift the earpiece, listening to make sure no one else was talking. If the line was free, they would turn the crank, thus alerting the operator that they needed to make a call. They were notified of an incoming call by the number of rings. There were three downsides to the telephone arrangement. First, every call on that party line rang into their phone. Second, everyone on the party line could listen in. Lastly, the service was very poor, and oftentimes it was difficult to hear the other party.

★ ★ ★

Rolla was a very hard worker and always looked for a little extra money. At one point, he found employment with the local school board.

Posey County sits in the extreme southwest corner of Indiana, nestled neatly between the Wabash and Ohio rivers. Being mostly rural farmland, it was difficult to expect that every child would somehow find a way to school. Between the extreme distances and chores around the farm, children often did not attend school. The tendency was for children to do their farm chores first and schooling later. As a result, the Wadesville School Board decided that they needed to do something to address the problem. The solution they decided upon was the school wagon, a concept already used in other parts of the country. This converted buckboard provided enclosed seating for students and a teacher. The concept was that the wagon would travel a prescribed circuit, picking up children and delivering them to school, much like today's school buses.

Because of the distances and the slow, horse-drawn travel, not every child went to school every day. In the summer, the wagon never went to the school. Instead, it picked up boys and girls and stopped at some shady spot so the teacher could provide a few hours of lessons. Then the wagon would return them home. The next day the wagon would take a different circuit.

When the school board started looking for someone to drive the wagon, they heard that Rolla was interested in the job. Because the Schneck family was greatly respected in the community, Rolla was hired. He drove the school wagon for two years before it was replaced with a gas-powered bus. In the winter months, Rolla would lay heated bricks on the floorboards to help keep the children's feet warm. In the summer, he undoubtedly eavesdropped on the lessons as he developed an acute understanding of the importance of education. He became committed to making sure that his own children got through high school and went on to further their education if they so desired.

★ ★ ★

Neither Jessie nor Rolla liked to have their picture taken, but on special occasions they would give in to the request. This picture was taken at Ralph's twenty-second birthday celebration, which was held on November 9, 1941, in their living room. His actual birthday is November 11.

Jessie, Ralph's mother, was a typical farmer's wife. Her duties were to take care of the house and make sure everyone got fed. She always cooked three meals every day. Every morning she was up before dawn and had breakfast on the table when Rolla, and eventually Ralph, returned from the field with the cows. As soon as breakfast was over, she would start on lunch, usually getting help from Juana and Marcia, who would bring in water from the well or tote firewood. Cooking on a wood-burning stove was a hot process and took a lot out of everyone in the kitchen, so it was common to take a long break after lunch, usually sitting on the summer porch when it was not too cold to do so.

In those days, several flour and grain companies packaged their product in colorfully designed cotton bags. The material could be used to make everything from shirts to dresses and patch up coveralls. Jessie could always be found in or near the kitchen wearing an apron she made out of flour sacks. In between cooking and other chores, she enjoyed using the flour sack material to make quilts.

Jessie also contributed to the family income by raising chickens and selling eggs. She maintained a kerosene-heated incubator in the mudroom and called upon the kids to take turns rotating the eggs three times a day. When the chickens hatched she would sell some of the chicks, while others were raised as layers and fryers. Even some of these were sold or traded in a pinch.

The chickens provided a source for family humor as well as a point of contention within the household. With a constant supply of fresh chickens, Jessie never hesitated to serve them for just about any meal. Her expertise was in the single-twist head removal, cleaning, and then frying them to perfection.

Sundays were special around the farm. Rolla only did the daily routine, and he planned something special to do, like going to town or taking in a baseball game. Jessie would have preferred to go to church, but since she did not drive, she relied on someone to take her. Rolla was not a church-going man, and until the kids grew up, he was her only transportation. Even then, Rolla made sure that he got Jessie to church at Christmas and Easter.

Every Sunday, Jessie cooked fried chicken, mashed potatoes, and milk gravy. Since she never wasted anything, everything that was edible was fried and placed on a large platter in the middle of the dining room table. After the blessing, Rolla would reach in and take the first piece. After that it was a free-for-all as everyone reached for their favorite piece. Everyone except Ralph, that is. It seems that since Ralph was the youngest, he had the shortest reach, so he had to wait for someone to push the platter his way. By the time it got to him, the back and neck were about the only pieces left.

The humor came as he got older, because Jessie realized that his arms were getting longer, and she started placing the platter just out of his reach, forcing him to still wait for someone to push it to him. Occasionally, one of his sisters would feel sorry for him and scoot the platter in his direction before everyone arrived.

As Ralph grew up and left home, he vividly recalled his experience with eating chicken. As a result, for many years, he ate very little chicken, and when he did, he was very particular about which pieces he chose. After leaving home, he never ate a neck or back again.

The contentious part of the chickens involved the only gun in the household. Rolla had pacifist tendencies and did not see a reason to have a gun around the house. However, Jessie insisted that she needed one to ward off anything or anybody that might try to get to her precious chickens. Rolla could not argue with the logic. No matter how obliged he felt to help someone in need of a chicken, the idea of someone stealing one rubbed him the wrong way, so he grudgingly relented. Rolla selected a double barrel side-swing model that mostly sat in the corner of the mudroom. No one, except Jessie, knew where the shells were kept.

Living on a farm in the 1930s could be quite lonely, and for Jessie one of the highlights of the year was the fall wheat thrashing. This event brought all of the local wheat farmers together to share in the cost of bringing in a steam-powered thrashing machine. It was an all-day event as each farmer took his turn at the thrashing machine. While all that activity was going on, the wives prepared lunch, dinner, and afternoon snacks. Jessie enjoyed all the conversation, seeing everyone's kids, and, of course, showing off her three. She was always one of the organizers for the event, calling around to make sure every woman brought her specialty. And when the day came, Jessie's food took center stage. After all, she had all the chickens.

★ ★ ★

When Ralph was two years old, he almost died in an accident. He was upstairs in the girls' bedroom while Jessie, Marcia, and Juana were cleaning his bedroom. The second floor had very low ceilings, but the windows were full sized. This caused the windowsill to be just a few inches off the floor. The screens for the upstairs windows were the type that came in two pieces and expanded to fit the opening. The only thing holding them in place was the small track that guided the top window.

Rolla was returning from town when Ralph spotted the car coming down the lane. In his excitement, Ralph put his hands on the screen and pushed it out of the window. Ralph stumbled as he and the screen both tumbled to the ground.

Jessie screamed and everyone came running to Ralph's aid. Without exception, everyone thought he had died. Surviving that kind of fall would be miraculous for an adult and even more astounding for a child. However, the screen landed on the ground on one side and rested there for an instant. Ralph then landed with his chest firmly smacking the screen, which broke apart from the impact.

Ralph just had the wind knocked out of him, though he sported a long bruise that ran from one shoulder across his chest to his hip.

★ ★ ★

Falling from the window was not the only excitement that Ralph experienced as a child. When he was four years old, he fell ill with a high fever. Jessie was very concerned and sent Rolla to fetch the doctor.

After the doctor concluded his examination, he proclaimed that Ralph had scarlet fever. No vaccine had been developed, and treatment methods varied from doctor-to-doctor. In some parts of the country, death was almost certain. Fortunately, whatever treatment this doctor prescribed worked wonders as Ralph survived. Nevertheless, the illness left him weak and sickly for a few more months.

★ ★ ★

When Ralph was six, Juana left home and enrolled at the Indiana State Teachers College,[9] entering a special two-year program that was instituted to address the extreme shortage of teachers. By the time Ralph turned ten, she had graduated and was in her second year of teaching at Coonrod[10] School, a nearby one-room schoolhouse, where she was only two years older than her oldest student and had to do everything from dusting the erasers to keeping the fire going. In that same year, Marcia left home to enroll in Lockyear Business College in Evansville.

With both sisters gone, Ralph had little to do around the farm except to follow his father. He had his own chores, but when he was not in school or doing those chores, he would hang around and wait for Rolla to ask him to do something. Rolla almost never told him to do anything. Instead, he preferred to ask, sometimes being very persuasive. This was a trait that Ralph took note of and carried with him for the rest of his life.

This time alone with his father was very productive. Ralph quickly learned that Rolla had an opinion on just about everything. Not just a thought or a point of view, but generally, a very strong opinion. Ralph had seen his oldest sister, Juana, argue with him but never thought anything of it. But now he was alone with his dad and had his own opportunity to question things. From this, he learned the art of negotiating a common position so his father could lose without saying so.

★ ★ ★

When Prohibition began, Rolla decided that he would make his own moonshine.[11] He set up a small still on the back side of the barn. Every once in a while, he would fire up the still and fill a few Mason jars for he and Jessie to enjoy. Occasionally, he would sell one or two to neighbors and friends or use it for trade. One day, while in Wadesville, he heard that the sheriff was starting to go after folks making their own spirits. Rolla feared being caught and decided to stop production.

After that, every Friday, almost without exception, Rolla would pay a visit to the local moonshiner. He would return the Mason jar from the previous week and pick up another for the week to come. Sometimes he paid in cash, but on other occasions he would barter with corn, eggs, and chicken. Occasionally, he would deliver a pie or a loaf of bread. On warm summer evenings, Rolla and Jessie would sit on the front porch, sip from the Mason jar, and listen to the corn grow.[12] When the weather turned cold, they would sit in the living room after dinner and watch the fireplace.

Rolla was always careful about keeping alcohol in the house. While he did not mind buying it, he was concerned about getting caught with it in his home, so he devised a simple noose contraption that would hang the jar about three feet down the inside of the well in the yard just outside the mudroom door. He was very deliberate about retrieving the jar and about putting it back when they were finished for the evening.

One day in the late summer of 1933 Ralph, now fourteen, had finished his chores and was following Rolla from the barn to the house when they saw two Ford Coupes pull off the main road and slowly head their direction. Ralph and Rolla waited for them in the front yard. They greeted three men and two women who said they were traveling to St. Louis and wondered if they could trade some farm chores for lunch. Rolla went into the house and asked Jessie. When he returned, he said they could chop some firewood in return for lunch. The men agreed, and Rolla led them around the back of the house to the woodpile. He watched for a minute as the men slowly got things organized and the women sat on the summer porch and watched.

When one of the men went to the back door to ask for water, he took note of the shotgun, which Jessie had moved next to the stove. After about a half hour, Jessie took out a platter of chicken, some more water, and bread. When they finished eating, they all walked back to the front of the house and found Rolla and Ralph waiting for them. Jessie was standing in the mudroom doorway, with the shotgun nearby. One of the men thanked them for the lunch, apologized for not chopping more wood, and asked if they could get some water for their radiators. Rolla pointed to a bucket at the horse trough. They topped off their radiators and made their way back to the main road, turning west toward St. Louis.

When Jessie went to the porch to clear the dishes, she found two dollars neatly tucked under the chicken platter. Without wondering why they pretended to chop firewood instead of paying, she scooped up the bills and stuck them in her apron. Later, she would put the cash with her egg money.

After lunch, Ralph and Rolla were headed back to the barn when the sheriff's car pulled onto their lane, followed by two black Chevrolet sedans. Rolla stopped, looked at the three cars, then turned to Ralph and said, "Feds."[13]

The sheriff got out of his car and greeted Rolla, then introduced him to the other four men, saying they were federal agents. Pulling one of them forward, the sheriff said, "And this is Mr. Purvis.[14] They have some questions."

Purvis went on to explain that they had a tip that John Dillinger[15] was in the area and may have stopped by Rolla's farm. He said that they were traveling in two cars and there may have been three men and two women. Finally, Purvis said, "Have you seen anyone like them?" Without waiting for a response, he asked if his men could look around.

The whole time Purvis was talking, Rolla and the sheriff were leaning against the well where Rolla's weekly stock of moonshine was hidden. Jessie stood in the door to the mudroom and watched, while Ralph stood next to Rolla with his mouth open, taking in the whole experience. Rolla looked at Purvis and told him his men could look anywhere, at which point, Purvis pointed to the barn and two of the men started in that direction. The third headed for the back of the house. Rolla asked, "Have you boys been on a farm before?"

Purvis said he was born and raised on a pig farm and that his men knew all too well about avoiding the cow patties, because they learned the hard way. Everyone chuckled at that.

While they waited for the men to return, the sheriff mentioned that Rolla was one of the most respected men in the county and that he ran one of the best farms around. Rolla thanked him for his comments. Purvis asked some farm-related questions, showing that he really did know a lot about being on a farm. The sheriff yelled over to Jessie and asked if he could get a dozen eggs before he left. She told him she would get them ready.

The men returned and reported to Purvis, who thanked Rolla and started to walk away. He turned back and said, "So I guess you didn't see these folks?"

"No, I didn't see them," Rolla responded.

Purvis thanked him again and headed for his car. The sheriff said he would be right with them as soon as he had collected his eggs. Purvis and the others got in their cars while the sheriff and Rolla walked to the back door. Ralph was right in stride, almost stepping on their heels as he tried to hear everything. Jessie greeted them with the eggs. While the sheriff fumbled around for some change, he asked, "So which way did they go, Rolla?"

Rolla said Purvis had it right—two women and three men who said they were on their way to St. Louis. They made a mess of the woodpile and Jessie fed them lunch. They had been gone about an hour and a half to two hours. The sheriff paid Jessie, thanked the couple, and headed for his car.

Rolla and Ralph watched as the three cars drove down the lane, led by the sheriff. They stopped after about three hundred feet. The sheriff got out of his car and walked back to talk to Purvis, who was seated on the passenger side in the first car. When they finished talking, Purvis looked back at Rolla and waved.

Later that evening, Ralph asked his father why he had lied to the federal agents. Rolla explained that they would get their information, but from the person that counted the most: the sheriff. Rolla went on to say that the federal agents would be gone shortly, but the sheriff would be around for a long time. As far as he was concerned, it was very important to make the sheriff feel like no one could just waltz in, start asking questions, and take over the sheriff's duties and his territory.

Rolla went on to tell Ralph that people have to consider what is important before they open their mouths and start talking. That was another lesson that Ralph would apply throughout his military career; however, he still thought his father was wrong for lying.

★ ★ ★

There was always plenty to do on the farm, and no one ever lacked for something to keep them busy. But, on those occasions when chores seemed to be caught up, the entire family would get dressed up and go to Wadesville on a Saturday afternoon.

Wadesville was a very small town that consisted of a general store, a gas station, and a tavern as the main businesses. On Saturdays, a local church group always had an ice cream social under the big canopy in front of the general store. It was Rolla's favorite place to go. Not belonging to any church and not openly subscribing to any faith, this was as close to religion as he cared to be, although he escorted Jessie to the local Methodist service on Easter and Christmas.

Ralph's favorite place to go was the tavern, diagonally across from the general store. He would routinely visit for a three-cent soda pop. In front of the tavern was a long bench where, it seemed, the same old men sat every Saturday afternoon. They must have felt it befitting or perhaps their duty to engage young folks in conversation. They would always ask Ralph what he wanted to be when he grew up.

Most boys Ralph's age wanted to get a job in a factory or stay on the farm, but Ralph had a different perspective. In the late 1920s, his answer ran the gambit from a drummer in a band to a train engineer, a baseball player, or running a steam wheat thrashing machine. Flying was never a consideration, perhaps because, at that point, he had never seen an airplane.

In 1934, the year John Dillinger was gunned down in Chicago, Ralph had made up his mind that he wanted to become a federal agent and join what would later be called the Federal Bureau of Investigation. That lasted for about one year.

In the early 1930s, Eastern Airlines began offering regular flights between Evansville, St. Louis, and Louisville. Their aircraft flew directly over the Schneck farmstead. Ralph was very intrigued by the airplanes, and whenever he could get away, he would watch the planes from one end of the sky to the other.

★ ★ ★

The largest city in the area was Evansville, which was about eighteen miles away from the Schneck farmstead. It offered all the conveniences of larger, more metropolitan cities in the east. While some shopping was available in Wadesville, the stores offered only limited selections, and some items were simply not available. Consequently, Rolla and Jessie would carefully plan shopping trips to Evansville.

Preparation was a necessity, because Rolla still had farm chores to complete, and he did not like driving at night. Getting to the right store when it opened allowed time for lunch and a movie before returning home. These trips were always an exciting event and never taken lightly.

Evansville also provided the nearest schools for higher education. The Evansville College[16] was a four-year school that provided a well-rounded education. The Lockyear Business College[17] provided a two-year degree in business.

In 1934, Evansville was home to six breweries. Prohibition had been lifted, and it was back to business as usual. Prior to Prohibition, all of America's breweries relied on grain from local farms as well as that which was brought in by rail from the Great Plains. During Prohibition, the brewers redirected their efforts to make products that did not contain alcohol, such as "near beer." These new products did not have the demand of those they replaced; consequently, the need for grain was far less.

Now that Prohibition was lifted, there was a huge national surge in the need for grain. Unfortunately, the drought in the Dust Bowl states put a great deal of stress on the ability of local farmers to meet the demand. As a result, every brewery reached out to local farmers to step up their efforts.

Rolla heard the call. It was another way to bring money into the household. However, he did not own a truck, and for him to take grain to the Evansville breweries meant hitching up a team of horses and spending a day delivering one wagonload of grain. Nonetheless, when he had grain, he would make the trip two to three times a month, weather permitting.

Jessie would plan the trip so that Rolla and Ralph could also run her errands while they were in the big city. The night before, father and son would load the wagon and cover it to prevent spillage. They would get up early, hitch up the two-horse team, and head for the Sterling Brewery on the west side of Evansville. After they delivered their grain and got paid, they would set out to do whatever was on Jessie's list. At some point during the day, they would venture into the German and Jewish sections of town, usually for lunch and to buy tools.

Before heading home, they would go back to the Sterling Brewery to pick up brewer's grains[18] for the livestock. The breweries had plenty of by-product, perhaps more than they knew what to do with, so they welcomed anyone that wanted to carry some away. Rolla and Ralph would load the wagon with the dregs and head home, fighting the bees and flies all the way. Upon arrival, the knowledgeable livestock would come running to line up for the best meal of their life. Ralph always thought he could see a smile on their faces after they finished eating and teetered off for a nap.

★ ★ ★

Even though Wadesville High School was very small, with a total enrollment of about forty-five, it tried to provide a well-rounded education. One of the subjects—aside from reading, writing, math, and science—was music. The students would listen to recordings, pick out the sounds of various instruments, and learn about famous composers.

The local blacksmith owned a full set of drums. However, he lived in a very small house and did not have any place to put them. He had asked the high school if they could store them, in return for allowing someone to learn to play the drums. The high school agreed and put the drums in a closet in one of the school rooms.

Ralph had overheard one of the boys talking about how he and his brother and sister were forming a small band. Ralph had seen the drums in the closet and asked if the group was looking for a drummer. The next thing Ralph knew, he was talking to the blacksmith to get approval to play the drums. After a quick trip to Evansville to get drumsticks, he was taking his first lesson.

The band was comprised of Al Strauss playing the trumpet, Ken Strauss playing the trombone, Lila Fay Strauss playing the piano, and Ralph on the drums. Al, Ken, and Lila Fay were all very accomplished musicians, as their father had once played first chair trumpet with the Philadelphia Orchestra and had taught each of his children to play various instruments.

About three or four times during the year (and between sports seasons), the little group would put on a concert. They were called the Wadesville High School Concert Orchestra. While the orchestra part may have been a stretch, considering they made up about 10 percent of the student body, it was acceptable.

In later years, Ralph would reflect on that experience, saying, "We weren't very good, but people came anyway, mostly for the Strauss kids, and they applauded every number we played."

★ ★ ★

Ralph's view of the outside world was extremely limited as a teenager. Trips to Evansville and baseball and basketball road trips were just about the only things he had to fill his little world. His sister, Juana, tried to change that.

As Ralph grew up, he became very close to Juana. Before she went off to college, they spent a lot of time together. She had turned the older-sister household chores over to Marcia as Juana preferred to spend time helping Rolla tend to the farm. As Ralph grew older, she began grooming him to take her place. When she went to college, she would come home and entertain Ralph with all the worldly things she was learning. The images she painted for him filled his head with imagination and wonderment. He could not wait to get out into the real world and see everything for himself.

★ ★ ★

Occasionally, Ralph would take a job helping one of the local farmers. He and another boy were hired to move hay bales from the field to the barn. They had done this before, and it had been a leisurely job. They followed the farmer as he drove a horse-drawn hay baler and waited for the bale to drop out of the machine. They had plenty of time between bales, and they took turns heaving them into their wagon. When the wagon got full, the farmer would take a break and help them move the bales from the wagon to the barn. The farmer's wife fed them three meals a day. At the end of the day, the farmer would take the horses home, and the boys slept under the wagon, in the field.

During Ralph's last baling season, he had an epiphany. When the boys arrived, they were greeted with the sight of a tractor and a new baler. It seemed like they all started together, but the farmer, driving the tractor, began to outdistance the horse-drawn wagon. It was not long before the tractor was at the far end of the field and what waited for them were hundreds of bales tossed about by the new baler. There would be no help in moving the bales from the wagon to the barn. Before falling asleep under the wagon that first night, Ralph began to think about how the tractor sure made things easier. He would not dwell on the situation at that moment, but he knew his father really needed one.

★ ★ ★

There were no gyms and very little physical education taught in school, but working on their family farms put muscles on just about every kid. Ralph was no exception, and as he grew older he developed a very athletic frame.

Rolla loved baseball and would often take the family to watch the local teams play in Wadesville. Sometimes, on a Saturday or Sunday afternoon, they would watch two or three games. Ralph developed an interest in the sport, and when the time came, he asked if he could try out for a team. Rolla was elated. He said he would make sure that Ralph got to every practice and to every game. He was true to his word. Through the years, Ralph never missed a practice or a game for lack of transportation.

As he grew older, the baseball coach took note of Ralph's long arms and lanky physique. They put him at first base. Rolla saw to it that he had the right glove for the position.[19] In those days, each player had to provide his own uniform,[20] and Jessie made sure that Ralph's always fit right and looked great.

Ralph developed quickly, learning the nuances of first base. He also became a quick study at batting practice. It did not take long before everyone considered Ralph to be the best first baseman in the county and one of the top batters. He had a reputation of never letting a ball get past him. With

Ralph's first love in sports was baseball. Here he is seen in the 1934 Wadesville High School baseball team photo. Pictured are (standing) Coach (and high school principal) Curley Melton, Mylowe Heckman, Charles Heal, Edsel Thornburg, Ralph, Jesse Marse, John Wentzel, Francis Earl Knowles, Coach Ed Glenn, (kneeling) Elbert Wade, Maurice Wade, Kenneth Strauss, (sitting) Lloyd Mills, Carl Owens, June Heal, Jesse Hanes, and Herbert Zenthofer. The "P" on Ralph's uniform stands for "Posey" as he and John Wentzel also played for the Posey County American Legion during the summers.

exceptionally long arms and standing tall at over six feet, he could snag the most errant throw or sloppy pop-up and never take his foot off the bag.

At this point in Ralph's life he had a full head of hair. Somewhat different from the rest of the family, including his ancestors, Ralph's hair was red. Some of his teammates began calling him "Carrot Top." Rolla did not like the carrot reference and began calling Ralph "Top." The team picked up on that and the nickname stuck.

Each summer, the high school baseball coach, who also coached basketball, would make the rounds of local games to check out his players. Early on he had been watching Ralph develop and knew he would be a starter on his baseball team. But after one of those games he approached Ralph to see if he had an interest in playing basketball as well. Although Ralph had played basketball almost as long as baseball, he had never considered it because he did not think he was very good at the sport. Baseball was his first love; however, when school started, Ralph showed up at basketball practice. In a scene reminiscent of a Hollywood movie, Ralph stood at the free throw line and tossed some air balls and some bricks. The coach started working with him. Before practice was over, Ralph was hitting baskets. From that point on, he was the starting center on the team.

Ralph also loved to play basketball. He is shown here in the 1935–1936 Wadesville High School basketball team picture. Pictured are (top row) Coach (and high school principal) Curley Melton, Francis Earl Knowles, Edsel Thornburg, Ralph, Coach Ed Glenn, (middle row) Lloyd Mills, Charles Heal, Carl Owens, John Wentzel, (front row) Maurice Wade, June Heal, Herbert Zenthofer, and Wayne Joest.

★ ★ ★

In 1934, the high school hired Curley Melton as the new principal. Melton also took over the coaching duties of the baseball and basketball teams, with Ed Glenn as his assistant coach. In those days, a high school principal had the latitude to design the school curriculum in any manner he felt would better serve the students. Melton decided that before he made any changes, he would interview each student. One question he asked was, "What do you want to do when you graduate?"

When he met with Ralph and asked the question, Ralph answered without hesitation that he wanted to be a flier.

Melton laughed and told Ralph that flying was a very dangerous profession and that he should choose something more realistic.

He did not fool Ralph. "More realistic" meant that Melton did not think Ralph was smart enough to learn to fly. But Ralph went along with it and told Melton, "In that case, I want to be a farmer," to which Melton replied, "Following in your father's footsteps, eh? That's a good idea."

Ralph smiled, but he never forgot about flying.

That same year, while Ralph was playing first base, the Wadesville High School baseball team made it to the Indiana High School State Championships. To celebrate, they purchased new uniforms. The new uniforms did not help, as they lost to a bigger and faster East Chicago team.

★ ★ ★

As Ralph entered his senior year of high school, in 1936, Rolla began to ask him what he planned to do with his life. This was not the first time Ralph had been asked this question. Until now, every mention of being a flier was greeted with ridicule and laughter. His own high school principal even inferred that Ralph was not smart enough to be a flier, and Ralph even doubted his own capabilities. So Ralph told his father that he had no idea what he wanted to do, and Rolla let the issue drop. A month later, Rolla asked once more. Again, Ralph had no answer, but the importance that his father placed on the question set Ralph's mind in motion.

The third time Rolla asked, Ralph had a reply. "I'm not sure," he said. "I have several options."

"Like what?" his father asked.

From there a long term discussion began. Ralph had given it some thought and decided that he really did have several options. He could stay on the farm and eventually take it over; he could go someplace and get a job; or he could go for more education. But Rolla wanted details. Where would he *work*, and what would he *do*? What would he *study*, and how would he *pay* for it? There was no winning for Ralph. The discussion went on for months and sometimes became heated. It always came back to staying on the farm, which was something Ralph was not sure he wanted.

At one point, he asked for advice from his two sisters. They had both left the farm and never looked back. They explained that he had to do what he thought was right, and they cautioned, "Do not blame it on us . . . whatever it is." But from this conversation came a partial solution. Herb, Marcia's husband, owned a Standard Oil gas station at the corner of Kentucky and Washington in Evansville. He promised Ralph that if he decided to come to Evansville, he would always have a job working at the gas station.

A little while after that, Rolla cornered Ralph again and asked if he had made up his mind. The discussion went on for about an hour, and finally, Ralph said that he would not mind staying on the farm. In fact, he had some ideas about how the farm could be expanded and become more profitable. Rolla paused for a moment, taken by complete surprise, then said, "Like what?"

"Well, I think we need a tractor."

Rolla did not want a tractor. Maybe he did not believe in them. Maybe it was the money. Maybe it was the thought of change. No one really knows for sure, but he told Ralph that there was no way he would ever buy a tractor and replace the horses. Ralph told him that adding a tractor was the only way he would stay.

There was a very long silence—a point where neither man said anything or looked the other in the eye. June bugs would have stopped flying. Corn would have stopped growing. The water in the pond would have stood deathly still.

Rolla broke the silence, "Well, I guess you better go to college."

★ ★ ★

Ralph graduated from Wadesville High School on Thursday, April 22, 1937. Commencement was held at the Wadesville Community Build-

During March 1936, the family gathered at the farm to celebrate Rolla's fifty-second birthday. Marcia's husband, Herb, took this picture of Juana, Ralph, and Marcia. By this time, Ralph was well over six feet tall, and his height really shows here. In the background is the barn.

ing. There were twelve[21] students in the graduating class. They had adopted the following motto: "Life is what we make of it."

★ ★ ★

Even though Rolla lost his argument for Ralph to stay on the farm, he was instrumental in making sure Ralph was cared for in Evansville. He knew Herb would give him a job at the gas station, but he still wanted Ralph to be secure. After all, he did not own a car and did not have much money with which to start out. He was also shy, naïve, and had trouble talking to strangers.

Shortly after the final discussion, Rolla announced that they were going to Evansville to run some errands. Jessie planned the trip and off they went. They stopped at a couple of shops, had lunch, and then went to see Addison (known simply as Add or AG) and Stella Beeler, longtime acquaintances.

Add had recently retired from the postal service. For many years he had run the parcel post window at the post office. He virtually knew anyone and everyone who had ever mailed or received a package. Over the years, he had struck up a friendship with Rolla and Jessie as a result of the egg business. Before Jessie bought her incubator, she would have her chicks shipped from a mail order company. Add took extra care to make sure the chicks reached her before any could expire. In the process, he would always come home with fresh eggs and chicken.

Rolla had placed a call to Add earlier in the week and asked if he knew anyone that had a room to let. He explained that Ralph wanted to come to Evansville for school and would need accommodations.

Add replied that he and Stella had a room that had recently become vacant and suggested that Ralph come by to have a look. The rent was three dollars a week.

It was a single upstairs room with a bath in the hall, located at 314 Powell Avenue.[22] It had one window that overlooked the backs of other homes. In the summer, Ralph could get a little breeze by cracking the door and opening the window. The furnishings were sparse: a bed, a small desk, a dresser, and a couple of chairs. No matter what the view looked like or how it was furnished, Ralph was happy with the room. But mostly he was happy to know that he had friends, as the Beelers were almost part of the Schneck family.

Not much of a view from Ralph's bedroom window at 314 Powell Avenue in Evansville. He overlooked everyone's backyard and a very small alleyway. Add Beeler had been burning trash and doing some yard work when he took a break. He is leaning against the utility pole.

Having a young man around the house was nothing out of the ordinary for the Beelers. Their own son, Jerry, was eight years older than Ralph. He had left home several years earlier, and it was his room that Ralph was now occupying.

★★★

In the early summer of 1937, at the age of seventeen, Ralph backed the family car up to the mudroom porch and packed all of his worldly belongings. Rolla and Jessie drove him to the Beeler family's home and helped him unload his things, lugging them up to the second floor.

There was a short good-bye and lots of tears. Then his father and mother got in their car and drove home. Ralph was now completely on his own, and for the first time in his life, he was scared.[23]

★★★

Herb fixed Ralph up with a blue uniform, a leather bow tie, and a chauffer's hat and put him to work at the gas station. He would greet every car that came in, pump the customer's gas, clean the windshield, check the tires, and top off the oil. It was a great experience for him because up to that point, he had very little contact with strangers and needed to cultivate some social graces. To say that he was shy or backward was an understatement. The fact is that Ralph normally did not talk to anyone he did not already know. But, as with sports, he was a fast study and quickly developed some loyal customers.

He made a trip to Lockyear Business College and put in an application for the start of the fall term. When he discovered how much tuition would cost, he realized that his meager pay from the gas station would not be enough and started looking for another job.

One of the largest employers in the city was the Servel Company. Servel made washing machines and refrigerators. Their refrigerators were unique for the time because they did not run on electricity. Instead, they ran on natural gas. Many homes, especially in rural areas, did not have electricity, so the Servel refrigerator was in great demand.[24]

Ralph took the bus to the Servel plant, located on the north side of Evansville near Garvin Park, and applied for a job. He asked if he could work second shift. They had an opening in the forming department and put him to work. His job was to remove the hot, newly formed refrigerator lining from the overhead conveyor and stack them on pallets. He worked from two in the afternoon until ten at night and was paid between $30 and $40 a week.

After school started, Ralph settled into a fairly domestic routine. He would get up early each morning and walk to Lockyear Business College. He would pass through the Jewish section of town, usually stopping for a bagel or a muffin and juice. He would spend all morning in class, then rush home, grabbing a sandwich on the way, and change into his work clothes. Next, he would walk to Zales Jewelers on Main Street, where he would catch a bus to the Servel factory. Ralph would get off work just in time to catch the last bus back to Zales, and he usually arrived home around eleven at night; however, if he missed the last bus, he had to walk all the way home.

The management at Servel was very nice to Ralph. Occasionally, the plant would shut down the refrigerator line and send people home. However, Servel had a good relationship with a number of companies in the area, so when they would close the line, they would loan Ralph to the Hoosier Stamp and Metal Company. That was fortunate because it meant that Ralph always had a paycheck on which to rely.

In addition to this job, Ralph continued to work at the gas station. He usually worked on Saturday and Sunday so Herb could spend time with his family. Between the two jobs, Ralph made enough money to cover all of his college expenses and had enough left over to enjoy a very comfortable life.

★ ★ ★

Ralph never missed an opportunity to go back to the farm and visit his mother and father. The problem, however, was that he did not have a car. In fact, there were only two people in the family who owned automobiles at the time: his father and Marcia.

Since the farmstead did not have running water, all of the laundry was done on the summer porch using a washboard and a manual wringer washing machine. It was a very labor-intensive contraption that was sometimes difficult to master, and Jessie hated using it.

When Marcia married Herb, they lived in a town where almost everyone had electricity. They bought a new washing machine, and Marcia offered to do the family laundry. She would drive out to collect the dirty clothes and drive back a few days later to deliver them. She would always contact Ralph to see if he had time for the trip, sometimes calling the Beeler family to leave a message and sometimes just stopping by. Additionally, Marcia would always ask Ralph if he had anything that needed washed.

If he was available, he would bundle up his dirty clothes and join Marcia for the ride.

★ ★ ★

After eighteen months of school and working in a factory, it came time to graduate and move on. With his newly minted accounting degree, Lockyear found Ralph a job as a bookkeeper at Rice's Motors, a Ford dealership.

He had not been there long before he noticed that the reports sent to the Ford Motor Company did not match the records he was keeping. In those days, dealerships made some of their money from a commission paid by the auto manufacturers. Each month, the dealer sent a report that showed the number of cars sold and the price for which each one sold. One way to make a little extra was to skim money off the sale price and not report it to the manufacturer. This practice was not condoned by the auto companies, and Ralph questioned the discrepancy with management. He was told that he had a lot to learn about the auto business and to just keep doing what he had been doing and everything would be okay. After only six weeks of fudging reports, two men from the Ford Motor Company arrived and closed the business.

Ralph hit the streets, looking for another job. He figured that he might know something about the auto business and went to other dealerships first. He ended up at a Chevrolet dealer who was familiar with what had happened to the Ford dealer. The owner decided to take a chance on Ralph and hired him as an assistant bookkeeper.

Everyone at the Chevrolet dealership was paid based on the number of cars sold. If they had a bad month, then everyone received a little pay; however, if they had a good month, then everyone received a lot of pay. After a month or so of suffering through some very low paychecks, Ralph decided to move on. He had heard about an opening at L. A. Parker and Company from a friend who already worked there. Ralph put in an application and got the job.

L. A. Parker and Company was the largest grocery wholesaler in the area. The company had been started by Lewis A. Parker, a self-made businessman who started out as a door-to-door salesman. He started out selling brooms, but one thing led to another, and he eventually wound up with one of the largest and most respected grocery brokerages in the Midwest. He was on the board of directors of Sterling Brewery and served as a director of both the National Food Brokers Association and the National Sugar Brokers Association. Parker was an influential community leader who was extremely well liked. Known for his philanthropic endeavors, he was often asked to help raise money for local charities. Over the years he was involved with the Evansville Association for the Blind, Boy Scouts of America, American Red Cross, Family Welfare, and Community Chest.

Lewis Parker was a very well-liked person who made it a priority to take care of everyone around him. In July 1940, he threw a company-wide picnic at Mesker Park in Evansville and invited his friend, C. B. Newman, of Lamborn and Company. Here they are pictured together while Newman pays off a bet. L. A. Parker and Company purchased sugar from Lamborn and Company.

Parker provided groceries from Cincinnati west to St. Louis and Indianapolis south to Nashville. Ralph took a position in the accounting department and was their only bookkeeper. He worked five and a half days a week and was paid a meager $12.50 a week. Finally, however, he had secured a job that he really enjoyed and one where he could put all of his talent to good use.

★ ★ ★

In the spring of 1938, Ralph went on a double date one Saturday evening. They walked through Garvin Park, got something to eat, and then went to see a movie. Showing that evening was the film *Test Pilot*, starring Clark Gable, Myrna Loy, and Spencer Tracy. The plot was simple: test pilot meets girl, girl marries test pilot, test pilot's best friend dies, everyone is sad. Ralph did not ever remember any of that. What he did remember was thrilling scenes of a new Boeing bomber identified as the Y1B-17, which would later become the famed B-17 Flying Fortress.

Ralph was intrigued by the idea of flying a big aircraft like the one in the movie. Of course, it looked bigger than it really was, but the image stayed with Ralph for weeks.

★ ★ ★

After working at L. A. Parker and Company for several months, Ralph took an interest in purchasing a car. Up to that point, he had walked, taken a bus, or relied on friends to get around. Owning an automobile produced an air of independence and maturity. It was time, he thought, to join the human race and buy a car.

Having worked at two dealerships, he had an acute appreciation for how much autos cost, and he knew he did not have the money. Nonetheless, every day he walked past a Chevrolet showroom and admired a used car that sat in front of the building. Then one day, a curious thing happened. While Ralph was looking at the car, Lewis Parker brought his wife's automobile in for repairs and noticed Ralph standing outside. Parker approached Ralph and asked if he liked that particular car. Ralph said he did and he was saving his money so he could buy it. Parker told him to keep working at it.

A couple of weeks later, Parker saw Ralph at work and asked him if he had bought the car yet. Ralph said he was still saving his money. Parker told him to stop by the dealership after work and talk to the owner to see what kind of deal he could get.

That afternoon, Ralph went in and asked to see the owner. Parker was there, and the three men talked, finally agreeing on a price of $325. The next day, Ralph picked up his first car: a 1938 Chevy Coupe, which had only been used by the dealership to provide their customers with a test drive. Parker had loaned Ralph the rest of the money he needed to buy the car, and Ralph agreed to pay him back and to use the car for company business.

Soon, Ralph was traveling to the far reaches of Illinois and north toward Indianapolis to personally visit Lewis Parker's clients.

This is Ralph's first car, a 1938 Chevy Coupe that Lewis Parker helped him buy. It is parked in back of the farmhouse. The front porch can be seen on the right and the summer porch on the left. While the window at the top of the picture is not the one Ralph fell from, it is the same height from the ground.

★ ★ ★

By the time Ralph saw *Test Pilot*, Adolf Hitler had taken control of Germany, the civil war in Spain had ended, and for what it was worth, all of Europe was in turmoil. Japan had invaded China and was expanding their hold on the north Pacific, but nobody paid much attention to them because they were "too far away." Ralph did not have to go very far to be reminded of these international events because the *Movietone News*[25] footage, which was shown at movie theaters, dwelled on current events and the possible future. The thought of another war in Europe was on everyone's mind.

Lewis Parker had a friend, H. E. MacConaughey, who was a top executive in the Hawaiian Pineapple Company in San Francisco. In the summer of 1939, MacConaughey had just returned from sailing around the world and had written a travelogue of his exploits. Parker had received a copy and sent it around for some of his employees to read. Ralph studied the document—all thirty-three pages. Of particular interest were the comments about the prospect of an impending war. During his travels, MacConaughey interviewed Chinese, Italians, and others about their feelings regarding the state of the world at the time. MacConaughey included their comments as part of the travelogue, then he concluded:

> I could go on for pages telling you more but the sum and substance of it all is that the people are not happy. All along the line, from the beginning of the journey to the end, there was the talk of war—the fear of war—the prayer that there will be no war—but the definite belief that there must be and really, it is a terrible thing to visit many lands and talk with many people whose first thought is war—death.[26]

Ralph had kept up with all the reports coming out of England. Herb had given him a Standard Oil world atlas, which he routinely consulted. He knew, just knew, something was going to happen. He started listening to reports from Washington, but they did not sound right to him. Most of the Washington politicians wanted to pretend that any conflict in Europe would not involve the United States, but Ralph wondered, "How could it not?"

Finally, in September 1940, the military draft was approved by Congress. Ralph saw this as absolute proof that even the politicians in Washington were preparing to go to war. Many of his friends flocked to the recruitment office to volunteer, because at the time, volunteers got their choice of assignments.

Whenever Ralph returned to the farm he would try to engage Rolla in a conversation about another war. Rolla would have nothing to do with it. He believed the United States should have closed its borders and locked the rest of the world out, letting them fight their own battles. The two argued over the role the United States would play. Like previous discussions, this one went on for a very long time.

Ralph had made up his mind. If the United States entered into another war, he was not going to march in it; he was going to fly in it. And not fly just anything. He wanted to fly the Y1B-17. But how and when would he break the news to his mother and father?

★ ★ ★

During the fall of 1939, England declared war on Germany and civilians began an evacuation of London. Poland fell to the Nazis and Canada declared war on Germany.

★ ★ ★

In the summers, Ralph continued to play baseball, making the trip back to Wadesville to play for the local American Legion-sponsored team. Sometimes the trip was made with friends, including his girlfriend at the time.

When he was not playing baseball or working, he still managed to keep busy. He would take a group of friends to Garvin Park or to the airport to watch the airplanes land. There was always plenty to do, and Ralph was always ready and willing.

He had become very popular with the ladies. As shy as he appeared, he had no problem getting a date. Additionally, it seemed they all had cameras and wanted to get their picture taken with Ralph, especially when he was in his baseball uniform. There was Evelyn, Aline, Doris, Elsie, Gene (with the beautiful legs), Mary, Peggy, three different women named Dorothy, and Margaret Rose.

★ ★ ★

**In 1940, the British began rationing.
Denmark, Norway, France, Belgium, Romania, and the Netherlands all fell to the Nazis. Greece, Egypt, and East Africa fell to the Italians. The Battle of Britain took place, and the Germans began bombing England.**

★ ★ ★

One day in 1940, Ralph was playing first base and knocking the cover off the ball. After the game, a man approached, said he was with the St. Louis Cardinals,[27] and that he wanted to invite Ralph to a team tryout to be held in the spring of 1941. He got contact information and over the winter they sent Ralph a letter confirming the arrangements.

After Ralph graduated from high school, he continued to compete in baseball games, playing for the Posey County American Legion. In the late summer of 1940, he was invited to try out for the St. Louis Cardinals. He is pictured here with teammate June Heal.

When spring rolled around, all the girls at L. A. Parker and Company wished him luck. Even Lewis Parker stopped by to shake his hand. Ralph had packed a few things, including his uniform, glove, and favorite bat. Herb drove him to Terre Haute, Indiana, where the tryouts were taking place.[28]

It was a cold three days, and Ralph gave it his best. There were about 120 boys attending the tryout, and Ralph made it to the third day; however, when the tryout was over he was told to go home, put on some weight, get a little faster and stronger, and play as much baseball as he could. They told him his fielding and batting was some of the best they had seen, but they played a grueling schedule[29] compared to what Ralph was accustomed to, and they thought he would fade without more weight, strength, and speed. They told him he would be invited back in 1942.

★ ★ ★

In October 1940, Ralph heard that the US Army was recruiting men for pilot training. The article in the paper said that anyone interested had to meet certain qualifications. They had to be a citizen of the United States, single, between the ages of twenty and twenty-seven, with two years of college, of exceptional character, sound physique, and excellent health. Ralph met all of the qualifications except the two years of college. He had graduated after only one and half years. Nonetheless, he visited the recruiting station to explore the notion.

At the recruiting station, Staff Sergeant J. E. Pettay told Ralph that if he passed a qualification exam the US Army would waive the two-year college requirement. The sergeant went on to say that the Junior Chamber of Commerce was sponsoring a refresher course for those interested in taking the exam and asked if Ralph would like to sign up for it.

Ralph had been talking about becoming a pilot for a long time, so after he signed up for the course, he convinced some of his buddies to follow suit. The refresher course started on February 24, 1941 and ran for ten weeks, meeting every weekday night for three hours. The instructors were recruited from the local high schools. They covered all of the topics that would be on the exam: history, English, geometry, geography, trigonometry, physics, and chemistry. The volunteer instructors were provided by the Evansville schools under the direction of Ralph Becker.

Ralph had never had any trigonometry, and his physics and chemistry background derived solely from book learning as Wadesville High School had no laboratories. He was at a distinct disadvantage starting out. Plus, working five and a half days a week, putting in long hours, he had little time to study.

Of the twenty-three boys who had signed up for the course, nine failed their physical and two others dropped out, leaving twelve.

Ralph and his two friends showed up at the recruiting station to take the three-day test.[30] The test was administered by three US Army personnel,

Staff Sergeant J. E. Pettay, and Tech Sergeant Frank Raines from the local recruiting station and Major H. B. Perkins from Fort Benjamin Harrison outside of Indianapolis.

Ralph worked through the battery of tests for three days, leaving some questions on each test unanswered, always thinking that he would come back to them later. Unfortunately, time would always run out, and he never finished any part of the exam.

The exam papers were taken by Major Perkins, who forwarded them to Washington, DC for grading.

★ ★ ★

Several weeks later, a secretary at L. A. Parker came to see Ralph, telling him he had a visitor in the lobby. Ralph went down to the front desk and was greeted by Staff Sergeant Pettay. The sergeant told Ralph that the results from the test had returned, and he wanted to personally tell Ralph that he did not pass the test and would be getting a letter from Washington. He went on to say that only three boys had not passed. He told Ralph that another test would be given in several weeks, and he encouraged him to take it again, saying that Ralph had very good scores, and he thought Ralph stood a great chance.

Ralph said he was not sure and asked why the sergeant thought he would pass it the second time. Pettay said he was sure Ralph would pass because he was going to help him, if he wanted the help. Ralph said he would be glad to have all the help he could get.

Pettay told Ralph that the Evansville Junior Chamber of Commerce was going to conduct another refresher school for selected prospects; however, this time the instructors would be college professors from Evansville College. He told Ralph that only twenty-five boys would be in the course, and he would make sure that Ralph was included. He also told Ralph that he had a friend who owned an airplane, and he had agreed to give Ralph flying lessons, provided that Ralph paid for the fuel. Ralph did not know what to say except, "When do I start?"

The sergeant told Ralph to be at the airport early on Saturday and be ready to fly.

★ ★ ★

Ralph worked hard at his flying skills. Paul Schlundt was the sergeant's friend and, as it turned out, was also a friend of Herb, Marcia's husband. He owned a Culver Cadet[31] and gave flying lessons. At the end of the day, if he had gas left, he would take Ralph up and give him a lesson. In between these lessons, Ralph studied for the ground school portion. By the time the next exam date approached, Ralph had become proficient and hoped he would be able to solo and get his private pilot license.

Between refresher courses, Ralph took flying lessons from Paul Schlundt in a Culver Cadet. Ralph is standing next to the plane, which is parked at a hanger at the Evansville Municipal Airport. The Cadet was a tiny plane, standing only about six feet tall, with a wingspan of twenty-seven feet.

At the same time the flight lessons were occurring, Ralph began the refresher course. As before, there were five classes each week, Monday through Friday evening, for six weeks. When the refresher course started, Ralph joined twenty-four other prospects from around the area, including his cronies, to prepare for the entrance exams. Again they studied algebra, trigonometry, English, history, geography, physics, and geometry.

At the conclusion of the six weeks, only seventeen students[32] had passed the physical exam and were ready to be tested.

★ ★ ★

The exam was given in the Evansville Armory by Major Perkins and the same sergeants as before. The desks were arranged so that everyone sat at least ten feet from each other. They were given two hours for each exam, except for trigonometry and geometry. For those two subjects they were given three hours.

Ralph sat down to take the exam a second time along with the other boys. When the door opened from the outer office, Major Perkins appeared just as he had before. Perkins stood before the room and looked at each person, finally turning to Sergeant Pettay, asking if some of the people had already taken the test and failed. The sergeant looked around the room and nodded his head. Major Perkins asked why they were taking it again, because he believed they would never pass it. The major and the sergeant left the room to discuss the situation. After a few minutes they returned, and the exam began.[33]

This time, Ralph finished every portion of the exam with time to spare. By the major's instructions, he put his pencil down, folded his hands, and waited for the time to expire. The major would look over at him and ask if he was finished. Ralph would nod his head.

The major would ask again, "Completely?"

Ralph always answered, "Completely."

By the second day no one bothered to look up to see who the major was talking to.

When time expired, the major would walk over to Ralph, pick up his papers, and quickly scan them. He always acted surprised that every question had an answer.

★ ★ ★

A few weeks later, Staff Sergeant Pettay came to see Ralph at L. A. Parker. He told him that it would take the War Department quite a while to grade all the exams; however, he said, it was customary for the local US Army Post to look them over before they were sent to Washington. Pettay said he and Major Perkins had looked over all the exams, and they felt Ralph had passed. In fact, he said that Major Perkins thought Ralph would have the highest marks he had ever seen.

Ralph asked about his friends, but the sergeant said he was not sure. All he knew was that Perkins told him that it looked like only nine people had passed.

Ralph told Sergeant Pettay that he was worried that the sergeant was going to get fired for letting them take the exam a second time. Pettay laughed and said, "They can't fire me. Sergeants run the Army. Officers, like the major, are just paper pushers."

Ralph asked about the next step and was told to sit tight and let things take their course.

★ ★ ★

Rolla, Jessie, and the rest of the family knew Ralph was taking flying lessons, but they did not know exactly why. Ralph had confided in his sister, Juana, and he figured that his other sister, Marcia, had figured it out, but never said anything. Now the time had come to tell his mother and father.

In April, Ralph had a date to see a movie. Again, there was the walk in Garvin Park or a trip to the airport, followed by something to eat. On this evening, the film was *I Wanted Wings*, starring Ray Milland, William Holden, and the beautiful Veronica Lake. This time Ralph followed the plot closely as it told the story of three recruits and how their lives unfolded in the US Army Air Corps. He fell in love, again, with the B-17, the uniforms, Randolph Field, the way they talked, and the romance.

The next day, he decided to invite his mother and father to come to Evansville for a movie. He planned to take them to see *I Wanted Wings* and to tell them what he had in mind. He made a call to the farm to set everything up.

The following Saturday, Ralph met his parents at Add and Stella Beeler's home. They all piled into Rolla's sedan and drove to the theater for the matinee. Ralph bought everyone popcorn, and they settled into their seats to watch the movie. Jessie sat between Ralph and Rolla.

The movie opened with a mock air attack on Los Angeles and included some discussion of being prepared in case the United States was attacked. At this point, it was all fantasy. The attack on Pearl Harbor was months away.

During the movie, Ralph would occasionally turn to see Jessie's reaction, then lean forward a little to see his father's. Jessie was very engrossed in the film. She followed every word of the story and seemed to enjoy the airplane footage and flying sequences. Rolla, however, sat in the same position for the whole movie. He never so much as shifted his weight, and he displayed the expression of someone with a toothache waiting to see the dentist.

After the movie, they went for a sandwich. Ralph asked what they thought of the film. Jessie said she loved it. She especially liked all the action and thought Veronica Lake was beautiful.

Rolla said he did not care for it. It was too much like war, and he did not like the subject. Ralph asked if he liked the airplane footage. "No," said Rolla.

After a moment of silence, Ralph got up his nerve and told them the real reason he was taking flying lessons; he wanted to join the US Army Air Corps. Jessie was excited and told Ralph how wonderful she thought his plan was.

Ralph went on to tell them that he had taken the entrance exam. Jessie again told her son how great that was and asked for all the details. He told them the whole story as they finished their meal.

His father said nothing until they dropped him off at the Beelers' home, and then it was only, "see you later."

★ ★ ★

The *Movietone News* showed that war was raging in North Africa, Greece, and Yugoslavia, with Nazi Germany firmly in control. Great Britain, especially London, was being bombed every day, and the United States was standing behind its declared neutrality.

★ ★ ★

On November 7, 1941, Ralph received a letter from the War Department saying that he had passed his mental exam to become an air cadet in the US Army Air Corps. The letter closed by saying that orders would soon follow.

A few days after his birthday on November 11, Ralph received bad news. The local Draft Board contacted him, saying it was time for him to take a physical; he was going to be drafted. Ralph called Sergeant Pettay and asked about being drafted. The sergeant told him there was nothing he could do. He also said that once he was drafted, it would be hard to make the jump to the US Air Corps.

To make matters worse, Ralph had traveled to Madisonville to meet a good friend of Paul Schlundt who was flying for the British Armed Forces' Royal Air Force. He told great stories about flying and the English people. Then Ralph received a letter from his close friend, Carl Beggs, with whom he had taken the first refresher course and exam. Carl wrote telling Ralph he had soloed and that he loved the US Air Corps, while it now appeared that all of Ralph's hopes and dreams would be dashed.

Ralph was in a panic. He started asking around for advice. One friend suggested that he get a congressman to write a letter to the War Department on his behalf. Ralph turned to Jerry Beeler, Add and Stella Beeler's son, for help. Jerry served on the Indiana Governor's Committee on Truck Transportation and was connected to local politics. Jerry wrote a letter to Congressman John Boehne, Jr., saying that Ralph was about to be drafted and asked him for his assistance.

Meanwhile, Ralph took the draft physical and the draft exam.

★ ★ ★

Ralph made many trips back to the farm, and occasionally, he would try to get his father to talk about his decision to join the US Army or the war in Europe. Rolla did not want to talk about either and usually mentioned to Ralph that it was not too late to come back to the farm. But Ralph's mind was made up.

The more news he heard from England, the more he was convinced of the necessity for the United States to enter the fray. Things were desperate in England. They had lost the battleship *Hood*, sunk the *Bismarck* then lost the aircraft carrier *Ark Royal*. The German army had invaded North Africa and seemed unstoppable as they continued to roll across Europe. Additionally, reports were starting to surface about the imprisonment of Jews in Poland.

★★★

One morning in early December 1941, Americans everywhere were enjoying a lazy Sunday. Thanksgiving had occurred two and a half weeks before, and Christmas was two and a half weeks away. For the Schneck family, it was a special day, as Jessie celebrated her fifty-fifth birthday. To celebrate the occasion, Herb and Marcia invited everyone to their house[34] for lunch.

It was Herb's turn to work at the gas station. He planned on going home for lunch and then returning to finish out the afternoon.

Rolla and Jessie arrived around half past ten in the morning. Jessie went into the kitchen to see if Marcia needed any help. Rolla sat on the couch playing with his granddaughter, Sandra Jane, who was seventeen months old.

After a few minutes, Jessie joined Rolla on the couch.

Ralph arrived a little before eleven and sat in Herb's favorite stuffed chair, talking with Rolla and Jessie, filling them in on his week at L. A. Parker.

Herb left his gas station shortly after noon and returned home for lunch. Marcia had prepared her best dish of stuffed pork chops, riced potatoes, and green beans, which she had canned at the end of the summer.

After lunch, Ralph helped Marcia clear the dishes. Herb and Rolla went back to the gas station to finish out the afternoon. Sandra went for her afternoon nap. Marcia began making dessert—homemade fritters.[35] In the afternoon calm, Jessie sat on the couch and nodded off to sleep.

Ralph decided to take advantage of the peace and quiet. Chicago's WLS radio station usually had a Sunday afternoon show, broadcast live from the Aragon or Trianon ballrooms. Eddy Howard and his band had been headlining at the Aragon, and Ralph hoped to tune in for the show. When the radio came on, WGN was broadcasting a football game between the Bears and the Cardinals. He listened for a minute or so, then spun the dial, finally landing on WLS just in time to hear the announcer say that they were broadcasting live from the Trianon Ballroom. He then introduced the Jimmy Dorsey Orchestra.

Ralph had just settled into Herb's chair. He was enjoying the music and working on the beginnings of an afternoon nap. He was at the top of the world. He had just turned twenty-two a few weeks earlier and life could not have been any better. Jimmy Dorsey introduced a young lady, Helen O'Connell, to sing. The music started up, and she had just begun when it suddenly stopped and the radio went silent. This sometimes happened, so Ralph did not think anything of it, until a different voice came on the air saying, "We interrupt this program . . ."[36]

Marcia yelled from the kitchen, "What was that?"

Jessie sat up to find out what she had missed.

"The Japanese have bombed Hawaii," Ralph said.[37]

Marcia was frying the fritters and just removing a batch from the pan. In her excitement, she became totally distracted and poured hot grease on her right hand, severely burning it. She came into the living room with her hand wrapped in a dish towel. Jessie went to her aid.

Ralph moved to the radio and turned up the volume. Everyone listened intently as the reports began coming in.

After about fifteen minutes, Ralph said he was going to tell Herb and Rolla, just in case they did not have a radio turned on.

At the gas station, he found Herb sitting behind his desk with Rolla sitting in a chair nearby. Ralph walked in and asked if they had heard the news. They had not.

It did not take Herb long to get the radio turned on and tuned into WLS. All three men listened to the reports.

Herb brought the unsettling news back home when he turned to Ralph and said, "I suppose you will be hearing something from the Army."

Instead of answering, Ralph looked at his father. Rolla looked at him eye-to-eye. It was one of those poignant moments in life when a boy becomes a man in the eyes of his father. Rolla smiled and slowly nodded his head.

Ralph did not need any approval to enter the US Army, but he certainly sought it. Jessie had been very supportive and enthusiastic. His sisters knew it was the right thing for him to do. But Rolla had been just the opposite, until that moment.

Ralph nodded back to his father. The two men had just settled months of arguments and debate without speaking a word.

A few minutes later, Ralph said he needed to head home. He told his dad that he would keep everyone apprised of any progress. On his way home, he thought about what could possibly happen in the coming days and weeks. The events of that day had set a new course for him, and he did not know where it was going. He had already taken the draft physical and their exam, and to add to his consternation, he still had not heard any official word from the US Army Air Corps.

When he got home, he pulled out his world atlas and turned the pages to the Pacific Ocean, looking to see exactly where Pearl Harbor and Tokyo were located. They were a long way from where he expected to go. They were a long way from England.

★ ★ ★

"Then I heard the voice of the Lord saying, 'Whom shall I send? And who will go for us?'"

"And I said, 'Here am I. Send me!'"[38]

★ ★ ★

NOTES

1. Opening to *I Wanted Wings,* Paramount Pictures, 1941.

2. Until 1939, World War I was called the "Great War" or the "World War." The United States lost 117,000 soldiers with almost 206,000 soldiers wounded.

3. Between January 1920 and December 1930, 26,897 people died from tuberculosis in the state of Indiana alone. Many more suffered through the disease and lived.

4. Pronounced "rollie."

5. Henry insisted that everyone speak English outside of the home. With the outbreak of the Great War in Europe, most German-speaking immigrants and their families, including the Schneck family, stopped speaking German entirely.

6. Ralph would grow up carrying this legacy.

7. Pronounced "waana."

8. When this home was built, it was common practice to provide for the eventuality of mourning the deceased. Friends wishing to pay their respects to a recently deceased family member would enter directly into the bedroom, where the body lay in repose, and then proceed into the living room and dining room for refreshments before going home. This type of home construction is still used today in America's Amish communities.

9. The Indiana State Teachers College became Indiana State College in 1961 and Indiana State University in 1965.

10. Pronounced "känrad," although all the kids sarcastically called it "coon•rad," with a distinct emphasis on "coon."

11. During Prohibition, from 1920 through 1933, the production and sale of alcoholic beverages was illegal in the United States. Moonshine, although illegal, was typically the only alcoholic spirit available.

12. This is an Indiana colloquialism. Many farmers believe that in the evenings one can hear the popping of the corn stalks as they grow.

13. Everyone who had been to the movies knew that the "Feds" drove black Chevrolet sedans.

14. Melvin Purvis (1903–1960) was an FBI agent who was in charge of tracking down notorious felons in the Midwest.

15. John Dillinger (1903–1934) was the most notorious of all Depression-era criminals. He was born in Indianapolis, but around 1920 his family moved to Mooresville, about one hundred miles northeast of the Schneck farm.

16. Evansville College became the University of Evansville in 1967.

17. Lockyear Business College closed in 1991.

18. Brewer's grains (also called dregs) are the remnants from the brewing process, containing the remains of the grain and a considerable amount of alcohol.

19. In the 1930s, it was common for first basemen and catchers to use the same glove.

20. Most families could only afford one uniform; hence, summer leagues never had matching uniforms.

21. Allyn A. Becker, Paul M. Campbell, Janice L. Cartwright, Lela Anita Gibson, Loyetta P. Miller, Elizabeth K. Rice, Henry Schnarr, Ralph H. Schneck, Lila Faye Strauss, Elva Ruth Wade, Maurice E. Wade, and Alvena C. Wentzel.

22. Powell Avenue was removed in the 1950s as part of downtown renovations. It was located near the east end of Washington Avenue.

23. This scene was repeated in 1965, when Ralph drove his oldest son to college and helped him carry his belongings to the eighth floor of a dormitory. Ralph always compared the two events.

24. Servel refrigerators are available today, manufactured by the Dometic Group. They run on propane gas or kerosene.

25. *Movietone News* was a newsreel with sound and music, produced by 20th Century Fox. The footage was a staple at movie houses all across the United States. It was always timely and was usually the only way to actually see what was going on in the world.

26. One of two closing paragraphs to H. E. MacConaughey's travelogue dated July 28, 1939, written on Hawaiian Pineapple Company stationery. The Hawaiian Pineapple Company was renamed the Dole Food Company in 1991.

27. The St. Louis Cardinals was, and still is, a baseball team in the National League.

28. Herb was concerned that Ralph would be too tired to drive back every day. So Herb drove Ralph to the tryouts and stayed to watch. At the end of each day, Ralph was exhausted and slept most if the way back to Evansville.

29. The St. Louis Cardinals played 156 games in 1940. Ralph played about thirty.

30. The battery of tests were called "mental exams" by the US Army and were given over a three-day period. They covered algebra, geometry, history, English, physics, trigonometry, and geography.

31. The Culver Cadet was first manufactured in 1939. It was a very small, two-seat monoplane, just short of eighteen feet long, with a wingspan of twenty-seven feet, and standing only five and a half feet tall. It had a top speed of 142 miles per hour and a range of 500 miles.

32. The remaining boys that qualified to take the exam were: Richard Boink, Donald Carver, Harold Carver, Arthur C. Dwyer, Paul S. Henrich, Robert Logan, Ralph H. Schneck, Kenneth M. Silverman, and William Wimsatt from the Evansville area; William Moll and Welborn L. Wells from Mount Vernon, Indiana; Carl Beggs from Princeton, Indiana; Don Whittaker and Donald Yoho from Lawrenceville, Illinois; Paul Phillips from Paducah, Kentucky; William T. Anderson from Madisonville, Kentucky; Wendell Sanders from Henderson, Kentucky; and Jean F. Crabtree from Ada, Oklahoma.

33. It should be noted that Major Perkins was an artillery officer. In US Army tradition, he would have held some resentment about being sent from Indianapolis to recruit flyers.

34. They lived at 1032 Ravenswood in central Evansville.

35. Corn fritters are not usually a desert item unless they are covered in syrup or served with something sweet. Marcia had planned on covering them in powdered sugar.

36. The program was interrupted at approximately 2:28 p.m.

37. Truthfully, not many people, and certainly no member of the Schneck family, had ever heard of Pearl Harbor until this very moment.

38. From Isaiah 6:8.

Chapter 2

CLASS 42F: THEY CALL US DODOS

★ ★ ★

"I ask that the Congress declare that since the unprovoked and dastardly attack by Japan on Sunday, December 7, 1941, a state of war has existed between the United States and the Japanese Empire."[1]

December 9, 1941[2]

Dear Juana,

Well, it looks pretty bad doesn't it. I haven't heard anything further. I hardly think I'll have to go Dec 20 but you never can tell. Two of the boys that passed the same time I did have to be in Indianapolis on Dec 13. They are to train in Calif.

I got a letter from Carl[3]—he is getting along fine.

I just heard a report over the radio that New York City is being bombed, but I think it is just rumors.

I am ready to go any time now and I don't imagine it will be very far off.

Well I will write when I have more news.

Ralph.

★ ★ ★

While it took Washington quite a while to come to terms with the surprise attack in Hawaii, the US Army wasted no time gearing up for war. In fact, the Army had been preparing for such an event for a long time, and they were ready to grow both the Army and the Air Corps. They had already leased land for training facilities, and their designs had been prepared. While they did not have enough aircraft, they had issued design requests to manufacturers for all sorts of planes. All they needed now was the money and men to put everything in place.

On Monday, December 8, Ralph got a call from Staff Sergeant Pettay, telling him to stay close because he was going to be called up any day. On Tuesday, shortly after he dropped a letter in the mail to Juana, the sergeant called again, telling Ralph that his physical for flight training had expired[4] and he needed to take another one on Thursday, December 11.

★ ★ ★

December 9, 1941

Adolf Hitler declares war on the United States.

★ ★ ★

Wednesday, December 10

Ralph woke up early. He had slept well, even though he had a lot on his mind, and he had a clear idea as to what he needed to do. He suspected that he would be notified either that day or on Thursday and that he would be leaving within a week. He went down to the kitchen where Add and Stella were having coffee. He sat down to tell them what was going on.

After the conversation, Ralph went back upstairs, put on his best-looking tie and nicest coat, and left for work. He arrived right on time and walked in to see his boss, without stopping at his desk or to say "hi" to any of the girls in the office. Everyone knew something was up, and they loitered nearby, waiting for him to emerge. After a few minutes, Ralph came out of the office with a somber look on his face. His boss told him they would miss him and to take care of himself.

Ralph went to his desk and one of the girls came over, asking, “You’re going, aren’t you?”

He looked up and said, “Any time now. I’m just waiting.” The young woman gave him a hug and told him to take care of himself. Ralph would never admit that he became emotional, but in his later years he would say that was one of the hardest conversations he had ever experienced.

Ralph started cleaning his few personal items out of his desk. He was only in the office for a short time, but there was a constant flow of well-wishers. Many of them handed Ralph their personal good-luck charm and asked him to stay in touch. He told each person that he would carry his or her good-luck charm wherever he went and that he would do his best to stay in touch.

Just before he left, Lewis Parker showed up. Parker was not known as a flamboyant person. He patiently waited his turn to see Ralph. Very quietly, Parker congratulated him for answering the call to serve his country. He told Ralph that he would be sorely missed in the company and that he would have a job waiting for him when he returned. He shook Ralph’s hand and handed him an envelope containing his last pay. As he did so, he leaned closer and softly said there was a “little something” included for good luck. Several hours later, when he finally got around to opening the envelope, Ralph found his pay and a brand new fifty-dollar bill.

Ralph returned to his room in Add and Stella Beeler’s home and began packing all of his belongings.

★ ★ ★

December 10, 1941

Japanese bombers sink the British battleships *Prince of Wales* and *Repulse* in the Gulf of Siam. Japanese forces capture Guam.

★ ★ ★

Thursday, December 11

One of the other boys in Ralph's exam class drove several of them to Indiana University at Bloomington. They arrived around nine in the morning and got in line with a number of flight training prospects at the Indiana University Flight Training facility.

Everything went great until Ralph was ordered to strip to his shorts and enter an exam room. The Army doctor looked Ralph over, then told him to walk across the room and sit down. Ralph followed the instructions, but the doctor stopped him, asking. "Why are you walking that way?"

Ralph explained that he had worn size twelve shoes since he was fourteen. During his first physical examination, the doctor had told him he had low arches and might not qualify for flight training. Ever since then, he had walked on the outside of his foot, curling his toes under, to give the illusion that he had high arches.

The doctor laughed and said there was nothing wrong with his feet, but there would be if he kept walking like that.

When the examination concluded, Ralph and the others had all passed and were handed orders to report to Fort Benjamin Harrison on Saturday, December 13. It was a loud and boisterous trip back to Evansville.

★ ★ ★

December 11, 1941

Germany, Italy, and Japan sign an agreement on joint prosecution of the war against Great Britain and the United States. Italy declares war on the United States, while the United States Congress declares war on both Germany and Italy.

★ ★ ★

Friday, December 12

Ralph packed his car and moved out of his room in Add and Stella Beeler's home. He thanked them for everything they had done for him. They asked him to stay in touch and that they would be talking with his mom and dad from time-to-time.

He made the trip back to the farm for the last time as a civilian.

At lunch, the conversation turned to what Ralph was going to take. Sergeant Pettay had told him that the Army would take care of nearly everything, but he should bring a few personal items with him. Ralph was a little concerned because he did not own a suitcase. Jessie said he could take one of theirs, but he did not know how to get it back to them. Rolla suggested they get a sturdy box, for which he would craft a handle.

Punch,[5] Juana's steady boyfriend, drove to Richmond, Indiana,[6] to pick her up. She had managed to get a substitute teacher for the afternoon. She and Punch headed for the farm, arriving around six. Punch dropped her off and departed after giving Ralph his regards.

Herb, Marcia, and Sandra Jane arrived in mid-afternoon and stayed for dinner.

That afternoon, Jessie gave Ralph a heavy-duty cardboard box with a sturdy lid. Standing at the dining room table, Ralph packed some street clothes, socks, underwear, and toiletries. After he made sure he had room, he threw in his Standard Oil world atlas and the good-luck charms[7] everyone had given him. When he was done, Rolla tied the box with fishing line and fashioned a loop for the box to be carried. Lastly, Ralph put his name on the box and set it by the mudroom door.

At dinner, Juana asked Ralph what he was going to do with his car. He said he would probably leave the automobile for Rolla to sell. Juana told Ralph that she needed a car because she could not keep asking Punch to drive her around. She offered to buy his, inquiring about the asking price. Ralph said he hoped to get about five hundred dollars for it. Juana replied that she did not have that much money, and after a few minutes of good-natured bickering back and forth, they settled on four hundred dollars. Juana paid him in cash,[8] and Ralph handed her the keys.

After dinner, Rolla threw a couple of logs in the fireplace and retrieved a bottle of whiskey from the mudroom.[9] Everyone sat around the fire and reminisced until there were just embers and the house started to cool off.

★ ★ ★

Saturday, December 13

Ralph got up early, dressed, and headed downstairs for breakfast. Rolla normally would have already been in the fields to herd the cows back toward the barn, but this morning he delayed his normal duties. Jessie had been up for a while and had a hot breakfast on the table when Ralph came downstairs. They ate almost in silence by the light of a kerosene lamp.

After breakfast Ralph said his good-byes to his mom and dad. Juana had already gone to her new car and had it all warmed up. Ralph picked up his sturdy box that contained all of the things he thought he would need and walked down the steps from the mudroom porch. At the bottom of the steps, Shep and Trixie, the dogs of the farm, were waiting for him. Ralph tugged on their ears, scratched their heads, and got in the car with Juana for the ride to Evansville.

At the recruiting station, Juana hung around for a few minutes to make sure everything was okay. When it was time for the boys to leave, she said good-bye, cried, and waited for their car to disappear before returning to the farm.

There were four boys from the Evansville area who were traveling to Indianapolis to join the US Air Corps. They met at six in the morning at the Evansville recruiting office. It was cold and foggy. They were given some papers to take with them, and Ken Silverman's father volunteered to drive the group to their destination.

It was a slow trip due to visibility and weather, plus they stopped for lunch in Terre Haute. It was drizzling rain when they arrived at the gate of Fort Benjamin Harrison. As the boys retrieved their belongings from the trunk, Ken's father went into the guard house and came out with a sergeant who asked to see their papers. He showed them to another guard, who asked, "Air Corps cadets?"

"Yes," they replied in unison.

"Wait here," the guard said. He took their papers and walked across the street to the adjacent building. A few minutes later, he emerged, handed them their papers, and told them his sergeant would be with them shortly.

This was when Ralph began to understand the meaning of "hurry up and wait." It had been a long drive from Evansville, it was raining, it was cold, they were told to wait, and it seemed like an eternity before a sergeant walked from the building. He was much older than the other soldiers, wearing a dark olive drab, wool uniform and an old wide-brimmed campaign hat. He checked their names with the names on their papers, then said, "Follow me."

After thanking Ken's father, they walked to the adjacent building and entered a small classroom. The sergeant asked if they were all going to be Air Corps "Key Dets." They said they were, and he muttered something about how they would be sorry later on. He then asked them to raise their right hand and repeat after him as he administered the "Oath of Enlistment." Within a few minutes, they were members of the Army.

After they signed some papers, the sergeant took them to the supply building. Along the way, he pointed out the Mess Hall and told them they could eat anytime it was open. After another long wait at the supply building, they were given a mattress cover, pillowcase, two blankets, two sheets, a towel, and washcloth. Sarcastically, the sergeant explained that normally they would get uniforms in the morning, but they were all out of "Junior Bird Man" uniforms, and they would receive those later on.

After another wait, they were escorted to a barracks and told to pick out a bunk. All of the boys were worn out. Not only were they cold, wet, and hungry, but they all had trouble carrying the Army's bundle and their own luggage. They were surprised to find six other boys who had arrived earlier in the day. One was from Ohio, one from Michigan, one from Illinois, and the other three from northern Indiana. After a brief greeting, they each choose a bunk and settled in for the night.

★ ★ ★

December 13, 1941

Bulgaria and Hungary declare war on Great Britain and the United States.

★ ★ ★

They were awakened by the sound of a bugle at five-thirty in the morning. It was still dark, and the building had cooled off considerably during the night. The radiator hissed as they rose to look out the frost-covered windows at some people scurrying about. One of the boys asked aloud what they should be doing. Another said, "Go back to bed." So they did.

About an hour later they finally got around to waking up and dressing. They decided to go get something to eat, so they walked to the Mess Hall. What the sergeant failed to mention the night before was that on Sundays, the Mess Hall was only open for breakfast from 5:30 to 7:00 a.m. It was 7:10 when they arrived. Before leaving, they made sure what time it would open for lunch, as they planned on being first in line.

That afternoon, a bus pulled up in front of the barracks, and the sergeant came in to talk. He said that all but four of them were leaving immediately, and the rest would leave the next day. After the other boys boarded the bus, the sergeant told the last group that he was going to take them into Indianapolis for the evening. The last group of air cadets included Barney O'Hara from eastern Ohio near Pittsburg; Kenney Ross from Jeffersonville, Indiana; Walt Simon from Washington Court House, Ohio; and Ralph.

Two of the boys had been to Indianapolis before, but they were still thrilled, at least until they got off the bus and found that on Sunday evening, almost nothing was open. They all ended up at a drugstore sitting at the soda fountain waiting for the sergeant to take them back. While he waited, Ralph found a pay phone and called home with the news.

★ ★ ★

Ralph got up early the next day and started packing his box. The sergeant arrived and gathered the group. He told them there was a delay; it looked like they would be at Fort Benjamin Harrison one more night.

Ralph and his newfound friends sat and waited.

That evening the sergeant picked up Ralph and the other boys in a staff car and drove downtown. They went to a small bar for a beer, then to a local steak house for dinner. Before returning, they ventured to the Indiana Roof Ballroom to listen to a band. The sergeant must have been a regular at all of the places the group visited, because everyone was familiar with him. When people would look at his four protégés, he would politely say, "These birds are with me." It was a private joke that only the five of them really understood.

When they got back to their barracks, they thanked the sergeant for a nice evening. He told them he would not be around to see them again unless there was another delay. The sergeant continued, saying, "I am sure you cadets will all do well. And when you are done, kick some ass for me." It was an order, not a request.

To Ralph, the sergeant had paid them the greatest compliment by calling them "cadets" for the first time. Up to that point, he had constantly made fun of their desire to be in the Air Corps. Ralph was always up for a good ribbing, and he took the jabs in stride, but now the sergeant was serious, and Ralph had developed the utmost respect for this man, and perhaps for all the sergeants he would meet in the future.

★ ★ ★

The next morning, before the boys could get anything to eat, a bus pulled up to the front of the barracks. Ralph was excited by the prospect of a long train ride and all the things he was about to see. He would only be the second person in his family to ever see the West Coast. His father was the first. And Ralph was excited.

At ten-thirty on the morning of December 16, 1941, just nine days after the attack on Pearl Harbor, Ralph boarded a train for King City, California. A naïve kid just barely off the farm, he joined the ranks of thousands of young men just like him. Full of wonderment and an imagination filled with the dreams of flying, he carried his cardboard box, still tied with fishing line, and headed into an adventure, the likes of which no man had ever witnessed before.

★ ★ ★

★ Postcard ★
December 16, 1941[10]

Dear Juana.

We were held over another day on Indpls. We left this morning at 9:40 AM. We go N.YC-RR to St. Louis, Missouri Pac to Kansas City. Then we catch our Pulman[11] on the U. Pac to San Francisco. We go thru Ogden Utah. We arrive Fri. noon

Will write more when we have a nice stop over. There are 5 of us going together.

Ralph

★ ★ ★

★ Postcard ★
December 16, 1941

Dear Folks

We are now stopped at Terre Haute. We were held over until this morn. We go N.Y. Central to St. Louis Union Pacific—Pulman to San Francisco. We have already received our meal money for the trip. We get to King City Fri noon.

Will write more later when we have a nice stop over. I doubt if you can even read this.[12] There are 5 of us together.

Ralph

★ ★ ★

★ Postcard ★
December 17, 1941[13]

Dear Mom

We are stopped for Breakfast in Ellis Kan. We get to Denver Colo. about 3:30 PM this after noon. Having a swell time.

Ralph

★ ★ ★

December 17, 1941[14]

Dear Folks

I just wrote you a card in the diner. But I had a little time so I thought I had better write you a good letter. We left Indpl's. yesterday at 10:20 AM. We got to St. Louis & changed to the Missouri Pacific. Then to Kansas City where we changed to the Union Pacific. We will get to Denver about 4:00 PM then we will change to the Southern Pacific. I slept in a Pulman last night. It wasn't as bad as I expected.

We are going through Kansas now.[15] We have already passed Topeka. This is the flattest country you ever saw you can look for mile & miles and never see a hill. I have had breakfast and am now sitting in the club lounge car. There is easy chairs big over stuffed lounges radios writing tables all the latest magazines. Barber shop—its wonderful.

We met an aviation cadet last night. He had already had 15 wks. & was going to Denver to some field there.[16] He said they were really hard on them and we wouldn't have much time to do anything. So if you don't hear from me very regular don't think I don't want to write.

This train is moving so darn much I can hardly write. We have already learned we are not allowed to wear civilian clothes at all. So I will bundle them up & send them home. Unless we hear different. I learned than we will make more than $75 while we are training. That is $75 on an Army field. As this is a civilian field the pay is around $140 per mo. Then when we are 2nd Leut. the pay is only $175 per mo if we are on an Army field & $302 if on a civilian field. The $245 per mo is flight pay & risk pay & you don't have that in case of war because everything is risk. After the war our pay will be $245. I will draw close to $70 for this half months pay.

We are gradually going up the last stop was 1870 ft. This is a wonderful climate. Everything is all decorated for Xmas & it isn't even cold.

Please don't send me anything that I can't carry in my pocket and don't send anything until you hear from me. Now if you don't get any Xmas letter from me—understand I won't have time.

Love
Ralph

★ ★ ★

December 17 and 18, 1941

Japanese forces invade Borneo and then invade Hong Kong.

★ ★ ★

King City was founded in 1886 by Charles King, an entrepreneurial rancher. He teamed up with the Southern Pacific Railroad to bring agriculture to the Salinas Valley. Until then, the Salinas Valley was considered unfit for farming, even though the Salinas River wandered down the middle. Because of King's farming success, the Southern Pacific Railroad ran a spur from Soledad that terminated at a new warehouse. From this single building, King City began.

By 1942, King City had a population of about 1,800, with US Highway 101 running along the outskirts of town. The city's economic base was still largely dependent upon agriculture as the primary source of employment as the city was now surrounded by rich farmland that produced a wide range of fruits and vegetables.

King City's air training facility may have been the best Air Corps training field available at the time. Brand new and situated absolutely in the middle of nowhere, it provided plenty of wide open spaces and was near a very small town where no one could get into much trouble. The Pacific Ocean was about thirty miles to the west and the Big Sur Mountains lay to the east. The weather provided nearly year-round clear skies, which meant very few non-flyable days.

The training facility was located at the Palo Alto Airport, which opened in 1940, on the edge of King City. At the time, England was already at war, and the Japanese were causing problems for the Chinese and making threats against the United States. In March 1941, the Army Air Corps, forecasting a need for pilots, entered into a contract with Palo Alto Airport, Inc. to provide pilot training. Additionally, there were four auxiliary fields located nearby. These fields were used for emergency landings, for practice landings, and for basic navigation training. The fields were called Bernard, Hanson, Sorenson, and Trescony, although the cadets referred to them as fields two, three, four, and five.

The hard surface runway at the airport ran in a general northwest to southeast direction. Initially, instruction was done using the Stearman PT-17 Kaydet[17] and the Fairchild PT-19 Cornell.[18] However, they quickly switched to the Ryan PT-22 Recruit[19] when it became available.

The city began just outside the main entrance to the airfield, although the center of town was about a mile away—still close enough for an eager cadet to walk if he did not want to wait for a taxi. A taxi ride cost ten cents each, provided there were three cadets riding together. The city proper had several restaurants, the Hotel El Camino Real, the King City Hotel, and the Hotel Vendome. It also featured an ultramodern Standard Oil service station, electric streetlights, and the Reel Joy movie theater. No one had very much time for leisure activities, so the movie theater was rarely visited by the cadets. There were no bars or taverns in King City, as the entire area was dry.

Other Air Corps training facilities called King City the "Country Club" because of the atmosphere and the integration of the city with the airfield. Cadets were treated as if they were there to only learn to fly. The Army commander was a 1st Lieutenant, whose primary responsibility was to post guards and provide security around the field. For this he used the cadet corps. There were three Army instructor pilots that gave check rides to the cadets after every six hours of flying time. Without much Army presence, there was almost no hazing, which was prevalent at other facilities, although upperclassmen bent the rules when they could.

During spare leisure opportunities, cadets could freely go into town for a few hours or, in some cases, the town came to them. The Reel Joy movie theater, for instance, would sometimes bring movies to the airfield. Additionally, stage plays, some by the high school, were presented at the field.

The USO opened a facility in an old hardware store in King City on December 20, and everyone was required to attend. On a stage at the back of the building, a three-piece country and western band played for about an hour. Ladies from town served cake and punch all evening. All of the chairs were occupied by a bunch of old men, who apparently were the husbands of the ladies serving punch. The townspeople had no idea what to expect when all the Army recruits showed up on opening night, so they had two local police officers, three sheriff's deputies, and one state trooper as a greeting party. All of the cadets had to be back in their barracks by 10 p.m., so it was a very short evening. After opening night, the USO was open only on Saturdays from 10 a.m. to 10 p.m.

Life on the post was as good as it could get. When Ralph showed up, nothing was more than a year old. In fact, some of the buildings were just being completed. The barracks were all single-story structures that encircled the headquarters building. Headquarters, the only two-story building, had a flagpole in front, surrounded by a paved parade area. This paved area is where cadets walked tour when they had to parade back and forth, sometimes with a weapon on their shoulders, as punishment for some wrongdoing. All of the buildings had a concrete foundation and concrete walls for about the first four feet. Above that, they were all wood frame construction, with large buildings, like the Mess Hall, having open ceilings revealing the rafters and trusses.

King City was called a "country club" by cadets at other facilities because the boys had it so good. A row of barracks with their covered walkway is shown on the left. The Administration Building is shown on the right (it is also barely visible in the first photograph). Some cadets are "walking a tour" in front of the Administration Building.

There was a Post Exchange (PX), of sorts. It occupied a single room in one of the administrative buildings. They only sold paper, pencils, razor blades, and other basic essentials. On larger installations, the PX was the on-post department store, selling almost everything a soldier could want or need. Some items sold in the PX were not available to the public.

The barracks all featured a covered common porch to help provide a little shade. The headquarters building also had a covered porch on three sides that was connected by a covered walkway to the barracks. The grounds were landscaped to perfection, and the entire campus resembled one of the many new motels that were springing up along Route 66.

The main crop in the area was carrots. The dining hall could obtain carrots inexpensively at any time. As a result, the cooks became experts at devising many different ways to prepare them, and carrots made frequent appearances at mealtime.

There was a great deal of confusion about the actual name of the facility. Army personnel, including cadets, referred to the field or post as King City Army Airfield. However, the contract called it Mesa Del Rey. To make matters more confusing, the Palo Alto Airport, which housed the facility, was not in Palo Alto, California, which is about 120 miles to the northwest. Finally, a brochure titled "Army Pilots in the Making," published by the facility management, shows the name of the facility as "Mesa Del Rey, Palo Alto Airport, Inc., King City, California."

King City Army Airfield was constructed and operated by civilians. The boys who trained there had no idea what a good situation they experienced. It was a comfortable setting for Ralph as he tried to settle into a routine, balancing his personal chores with schoolwork and, of course, writing letters. All of the letters from King City were written on "Air Corps Training Detachment" stationery as he did his best to keep up with the demand for information.

★ ★ ★

On December 19, the boys found themselves in San Francisco, waiting to go to King City. They were supposed to leave around noon, but there was a blackout in effect. This meant that the trains would run only at night so no one would be able to determine any type of schedule. The boys finally left at 5 p.m., arriving at King City around 10:30 p.m. in complete darkness. The only light was from a lantern held by the stationmaster. The new cadets were the only people who disembarked. The stationmaster called the airport, which sent a truck to pick them up.

They were dropped off in front of the headquarters building, which they could hardly make out in the darkness. They groped their way to the front door where they were greeted by a sergeant major who escorted them to the commandant.

The commandant was a skinny man with a thin mustache, wearing an Army uniform with jodhpurs[20] and a Sam Browne belt. He told them they were the last four boys to arrive and that the facility was now at maximum capacity. As the sergeant major led them out of the office, Ralph could not help but take note of the nameplate on the desk. It ran almost the entire width of the desk, proclaiming the name of the commandant in gold capital letters: 1st Lieutenant Perry M. Hoisington III.

The sergeant major took the group to supply to obtain bedding for the night, and then he led them toward their barracks. He pointed into the darkness and told them to go to the last door, which would lead into their room for the night. As the boys stumbled in the darkness, they heard a voice say, "Halt, who goes there?"

One of the boys replied, "You think he's talking to us?"

"Who goes there?" asked the voice. "Halt or I'll shoot."

Ralph thought, "Oh my God. I'm going to be shot before I ever see an airplane."

"Step forward and be recognized," the voice continued.

The sergeant major came up behind the boys with a flashlight and talked to the guard. He then took them to their room and told them not to leave the room for any reason until he came to get them in the morning.

The boys got to bed at 1 a.m., only to be awakened at 5:30 a.m. to start their day.

★ ★ ★

December 21, 1941[21]

Dear Mother & Dad—Folks

Well this is my first weekend in the Army. You'll have to excuse the pencil as I have run out of ink. We had a wonderful trip out here. Kansas was so awfully flat and dry no trees over 10 ft high. Kansas City was the smokiest place I ever saw. But we have had no smoke since then. We came thru Denver which is a nice city. It was fairly cold but it was such high altitude you couldn't see your breath. Then Ogden, Utah and on thru the Great Salt Lake. The Bridge itself is 12 miles long but the tracks are on a levee 35 miles long—the distance across the lake. By the time we got to Denver there were mountains. Our train was blacked out[22] from Denver on. From the great Salt Lake we went to Reno, Nev. The train is there for 15 min. and everybody runs across the street to the Palace Inn.[23] The largest gambling place in town. You see rich men and beautiful women in fine clothes—Furs, silks, diamonds you see prospectors with long beards & ragged clothes, cowboys with boots & 10 gal hats. It is 1 large room with everything from slot machines to roulette. It was a most beautiful building inside. Then we went thru Dunher Pass[24] where the wind blows at a 70 MPH gale all the time. It was the highest part of our journey almost 7000 ft high and it was so steep that we had to put on two engines to get over. Then there was Trukey[25] the beautiful winter resort. And finally Calif. The trees are big the mts are big everything is big. The train brings you to Oakland, then you have to take the ferry across the bay to San Francisco. You see all kinds of boats & you go under the beautiful Golden Gate bridge & you can see Alcatraz.

Frisco is a very beautiful city. All the buildings are white or light tan and most of them are rather new, having been built since the earthquake. Everybody rides the cable car up the hill & goes in the Drake roof garden[26] which is up 32 stories[27] in the Hotel. You can see all over the whole city for miles & miles. You are almost 1 mile above the main St., Market, which is only 5 blocks away. So you know it is a large hill. Then there is China town. I could write pages & pages but I couldn't tell you exactly how it is on paper. There is no smoke but there is fog until about 10 AM.

We arrived in King City about midnight Fri. Our train was late. King City is a small town about 2000 pop. Everybody wears cowboy boots & hats. There are quite a few Mexicans.

Palo Alto Airport is about 1 mile from town. It is a beautiful place. All new buildings built within the last 6 mos.

There are 4 cadets in a room. 2 tables & 4 chairs. 4 beds. 1 bathroom with 2 wash basins 1 shower and commode. 4 built in lockers. 1st reveille is at 5:25 Breakfast at 6:00 AM. I couldn't be treated any nicer if I was at home. There are very few upper classmen & they are not Cadets. They are Aviation Students. They are enlisted men & will be called Flying Sergeants[28] when they are finished. They will not be commissioned officers like we will. They pay very little attention to us. I understand they have cut out hazing & initiation like stuff all together. There is a public address system & we receive our orders over the loud speaker. Of course we have to salute our superior officers & you have to know when, where & who to salute.

All our clothing so far has been G.I. clothes. I have 2 pr. coveralls, 1 heavy wool slip over sweater, 1 gym sweat pants & shirt, 2 T shirts, 1 pr gym shoes, 2 pr wool socks, 1 cap like a baseball cap. We have to wear a piece of white tape across this until we solo then we can take it off. Then we have 1 helmet, 1 pr. goggles, 1 heavy leather jacket sheep skin lined, 1 pr. sheep skin lined leather flying boots, 1 pr fur lined mittens.

We met our instructors yesterday. Mine is L.C. Hale.[29] We start flying tomorrow. We fly low wing Ryan PT22. They have 155 HP engines and have top speed around 160 MPH.[30] There are quite a number of these ships here, they are brand new. There are some other airplanes here also. They have all been explained to us. Our instructors warned us about talking about the planes, there instruments & other gadgets. So I had better not say anymore. If you have any questions ask them & I will try to answer them if I can.

All cadets have to take turns walking guard duty. I am on tonight from 8 PM to 10 PM & then again from 2 AM to 4 AM. You are on 2 hrs off 4hrs & on 2 hrs more. I have had instructions on how to use the Gererand rifle.[31] We have instructions—if someone fails to stop when we challenge them to shoot & shoot to kill. I hope everybody stops for me.

We are in a valley here & there are mountains on all sides of us. We can fly in a 10 mile radius of the airport. There is 1 mt. that is real close to us.

Some Sunday I am going to climb part of it. We will be here 10 wks. & will receive around 60 hrs. of flying. We had open post last night. Which means you can leave the post when you get thru Sat & be back Sunday by 7:00 PM. Unless you walk guard Sat night then you have to stay in. You can sleep as late as you want on Sun. & you have to answer no calls.

The U.S.O. has a very nice building in King City. They were dedicating it last night. They had a Dance. I stayed until about 10 PM then I came back to the post as I wanted to get a goods nights sleep to prepare myself for tonight. Our meals are very good. We have tables[32] & the food is set on the table home style. We can talk & we do not have to sit on edges of our chairs. We can eat as much as we like. Last night we had large T bone steaks, fried potatoes, lettuce & dressing, cake, fruit Salad & coffee or water. We have milk only at breakfast. There is a PX on the post where we can buy things. There is bowling alleys, pool tables & ping pong tables there also.

I have just signed my insurance policy. I have named Mother as benificiary & Dad as alternate. I am having it sent home so be on the lookout for it. I understand that we are to get dress uniforms & shoes & shirts, etc. next week & I will send my civies home as it will be impossible for me to wear them until the war is over. I think we get 2 days off Xmas. Please let everyone read this letter as I do not want to write it over. I won't have any time to write except on Sun. You can address me either as a/c or Cadet.

Merry Christmas to all.

Love
Ralph.

★ ★ ★

December 21, 1941

A German submarine torpedoes and sinks British carrier *Audacity*.

★ ★ ★

During the evening, aircraft were covered with tarps to keep the dirt out. Here, Ralph is uncovering a Ryan PT-22 Recruit for a morning flight. This picture was taken before he soloed; his white dodo stripe is clearly visible.

December 25, 1941

Dear Mother, Dad & Juana,

Well, it is Christmas Day. We have 4 days off. Thur, Fri, Sat & Sun.[33] I have just finished eating Supper. We had Turkey & dressing, Peas, Mashed Potatoes & Gravy, Celery, olives, Pickles, etc. Cranberry sauce, fruit salad, Fruit Cake, Mince Meat pie, ice cream. I sure am full.

All of those who had relatives near hear were excused and got to go home. The rest of us take turns leaving the post. I was in town last night and I can leave Sat night if I want to. I am on guard Fri night & again on Sun. in the day time. We ordinarily don't have guard duty in the day time—only on holidays such as this. This makes it pretty hard on us fellows here on the post, but we won't have to do it for about 2 wks again. I have an hour and 9 min flying time in. We only got to fly 2 days this week. It rained the other day. Oh! Pardon me, it never rains in Calif.—just a heavy dew.

There was a notice posted on the board—the upper classmen will leave Jan 16, 1942 or before. Which will make me very happy, for then I will be an upper classman. I am so darn sore all over that I can hardly move. We really have to move around. This week my day consists of Revielle 5:25 AM, exercises 5:30 AM (they last 10 min), Breakfast 6:00 AM, ground school 6:45 AM to 9:20 AM, Physical Ed. 9:30 AM to 10:20 AM, Lunch or dinner 10:40 AM, Flying line 12:15 PM to 4:00 PM, Drill 4:30 to 5:10 PM, Supper 6:00 PM, studying period (confined to quarters) 7:00 PM to 9:00 PM, release from quarters 9:00 PM, lights out at 9:15 PM. There are 2 flights B & D & next week all by morning classes will be in the afternoon & all afternoon classes will be in the morning. I guess I am getting along all right. My instructor hasn't boiled me out about any thing as yet. I got Marcia's letter yesterday. It took just 2 days to get here. She said Lewis Parker[34] had to go sort of sudden like also. That really makes me feel good. I am going to try to write everybody a letter this week & get that caught up. I won't write Juana any at Richmond because she can read this one there at home. I am also trying to catch up on my studying. The following are books that are issued us and we will have ground school in. Air Navigation; aircraft engines; aircraft induction, fuel and oil systems; weather manual for pilots; aircraft electrical systems; Elementary

Map & Aerial photography reading; Aircraft Engine operation & test; Airplane structures; Airplane Hydraulic systems & Miscellaneous Equip; aircraft propellers; Airplane inspection guide; Theory of flight; and Instructions for Airway meteorological service. Of course we have just 3 periods a day but we will have classes in all of these before the 10 weeks are up.

One of the boys here in my room has already washed out. I came in the other day (Monday) and he was laying on the bed shaking all over. He said he just didn't have the nerve to go up in the plane. He went to see the Flight Surgeon & he told him to just forget about flying. He is writing for his release now. I kind of feel sorry for the boy. The fellows I stay with are really a fine bunch of fellows. 1 is from Texas, 1 from West Va. and 1 from Colorado. None of them smoke or drink, they are clean and a pretty good bunch of boys.[35]

This is supposed to be the finest primary school in this end of the country. There are 6 lieutenants here who have received commissions in other branches of service and are starting to fly here. So if the Army sends their own men here it must be pretty good.

We haven't received our uniforms as yet. The Army, especially the Air Corps, is usually pretty slow on things like that. The uniforms are to be regular officers uniforms. Dark green coats & trousers about 3 shades lighter. It is a different color from the enlisted men and of a much nicer material. Our cap is a regular officers cap only while we are Cadets we will have to wear a blue band around it. Then we get an officers short coat, shirts, socks, etc. Well, I'm getting ready to go to bed. If I think of anything between now & tomorrow I'll put it on. I got the telegram. Thanks a lot.

Love
Ralph

Please send me my best brown shoes, the best protractor[36] which was in the table drawer at Beeler's, and the large brown celluloid box which I took out of my fitted military case and if there are any more of the Dixie Crystal[37] blotters which were in the table drawer send a few of them also include about 6 wire coat hangers. There is no particular hurry anytime in the next 2 weeks. Thanks a lot. Ralph.

★ ★ ★

December 25, 1941

British forces in Hong Kong surrender to the Japanese.

★ ★ ★

December 31, 1941

Japanese submarines shell Hilo, Nawiliwili, and Kauai, Hawaii.

★ ★ ★

January 1, 1942

Dear Juana,

I am so glad you liked the pajamas. Did you get the monogrammed cards? I left them there at home. Marcia wrote me that she liked her table just fine. I didn't get my watch for Xmas. I still have $60 set aside for it. You can hardly get chronographs anymore. Most of all of the works were swiss and we can't get them anymore. However, I'll keep trying and maybe I can get one thru the Army at a reduced price.

Our bldgs here are concrete up about 4 ft and then they are frame. On the inside the walls are white plastering. The windows doors & closets are light green, the beds tables chairs are light maple and cream color venetian blinds with dark Red floor. The rooms are really nice. We can regulate our own heat. And we have our own private bath.

We have to furnish our own soap, towels, shoe polish, etc. We are charged 75¢ for laundry whether we send anything or not. For the 75¢ we are allowed 1 pr coveralls, 1 pr pajamas, 6 pr socks, 3 pr shorts & shirts, 3 dress shirts, 6 handkerchiefs, 3 towels and wash rags. Anything over that costs you more. But I think that is very reasonable.

I have received all the letters & Telegrams. However, I did not receive the Tel until Dec 26.

We are allowed radios but I don't want any until I am an upper classman and then I don't want any if I have very much studying to do at night. I want my work here to come first.

There were 3 other boys came here from Indiana with me.

We were measured for uniforms this week. Officer hat, Flight caps, shirts, pants, blouse or coat, belt, socks, shoes, underwear, over coat, gloves and rain coat. We will not have to pay for these and they will be regular officers clothes. When we get these we will put them on every night & stand inspection before we eat supper.

I am glad you ask a lot of questions because then I can tell you what you want to know.

Will write more later. You can do what you want with the auto & you don't owe me any money.[38]

Thanks a lot for all you have done for me. If there is anything I can do for you let me know.

Love
Ralph

★ ★ ★

January 1, 1942

Dear Dad,

You were right when you said you guessed I was learning lots of new things. Everything is so much different than it is in a civil life.

The Rockies are a wonderful sight. I think it would be well worth any bodys time and money to make a trip west. There is snow on some of the mountains here. But they are about 8 or 10 miles away. However they look about ¼ mile away. You see we are between 2 ranges here and the mts that are close are only about 1000 or 1500 ft high whereas the ones further off are higher and are probably 2000 or 3000 ft high and they are the ones which have snow. There are mts on all sides of us and no matter where we look up we see mts. We have not had very many pretty days since I have been here. It has either been pretty cold or raining. You see this is their winter here and it snows in the mts. and rains here. 9/10 of the yearly water fall comes in the months of Dec & Jan. And it sometimes gets as low as 45°. However we have green grass and the flowers are blooming.

You asked about the upper classmen. You see there is a class comes every 5 weeks and they stay for 10 weeks. When we came here there had already been a class here for 5 weeks and they are upperclassmen. They will be leaving about Jan 16 and then we will be upperclassmen the next 5 weeks.

We are called Dodo[39] until we solo. A dodo is a bird that can't fly and until we solo we are called Dodos. I expect to solo the end of next week or 1st part of the next if the weather holds good. I have a little over 2½ hrs. This Army flying is a lot different than civilian flying. There at Evansville when we came in for a landing we glided in very gentle and easy. like this [drawing of a long glide path] at 500 ft high. In the Army you come in at 500 ft and when you get to the edge of the field you just head it towards the ground and when you get about 20 ft from the ground you level out like this [drawing of short glide path]. However my instructor said I was getting along alright. They don't give you very many compliments but when they do you can rest assured they mean it. My instructor is the best out here at Palo Alto. He is the commander of the instructors. Every so often he has to take all the other instructors up for a check ride to see if they can still do all the manuevuers they are suppose to do. He doesn't teach any Cadets unless they get a little short in instructors. He is only teaching 4 of us, all the other instructors have 5. He is really a swell fellow.

They have a very sensitive altimeter on these planes to measure the height. And when he says we will practice 360° turns at 1000 ft. We will make the turns at 1000' and not 1010 ft or 990 ft. They will allow us 5' gain or loss on one turn so you see we have to be pretty accurate and we keep on practicing 360° turns until they are perfect then we will go on to something else.

I am beginning to feel like a man. We have 1½ hrs of Physical Ed each day. We do exercises to strengthen all the different muscles especially the chest, back, stomach & leg muscles for 45 min. Then we can play the rest of the time. I am on a basket ball team, we have 5 teams. I eat like a horse and I am not getting fat. My muscles are getting hard, I get at least 8 hrs sleep every night, I am hungry all the time and I really feel good.

On the way out here we were allowed $1.00 per day which wasn't nearly enough until we got to Kansas City. Then we could eat on less than $1.00 as food got cheaper. I will write more the end of the week. I have to pull guard from 12 N to 2 PM and I have some studying to do. Thanks a lot for taking care of my clothes and everything.

Love,
Ralph.

★ ★ ★

January 11, 1942[40]

Dear Mother & Dad.

Boy am I feeling good. After 6:40 min of dual instruction my instructor said, "It's all yours." I soloed Thursday.

We have 5 different fields here. Number 1 is here at the hangers. It is hard surface all over and is the largest of them all. The rest of the fields are in different places up and down the valley within a radius of 15 miles of here. We were over on #3 shooting landings. We had made 4 landings and were Taxing back up the field & Mr. Hale (my instructor) was explaining about traffic when taxing on #3. When we got to the end he said "Do you think you could fly this by yourself." I said "I don't know." He said, "you'd better because that's just what you are going to do." He climbed out of the plane & I was on my own. It sure is a funny feeling up there by yourself the first time. I wasn't scared or a bit nervous but I just had a funny feeling. I made 4 landings and came back & picked him up. All the landings were perfect he said. When we landed back at #1 everybody saw I had my Dodo strip off my helmet and when I stopped the plane most all the boys I knew ran out & congratulated me, shook my hand, slapped me on the back and all that stuff.[41] It really made you feel good. I think Mr. Hale was more anxious to get the Dodo tape off my helmet than I. He pulled it off after my first solo landing. The hard part of it all was they start giving check rides at 6 hrs. These are taken with civilian instructors and are given to see if you know what you should for the hrs. you have in the air. If you come up to par you are OK. If you don't they put you up for a washout ride with 1 of the 3 Army Instructors here and if you don't pass that check out you go.

It so happened I was up for a check ride the day I soloed. We were out 23 min and when we came back he congratulated me on the way I looked around, watching for other planes. He said failing to look for other planes was a bad common fault with most pilots. He said the only thing wrong was I glided a little too fast when losing altitude. So that made me feel pretty good. It so happened that I was guard the night before and only got 3 hrs sleep. So when taps sounded at 9:15 PM Thur. night I was really ready for bed. Friday we didn't get to fly on account of fog. But Saturday I soloed from

After Ralph received his uniform, he owned more clothes than he ever thought possible. This is one of a group of pictures he sent home where he models all of the clothing the Army had given him. The picture was taken in front of his barracks.

field #4. You have to solo from 3 different fields then you can go to the dispatcher and check a plane out myself. I imagine if we can fly on Monday I will get to solo again then I can check a plane out anytime I feel like flying. I was the 9th man to solo in this class. All the other men had more hrs. than I when I soloed. I know some boys here who have had 100 hrs previous flying and who has more hrs than I, here, and have not soloed. However, I do feel that what little flying I did have has helped me a lot.

We are really getting into swing of the war out here. We have had several blackouts here. some of them lasting 1hr 10 min. but nothing has happened. I told you in the previous letter that we had been issued gas masks. We received orders that every Army man on the post, including officers, Has to wear these at all times. No matter where we go. These masks are in a little canvas packet about 12" X 12" X 4" and have 2 straps on them 1 goes over your shoulder and 1 around your waist. They fit behind right at the small of your back. They are quite a nuisance. We can get out of Post only on weekends and then ½ goes on Sat night and the other half goes on Sunday. We can only be gone 6 hrs. at a time and can go no further than King City, and there is nothing there. So you can see we have some very, very exciting times.

They are washing them out right and left here. There were about 20 washouts this last week. 1 of the boys who washed out was a regular on Stanford's football team last year.

Our Physical Ed. director was an all American about 3 yrs. ago for Southern California.

I received both the boxes and I want to thank you very much. The cookies weren't very good. They had been shaken around so much that there was nothing left in the box but crumbs. The candy, although it was broken up in little pieces was very, very good. The Army does furnish shoes but so far I haven't gotten any yet. All the clothes anybody has so far is underwear, sox, toothbrush, shaving brush & razor, which I don't use, barracks bags & rain coat.

We have small wooden beds we sleep on. We are allowed to take pictures & I am sending Marcia money today to get some film, because It would be easier for her to get it than you folks.[42] I will send the pictures to Cin.[43] and will have them sent direct to you.

We have taxi service in to town. They charge 10¢ a head. I have not seen any graveyards[44] out here.

I will send the tin boxes back when I send the clothes. But I won't send them until I get my uniform.

We have cooks who do the cooking & waiters in white clothes who serve the food on tables. We have to do no cooking or dish washing.

Thanks a lot for the newspaper clippings. I enjoy reading them. We are allowed newspapers. The only ones we can by at the PX are San Francisco papers. I would enjoy reading some of the Evansville Sunday papers once in a while.

Everybody seems to be hit pretty hard on auto tires. I guess people will have to sell their cars.

I am sort of glad I am not in the snow. It was chilly here for a few days but we are going without shirts again now.

I wouldn't do anything about the Insurance Policy. They will mail it when they get around to it. But don't worry I have already signed it and if anything should happen to me everything will be taken care of. The Guardian Insurance comes due every six mo. and when you get the notice let me know & I will send you the money.

I think Dennis John is doing the right thing in joining the Navy.

I am sending 3 pictures and will send some more when I take them. The one where I am about to get in the plane you can see the white tape on the helmet running from my forehead back. It isn't on there anymore. These were taken on Sunday and we had to uncover 1 of the planes. You can still see the ropes and canvas.

Love
Ralph

In a letter to Juana written the same day, Ralph adds:

I have already ordered a watch from here. It is a Jardur.[45] It is listed as $105 watch and I am getting it for $59.95 including tax and everything. Several of the pilots here have them and they say they keep excellent time and are very good watches. . . .

We have been taking shots. I have had 2 typhoid shots & I have 1 more to go. On the first shot my arm got real sore and I was pretty sick for about a day but this last one hasn't bothered me much. They say we have to take lockjaw & some other shots also.

★ ★ ★

January 13, 1942

Germans begin a U-boat offensive along the East Coast of the United States.

★ ★ ★

January 18, 1942

Dear Juana,

I got the fruit cake and it was delicious. I certainly enjoyed it. I ate so much at one time I was afraid I would get sick but I didn't.

It hasn't been very cold here. In the daytime it warms up quite a bit but in the night it gets pretty chilly.

We are upper Classmen as of tomorrow. At the end of the week the new class will come in. There will be around 200 of them. We will have a hot old time drilling them & making them walk the line.

I haven't received any demerits yet. You get gigs here and 1 gig is equal to any number of demerits, usually 2, according to the seriousness of your fault or error.

We received our uniforms this week. 1 Blouse, 2 wool shirts, 3pr. Trousers, 2 pr shoes, 1 garrison cap,[46] 2 flight caps,[47] 1¾ long overcoat, 1 pr gloves and our jewelry. However I had to have mine altered and it is not back from the taylor shop yet.

I haven't received my watch as yet. But I will the first part of this week, unless they are out of them. It will be stainless steel case. They are suppose to be more durable than gold and will have an ordinary leather band. However, when I can get to a government PX where prices are cheaper I will get a silver band with the Air Corps insignia and my name on it.

We signed the payroll sheet Thur. night & we get paid the last of the month. I have enough money to last until then.

I have about 17 hrs in the air now. I get on the average of about 2 hrs daily.

One day when I was up solo, I was up to 3500 ft practising stalls & spins and just for curiosity I climbed up to about 5500 or 6000 ft. It was a very clear day and I could see the ocean about 40 or 50 miles away. You could tell it was the ocean only by the horizon which was a straight line. However, I could see Mt. Whitney, the tallest mt. in the U.S., which looked about 30 miles away but actually was about 200 miles.

It doesn't seem as if Evansville College is doing so well in basketball this year.[48]

I guess you have been pretty busy with test & grades, etc.

We have a test every Friday in all ground school subjects.

I saw the stage show Hellzapoppin.[49] It was very good. I haven't seen the picture by that name.

I got a letter from Lela Johnson[50] this week.

Mother wrote & said she was mailing me a cake Lela had baked. But so far I haven't got it.

Well I can't think of anything more & thanks again for the cake.

Ralph.

★ ★ ★

Ralph was always amazed at the amount of paperwork the Army required. With the dodo stripe gone, he fills out papers for his very last flight at King City, a one-hour and ten-minute solo flight to the auxiliary fields.

January 18, 1942

A German submarine torpedoes and sinks Canadian passenger freighter *Lady Hawkins* 250 miles off Cape Hatteras, North Carolina.

★ ★ ★

January 24, 1942

Dear Juana,

It is raining so I'll drop you a line & hope I get it finished before I'm called for something.

Our new class of 200 Cadets just arrived and we have to look after them, help them fix their rooms, lockers and tell them what they have to do. I have also been appointed "Right Guide" for "C" Company[51] and I have been studying my drill manual for we are going to have a parade review pretty soon.

It has been raining & general bad weather. I only have about 23 hrs in the air. We had a little storm here this week. Some of the planes were wrecked, etc. although no one was hurt.

Tell Mrs. Gay I enjoyed the popcorn[52] a lot. It was awfully good and nice & fresh. One of the boys got some apples the day before and we had a little party. It was awfully good.

I guess we will fly on Sunday from now on. They are going to cut the course from 10 wks to 9 wks.

One of the boys in the room got his radio from home so now we can keep up on the news. It seems funny that we listen to programs in the afternoon that we used to hear of a night.

I am anxious to hear how the tournaments come out. It seems as if Washington is going to take everything again this year.[53]

Will write more later.

Love,
Ralph.

★ ★ ★

January 26, 1942

The first American forces arrive in Britain, landing in Belfast, Northern Ireland.

★ ★ ★

February 1, 1942

Dear Juana,

Just got your letter and the clippings—Thanks a lot.

We flew today just as usually. I have 36½ hrs as of today.

I got the Candy. It was awfully good. Thanks a lot.

The only shirts we got were wool ones. When it gets warmer we can wear Sun Tan. These are the only two shirts we can wear until we are officers.

I will take some pictures just as soon as I have time. As we fly on Sun. we don't get any time off.

I really have a good watch. I set it the first day with the dispatchers time & I haven't had to set it since.

You asked about flying. The more I fly the more I like it.

I feel a little sorry for these farmers here in the valley. All of we Army boys flying around 500' doing pylon eights or elementary 8's[54] for 30 min at a time.

Well I have a few more letters to write & its getting close to supper. Thanks again for the candy.

I guess we will leave here in 3 more weeks.

Love
Ralph.

★ ★ ★

February 8, 1942

Dear Mother & Dad,

Well another Sunday another week. These weeks sure pass fast. We are supposed to be thru here in 2 more weeks. I think we leave on Feb 23. But I do not know where. Most of the Classes from here have been going to Moffett Field, near San Francisco, but I see that the Navy has taken that over, and I doubt very much if we go there. There has been talk of us going to Chico. It is further north around Sacremento, I think. If we go there we will be the first Class, as that is a new field just being completed. That would please me very much as we would have no upper Classmen there. But you never can tell where we will go, New Mexico, Arizona, Colorado, Washington, or Oregon. When I write you next week I will probably know where we will go.

We flew today the same as usual. The upper Class had open post last night until 12:00 PM. The U.S.O. had a picture show and the Salinas Junior College[55] tumbling team gave a performance and then there was dancing afterwards. Next week end there is going to be a 3 act play put on by Fox pictures. They are sending some of their players here for fri & Sat nights. Half of us will go fri & half Sat. nights. The next week end they are having a graduation dance for us upper Class. Several of the Sororities from Salinas College are sending a bus load of girls down here for the occasion.

I have 45 hr & 23 min as of today. I have just a little over an hour a day to fly to be done by the 23^{d}. I expect to be pretty well thru by the end of next week. We get 60 hrs here. I only have 14 hrs to go. The last five hours we get here will be acrobatic.

I have all my uniform. I sent my clothes to Marcia last night when I was in town. I sent them Railway Express Prepaid. If you see her please tell her so. It will probably be a week before it gets there.

Please put these income tax things in my green box. I am not going to pay the Fed. until I am out of the Army.[56]

I took some pictures yesterday in my uniform. I don't know if they will be good or not. I am putting the film in the mail today. It will be sent to you from Cincinnati. Please let me know if they are good.

I got the Candy. It was awfully good. I also got a cake form Juana yesterday which was very good. The next time you send me something please put in my alarm clock. You need not send it by itself. Any time in the next month will be alright. Both the boys here in the room have clocks but they make so much noise it sounds like a second hand jewelry store.

As for breakfast we average having hot cakes 3 mornings a week. I usually eat a pretty good breakfast. This flying sure develops an appetite.

The goggles we wear are just plain glass but they are ground like any glass lens. They do not magnify. They cost $12.25. They are charged to us but when we turn them in when we leave the charge is credited. However, if we break a lens we do have to pay for that. Each lens cost $3.25. So far I haven't broken any.

I thought I had written you about the clothes I got. We received 6 pr shorts & shirts, 6 pr cotton socks, 4 pr wool socks, 2 pr shoes, 6 handkerchiefs, 3 pr trousers, 1 blouse, 1 fingertip Overcoat, 1 garrison cap, 2 flight caps, 1 pr gloves, 2 shirts, 1 tooth brush, 1 comb, 2 towels, 1 razor & 1 shaving brush, 1 belt and 2 barracks bags. All of this belongs to me. I didn't have to pay for it and I take it where ever I go. We also received 1 pr coveralls, 1 sweater, 1 cap, 1 helmet & goggles, 1 flight jacket, 1 pr gloves, 1 pr flying boots which I will turn in here when I leave. I had to buy my gym clothes & shoes and I have a gas mask which doesn't belong to me but I have to keep it. If it is lost the Army charges me $24.00 for it.

It is really getting warm here. I usually use 1 blanket sometimes 2 when the fog comes in & it gets cold.

I guess the valley here is about 30 miles long. Of course it is part of the valley that runs between San Francisco & Los Angeles. We are restricted to about 12 miles each way up & down the valley [drawing].[57] It is about 7 miles to fields 4E & 4W & about 12 miles to 7E & 7W. These fields are so numbered that if you add 2 zeros to the numbers it gives you the altitude at which you fly the traffic pattern. You see some of the lands are higher than others. E & W Stands for East & West fields. These fields other than the home field are nothing more than cow pastures which have been rolled. We shoot stages and practice landings on these fields. The Home filed here is almost ½ mile long & 1/8 mile wide with a strip of tarvey[58] 300' wide & 1 mile long on the side. Next to the long strip is 13 bomb shelters for airplanes.

We have 1 drill period a day which lasts 40 min. The right guide marches in front of the platoon he is responsible for the Cadence & direction of the platoon. [drawing][59] We are going to have a parade this afternoon at 4:30. There are several visitors on the post. Mostly Legion people as the American Legion post is giving us some guidons.

I am sending you $40.00 keep enough for my insurance. You can do what you want with the rest. If you need any of it at any time please use it. We get paid once a month. Let me know if you get the money OK.

Love
Ralph.

★ ★ ★

February 17, 1942

Dear Mother & Dad,

I am sorry that I have not answered your letter sooner. We didn't fly Sunday so I took a trip. One of the boys here in the Room has an auto[60] so he (Ervin Rogers) and another boy from Huntington, Ind and myself went to Salinas which is about 50 miles from here. We got a nice juicy steak drove around a bit and then came back. It was a nice little drive. It sure does a fellow good to get off "the Ranch" a little while.[61]

We are just about thru here. I have about 3 hrs to go. I have an Army & School check ride and then I have a front seat ride with the instructor. This will take about 2 hrs. and I will finish the rest solo and I will be thru. If we have a good day tomorrow I will finish up.

Unless our orders change at the last minute I will be sent to Leamoor,[62] Calif. This is a new basic school and have had only three classes.

Three of our upper Classmen to be, were here from Leamoor Sun. They told us it was pretty tough and everything very military. It seems that all the officers there are from Randolph Field, Texas and they have tried to make this field as much like Randolph as possible. I am not for sure that this is where we go but unless our orders changed we will be there Feb 24. We are to leave here Feb 23. We started out with 150 men, about and so far about 40 percent washed out. There are between 80 & 90 left.

These new classes coming in are much larger but they are washing out a larger per cent of them. Our Dodos here have already 40% washed out. They have lowered the mental Requirements to let more men in but they don't spend as much time with them. Our Dodos have an average of less than 20 hrs per man. Another thing these new men are having their ground school cut down. My Class, 42-F, is the last Class to get the full course in ground instruction. All Cadets who enter the same time I did are in Class 42F no matter what school they go to. Class 42G and all others will have their ground school cut down. In ground school we are studying meteorology. Besides flying, this is the most interesting thing I have ever run across. Every day I try to predict the weather but most of the time I miss it a mile.

Did Grandma[63] have a nice funeral? Thanks for the valentine. I got the Candy & clock today.

I got a letter from Mr. Parker[64] last week & one from Mrs Elles (Miss Lannert). I haven't answered them yet. I guess I'll get around to it sometime next week.

I am sending you my duplicates on Income Tax. This is Federal & I am not paying this now. There was an income Tax man sent here to the post by the government and that is what he advised me to do. Please put the papers in the box for me.

I am not gaining much weight. I weigh between 170–175 lbs. Exercise doesn't seem to hurt me any more. We have tests in exercise the same in exercise as in any thing. We have standing broad jump, chinning, basket Ball free throw laying on your back & lifting your legs up. Laying on your stomach & lifting yourself up with your arms. 75 & 150 yd dash. We are given these every 5 wks & are supposed to show an improvement. I am tied with another boy from Ohio in BB free throw. I got 9 out of 10.

I think nothing of flying by myself. I have finished with acrobatics and can now fly in most any position whether upside down or sideways.

I mailed a film to Cin. have you got the pictures yet! You probably won't hear from me any more until I am situated at the new place. Will write and tell you all about it.

Love
Ralph.

In a letter to Juana on the same day, Ralph added:

I got the cake and candy. They were both very good. But you don't have to spend your money buying me things. You should put it in the bank & save it.

Mother & Dad or somebody sent me the Sunday Paper & it had about Lila Faye's marriage. I guess I'm the only one left who isn't married in my class. . . .

My average in all subjects in all ground school is about 91. I still have 2 finals to take this week yet and my grade might go down.

★ ★ ★

February 19, 1942

Japanese aircraft attack Darwin, Australia.

★ ★ ★

Evansville Feb 20–42

Dear Juana.

Marcia came by this morning and as Add wasn't here, left Ralph's letter and pictures, as I wanted him to see them. And I told her I would send them on to you.

We looked up "Leamoore" in the atlas, but found "Lemore" so imagine that is where Ralph will be sent. If you look at the map you will see Lemore is due east from King City, about 75 miles and is in Banford Co.

We were so pleased to see the pictures. Ralph looks happy & sweet. Just like he always looks when real pleased over any thing. Marcia, Add & I think the over seas cap[65] so becoming.

I imagine we would all be amazed at all he has learned and his varied experiences. He will be careful I know as he wants to do every thing right and is so eager to reach the top.

I rec'd your letter and was glad to hear from you. You very much over estimate our doings for Ralph. We felt he was one of us and never did hesitate to ask him to do little things for us. He required very little attention as he loved to be independent. But Add and I really love him and miss him. Ralph is made of fine qualifications, has a splendid family back ground. And I often told him—two sisters that were 100% in every way. We will always be glad he came into our lives and was one of us. Let us hope & pray that he will have a future as pleasant as his past has been. I wish you are well.

Love.
Stella Beeler

★ ★ ★

February 22, 1942

Dear Juana,

Well I am all packed & ready to leave in the morning just as soon as we get our clearance papers.

There are four of us driving over together.

I had some pictures taken and am sending them to Mother & Dad. I had a letter from Harold down at the offices[66] & he said that Bill Wimsatt turned a plane over 3 times & his instructor sent him up for a check ride. Then he was about washed out and he asked to have his instructor changed & he was doing better but they were holding him for the next class.

Well I have nothing more to write.

I don't know what the correct address will be. But mail will reach me like this:

Cadet R.H. Schneck
Class 42-F
Lemoore Field
Lemoore, Calif.

Ralph

★ ★ ★

With two finals to go, Ralph had an average grade of about 91 percent. He was concerned that after the last two exams, his grades would slip. However, through his diligent efforts and careful preparation his grades went up.

On Saturday morning, February 21, Ralph was summoned to the military commander's office. When he arrived he was told to wait and was directed to a chair in the outer office. While he waited, he watched the civilian head of the school, his flight instructor, and a few of the classroom instructors walk into the office. After a few minutes, he was told to enter.

He reported in, saluting and standing at attention. The commander told him to stand at ease and asked for his demerit book. Each cadet was allowed twenty demerits[67] during the course of the school. If they exceeded that amount they would go before a review board, which almost always resulted in being washed out. In order to keep track of their demerits, cadets carried a matchbook, which contained twenty matches. When they got a demerit, they would tear out a match. The number of matches left in the book told them where they stood. This book of matches was called the "demerit book" or "gig book." Ralph retrieved his from a shirt pocket and handed it over to the commander.

The commander folded the cover back, revealing all twenty matches, and held them up for all the room to see. While holding the book at arm's length he said that it was very unusual for any cadet to go through primary school without getting any demerits, at which point, one of the military instructors pulled out his cigarette lighter and set the matches ablaze. The commander dropped the matchbook in an ashtray and said, "Well done."

The commander then read off all of Ralph's grades, course by course, ending with the overall average of 96 percent. The commander explained that the Army did not keep official track of the highest grades attained, but unofficially, Ralph had scored the highest marks he had ever seen. The room erupted into applause and everyone congratulated Ralph.

In addition to those two honors, Ralph soloed with the fewest hours of any cadet in the class and finished tied in the basketball free throw contest.

★ ★ ★

"We leave them now with a feeling that we were one step nearer to those hoped-for-wings, a step that we realize was so important in our future as flyers. Knowing that soon, in a few short months . . . we, too, would carry on, doing our part. Returning bullet and bomb that those who had tried to stem that maniacal tide had taken—but not in vain. For before the finish is written in the books they too will know the sting and fury of the unleashed hell they have perpetrated on this earth.

"Then and only then will we dare to think of home and our loved ones, of peace and security as we had pictured it, . . ."[68]

★ ★ ★

NOTES

1. From President Franklin Delano Roosevelt's speech to a joint session of Congress on December 8, 1941.

2. Written on L. A. Parker and Company stationery.

3. This is in reference to Carl Beggs, who took the first refresher course with Ralph. Carl had passed the first examination and entered the Air Corps in September 1941. He and Ralph stayed in touch during the early part of the war. No doubt Carl's stories about the Air Corps fueled Ralph's dream of flying.

4. Flight physicals were only good for six months.

5. Punch was a nickname. His real name was Floyd Moye, but no ever called him that until much later in his life.

6. After Juana left Coonrod, she became a primary teacher at Thayer School in Newton County, near Rensselaer, Indiana. In 1933, she became a primary teacher in the Mishawaka school system. She moved to the Richmond school system in 1935. She had no personal transportation and relied on the train and Punch to get her between these jobs and Wadesville.

7. By the time Ralph packed, he had been given many good-luck charms, including a 1936 penny pressed into an aluminum horseshoe, a 1934 Chicago World's Fair medallion, a four-leaf clover preserved in a plastic case, a seashell, a very tiny pocket knife, and an oversized 1937 Indian nickel, which was actually a paperweight someone took off his desk. To these, Ralph added his own good-luck charm—a token from the county fair with his name and address on it.

8. In this era, banks were primarily savings institutions and not every bank offered checking. Even then, cashing a check drawn on a bank in another town was almost impos-

sible. Juana may have brought extra money with her in the event she could buy Ralph's car, but since she lived part of the year on the farm, she may have had an account at the Wadesville Bank and made a trip to town to get the money. Or she may have pulled money from her account and deposited it into Ralph's after he left. No matter how it happened, in Ralph's mind, she paid in cash.

9. After Prohibition, Rolla stopped storing his moonshine in the well.

10. These two postcards were written while on the New York Central Railroad and mailed from St. Louis.

11. Pullman cars were used for overnight train travel. The one Ralph rode in featured only bunk-styled beds with privacy curtains.

12. Ralph was concerned that the train was moving so much that his handwriting would not be legible.

13. Written on a Union Pacific Railroad postcard that features a color rendition of Yosemite National Park on the front. The piece of mail was postmarked in Denver.

14. Written on Pony Express stationery of the Union Pacific Railroad and postmarked in Denver.

15. Much to the boys' chagrin, Kansas was a dry state, so the bar on the train was closed while they went through the state.

16. This is probably in reference to Lowry Army Air Field.

17. The Stearman PT-17 Kaydet was a biplane used by the Army as a primary trainer (hence "PT"). It was introduced in 1936 and had a top speed of 124 mile per hour.

18. The Fairchild PT-19 Cornell was a single-wing trainer used by the Army as a primary trainer. It was introduced in 1939 and had a top speed of 132 mile per hour.

19. The Ryan PT-22 Recruit was introduced in 1934 as a sport trainer. It had a top speed of 125 miles per hour.

20. Jodhpurs are riding pants that were very fashionable in the 1930s and 1940s. They were standard uniform for the US Army Cavalry. Jodhpurs were tailored close to the calf with extra room around the thigh from the knee to the waist. Often, they featured a soft leather patch on the inside thigh where the rider's leg met the saddle.

21. This is the first letter from King City, California.

22. In the early days of the war, there were real concerns about being bombed again by the Japanese. With the damage to the fleet in Hawaii, no one knew for sure where any Japanese ships were located. There was strong speculation that they were off the coast of California, poised for another attack. This fear caused blackout orders for public transportation, large buildings, and anything else that could be a target or used as a landmark for navigation.

23. This was actually the Palace Club, which was constructed in 1888. It closed in 1979 and was torn down.

24. This is in reference to Donner Pass.

25. This is in reference to Truckee, California, in the Lake Tahoe region.

26. Sir Francis Drake Hotel, constructed in 1928, is still open today and is as beautiful as it was then. The Starlight Roof/Room is now a nightclub and still offers a great view of the city. In 1942, it was called the Top of the Mark.

27. Actually, the Top of the Mark was on the twenty-first floor, but, no doubt the folks back home were as impressed as Ralph. Top of the Mark was closed when they arrived, but the cleaning people let them in so they could look around.

28. These were enlisted men who would become glider pilots. They received the rank of staff sergeant, regardless of their previous rank. They went through the very same training as the aviation cadets, but in separate facilities. They were treated in a rough manner, but no one seemed to mind because this was a once-in-a-life opportunity for them. The practice of using enlisted pilots dates back to 1912 and was a temporary fix to addressing the extreme shortage of pilots during wartime.

29. Charles Hale was the instructor's instructor. It was his responsibility to make sure that all of the instructors were doing their job and doing it to the best of their ability. Ralph had the utmost respect for Hale and noted that he stuttered while on the ground but stopped as soon as he got in the plane.

30. Early on, Ralph seemed to get confused with all the numbers thrown at him. The Ryan PT-22 had a maximum speed of about 125 miles per hour, but it did have a 160 horsepower engine.

31. This was an M-1 Garand, a .30-caliber rifle that was forty-three and one half inches long and weighed about ten pounds. The cadets were not given any ammunition for the weapon.

32. There was some concern back home that meals were served outdoors and the men had to find a place to sit. This was the image shown on newsreel footage of Army recruits in the infantry. The other image they had back home was of old-school academy or military school training, depicted in the movies, being filled with rigid rules and a lot of hazing.

33. December 25, Christmas Day, was on Thursday.

34. This is in reference to Lewis Parker's son, who was called up for military service.

35. After this cadet washed out, Ralph was left with two other men as roommates: Ervin Rogers and Kenny Ross. At that point, all Army personnel of the same rank were assigned to quarters, classes, and nearly everything else alphabetically.

36. There was a little drawing on the edge of the page showing what a protractor looked like.

37. Dixie Crystals sugar was a brand carried by L. A. Parker and Company. They apparently gave Ralph some promotional items that included ink blotters.

38. After Juana drove the car for awhile, she felt bad about not paying Ralph his original full asking price, \$500. She purchased the car for \$400.

39. Pronounced "dough-dough."

40. Scrawled across the left corner is a note to save the enclosed newspaper clipping. Ralph had included an article from the *San Francisco Examiner*, "Army Schools Rush

Training of New Pilots," dated Sunday, January 11, 1941. The article is about the facility at King City. While the masthead incorrectly shows 1941, other dates on the back side of the page were for 1942.

41. Once on the ground, his pals also cut off his tie, in keeping with US Air Corps tradition.

42. The PX did not sell film with a mailer for the Midwest processing plants.

43. There was a Kodak processing plant in Cincinnati, Ohio, which would provide mail-order services that Ralph preferred to use when he could.

44. This is an excellent example of the strange questions folks back home asked, fueled by an innate thirst for knowledge.

45. Jardur watches were sold primarily to aviators. It was the watch of choice among pilots of the era.

46. The garrison cap is a flat cap with pleated fold down the middle.

47. The flight cap is a billed hat with a chinstrap that is functional but mostly used for decoration. They received two so that one could be worn during the day and one for flying. The one used for flying generally has the inner stretcher removed so that headphones will fit over it, giving it the nickname "crusher."

48. Evansville College finished with thirteen wins and six losses, then lost to East Central Oklahoma, 30–42, in the NAIB Tournament.

49. *Hellzapoppin* was a musical review that opened on Broadway in 1938 and closed at the end of 1941. The show went on to tour the country and was made into a movie.

50. Lela is Jessie's niece.

51. After the war, the position was renamed "guidon bearer." A guidon is usually a swallow-tailed flag on a staff. The bearer stands to the right of and slightly in front of the formation. As the unit marches, all the soldiers take their cue from the guidon bearer, who is appointed by the unit commander. Appointment is usually given to the one person that, in the commander's eyes, is the perfect soldier.

52. Popcorn was not as popular as it is today. It was primarily only available at the movies and at ballparks. The Gay family apparently grew their own and sent some to Ralph, already popped.

53. This is in reference to the Indiana High School Basketball Championships. Washington High School, located about sixty miles northeast of Evansville, had won the tournament in 1941, and they also won it in 1942, posting a record of thirty wins against one loss.

54. Figure eight turns are turns that start and end at exactly the same point and form a figure eight. In doing pylon turns, two points on the ground are selected, and the two turns forming the figure eight occur over them.

55. Salinas Junior College was renamed Hartnell College in 1948.

56. The federal government and most states with income taxes exempted active military from paying taxes until they returned from war.

57. This large drawing shows the valley and the relative location of the various fields he describes in the rest of the paragraph.

58. “Tarvey” or “tarvee” are other words for pavement, blacktop, or asphalt.

59. This drawing shows the detail of a company formation and the location of the right guide.

60. The automobile was a Chrysler Airflow.

61. Salinas was the nearest town of any size. While there, they met a couple of girls. The girls told them that they were told to stay away from the boys because they were flyers, which was very dangerous. So dangerous, in fact, the boys would not be around very long, so the girls should not waste their time with them.

62. This is in reference to Lemoore, California.

63. This is in reference to Anna Elizabeth Schneck, called Grandma Annie, who passed away on February 5. She was Henry Schneck's second wife. His first wife was Sara, who took Rolla to the Oklahoma Land Rush and on to California. Neither Rolla nor Jessie attended Grandma Annie's funeral, and to this day, no one knows where she is buried.

64. This is in reference to Lewis Parker, who continued to stay in contact with Ralph.

65. This is in reference to a foldable military cap that has straight sides and a creased crown. It is also known as a garrison cap, campaign cap (not to be confused with campaign hat), flight cap, fore-and-aft cap, envelope cap, and the flat hat. It was very popular and was often worn cocked to one side of the head.

66. This is in reference to L. A. Parker and Company.

67. Also known as “gigs.”

68. The closing paragraphs of “Army Pilots in the Making,” an undated publication of the Mesa Del Rey Contract Pilot School in King City, California.

Chapter 3

SURE ENOUGH IT WAS HENRY FONDA

"In the central part of California there is a valley. In this valley is a quiet, sleepy little town. It is called the San Joaquin.

"But today it is at war as are all American towns. In this industry, this building, this rippling and smoothing of the earth, has but one driving impulse; to produce airmen to man the wings of destruction that will carry the flaming hell of our vengeance to the foe who would encroach on what we call America."[1]

Lemoore had its beginnings in the early 1870s when a group of pioneers rallied together to establish a center for trading and commerce. The area was known for its rich soil and a steady availability of water. Most of the families derived their income from either ranching or farming. The original city comprised about twenty blocks with the unique characteristic that the east-west streets were named B Street, C Street, and D Street. As the city grew to the north, E, F, and G streets were added.

Not much had changed by 1942 when Ralph showed up. The city had grown to about 1,800 in population, and the town proper had retained most of its turn-of-the-century charm. The city featured Scally's Department

Store, several churches, the Oak Rooms Hotel, the Antler Hotel, Lucerne Hotel, and Legion Hall, which housed both the VFW and the American Legion. There were also a number of bars or saloons in town, but other than that, there was very little to do in Lemoore.

Fresno was about thirty-five miles north of Lemoore. It was a much larger city that had plenty of attractions for the cadets. Perhaps the most visited attraction was Fresno Junior College. The college had nearly closed because of a lack of students caused by the war, and its current students were comprised of a mostly all-female population.

Without many boys on campus, there was little need for a field house, so they turned it over to the USO, where there was a dance every Saturday night. At times, the city was overrun by military, with three US Army airfields and a large Army post nearby. The cadets were allowed to go to Fresno every other weekend. They could leave Saturday morning and had to return by Sunday afternoon. The Army ran a regular shuttle service from Lemoore to Fresno, using standard transport trucks.

Fresno was a very friendly place to visit. Many of the young men in the area had either been drafted or enlisted, so the town's people all knew someone who was away from home for the first time. They seemed to embrace the boys and opened their hearts to them like no other place.

Lemoore Army Air Field[2] was located about nine miles southwest of town on the south side of California Route 198. Like King City, this was another new facility, but that is where the similarity ended. The Army had started acquiring land in 1941 and began construction sometime around June of that year. Unlike King City, Lemoore would not have a paved runway. Instead, it featured two intersecting dirt runways or landing areas connected by a taxiway, forming a triangle called a landing mat.

There were seven auxiliary fields that were used for practice landings and navigation. These were named Huron, Indian, Murray, West, Summit Lake, and Helm; however, cadets referred to these locations as A-1 through A-7, with A-1 being a second airfield at Lemoore. These fields were also unpaved but had either an oiled or crushed stone surface. Twenty-two miles to the southwest was the Coalinga Municipal Airport, which was sometimes used for emergency landings.

West of the airfield was the training and housing complex that included a PX, gas station, barber shop, tailor shop, post office, motor pool, fire station, warehouses, mess hall, chapel, classrooms, cadet and officer quarters, a hospital, an amphitheater, and a swimming pool. The cadet barracks were all wood frame two-story structures. Other buildings, including officer's quarters, were single story. There was also a movie theater that was occasionally used for stage plays and large briefings.

All of the facilities were off-limits to cadets, except the PX. Cadets could visit the PX every evening between seven and eight o'clock.

Perhaps the biggest difference between Lemoore and King City was the military presence. Even though the boys had been through some training and knew how to fly, they did not know the first thing about being in the Army. Lemoore was strictly an Army post, built by the Army and run by the Army. There were no civilians on the post other than a few clerical personnel. At King City, a fellow only had to worry about washing out because he could not fly. At Lemoore, he could wash out because he was unfit to be in the Army.

Having already learned how to make new friends and to fit into a large class, Ralph quickly settled in. Letters from home asked for more and more information, which added to his increasingly hectic schedule. Most of the letters Ralph wrote from Lemoore were written on "Basic Flying School" stationery as he tried to satisfy everyone's curiosity.

★ ★ ★

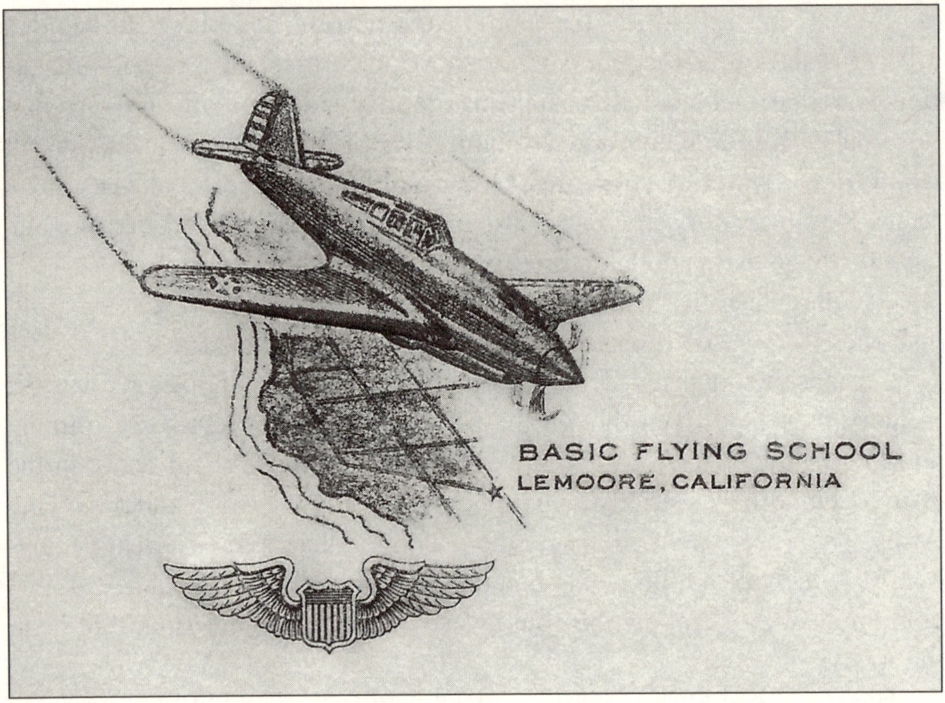

Image from letterhead stationery Ralph used while at Lemoore.

March 1, 1942

Dear Mother & Dad,

Happy Birthday Dad—

I am sorry I have been unable to get you something. Everything you looked at in King City was 2 prices higher than any place else.

We left King City Monday about noon. We took the mountain road and ended up in Fresno about 4:00 PM. After we had checked in at the Hotel we went for a drive and happened to see 3 girls riding a bicycle, you know tandem type. They looked pretty nice so we stopped and talked to them. They invited us out to their house that night. We figured we could always leave if everything wasn't right. They turned out to be nice girls. One girl lived at home and the other 2 lived with her. They all went to school at Fresno State College there at Fresno. Everybody is pretty nice to Cadets around here. At 10:00 AM Tues morning we reported to Lemoore Field which is about 12 miles west of Lemoore. Just as soon as we got in the field our upper classmen lined us up and made us stand at attention. Then they asked us our name, where we were from and what we were famous for. Everything had to be stated a certain way. If you said you were famous for nothing they made you stand & look at a cloud until you could think of something. All the time they were saying that men in the Air Corps were famous for nothing. After you thot of something they said, "Well now here is a big shot we will have to give him something special etc, so they had you either way. Then we were marched up to headquarters Bldg. where we reported in to our Tactical Officer. He assigned us to Barracks & room number. We drew our bedding then the upper classmen took us out to drill and we have been drilling ever since. We have drill 8 hrs. Then Thur. we would drill awhile and then we would listen to a lecture by one of the officers. We have had lectures on table manners, writing military letters, how to dress as officers, how to report to new fields after we are officers. We have had the articles of war read to us. These are our laws now. We pay no attention to civil laws. They are pretty strict on us and we don't have much time to play around. This is the real Army. And it is far different than the Country Club we stayed at in King City. Our rooms are plain wood and are not finished up. We have racks for our clothes and foot lockers for underwear, towels, etc. We do not have to walk guard although we have been issued rifles. There are no chairs or tables in our room. Our meals are very good. Much better than at King City.

There is always a Lieut. in the mess hall and if we do something wrong we have to stand at attention for a while. We have to eat with one hand at a time. We have to use our knife & fork a certain way and we have to lay them on our plate a certain way. Everything is strictly Army around here. The officers on the post are many. You can hardly walk 100 ft with out saluting one. Our class is a pretty large one. We are also twice a large as our upper class. This is the third class to go thru here so you can see it is almost a new post. They are strict on what we talk about. We are discouraged from talking about size, numbers, and strangely the Army. There are quite a few enlisted men here. But we are kept on the opposite side of the post from them. There is a large hospital here. There are several dentists and a lot of doctors & nurses here. There is a Post Exchange where you can buy anything from peanuts to radios. I have bought me a new electric razor. I got it for $9.85 with tax and in town it would cost about $15.00 without Tax. We can get everything we need here at a low price. It is operated by the Army at no profit. *If there is anything I can get you please let me know and if I can get it at the PX at a low price I will do so.* There is a post office, taylor shop, barber shop, church and many, many other buildings here. It is a small town all by itself. All week we did not even touch a plane I had begun to wonder if we were going to fly.

Then this morning we met our instructors. They are all Lieut. My Instrs. name is Lieut. Simon. He seems like a very nice fellow.[3] Our planes are BT13a's.[4] They have a 450 horse power engine and are really a big job. They weight 4300 lbs. They are full cantilever, low wing jobs. They stand about 12 ft high and instruments, my God, I never saw so many. There are about 50 and they all have to do with the operation of the plane. They have a radio set in them. Both a broadcasting & receiving set. We can talk to the ground at any time and also we can talk back and forth with our instr, who sits in the back seat. It has a transparent canopy which we pull up and it becomes a closed plane. It has hot & cold air so we can not get cold. We have more instruments in our cockpit than the instr has. The instr let me start the engine. You put one foot on the brake, one foot on the energizer,[5] one hand on the wobble pump,[6] one hand on the primer & you hold the stick back with your knees. Then when you get everything working you take your foot off the energizer & engage the starter. Then if you get every thing together the engine starts. They have a controllable pitch prop for low pitch & high pitch. Every thing is done by instrument. You can't do anything until the instrument which governs that control says you can.

As soon as we solo, which we should do in about 5 hrs, and we get a little time to familiarize our self with the plane—the rest of our time will be devoted to cross country hops, night flying, instrument flying and formation flying. We will also get several hrs in the Link trainer.[7] These planes have a top speed of about 165 MPH & cruise at 140 MPH. They are a real plane & there is a lot of it. But I have made up my mind I am going to fly it & not let it fly me. These planes are made by Vultee and we have quite a few of them. It will really feel good to get back in a plane after almost 2 wks out of them.

For our uniform we wear our regular wool shirts & wool trousers, brown shoes, black tie, overseas or field cap and when it is cold enough we wear our finger tip over coat. We wear this uniform all the time. When we leave the post we put on our blouse & Garrison Cap & gloves—these 3 items are considered dress as the Army is concerned. When we fly we wear the same shoes, shirt, field cap, trousers & black tie only we have gaberdeen[8] coveralls which we wear. These coveralls are just like the officers here wear—the only difference they have gold bars on their shoulders. We also have our own head phones which we wear while flying. In ground school we have, more navigation, meteorology, engines and 3 new subjects radio theory, military law, and radio code in which we have to learn to send & receive 15–5 letter words per minute. In the morning we will get up at 4:45 eat brfst at 6:00 PM.[9] Then we will have 40 min of drill, 1 hr of physical Tr. we eat at 12:00 noon & go to flight line at 1:00 PM We fly from 1 to 6 PM eat at 7:00 PM. Call to quarters at 7:30 PM. We cannot make our bed until 9:00 PM & we can not go to bed until 9:30 so you see we can't get over 7½ hrs sleep only on Sun. when we can sleep as late as possible. We have 4 companies here A, B, C, D. And on week ends 1 company stays in every week end. You can check out at Sat noon & you don't have to report back in until Sun nite at 7:00 PM. So we can really have a nice leave. I have had another complete physical exam. My eyes checked OK and my Schneider[10] was +15 which was very good. So I guess I am still alright.

Our flying area here is a square 22 miles by 22 miles. We did not get out this week end but will next week end. We will get 70 hrs flying here & then we will be sent some other place for advanced training. I weigh 168 lbs striped now am getting real freckled face. I am hungry most all the time. *Please don't send me anything to eat.* I can not keep it in the room & we are not allowed to have food in the room. I have a lot of regulations to read & memorize so this is the only letter I will write so pass it around. I can not begin to cover all so if you have any questions please let me know. Will try to write more in the week. Excuse the paper it is all I could buy.

Happy Birthday Dad.

Ralph

★ ★ ★

The Vultee BT-13 Valiant was the principle aircraft flown at Lemoore. It was affectionately known as the "Vultee Vibrator." Reasons for the nickname range from violent shaking just before stalling to the rattling of windows on takeoff.

March 10, 1942

Dear Mother & Dad

Well it has been raining all afternoon and we have had a couple of hours off so I got caught up on things.

I soloed yesterday. Our Stage Commander gave orders that he didn't want anyone in our stage to solo under 6 hrs. But there were a few of us who were ready & they said it was OK. I had 5^h 15^m when I soloed.

It really feels as though you are flying a plane now and you really have to fly the plane & not let it fly you. In the Ryan's we flew at Palo A.[11] you couldn't hardly make a mistake. If it stalled when you came in for a landing and only had 100 ft of altitude it wouldn't drop only 50 ft and you still had plenty of alt. Now in these BT's if you stall you will loose about 300 ft. and if you are coming in for a landing you are just out of luck. When we get ready to land we glide at 90 MPH. If you get under that it will stall out and it happens in a split second.

There was another Instructor & Cadet killed yesterday. This makes 4 deaths in 2 weeks. Everybody was standing in front of the hangers and we were getting in the plane. It was the first period of the morning and we were getting ready to go up. This plane took off just as I sat down in our plane. I noticed it taking off because It was the first one off. After it got up about 300 or 400 ft I heard its engine sputter a little and it turned back towards the field. I had my headset on so I plugged it in & flipped on the radio and the instructor in the plane was calling the tower to clear the field for a forced landing. As I was sitting there watching him he made a turn. It was a very flat turn, no bank, and he must have been holding bottom rudder so it would skid around the corner. Evidently he was holding the nose up so as to stretch his glide and he got it too high. It stalled & started nose first towards the ground and because he was holding rudder it started to spin. It went about one full turn & then hit the ground. They were both killed instantly. It took them 45^{m} to get the Cadet out of the plane because he was torn up so badly. Traffic was held up for about 30^{m} but then it went on as usual and no one said anything about the wreck.

Lemoore is about the same size as King C. But we can go to Hanford about 8,000 pop & Fresno about 90,000 almost as large as E'town.[12]

We will be sent some other place in about 6 weeks to finish if we get thru here. It is according to what they want to make of you where you will go. For instance—Instructors go to Mather Field, Pursuit & interceptors go to Luke field and Craig fields, Bomber and twin motor pilots go to Mather field—March field and Bakersfield. So I do not know where I will go.

We have had no black outs since I have been here.

You asked what color my suit was. I guess you mean my flying suit. It is olive drab green or Army green. It is gaberdeen and just like the officers wear. It has zippers up each leg to the knees, up each sleeve to the elbow and one up the front. It has 1 pocket on the chest and one on the leg between the knee & bottom. And of course we have a leather jacket we can wear. It is not sheep lined & I very seldom wear it. The planes are closed cockpits and have hot or cold air regulators. We did not get any extra clothes & I do not have or need a sweater. We wear the flying suit right on over our regular wool shirts & pants. In other words we are dressed up when we fly including black tie.

The parachutes weigh between 20 & 30 lbs. but we don't pay any attention to the weight. As you have guessed the only reason we wear them is to have something soft to sit on. I thot I would get you to make me a nice feather cushion to sit on instead of the chute, or do you think I had better wear the chute?[13]

I will not be able to take any pictures. Everybody is supposed to check in their cameras to the headquarters. I am also writing to Marcia & Herb & Juana & Mrs Beeler tonight so will close.

Love,
Ralph.

In a similar letter to Juana on the same date, Ralph adds:

I got your letter today and the stamps, thanks a lot. I thot I would take the hint & drop you a line tonight. I have forgotten when I did write you last so will apologize. I spent last week end in Fresno and had a very good time. I wanted to do a little shopping but out here all the stores close at 6:00 PM on Sat.....

I enjoyed the play by Fox very much. There has also been two plays put on in the theatre here at the post. Major Bowes[14] unit comes here next week I think. They charge us only 15¢ and they are well worth the money....

Richmond had tough luck in the tournament didn't they?[15]

Mother said the car was using oil. I very seldom had to add any oil, sometimes 1 qt between changes. Well it is getting close to 9:15 so I'd better close because I have to shine, shave & shampoo before lights out.

★ ★ ★

March 12, 1942

Allied forces in Java surrender to the Japanese.

★ ★ ★

March 29, 1942

Dear Mother & Dad,

Well at last I think I'm going to get a letter off to you. I don't know why but our new Dodos came in today and I have been out giving them heck. I never saw such a raunchy bunch in my life. Most of us had to change rooms last night. The barracks I'm in now is just across the street from the officers quarters.

I passed my 20^{hr} check ride last week[16] and all I have to worry about is my 40^{h} check. If I pass that I'm just the same is *in* because there won't be any more check rides.

I went on my first cross country trip Thursday. I went to Bakersfield, Wheeler Ridge, Taft and back to Lemoore. Wed. night I took my Regional map of the section and laid off my course and made notations of my check points. Then just before I took off I called the weather tower and got the wind direction and velocity and figured my drift angle. It was about 225 miles round trip. It took me between 1½ and 1¾ hrs to make the trip. This coming week we start night flying. The first 3 nights we have flood lights on the field we land on and after that we have black out landings with nothing but boundary flares on the field. Ordinarily our course here includes only 6 hrs night flying, 10^{h} instrument, 6 hrs formation and 10^{h} in link trainer but since these are the most vital phases we are supposed to get 10^{h} night flying, 20^{h} instrument, 10^{h} formation and 15^{h} in the link trainer. I have already had 3^{h} on instruments and it is a funny feeling. The instructor sits in the front and you sit in the back seat and there is a black hood which comes over the top so you can't see out. You will swear you are going in the opposite direction than what you are. I have had all kinds of manuevers under the hood including stalls & spins. Next week I will practise flying with the compass and clock. What you do is fly a course of 45° for 3 min then make a single needle width turn for so many seconds and fly a course of 285° for 3 min, etc. It is really quite interesting. When I get more proficient in it I will go on my night cross country. It will be the same one I went on Thursday. I have a little better of 40 hrs now. And with all the additional training we are going to get I expect to have about 80 or 85 hrs when I leave here. We will leave here about April 23. The instructor has only rode 20^{m} with me this week. (I ran out of ink)[17] The rest of my time has been solo. I got in 6^{h} one day this week but now we always get in 3^{h} or more every day.

There are 4 companies of we Cadets, A, B, C, D. We take turns staying in on weekends. Since it was Company D turn we stayed in this week.

There are very, very few negroes but you do see a lot of Japs,[18] Chinese, and mexicans.

We have always been permitted to listen to radios when we have time.

There are lots of flowers blooming now and the wheat is getting to be pretty good size now.

The beds are plenty long here but the mattresses could be a little longer.

I think there is some mistake about the Schettler boy. I talked with our Tactical Officer here and he said there was no way under the sun you could be a 1st Lt. without having at least 1 yrs. experience.

You asked if we hear any news about planes cracking up. We are usually the first ones to hear about it. The War Dept won't let the newspapers have it until all investigations are done. Then in ground school we usually study the weather, etc at the time of the accident and try to figure out what happened. You profit by the other fellows mistakes.

I hope you come out good with your soy beans[19] this year.

You mention about your chickens. We had fried chicken today but it didn't taste anything like what you have at home.

Well I guess I better quit, I will write more later.

Love
Ralph

★ ★ ★

Each morning cadets lined up for formation before going for breakfast. The lucky ones got to stand in the shade. Ralph is in the front group, in the second row, where he has labeled "Me." The two-story buildings are barracks for the cadets, and the one-story buildings are officer and civilian living quarters.

The following Honor Code was enclosed in a letter to Jessie and Rolla dated March 29, 1942. Written across the left corner, Ralph noted, "I helped write this."

AVIATION CADET HONOR CODE

With the sincere belief that every man accepted as an Aviation Cadet is honorable, we hereby set forth a guide to more firmly bind this, the Aviation Cadet Code of Honor, to our word as a gentleman and a future officer of the Army Air Forces. May our dealing with each other and those with whom we may have contact reflect credit to our country, our service, and our uniform.

- - - - - - - - - - -

A CADETS OFFICIAL STATEMENT, VERBAL OR WRITTEN, WILL ALWAYS BE THE COMPLETE UNALTERED TRUTH IN SPIRIT AND IN LETTER.

A CADET WILL NEITHER GIVE OR RECEIVE UNAUTHORIZED AID IN HIS CLASSROOM WORK.

A CADET WILL RESPECT THE PRIVACY AND PROPERTY OF OTHERS.

- - - - - - - - - - -

"Endow us with courage that is born of loyalty to all that is noble and worthy, that scorns to compromise with vice and injustice and knows no fear when truth and right are in jeopardy . . . Teach us to choose the harder right instead of the easier wrong and never to be content with a half truth when the whole can be won."

--Excerpts from the West Point Cadet Prayer

See your upper or lower class Company Honor Representative for clarification of the specific problems related to the Honor Code.

Written and administered by the Aviation Cadet Honor Committee[20] for the Aviation Cadet Battalion.

April 5, 1942

Dear Juana,

Well Im back on post after spending the weekend in Fresno. You asked about Fresno. Out here it is called the Raisin City. All the large dried fruit concerns have packing houses here. There are lots of vineyards here and the largest winery in the world[21] is located at the city limits of Fresno. Thursday last week I flew cross country from here to Clovis, to Tulare, to Wasco and back here. It was a clear day & I could see for about 10 miles. I noticed acres & acres of fruit trees throughout the valley. As you know this is the San Jouquine valley[22] & all fruit coming from here is called "in" fruit which means it comes from this valley all other fruit is called "out" fruit which means it is grow outside this valley.

You asked about a Schneider. It is a combination of blood pressure and pulse rate. They take both upon reclining, both 5 min after reclining, both standing, both sitting, both before exercise, both immediately after exercise & both 5 min after exercise. These rates are in a chart and certain combinations score points. A normal person will run from low 10 to the best you can get 18. Anything under 10 you probably have high blood pressure or heart trouble anything above 18 you are probably half dead & don't know it. I had my lungs xrayed Sat.

The trees are very green and the grass is up very big.

We start night flying tomorrow night. I have $52^{hr}5^{m}$ which includes $12{:}25^{hrs}$ dual, 34:40 solo, 5:00 instrument & 1:00 formation which is the hardest flying of all. I expect to leave here around the 23 or 26 of April but I don't know where I will go.

More later.

Ralph

★ ★ ★

April 9, 1942

American and Filipino forces in Bataan, Philippines, commanded by General Jonathan Wainwright, surrender to the Japanese.

★ ★ ★

April 18, 1942

The United States Army imposes a blackout of city lights on American East Coast cities to help protect ships from being seen by enemy submarines.

Sixteen American B-25 Mitchell bombers led by Lieutenant Colonel James Doolittle bomb targets in Japan. The planes are launched from the carrier *Hornet.* Seventy-three of the eighty crew survive as the planes land or crash in China.

★ ★ ★

April 19, 1942

Dear Juana,

Well another week-end is over and this is my last week end at Lemoore. I finished up flying last night and I will leave here either Wed afternoon or Thur. I will go to Stockton, Calif. for Advanced Training. I took my last ride here last night. It was my night cross country to Merced, Calif about 110 miles from here by air. Night Flying is a lot of fun and it gives you confidence in yourself and the plane. When you fly at night you have very little judge of distance. You cannot see the ground and the only way you can tell how high you are is by your altimeter. When we first started flying at night they had big flood lights that lighted up the field. But now we only have boundary lights around the field so we can tell where the field is. These lights are nothing more than oil flares[23] like all trucks are required to carry. They are placed about every 40 ft around the field. So they don't give out any light. When you come into land you line yourself up with the field and when you get within 200' of the ground you turn on your wing lights. Then you can tell wheather you are over or under shooting and make your correction with more flaps or a little throttle. At first it is a common mistake to level off too high and if you don't catch it in time you will drop in from about 5 ft. But with a little practise you can get as good a landing as in daytime. There has been several boys leveled off too high and as a result 3 landing gears & a couple of wings have been washed out but no one was hurt.

I like night cross countries a lot although they do get monotonuous (? spelling) as do all cross countries. At night you can see for miles & miles and a small town will show up big because of the lights. There are no vertical currents and the air is as smooth as silk. So all you have to do is trim the plane for level flight and watch the clock so you can find your check points at the time you are supposed to be there. I took off at 8 PM and at 9:50 I was back so it took me only $1^{hr}50^{m}$ to go the 220 miles.

I have 79 hours here and with the time I got at primary it makes a total of about 140 hrs. Of my time here 12:30 is Instrument, 5:00 Formation, and 8:00 night flying. Of all this time only $23^{h}55^{m}$ is dual instruction. The rest is solo. When I had about 40 hrs I changed instructors. And last week I saw my old instructor.[24] He asked how I was getting along. He said he had heard some good things about my flying. He said I had less dual instruction than any of the rest of my class of 250 Cadets. And you know at primary only 1 other Cadet had less than I. He said he was very proud of me. He was talking to my new instructor and they both agreed that I was the kind of pupil an instructor dreamed of. He and I had a little confidential talk and he gave me a few inside pointers. So I felt pretty good after talking to him. They have washed a few fellows out here because of disorderly conduct and not behaving in a military fashion. And most of these fellows had good grades in flying but Uncle[25] just thot he didn't want them for officers.

Stockton is a twin engine advanced school. Although most of us will fly a single engine AT6 at first. As our flight Commander said here they weed the men from the play boys. Most all of my friends, all of the boys I came out here with & all my room mates but one are going to Luke Field—Phoenix Ari. for Pursuit school. This other roomie of mine is going to Stockton. He has a brother who is a pilot for Pan American Airways.

You said you studied airplanes every week. We study silouettes and have to be perfect in recognising them. All information we receive on them is restricted. In Meteorology we study the Haw islands & Philup. & Australia & Alaska all this is put out by the War Dept & is very confidential. In ground school for here my grades are Military law 96, Navagation 94, Meteorology 99, engines 93 and Radio 95. It is bed time so will close

Love
Ralph

My new address will be
Cadet RH Schneck
Advanced Flying School
Stockton, Calif.

do not send anymore letter to Lemoore

★ ★ ★

April 23, 1942

German air raids begin against the cathedral cities in Britain.

★ ★ ★

Stockton was accustomed to being a boomtown. Up until gold was discovered in northern California, it was a sleepy village along the San Joaquin River. The river ran wide and deep from San Francisco to Stockton's doorstep, making it a popular destination for gold diggers of the era traveling by ship.

After the Gold Rush, Stockton began to develop for a different reason. The rich soil in the valley made the area ideal for growing a wide variety of fruits and vegetables. Much of what was grown needed to be transported to the bigger cities, so Stockton became a rail and shipping hub. In the years that followed, immigrants moved into the area, providing low-cost workers for menial jobs.

By 1942, Stockton had blossomed to about 55,000 as it braced for the onslaught of military personnel that would flood the town. Not only did the Army have a large training facility located nearby, the Navy had a substantial operation to the west of the city.

Even though Stockton was the largest city Ralph had been stationed near, it was only about half the size of Evansville. As far as Ralph was concerned, however, things were looking up. The city provided everything a young aviation cadet could ever want. And, if he was lucky, he could get to San Francisco, which was only about sixty-five miles away. Unfortunately, the Army had other plans.

Stockton Army Airfield was located a few miles to the south of the city. As with King City and Lemoore, the Army had entered into discussions with the city of Stockton to use its airport. These discussions led to lease agreements for the city to construct and operate a pilot training facility. Stockton Airfield was dedicated on January 11, 1941, as a US Army Air Corps Advanced Flying School. The field featured three runways, all paved, with a triangular layout. There were five auxiliary fields used for navigation and practice landings located at Kingsbury Field, New Jerusalem Field, Modesto Field, Tracey Field, and Franklin Field. New Jerusalem Field was shared with the Navy.

The living and training complex was located on the east side of the facility. Like Lemoore, everything was provided for the young aviators to be. This would be the group's last stop, as they were all hoping to graduate in June.

Stockton would provide a rude awakening to most of the young men stationed at the airfield. Stockton's growing population consisted of a large number of Japanese Americans. Even prior to the beginning of the war, there was a lot of prejudice against this ethnicity. So much so, that some Japanese families decided to live in one area of Stockton called "Japan Town."[26] On February 19, 1942, President Roosevelt signed Executive Order 9066, which established a military zone, called Military Area No. 1, that covered almost the entire western seaboard and inland up to 100 miles. This order set the stage for the internment of approximately 110,000 Japanese Americans, many of whom were born in the United States and were American citizens.

The roundup of Japanese Americans began in March, and by the time Ralph arrived in late April, it was in full swing. It was not something that was done in secret. Nearly every American knew what was going on, and there was plenty of controversy.

In total, about 4,500 Japanese Americans from San Joaquin County, which included Stockton, were interned in a prison camp. Most of them were sent to the Rohwer War Relocation Center in rural southeastern Arkansas, near McGehee.

Ralph never mentioned the internment in his letters. That was a sure sign that he did not totally approve of the situation. However, if the folks back home had asked about it, he would certainly have answered their questions. Since they apparently did not, they too were probably in disagreement. That is the way difficult topics were handled in 1942. People may have disagreed with the internment, but they knew why it was happening and kept their thoughts to themselves.

Another point of awakening for the cadets was the brutal schedule. The Army told them they could go to Stockton anytime they wanted to, but they had no time to do so. They flew or had classes on flying all day. They were starting to learn navigation and the use of the sextant. These classes were at night, along with classes on how to be an Army officer. They could still wash out for lousy flying or not being Army quality, but additionally, they had to worry about being good officer material.

Ralph was now seemingly roaming the California countryside. He had been on the West Coast for about five months and had been stationed at three different locations. No doubt this fueled the quest for more and more information back home. Many of his letters addressed only the questions that folks asked. Ralph's fondness for using letterhead stationery continued, as most of the letters from Stockton are written on US Air Corps Advanced Flying School stationery.

★ ★ ★

No country club here. Stockton was a new facility with no grass—anywhere. Dirt blew in every direction when it was windy. Here Ralph poses with his gas mask, which he was required to take everywhere he went.

April 24, 1942[27]

Dear Mother & Dad,

I stayed here[28] last night and I am taking a train this afternoon to Stockton. I have to report to the Air Base before 9:00 AM tomorrow. We were checked out and were released yesterday morn and then we received our special orders yesterday about noon.

We finished flying last Sat night with a night cross country to Merced and back. That trip was really a beautiful thing. You can see the lights of the cities for miles & miles. The lights from the autos on the highways look like small sparkling diamonds trickling down a path. The only way you can tell where you are is by the cities as you use these as check points.

The school here at Stockton is to prepare you for twin engine planes, however I doubt if we get to fly any twin engines while at Stockton. We will get a lot of night flying a lot of instrument flying and a lot of cross country trips because these are the things you use most when you fly bombers.

All the boys I roomed with here & at King City, with the exception of one, are going to Pursuit school, Luke Field, Phoenix Ari. They will get a lot of practise in formation flying and gunnery practise. This will require a lot of dual instruction.

I will get very little dual instruction after we are checked out in the AT6 everything with the exception of instruments is solo flying.

You asked about pork. We get roast pork about once every week & we get pork chops about 2 times a week then we have steak, lamb stew & roast beef and either chicken or turkey on Sunday. How are your chickens are they getting about big enough to eat?

You said you bet I got a thrill out of my cross country hops. On the contrary—they are very monotonuous. We usually fly at an altitude where the air is smooth and we have a tail wind. After you get this altitude you trim the plane & it flys by itself. All you have to do is set there. I usually take a long a couple of apples to have something to eat. I guess when you get your sugar cards[29] you will have to learn to drink black coffee.

I didn't get to see my xrays. I'll have to go thru another exam when I get to Stockton. And if there is anything wrong they will find it.[30] We do not do any actual work on the plane. However if something goes wrong with the plane we are supposed to know what it is. Then we write it up in the form 1A. The plane is then Red lined and cannot be used until this is fixed.

Last night I had a date with a girl by the name of Genevieve Sulente. She lives about 2 miles from Fresno. They raise all kinds of livestock. Her father is a meat cutter for Swift & Co. She works for a couple of lawyers. We went to the Fresno State College "Spring Swing Dance." We had a lot of fun and the Students put on a show on the Stage and the movie actress Jean Parker[31] was there.

Will close & write more later.

Love
Ralph

My address will be
Cadet R.H. Schneck
Air Force Advanced Flying School
Stockton, California

★ ★ ★

April 26, 1942[32]

Dear Juana,

I got Mother & Marcia a letter last night so I will get this one off tonight. Marcia wanted to know some things just in case you folks did decide to come at the last minute. I wish you all could come but I know it would be a long hard trip but you would enjoy it.

You asked about ladies dancing with men in uniform. She does not have to have a formal on unless it is a formal affair. And then she would have to be. A soldier when he has a sun-tan shirt, blouse black tie & Garrison Cap on is considered in dress uniform and this is suitable for evening dress or any affair. However, when on a military reservation, Army post or air base a lady may never take an officer's arm unless they are going to a formal party, formal dinner or a formal affair of some kind. However the latter applies only to officers and only when they are on a post, etc. When they are off the post they can do as they please unless they are on official business or armed. An armed officer never allows any one to touch him. He never removes his hat or gloves at any time and only under certain conditions does he salute anyone. This applies to officers. We are having announcements made for our graduation and I am getting 1 doz along with 100 calling cards.

We have had several lectures on the social duties of an officer as a bachelor and married. Also we have had a lecture dealing of the social duties of an officers wife. When an officer goes to a new post he has to pay a visit to the Commanding Officer of the Post. Of course the idea is—is to call when he isn't home and all you do is leave your card. But you have to leave a card for every member of his family & if you are married your wife has to leave a card for herself and for each of your children if any. Your wife has to leave 2 sets of these—1 for the Commanding Officer & 1 for his wife. Quite complicated isn't it? There is a lot of things we have to do like this.

I got a letter from Carl Beggs today his is in Norfolk Va. He is flying Curtiss P40F with the new Rolls Royce engines. I am cadet officer of the day tomorrow so I will have plenty of time and will write him.

This last week end this girl[33] at Fresno invited me down for the week end. We went to a dance Sat night & Sunday she came in after me and I went to her house for dinner. They have a small farm at the edge of town. They have a lot of vine-yards and orchards. They make their own raisins and dry their own fruit.

★ ★ ★

April 27, 1942

Dear Juana,

I've wrote every one but you so thot I'd drop you a line. I like this Post very much. It is by far the best one I've been on.

Everything is for our convenience. The Mess Hall, Library, PX, tailor and everything is within 2 blocks of our barracks.

I think there is a boy here from Richmond, Ind. but I can't think of his name right now.

The other night about 6 of we Cadets were in the Calif. Hotel[34] kidding a Cadet who started out on a cross country for Bakersfield, got lost & ended up in Santa Maria 120 miles away. A fellow came over & said he heard us & thot it was a good story. He said he guessed he'd better introduce himself. He stuck out his hand and said "My names Fonda" I couldn't think of anything to say so I shook hands & said "My names Schneck." Sure enough it was Henry Fonda.[35] He is one swell fellow. He told us his Pal Jimmy Stewart[36] just finished Flying Cadet training at Mather Field near Sacramento. He is going to be an instructor.

I met a girl in Fresno, Genevieve Sulento, she works for a couple of Lawyers, she is very nice. We went to a Fresno State College play Thur night. Jean Parker was guest. I was rather disappointed in her. I did have a good time though. We left Lemoore Thur morn & didn't have to report here until Sat morn.

We are planning our graduation for about June 20. I am going to order my officers uniform sometime this week. We are going to have several different ones[37] modeled by different firms Wed night.

The night before we are commissioned we are going to have a dinner party in town. Everybody is going to invite their Mother,[38] girl friend or family or any one they want. After the dinner there will be a dance until 12:00 PM. We are getting a good orchestra. At 12:01 we will all line up and the Colonel will swear us in as officers. Then we can have one of our guests pin on our gold bars. Then we will dance until 1:00 AM. The next morning we will be graduated & receive our Silver wings. The officers have agreed to let us wear our new uniforms that night.

We have been going to a lot of lectures lately. All are about military customs, dress and everything pertaining to us officers.

We get open post here 2 or 3 times every week. You can read Marcias letter about it.

I expect to be sent to a tactical unit immediately upon graduation. But you never know.

We can stay up until 10:30 now instead of the usual Army 9:30 but we still have to get up at 5:20 AM.

I want to get up to Yosemite some week end but I don't know if I'll have time.

Well I guess I better close as I want to write Mom & Dad.

Please pass this letter all around & ask to read the others as I have tried to tell each of you different things.[39]

Ralph.

★ ★ ★

April 27, 1942

Dear Mother & Dad,

Just a line to let you know I am all right. Well, I'm situated here. I like it swell. This is the best post I've ever been in. Everything is for our convenience. The food is very, very good. Yesterday we had Roast Turkey, tonight we had fried chicken.

We have been hearing a lot of lectures on Army, customs, dress and things that will apply to us as officers.

We expect to graduate about June 20. We are going to have a showing of uniforms this week & I will order them so I will be sure & have it when I graduate. I expect to pay about $120.00 for it. The Blouse will cost abut $45.00, 2 pr "pinks" trousers $12.50 apiece, 1 wool Garrison Cap $10.00, 2 wool shirts at $10.00 apiece. Then I want a new pair of shoes and I will need some gold bars and a gold officers eagle for my hat and a few other incidentals which run it to about $125.00 or more. We get $150.00 cash as soon as we graduate.

I wish you folks could be here when I graduate. We are going to have a little ceremony and I'm sure you would enjoy it.

These Army uniforms are pretty expensive but they will last a lifetime you can hardly wear them out.

You can read Juana's letter about our ceremony.

Last week I met Henry Fonda & I saw Jean Parker. I was very mush disappointed in Jean Parker. She wasn't a bit pretty with dirty red hair[40] & Freckles.

Pretty soon we are going to have to decide what we are going to do when we get thru here.

At the present time there are only two channels open. One is instructors job & the other Foreign service.[41]

This is the way I have it figured out. If I take an instructors job I will probably stay around 1 or 2 years until my turn comes up and then I will be sent across. I will still be a 2nd Lieut in all probability and in 1 or 2 years they will be killing them off like flies so that won't be so good. Because I will have to take my turn & go in actual combat when my turn comes. On the other hand if I sign up for foreign service I will probably be sent to a tactical unit here in the US for 6 months & will do nothing but practise what I will do in actual war & play war games.[42] Then I will be sent to some foreign unit at this time. I will be promoted to 1st Lieut and then when I get to active duty with the unit, I will be promoted to Captain. This will all take place in about 1 yr. and then as a Captain I can sort of sit back & take it easy. I figure the fighting isn't at a peak yet because things aren't organized but will be in about 1 yr. & by then I will be out of it more or less. Please let me know what you think of this. I imagine I'll have to turn in my preference in about 3 weeks so it can be sent to Wash D.C. Then they can get my orders where to go by the time I graduate.[43]

I have already filled out my application for commission and the Army took my picture which has to be sent in with it.

There are several boys here from Indiana but none from near home.

All the boys I came out here with are at Luke Field in Pursuit school.

They didn't have enough twin engine planes to go around[44] here so they drew names for those. I wasn't lucky & have to fly a single engine. But I don't mind. I don't much like the twin engine trainers they have here. However when I graduate here I will fly twin engine planes. The planes I fly are 550 HP AT6[45] they cruise at 145 MPH & are all silver & have retractable landing gear. They are really nice jobs. We will get lots of cross country, night flying & instrument flying.

Well guess I better close and go to bed.

Ralph

★ ★ ★

May 1, 1942

Japanese forces take Mandalay.

★ ★ ★

Ralph is seen here flying a North American AT-6 Texan in tight formation. It was probably scenes like this that led his instructors to think he was too tall to fly fighters.

May 3, 1942

Dear Mother & Dad

Well this is my first week here at Stockton and I can say truthfully that I have enjoyed it. I didn't go into town during the week because I wanted to get enough rest. I always want to be on my toes for the first 2 or 3 weeks and get a good start.

I'm glad you folks had a good time at the barbecue. I wish I could get some good Kentucky barbecue. They don't serve barbecue out here very much.

I have not flew any 2 motored planes yet. We have some here and I imagine I will get a few hours in them before I leave. I have no idea what I will do when I leave here.

Our graduation day has been set at June 23 with our dance on the night of the 22nd. I wish you folks could be here for it. Because it will be a nice affair and you would enjoy it a lot.

Always before the boys set their alarm clocks for midnight. Then when the new day started they pinned their bars on their pajamas. Because by an act of Congress they are officers as of that day. This way we stay up till midnight and are sworn in officially. This is going to cost us $6.00 apiece which will include the dinner & money for renting the orchestra, flowers for the ladies, etc. Life magazine is very much interested in the idea and maybe they will cover this party of ours. I trust you have read Juanas letter where I explained it to her.

I have been busy all week taking a physical exams & filling out Army red tape in preparation for the commission. Wednesday we had a showing of uniforms from the different firms.

I have mine all bought. It is going to cost me $134.00. All my clothes are to be tailor made and I'm sure I'll have a good fit. The tailor took my measurements. He said my right shoulder was ¼ in. lower than my left so he made allowance for it. He looked to see if I was bowl legged so he could make allowance for it.[46] My blouse will cost $46.00. I will get 2 pair "pinks" trousers, 2 wool gaberdine shirts, a cap, shoes, belt, set of insignias, and a rain coat. We will get $150 cash the day we graduate for this uniform allowance. All these clothes have to be tailored a certain way and they have to fit. Before we graduate we have to stand inspection before the Commanding Officer of the post and if he doesn't like our uniform we have to get another.

Well, Dad, I guess you have registered for the draft now. Do you think they will call you.[47]

We are only 74 miles from Frisco. There aren't very many big trees around here because this is low lands. The trees are in the mountains. Yosemite Nat'l park isn't very far from here and I hope I can get up there before I get out of this neighborhood. There is an awfully lot to see and just so much time to do it in.

I have just finished writing a letter to Uncle Arthur.[48] I went into town last night and had a very good time although I like Fresno much better. I am going to take some more snap shots pretty soon some Sunday and will send them to you when I do.

Mother—I haven't forgotten that next Sunday is Mother's Day and I want to tell you—I think you are the best Mother a fellow could have, I sometimes wonder how you put up with me so long. If I could steal one of these AT's I would buzz up there Sunday and we could go to church on Mother's Day. Again lots of love on Mother's Day and I'll be thinking of you.

Ralph.

★ ★ ★

May 6, 1942

Corregidor surrenders to the Japanese. All of the Philippines are now under Japanese control. All American soldiers are either killed or taken as prisoners.

★ ★ ★

May 8, 1942

Battle of the Coral Sea ends. This was the first major US sea battle of World War II and the first time Japanese expansion was turned back. This battle was the first naval battle in history where ships of the two forces never saw each other or engaged each other.

★ ★ ★

May 9, 1942

Dear Juana,

Well I'm spending the night on the post. Since our barracks didn't get a superior rating we didn't get off. However, I will get off tomorrow.

Did you get your school back? I would bet money that you did.[49]

A Tactical unit is a unit usually squadron which trains men for a special duty. In my case it would be learning to do a certain flying mission as bombing, pursuit or fighting. They get several men together, they learn them to do the special duty and how to work together. Then when they are highly trained they send them as a whole unit out to fight in the actual war. The idea is to specialize the men, learn them how to work together, get confidence in each other & then let them fight together.

There was a P-38[50] in the airport so—curious I went out to see it. It was all armed and I mean it was really loaded for bear. The pilot let me look in the cockpit. There were more gadgets in it than in a Chinese radio station. The Airspeed was red lined at 300 MPH. & yellow lined at 700 MPH.[51] He stopped off here to see his Father. So when he took off he had to show off a bit. He took off & climbed to about 4000 ft. (they climb more than 1 mile a minute) turned & headed for the field. When he passed over the field he was just a few ft off the ground. He was doing better than 300 MPH and the sound of the engines were way behind him. He was clear over the field before you could hear it. Sounds a little fishy doesn't it?

You asked if I had my suit ordered. If you mean my uniform I have my blouse, slacks, shirts, cap and insignias all bought. They are to be delivered the week before I graduate. We will all have to put them on and stand inspection before the Commanding officer of the Post and he puts a final OK on them. I will keep my old blouse & have braid put on the sleeves then I can wear in rain or when the other one is getting cleaned etc.

When will school be over? Will you be glad when it is thru? If I were there I could help you with your grades. Write when you have time.

Love
Ralph

★ ★ ★

Please thank Mrs. Gay for the stamps, they sure come in handy and I sure appreciate them.

May 11, 1942

The transport SS *Andes* arrives in England, carrying about 1,800 personnel for various 8th Air Force units. This is the first large contingent of US Army Air Force troops to arrive in England.

★ ★ ★

May 11 and 12, 1942

A German submarine torpedoes the 5,000-ton British freighter *Nicoya* and the Dutch freighter *Leto* at the entrance to the St. Lawrence River.

★ ★ ★

May 30, 1942

Operation Millennium begins. This is the first British 1,000 bomber attack on a German city. Gambling all available aircraft (front line, reserves, and much of the training organization), 1,047 bombers attack Cologne, dropping 1,755 tons of bombs. The British lose 41 aircraft. Over 12,840 buildings are destroyed, and 45,132 people are made homeless.

★ ★ ★

June 6, 1942

Japanese forces begin landing on Kiska Island in the Aleutian Islands off the coast of Alaska.

★ ★ ★

June 7, 1942

Dear Juana

Happy birthday—I know it's a little late but better late than never. I guess school is all over by now and I guess you are glad. I am about thru ground school & I know I'm glad its thru.

This weather out here is very peculiar. It gets real hot in the day and very cold at night. It hasn't rained for 3 weeks here. The rain period is over and there will be no more until around October so they say. You can't always believe the Chamber of Commerce out here.

You said in your letter not to write you at Richmond anymore so I am sending this home.

Now don't keep Punch up too late every night now you are home. After all he has a lot of work to do you know.

The explosion didn't amount to very much other than killing 14 or so men. The thing was they were cleaning guns with aviation gas and the pilot light on a gas burner ignited the fumes. There is nothing left on the inside of the bldg at all. Big holes were blowed in the roof and the windows are all broken.

Well guess I'd better close and once again Happy birthday.

Ralph.

★ ★ ★

June 7, 1942

The Battle of Midway ends. The Unites States loses the carrier *Yorktown*. The Japanese navy loses four aircraft carriers.

Japanese forces begin landing on Attu Island in the Aleutian Islands off the coast of Alaska.

★ ★ ★

June 15, 1942

Dear Mother & Dad,

I am sending this anouncement[52] but it is understood I want no presents or anything. It is merely a souvener. I am also sending one to Uncle Doc's[53] & Uncle Clarences and am telling them the same thing. I sent Unc Clarence's to Stewartsville. I remember them saying something about losing the Post Office at Stew'ville, but I guess they will get it just the same.

I have just looked at my service record and I have a rating of Excellent in all phases of military work including—Soldier, Pilot, Ground School, Character and all other things.

I don't know if you will hear from me anymore before graduation or not. I may find time & I may not so don't expect anything.

Love
Ralph

★ ★ ★

June 15, 1942

Dear Juana

I am sending this anouncement but it is understood I want no presents or the like.

We are almost finished up now but we are still very busy.

We have to check in all our G.I. equipment—ground school equip—get released and have to sign a lot of Red tape papers.

I have just finished signing my service record, Insurance papers, my release and honorable discharge from the Army as an Aviation Cadet.

Can't think of anything else so will write more when I have time.

As ever
Ralph

★ ★ ★

Two days before graduation, Ralph received a telegram from the West Coast Training Command stating that he could not graduate because he had not completed seventy-five hours of dual instruction. The commander made several phone calls explaining that Ralph had more expertise than most of the instructors, and with only sixty-five hours of dual instruction, he was a better pilot than those with the required tutelage. Finally, someone got the message, and Ralph was allowed to graduate on time.

Ralph attended the dinner-dance alone, as did most of the boys whose parents could not get to California. The commander made the point of pinning rank on those boys and congratulating them on their accomplishment.

When Ralph purchased his gold bars and wings, he also purchased "sweetheart wings" for his mother and sisters. These were wings just like Ralph had earned, but were only two inches long. Even though Jessie rarely got to town for anyone to see, she proudly wore them every day.

★ ★ ★

June 20, 1942

A Japanese submarine shells the lighthouse at Estevan Point on Vancouver Island, British Columbia, Canada.

★ ★ ★

"As we here at home contemplate our own duties, our own responsibilities, let us think and think hard of the example which is being set for us by our fighting men.

"Our soldiers and sailors are members of well disciplined units. But they are still and forever individuals—free individuals. They are farmers, and workers, businessmen, professional men, artists, clerks.

"They are the United States of America.

"That is why they fight.

"We too are the United States of America.

"That is why we must work and sacrifice.

"It is for them. It is for us. It is for victory."[54]

★ ★ ★

NOTES

1. Introduction to "Passing Light," a publication for class 43B of the Lemoore Army Flying School, circa 1943.

2. At this point the Army had not yet standardized the spelling of "airfield," so it appears as both one word and two words.

3. Lieutenant Simon had three cadets assigned to him. In later years, Ralph would recall he appeared to be afraid to fly and that he never took his hands off the controls.

4. The Vultee BT-13 Valiant was introduced in 1939. The BT-13A was the first variant after the basic airframe was in production. This variant had a different engine and some other minor improvements.

5. The energizer circuit provides power to the coil so the engine can initially be started.

6. The BT-13 did not have an electric fuel pump. Instead, it relied on an engine-driven pump that only worked when the engine was running. The "wobble pump" was a hand-operated fuel pump used to get the engine started or used in the event that the engine-driven pump failed in flight.

7. The Link Trainer was an aircraft simulator used between the 1930s and the 1950s. It was also called "Blue Box" or "Pilot Trainer."

8. Gabardine is a tightly woven fabric used in uniforms and other apparel. It is generally woven from worsted wool and is a heavy-duty fabric that wears well.

9. He means a.m. This shows how excited he was to share his new adventure.

10. The Schneider test for physical fitness measures the efficiency of the cardiovascular system and how fast it returns to normal after exercise. It is an early form of a stress test. Ralph explains more about the actual test in his letter dated April 5, 1942.

11. This is in reference to King City.

12. Evansville is sometimes shortened to "E'town" or "E'ville."

13. After describing the accident, Ralph probably thought a little humor was in order.

14. Edward Bowes (1874–1946) was an American radio personality who hosted a program featuring amateur talent. His nickname came from the rank he attained during World War I. *Major Bowes' Original Amateur Hour* was the most popular radio show during its eighteen-year run on NBC and CBS radio. The talent performing on his show included singers Teresa Brewer, Beverly Sills (opera), and Frank Sinatra.

15. This is in reference to the Indiana High School Basketball Championships and Richmond, Indiana, where Juana was teaching.

16. After the check-ride, Ralph and the other two cadets assigned to Lieutenant Simon complained to the senior instructor about Simon's nervousness and that he never took his hands off the controls. That afternoon, the commandant took Simon for a check ride. The boys were immediately assigned to a new instructor, Lieutenant Dougherty. Simon was transferred to non-flying duty within a week.

17. Ralph ran out of ink and switched to pencil.

18. In 1942, this was not an offensive reference.

19. Rolla was a corn and wheat farmer and had never planted soybeans until that season. However, before the war, trade disagreements with Japan had already drastically reduced America's supply of fats and oils needed in production and manufacturing. Consequently, in 1941 the US Department of Agriculture initiated price support programs to encourage farmers to plant more soybeans, the oil of which was greatly needed. Under this program, farmers were guaranteed to make a handsome profit. Rolla would never turn down a guaranteed profit.

20. One cadet from each company of upperclassmen was appointed to this committee. It was their responsibility to write and enforce the code. As new upperclassmen took over, the code would be rewritten. While the actual words could vary from class to class, the spirit never changed.

21. Roma Vineyards, owned by the Cella family, was at that time the largest winery in the world. In 1942, it was purchased by Schenley Industries. After a few years, Schenely got out of the wine business and sold all of the Roma facilities and land.

22. This is in reference to the San Joaquin Valley.

23. Also known as a smudge pot or Anthes Flame, an oil flare is a round container with a flat bottom and a wick. The container is filled with a flammable liquid, usually kerosene, and then lit.

24. This is in reference to Lieutenant Dougherty.

25. This is in reference to Uncle Sam.

26. Nicknamed "Jap Town" by the locals.

27. Written on Hotel Californian stationery.

28. The Hotel Californian in Fresno opened in December 1923 as a three-star luxury hotel, at the corner of Van Ness and Kern streets. While the building still stands, it no longer functions as a hotel. It now provides low-income housing.

29. The government had announced that sugar was going to be added to the list of rationed food items. By the time this letter was written, no one knew when sugar rationing would begin. It actually did not take effect until November 1942.

30. This is in reference to the fall Ralph had when he was a child. There was always concern that he had really injured himself internally, even though there was no physical reason to believe so.

31. Jean Parker (1915–2005) was a movie, television, and stage actress. By the time Ralph saw her, she had already made forty-six movies. Her latest film at the time, *Hello Annapolis*, was released on the same day as the Spring Swing Dance. Parker and her second husband, Doug Dawson, managed an airport and flying service in Palm Springs, California, until the start of World War II. During the war, she toured veteran hospitals throughout the US and performed on the radio.

32. Ralph started this letter to Juana on April 26 and apparently became distracted and forgot about it. He writes her on April 27 with much of the same information. He apparently discovered the first letter and enclosed both letters in the same envelop with no explanation.

33. This is in reference to Genevieve Sulente.

34. This is in reference to the Hotel Californian in Fresno.

35. Henry Fonda (1905–1982) was an American screen and stage actor. Mostly recognized for his movie roles, Fonda made 115 films in his lifetime. By the time Ralph met him, his twenty-ninth film, *Rings on Her Fingers*, had just been released. At that point in time, Fonda's greatest role was that of Tom Joad in *Grapes of Wrath*.

36. James "Jimmy" Stewart (1908–1997) was an American movie actor. Five of his ninety-five films are included in the American Film Institute's list of the one hundred greatest American films. By this time, Stewart had appeared in thirty films. Stewart was allowed to join the US Air Corps, even though he was over the maximum age. He used his influence and personality status to get moved into a combat role.

37. At this point, the Army lacked consistency in their uniforms. Individual commanders had the flexibility to make minor changes in the uniform to suit their own preferences. As a result, individual companies had the latitude to make slight design changes that could make their uniforms more desirable. "Pinks" were a direct result of one such company's alterations in color even though the Army had assigned "standard color" numbers to each color. The pants and shirts were not actually pink, but were a shade of tan or taupe that took on a pinkish hue. Pinks were only worn by officers.

38. Ralph really wanted Jessie and Rolla to come for graduation. He knew Juana would be off for the summer from her teaching job and could accompany them. In the next letter to Jessie he intentionally leaves out details of the graduation and tells her to see this letter, hoping that they would then start talking about coming. Unfortunately, within the next month, gasoline would be added to the growing list of rationed items, making it almost impossible for them to make the trip.

39. Ralph had finally awakened to the idea that he did not need to write individual letters to everyone. From this point forward, he asked that the letters be passed around for all to read.

40. This is in reference to the color of her hair.

41. None of the Cadets really knew what "foreign service" meant. Some thought it was fighting alongside another countries' air forces, while others thought it might be more of a diplomatic service. Few recognized that they would be deployed to war in a foreign country.

42. At this point in time, the 8th Air Force had not established operations in England. Outside the United States, the 5th Air Force was operating in the Philippines, the 6th Air Force was headquartered in the Panama Canal, the 7th Air Force was still in Hawaii, and the 10th Air Force was working the China-Burma route out of India.

43. This whole discussion was prompted by a conversation among roommates. The general feeling was that the fighting would not really get underway for quite some time, and everyone was trying to figure out his best chance of survival. Ralph was no exception. While he loved everything about what he was doing, he still wanted to come home alive.

44. Up until that point, Ralph had not seen the shortages that were prevalent throughout the military. The fact that these men were at a school to teach them twin engine flying

and they did not have enough twin engine planes put an exclamation point behind the previous conversation on surviving the war. When he said things were not organized, he was talking from experience.

45. The North American AT-6 Texan was one of the most popular trainers made during the war. It first flew in 1935, and the combat variant saw action during the Korean and Vietnam conflicts.

46. Ralph was not bowlegged.

47. The Selective Training and Service Act of 1940 required all males between the ages of twenty-one and thirty-five to register with their local draft boards. When the United States entered the war, the ages were changed to include all males between eighteen and sixty-five. This is a tongue-in-cheek jab at Rolla. Although Rolla, then fifty-eight, registered for the draft, Ralph knew he took exception to it and would complain about it forever. In a way, Ralph was rubbing in the fact that he had won an argument with Rolla over the country's presence in the war.

48. This is in reference to Arthur Lawrence Johnson, Jessie's brother.

49. Juana had expressed some concern that when Richmond renewed her contract that she might be moved to a different school.

50. This is in reference to the Lockheed P-38 Lightning.

51. Apparently Ralph has this backward. The redline airspeed indicates the absolute maximum, never to exceed, airspeed. The yellow line indicates a range for normal operation. Ralph obviously wanted to impress Juana. The actual redline airspeed is about 440 miles per hour and the climb rate is 4,750 feet per minute.

52. Enclosed was an engraved invitation to the graduation ceremony of Class 42-F, to be held at 10:45 on the morning of Tuesday, June 23, 1942, at Stockton Field, California. Ralph also enclosed one of his calling cards.

53. This is in reference to Dr. Soreno Watson Schneck and his son, Dr. Robert Jacob Schneck, both of Mount Caramel, Illinois.

54. Closing remarks by President Franklin Delano Roosevelt, Fireside Chat 21, delivered on April 28, 1942.

Chapter 4

NOTHING TO DO BUT FLY

★ ★ ★

"There never has been—there never can be—successful compromise between good and evil. Only total victory can reward the champions of tolerance, and decency, and freedom, and faith."[1]

Mather Field was a long-established facility that opened in 1918. Located east of Sacramento, California, the field was closed in the 1930s because the US Army did not need it for the organization's meager Air Corps; however, in May 1941, the field was reactivated, and the Army expanded it from about 900 acres to over 4,400 acres. The field consisted of two parallel runways. All of the training facilities, living quarters, and operations were located to the east of the runway complex.

Among other things, Mather Field was the principle instructional facility on the West Coast for future instructor pilots flying multi-engine aircraft. There they learned how to be an instructor, mentor, tutor, and wash-out specialist. Nearly all multi-engine instructor pilots in the western part of the United States, regardless of aircraft type, came to Mather for a brief period before going to their next assignment.

Ralph's room in the barracks was located about five feet from the pay telephone in the hall. Shortly after settling in, the phone began to ring incessantly. Finally tired of listening to the clanging, Ralph went to the phone and answered it. A young girl on the phone asked to speak to "Jimmy Stewart." Ralph thought it was some kind of joke but decided to go along with it, so he held the receiver at arm's length and screamed at the top of his lungs for Jimmy Stewart. Just as he was about to hang up, the door directly across from Ralph's room opened, and sleepy-eyed Jimmy Stewart came out to take the call. Afterward, he stopped by Ralph's room and thanked him. Stewart hung around for a few moments, chatting with Ralph, and then returned to his room. Stewart was assigned to Mather as a twin engine flight instructor and visited with Ralph whenever he had a chance.

After that, Ralph's time was very hectic. The training course was supposed to be four weeks, but it was shortened in order to get instructors to their assignments as fast as possible. The boys checked in, received their room assignments, and were given a five-day pass, although the pass came with many travel restrictions that limited where they could go. It was not until they returned that they found out about the change in the course. They were thrown into lecture after lecture, numerous reading assignments, and flight instruction on how to wash out the poorer performing cadets.

Leisure time was almost nonexistent. Ralph never got to Sacramento. There were no dances. The USO never came out for a visit. No plays. No time for movies. And absolutely no pomp and circumstance when they finished up. All in all, Mather was a blur of instruction.

About the only thing Ralph and the boys had time to do was to make a single trip to Los Angeles. Everyone in the country knew about Los Angeles, or more correctly, they knew about Hollywood. Ralph was no exception, and he jumped at the chance to stay in the middle of the excitement. One of Ralph's roommates, Bob Saunders, worked for a movie booking agency in Cleveland. He owned a Ford Deluxe Convertible Coupe and said he had "contacts" in Hollywood. Saunders invited Ralph and their other roommate, Stuart Swaggerty, to spend their leave in Los Angeles with him. They stayed at the Hollywood Plaza Hotel, located at Vine Street and Hollywood Boulevard.

Image from the Hollywood Plaza Hotel letterhead.

★ ★ ★

June 28, 1942

A German submarine shells and sinks Canadian merchant ship *Mona Marie* in the Caribbean.

★ ★ ★

July 1, 1942[2]

Dear Mother, Dad, Juana, Marcia, Herb & Sandy,

Well Graduation is all over and I am now a Junior Birdsman. I don't feel so much different although it does feel funny having to salute all the enlisted men and being called Lieutenant and Sir all the time.

The telephone call only costs $10.05 which wasn't bad at all and I enjoyed talking to all of you. I was recommended as an instructor so I guess I'll spend the rest of my Army days teaching some dumb dodo how to fly an airplane. So I am going to instructor school where I will be checked out in all training planes. We will be taught a little Psycology (spelling)—how to get the best work from your students. What to look for in a flyer, how to correct his faults and encourage his good points without him getting a big head. How to grade your student and know when he is failing and when to wash him out. This school only lasts 4 weeks then I will be sent to some training field.

Mather is the largest field I have been on. I am living in the B.O.Q.[3] I walk out the front door and am in the officers club and out the back door in the officers mess. We are 11 miles from Sacramento. It is a very pretty town and is a rather old town.

The Army finally decided to give us a 5 day leave but they limited it to 500 miles and we can't ride on the train, buss or airlines from June 30–July 7. So I couldn't come home. 2 other boys were driving down here so I came along and I don't regret it.

This is really a wonderful place. Tues nite I went to NBC, which is just around the corner, and saw the Johnson Wax program with Harlow Wilcox[4] and Meredith Wilsons[5] Orch. Last night I went to Coconut Grove where Harry James[6] & his Orchestra is playing. That is really a beautiful place and music as you've never heard before. One of the boys knew a girl in L. Angeles and she got me a date with one of her friends. She is a cute little trick—Georgia Corrigan, whose Father is quite well to do—they own a large Mansion in Beverly Hills. Naturally, I would have to get shot with romance. Her Mother came from Louisville and she knew all about the country back home.

There are lots of places I want to see yet. Grummans Chinese theatre is just across the street and the Florentine gardens, Paladuim, Earl Carrols are right close.[7] Today we went out to R.K.O. Buddy Clark,[8] who used to sing on "Lady Ester" program[9] saw us and invited us in the lot. He introduced us to Mr. Lewis[10] who is the director of the picture, which happens to be an Army picture.[11] Then he introduced us to Victor Mature.[12] They introduced us to all the boys & girls there on the stage and we had a good time. Then Mature had to have a picture of all us together. So, he, a miss Heath[13] and we 3 boys all had our picture taken together. He told us to look him up anytime we were in town and he would do anything for us. Then we went over to MGM. One of the boys knew a lady who worked there. She is secretary to Major W.S. Van Dyke II[14]—the director. He took us out to the set and we watched them shoot a few scenes from "Journey for Margaret" then he introduced us to the stars—Robert Young[15] and Larraine Day.[16] They are fine folks too. I think we are going back out there tomorrow as we didn't get to see all of it. This lady at MGM wants to take us to some Country Club on the beach for swimming Fri afternoon. This evening an assistant director, Tommy Conners, whose Father is vice pres of Fox films, had us out to his house for dinner. We had fried chicken and all the trimmings. He said the next time we come to town to look him up & he would be hurt if we stayed at a hotel. They had 7 bed rooms in their house and they liked company. There are still several places I want to go & see. I want to go to NBC Fri nite and see the Dinah Shore[17] program.

I guess I will just have to forget about the car for awhile. Because, when I get back from this trip I will have only about $100.00 extra besides what I will need to live on. I won't get paid anymore till Aug 1. Then I will draw close to $400. I will get last part of June & all of July. I will also be transferred about that time I imagine.

There were only 12 of our class which were made instructors. Some of them went to N. Carolina to fly pursuit—some went to Arizona—Salt Lake—Denver—to fly bombers. I don't know why I should get stuck with an instructors job but there isn't much I can do about it. Please let everybody read this as I don't want to write is all over again.

Love Ralph.

★ ★ ★

What Ralph did not mention about the trip to Hollywood was that they were in full uniform and Mature insisted that the boys appear in the movie, playing soldiers along with uniformed actors playing the same roles. In their scene, they were positioned in the back row of an audience of soldiers and sailors for a musical number where Victor Mature and Mapy Cortes sing and dance through a song called "You Speak My Language." As the camera stops on Cortes drumming on suitcases, Ralph and the boys can be seen on the left side of the screen. The director was not too keen on the idea. Ralph was so sure that they would be cut, he did not tell anyone about it until after he had seen the movie.

★ ★ ★

One of Ralph's roommates worked for a movie booking agency and had connections in Hollywood. Here they are on July 1, 1942, on the set of Seven Days' Leave. From the left are Stuart Swaggerty, Victor Mature, Ariel Heath, Ralph, and Robert Saunders.

Just prior to leaving Mather, Ralph ran across his first flight instructor, Charles Hale. During the conversation, Hale told Ralph that he had never flown a twin engine aircraft. Immediately, Ralph took him to operations and got permission to take Hale up for a ride in a Curtiss AT-9 Jeep. Ralph put Hale in the left seat (where the main pilot sits) and talked him through takeoff and landing. While they were in the air, Ralph put him through some spins, stalls, and loops. It was his chance to show his first flight instructor something new, how much he had learned, and how good he had become. Hale got out of the plane with a big smile on his face and thanked Ralph for the ride.

★ ★ ★

July 4, 1942

Six bombers from the 15th Bomb Squadron, flying British Boston IIIs, flew the first American mission against Germany.

★ ★ ★

Will Rogers once called Roswell, New Mexico, "the prettiest little town west of the Pecos." He probably knew what he was talking about; however, when Ralph stepped off the bus from El Paso at Fifth and Main streets, he didn't think much of it. He was greeted by cowboys, American Indians, and Mexicans.

Roswell was a town of about 14,000 and situated at the confluence of the Spring, Hondo, and Pecos rivers. The city and, in fact, all of Chaves County, lay completely within the original homeland of the Mescalero Apaches, including the hunting grounds of the Comanche. Through the years, Roswell had become a steadfast ranching community as the white man learned to live side-by-side with the American Indians who lived in the area.

The town consisted of the usual business district of stores and government buildings, and it had all the conveniences a cowboy, just off the trail, could enjoy. There was a movie theater, several bars and saloons, some barber shops, a couple of hotels, and a very rough district reserved for "gentlemen" seeking companionship—strictly off-limits for the military. Roswell offered some local attractions like the Bottomless Lakes State Park and the New Mexico Military Institute. Beyond that, there wasn't much to see or do. It was the normal place to locate a military flying school—in the middle of nowhere, with little to offer that would get the boys in trouble for the short time they were there. That was the ideal situation: nothing to do but learn to fly.

Ralph had just completed a long trip to get to Roswell—a trip that was longer than seemed necessary. He had been given a ride from Mather Field near Sacramento to Phoenix, through Los Angeles. He had expected to get a bus or train from there to Roswell through Albuquerque; however, much to his surprise, there was no such connection. Instead, he had to take a bus to El Paso, lay over for most of a day, and then connect to another bus to Roswell. It took three days to get from Phoenix to Roswell, and when he arrived, he was tired. All he wanted to do was find the airfield, report in, and get some rest.

There were several other boys on the bus headed for the airfield. After a short wait, an Army transport truck arrived and loaded them into the back for the five-mile trip.

★ ★ ★

Roswell Army Air Field had its beginnings early in 1941. The Army fully expected to encounter problems with heat, dust, and insufficient civilian housing; however, the need outweighed these potential problems, and construction began in June of that year. Enough of the construction had been completed for the base to become active on September 20, 1941. It became fully operational in early 1942.

The Roswell Army Flying School provided primary flight training and bombardier school. Because of New Mexico's excellent flying conditions, the facility was initially designed to be large and expansive. The airfield plans called for seven runways all paved in concrete.

The facility included a bombing target adjacent to one of the runways, but it was only used for dropping bags of sand or flour. The actual active practice bombing and gunnery ranges were due south of the airfield, on

Matagorda Island off the coast of Texas. Additionally, there were nine auxiliary fields used for overflow and landing and takeoff practice.

The runways were situated entirely to the south of the facility. Just north was the parking area and hangars. The office complex, housing, and all of the other facilities were located on the far north side of the facility. Like other new facilities, it was supposed to have had all the comforts of home—military style, of course. But this airfield was very new, and it seemed that everything was still under construction. There were almost no paved roads, no grass, and no trees of any kind. While the barracks were new, each room only had one window and a transom above the door for ventilation. When the wind blew, or even a slight breeze, the sand and dust flew everywhere.

Ralph never complained about any of this. As far as he knew, this would be his home for the duration of the war, and he was eager to settle in.

★ ★ ★

While Ralph was at Roswell, his family came for a visit. They had driven from Evansville to Roswell and stayed for a few days. It was a long, arduous trip. They took Herb's car, as it was the largest. He, Juana, and Rolla split the driving. Beginning in May 1942, gasoline was rationed. In most cases, farmers were given extra coupons for their farm equipment, and since Rolla did not have a tractor, he made out quite well. Nevertheless, in order to make the trip, everyone needed to combine their coupons. The trip served two purposes: to see Ralph and for Rolla to get some fresh dry air, which did wonders for his respiratory problems.

Rolla was especially eager to go because he had been through the area on his trip to California as a boy, and he wanted to see the sights again. The trip was quickly organized when it was discovered that Ralph could be sent overseas at any time. Juana's teaching duties made it imperative that the group visit Roswell before the start of school. As a result, planning and coordination with Ralph also was done over the phone.

★ ★ ★

Most of Ralph's letters from Roswell were written on letterhead stationery; one example is shown here.

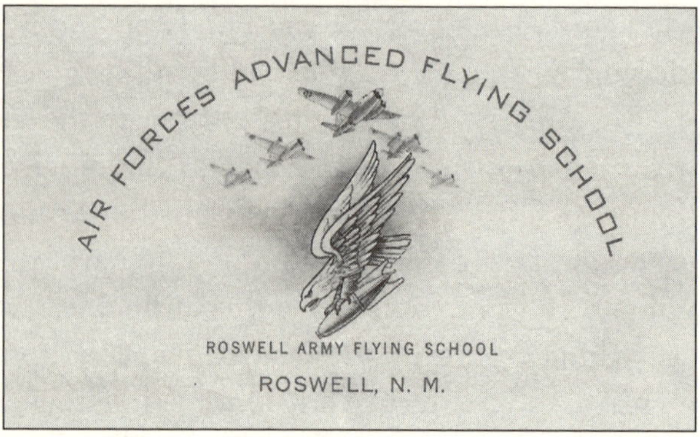

August 3, 1942

Dear Mother & Dad,

We drove dove down here[18] yesterday from L.A. We stayed here last night and I have to take a bus from here to Roswell. I am taking one at 7:40 PM[19] and that will save me from riding in the heat today. I will go to El Paso, Texas and get to Roswell at 3^{30} PM tomorrow. My room here[20] is the coolest place I've found here. I gave Bob[21] $20.00 for the ride down here and it will cost me about $13.00 on to Roswell. The Army will pay me 8¢ a mile which will amount to about $90.00 so I will make a little money on the deal. In Calif before we started on the desert you could buy all the orange juice you could drink for 10¢. We found that natural fruit juices quench your thirst better than anything else. So we bought a gallon jug of orange juice. It only costs 70¢ jug and all and it was pure juice because we watched them squeeze the oranges. This Arizona is some place. I never was so sick of black, dirty mountains, big rocks, cactus and hot weather in my life. There is very little that is green only the cactus & some sage brush and the wind is so hot that it burns you. We rode with the windows closed on the car because the wind burned so.[22]

Now in answer to the question about doing all the acrobatics. I know how to do most all of them including, spins, loops, rolls, immelmans[23] and Cuban eights.[24] But there is some ships which you can not do acrobatics in. The twin E AT9[25] is a restricted ship and if you do any violent maneuvers in it it is liable to come apart. I know I completely stalled it one day. I was keeping the plane level with the rudders and the forward speed was almost nothing and it shook so much that some of the rivets on the gas tank came loose and I just did have enough gas to get back to the field.

It is too bad about Margaret Bolin's husband not wanting to be an officer and I'm sure he won't have to be one if he doesn't want to.

You don't need to show Margaret Rose any of my pictures. She has no strings on me and I have none on her and doubt very much if I ever do, so you can just keep the pictures in the album.

We ran into a dust storm yesterday that lasted for about 10 miles sometimes we would just have to stop the car because you couldn't see the road.

You go ahead and pay the insurance[26] this time. I am going to write Jim Wade & Elles and get a monthly rate on my insurance and have it deducted from my pay and the gov't will send them a check each month. It won't cost any more this way and it will save you folks a lot of worry. I will take care of it and will let you know when it takes affect. Also when I get to Roswell I will complete my personal file and my overseas file and will send you a list of all my papers and my *will*. And the proceedings to go thru in case something happens to me so that you can get all the money that is coming to you. Now to complete my file you'll have to send me a list of important papers, such as insurance papers & policies and when the premiums are due and where these papers are kept also how much money I have in the bank[27]—whose name it is in and the correct name of the bank—also 6 blank checks on that bank.

We are the last bunch of officers who are to be instructors. From now on it will be civilian pilots who will be instructors. They expect to replace all Army instructors in about 6 months and from there I don't know what will happen. However, I am getting my affairs set up so you will know what is what and if I have to go overseas I will have my pay allotted. I will write & explain all this when I get to Roswell. I will sure be glad to get back to Calif. I'm sure this climate would be good for Dad.[28] Will write more later.

Love
Ralph.

★ ★ ★

Image from the Hotel Adams letterhead.

August 6, 1942

Dear Mother, Dad and Family,

Oh! Happy day. I am now well situated in Roswell, N.M. As you know we stayed 2 days in L Angles. And I stayed 1 night in Phoenix. Then I took a bus on to Roswell via El Paso, Texas. There isn't much at El Paso except Fort Bliss.

Roswell is stuck out here pretty much by itself. It is better than 150 miles to the nearest town of any size. But there is some green vegetation here and it does *rain* here and there are some real big clouds every once in a while. On the way here from El Paso we had to cross a range of mountains and went up to about 6000' elev. On top of these mountains is some very beautiful country. There is a lot of fir trees and lots of green grass & flowers. It is rather cool up there. It took about 2 hrs to cross the range and it rained for almost an hour up there. I was so happy I got out and walked around in it at every stop. It was a good hard rain. *It is the first rain I have seen of any kind since Feb 15.* They have a fairly nice swimming pool here. But there is practically nothing else to do in the way of amusements. There are 3 picture shows here in town and they all have pictures which I saw 6 months ago. For those who like to drink there is no liquor restrictions. In Calif and Ariz. you could drink beer from 2 PM–2 AM and hard liquor only from 6 PM–10 PM. In N.M there is no restrictions on any kind of liquors.

The town is full of cowboys with jeans & high heeled boots and lots of places to by Indian—silver jewelry, blankets, hats, etc. It isn't so awfully hot here usually around 100° in daytime but at night it gets real cool—sometimes drops as much as 30°.

The field is about 4 miles from town. It is a new field as it graduated its first class of Cadets last Sunday. It undoubtedly has the largest runways of any field I have been on. Most of them 500 ft wide and over 2 miles long.

After spending 4 weeks in instructor school I am not going to be an instructor. When I reported to Capt. O'Phiel,[29] the Director of Flying, he said I had a very good record in instructors school and asked me if I would like to go to school for 2 or 3 weeks more and learn to be Bombadier Pilot.[30] He said they were rather short on these Pilots and you had to go to school and take practically the same course as the bombadiers take. So I am now going to ground school and taking transition flying in the AT 11,[31] which is a twin engine plane. The boys who were made instructors here had to go back to flying the AT 6,[32] a single engine plane. This AT 11 I will be flying has 2 450HP engines. At 10,000 ft or above you can get between 160 & 180 MPH cruising. It has a glass nose for the bombadier to sit in and carries quite a few bombs. In ground school we are learning all about the famous Norden Bomb sight you read so much about. We have an expert come out from the factory and tell us all about how it works, which is something the bombadiers don't even know. We have to spend 8 hrs just playing with one of these which is rigged up on a stand and learn to synchronize it's instruments with the airspeed, groundspeed and altitude of the plane. Then we learn all about the Automatic Flight Control equipment. Then we will go up and actually drop some bombs. These bombsights are uncanny in the things they do. You wouldn't believe it if I told you all the things they will do. After we have finished all the ground school and thoroughly understand all the equipment we will use—I will be assigned a plane of my own. I will get my own maintenance crew of 3 men—I will have to see that I get my plane inspected regularly that it is kept in tip-top condition. I will be issued my own bomb sight and automatic Flight Equip. I will have to see that it is locked up in the guarded vault when not in use. I will have my own students which I will take up and we will practise dropping bombs on 1 of the many targets they have set up out in the desert 200 miles north & South of Roswell. The bombs we drop will be practise bombs with a 5 lb charge of powder. You and your students will fly every other afternoon, morning

& night. That way when you fly at night you don't have to fly till the next afternoon.[33] Every other day is an altitude bombing mission and you bomb anywhere from 14,000 ft to 20,000 ft according to the weather. The absolute ceiling on this AT 11 is about 20,000 ft in normal weather. I have already been issued my own oxygen mask and all the equipment I will use. I think I am getting some more valuable training and if I should ever be put in a bomber in actual combat I will certainly know what it is all about. It is just as the Capt said as long as you show that you can learn, want to learn, make good grades, the Army will send you to school so you can learn. I will get to fly a bigger & faster plane, will learn how to use oxygen in high altitudes will learn all about bomb sights & bombing.

This training is something every pilot in the Army doesn't get and I think I am very fortunate. I doubt if I will get a furlough because they are in need of us very bad now. I received $99.04 travel pay down here and it only cost me $35.00 so I made a little money on the deal. I think I will buy me an automobile very soon now. Please let every one read this letter as I do not want to write it over also Mr & Mrs Beeler. You can divide the pictures up among the family & can give Mr & Mrs a GB[34] one if they want it. I have some more here I can send if there isn't enough to go around. If you have any questions I will be glad to try & answer them. I am glad to hear that you are feeling so well, Dad, and hope that this will cure all your troubles.

Love
Ralph.

★ ★ ★

Roswell Army Air Field was desolate and foreboding, with dirt roads. Pictured here is Ralph's barracks on the left, with high-ranking officer and civilian housing shown on the right.

August 7, 1942

Allied forces, led by US Marines, land on Guadalcanal.

★ ★ ★

August 17, 1942

8th Air Force Mission 1.
The 97th Bomb Group made the first US heavy bomber raid. Twelve B-17s, escorted by RAF Spitfires, attacked the Sotteville railroad yards at Rouen, France, while six other B-17s made a diversionary sweep along the French coast. All planes returned safely.

★ ★ ★

August 22, 1942

Dear Mother & Dad & Juana

I got your cards and letter saying that you got home all OK.

I am awfully glad you folks could come out here. I was glad to get to see you.

There hasn't been anything doing since you left. I have flown about 1½ hrs every day since you left and that is all I've done. I flew 1½ hrs this morning and I don't have anything to do until Monday night at 9:45. We start night flying Monday nite. All of boys who graduated in the last class here and who had never received orders were shipped out Thursday. They were sent to San Francisco and were going to be sent over. Australia they thot.

They left by airplane and they couldn't drive their cars. One of the boys left his in a garage down town. The car is in his Fathers name. He said his Father would want to sell it because he wouldn't come down after it. It is a 1937 Chev. Coupe and has 5 new tires. The spare has never been on a wheel yet. I think I am going to buy it for $250.00 and I may write a check on the Wadesville Bank for about $30.00.

Well, I guess thats about all the news will write later,

Love
Ralph

★ ★ ★

Somewhere Ralph ran across this tongue-in-cheek letterhead for Roswell. It was not sold at the PX.

September 6, 1942

Dear Mother, Dad, Juana, Marcia, Herb, Sandra, Mr & Mrs Beeler,

I will try to make this one letter do the trick then I won't have to write so much.

There hasn't been anything very exciting happen with the exception that I got to take a couple of trips.

I acted as Co-Pilot on the oxygen ship to Albuquerque this week. We don't have facilities for making oxygen here as yet so we have to take our empty bottles to Albuquerque and leave them and bring back some full ones. We flew up about 7 AM and returned about noon. At the field there they had a A20C,[35] some B24F's[36] and a B17D[37] "Flying Fortress". I got to get into it and go all thru it. One of the pilots was with me and I got to ask a lot of questions. If you think it isn't well armed, defensively, you have another guess coming. There is machine guns and cannons all over the plane. There is 5 receiver and 3 transmitter radio sets. The pilot said they were getting ready to go across. Instead of having bombs in the bombays they had huge gas tanks which enable them to carry a safe reserve of fuel for the long trip across the Pacific. We went up front and I sat in the Pilots seat. There are dozens more instruments than on any plane I have ever flown. But I liked to sit up there and look at the huge wing and the four motors of 2000 HP each which at 30,000 feet altitude carry the plane faster than 300 MPH.

There are dozens of electrical switches which turn on, regulate and operate, generators, transformers and other electrical equipment that furnishes the current for the many lights—radios and the electric gun turrets. But I would give anything to fly one.[38] It is really some plane.

Then Friday I was lucky and got to go on a ferry trip. There was 13 of us went and we each flew an AT6 to Williams Field,[39] Ariz which is near Phoenix, Ariz. We took off at 1 PM Fri. and flew to El Paso, Texas. We landed there and gased. Nothing much happened on the way down. We did a little buzzing, some formation flying and some acrobatics. When we landed one of the boys had a flat tire so we had to stay there an hour getting it repaired. Then we took off for Williams Field. My engine had been running a little bad on the trip but I didn't think much of it because it had quite a few hundred hours on it and was due to be pulled for inspection. However, the thing that bothered me was that it burned a lot of gas and I didn't get any speed. At full throttle I only got 160 MPH.

About 30 minutes out of El Paso we ran into a storm. We couldn't fly around it because there was an overcast and the mountains were dangerous. It so happened that there was a ridge of mountains which were about 5000 ft high and lay in the shape of a horse shoe. So we figured if we flew up in the horseshoe the storm would pass over the mountains and they would break the strongest winds. So all we did for 20 minutes was fly as close to the ground as possible in one long "rat race."[40] The wind wasn't bad and all we got was rain. We couldn't land there because the land was so rocky and rough.

We finally proceeded on our way. About an hour out of Williams Field I noticed my gas was running low so I climbed to 8500 feet and leaned out my mixture good. When I landed I had 3 gals. of gas left. It's a good thing I didn't overshoot the field as I hardly had enough gas to go around the traffic pattern again.

We had some command cars take us into town where we ate supper. We were suppose to catch a train back at 10:30 Fri. nite. But it had a break down and was late. They kept telling us it would be in every 30 minutes. So we went up town and every 30 minutes we would call in and ask when we could get on. We finally pulled out at 2 AM Sat morn. It was one of these slow milk trains which stops at every cactus bush & road crossing in the desert. It took me 3 hrs & 45 min of actual flying to make the trip down and it took 20 hrs of riding to make it back. We went on the train to El Paso then we took a bus into Roswell. We arrived here at 8:30 PM Sat night. On the bus we came thru Lincoln County, New Mexico. The county—"Billy the Kid" made famous. There are all sorts of signs along the road which tell something about "Billy". There is still lots of shooting up there in the mountains. Almost every week you read where somebody has been fueding for so many years and someone killed someone else.

We got all our expenses paid on the trip with the exception of our meals and we got paid 5¢ a mile travel pay. So I figure I will make about $30.00 on the trip.

I haven't got the car yet. He hasn't written me that he wants to sell it for sure. I hope he doesn't change his mind.[41]

Well I hope everybody is alright and Dad's back is better.

I will write later on

Love
Ralph.

★ ★ ★

While at Roswell, Ralph purchased a 1937 Chevrolet Coupe from a pilot who was sent to the Pacific Theater. It was all white with black interior.

September 9 & 29, 1942

Japanese submarine *I-25* launches a Yokosuka E14Y floatplane off the coast of Oregon for two airstrikes. On both occasions, the plane bombed the region near Mount Emily with the intent of starting forest fires, which were contained by forest rangers. These events marked the only enemy bombing of the continental United States during the war.

★ ★ ★

February 5, 1943

Dear Mother & Dad,[42]

It is midnight and I just got off work. I want to get to bed early because I have to get up early. I am going to Albuquerque. Just a line to let you know I am a 1st Lt.[43] It came in the mail today. I guess that isn't bad. 7 months & a 1st Lt. It will mean about $30.00 a month increase in pay to.

Will write more later.

Ralph.

★ ★ ★

February 18, 1943

Dear Mother & Dad,

We have been having beautiful weather. Rather cool at nights but warm in the daytime.

How are the new teeth[44] coming? I am getting all my magazines now. Every officer has to take an hours athletics every day—5 days a week. If you miss you have to write a letter of endorsement to the Colonel.

Wadesville doesn't seem to be doing too well at basketball this year.

There are only 7 boys on this field who graduated in 42-F that are 1st LT. there are about twice that many 42-F men who are still 2nd LT. Also there are a lot of 42E men who graduated a month before I did who are still 2nd LT. Believe me we are none too popular with these boys because they feel they should have been promoted before we were.

Did you know that our field here is now considered the largest training field in the U.S.A. We train more bombadiers than any other field in the U.S. We also train more pilots here than any other field in the U.S. I am going to be transferred back to the pilots school pretty soon. I will go back to instructing cadets & teach them how to fly instead of flying bombing missions. I will also get to fly B-25's[45] which are the kind of planes Doolittle bombed Tokyo with.

I got the box of candy alright. Thanks a lot. It was very good. But don't go without sugar[46] just to send me candy because I can get candy & chewing gum & you folks cant.

Love Ralph

Would you like me to send you some gum.[47]

★ ★ ★

Ralph had barely gotten acquainted with the B-25 and had met his first class of students when orders came for him to proceed to Hobbs Army Air Field. Hobbs, New Mexico, is about one hundred miles southeast of Roswell and about five miles from the Texas state line. Back then, it had as much to offer as Roswell, especially if a fellow had a car. When Ralph went to the train station, took a look around town to see what was there, and saw the same things he had seen before, only smaller. As before, this was a great place to put a military training facility. Nothing to do but fly.

Ralph was sent to Hobbs to get acquainted with the B-17 Flying Fortress. It had been two years since he had seen the movie *I Wanted Wings*, and up until that point, he had only sat in one for a few minutes. Ralph had over one thousand hours of flying time and had yet to fly the plane that sparked his dream. One thousand hours was a milestone few other pilots had obtained. It meant that he had more experience flying military aircraft than almost anyone else. It put him in an elite class that included the best aviators in the military.

★ ★ ★

After settling in at Hobbs and becoming familiar with the B-17, Ralph was surprised to receive fourteen days of leave. He did not waste any time packing and heading for the train station. He had not been home since he left on December 13, 1941. There was a lot of catching up to do.

He arrived at the Evansville train station and was greeted by Marcia, Herb, and Sandra Jane. As they drove him to the farm, Marcia explained that the word was out that he was coming home, and the phone had been ringing off the hook. Ralph was going to be busy for the next ten days.

There were numerous parties in his honor and numerous requests for him to "stop by." He made the rounds, not wanting to disappoint anyone. Everywhere he went, folks wanted their picture taken with "the most handsome boy in town . . . all dressed in his Air Corps uniform."

One of the most important stops was to see Add and Stella Beeler. Of all the people he left behind in Evansville, aside from family, they were the ones he missed the most. He not only enjoyed their company, but he had the utmost respect for Add. He knew they were growing old, and he wanted to see how they were doing. Ralph spent a long time with the couple, patiently answering their questions and filling them in on all the details of his new life.

The rest of the time he spent at home. Juana engaged a substitute teacher and came back for a long weekend. Marcia, Herb, and Sandra Jane came out to the farm several times, and on one occasion, the entire family went to their house for dinner. Ralph also had the added bonus of being able to wear his old civilian clothes when he knew no one would stop by the house.

When it was all over, Rolla and Jessie drove Ralph to the train station for the return trip. Herb, Marcia, and Sandra Jane met them there. There

While on leave, Ralph posed for many pictures. On the left, he is pictured with his mother and father on the farm. The "sweetheart wings" that Ralph gave to Jessie can be seen on her coat lapel. On the right, he is pictured with his sister, Juana.

were lots of hugs, kisses, and tears. Although no one said it, everyone knew that this could be the last time they would ever see Ralph.

★ ★ ★

Whatever Ralph thought Roswell lacked, Hobbs was much worse. A newer facility, it was hastily thrown together. When he arrived, some buildings still were under construction. As with Roswell, there were very few paved roads and all of the buildings looked almost identical. Over four hundred buildings had been constructed in seven months, between June 1942 and January 1943. Grading on the four runways also began in June, with final paving completed in mid-September.

The field was originally designed to be a bombardier training facility, utilizing as many as six satellite fields. However, in the fall of 1942, the decision was made to make Hobbs one of three facilities that would be used to prepare pilots to fly the B-17 Flying Fortress. The first B-17s arrived in December, along with the first of forty-six pilots.

★ ★ ★

Ralph's passion for fancy stationery continued at Hobbs. Most of the letters were written on United States Army Air Forces stationery.

★ ★ ★

April 24, 1943

Dear Mother & Dad,

Well, I have been down here[48] almost a week now and they are really putting us through the paces. We haven't been too busy this week—only at times. But our next weeks schedule is really full. We fly every day and that includes Sunday. I fly in the morning (tomorrow morn) (Easter Sunday). I fly from 630 to 1130. We don't have much time to ourselves with ground school and athletics on our schedule also.

We are to be here only 4½ weeks or 30 days. At first we thought they were shortening our course because they needed instructors. Now they tell us that they need some men for combat duty in a hurry and so they shortened our course so we could get to combat duty quicker. But nothing is definite and nobody knows for sure. They probably won't know until we are ready to leave here.

I am not too eager to go to combat in such a short time but if I have to go I guess the B-17[49] is as good a ship as any. It is easy to land and fairly easy to fly. As you probably know it is 105 ft from wing tip to tip and about 80 ft long. The pilot sits 14 ft above the ground. When you come in to land you have to be able to judge the distance almost perfect or you will make a bad landing. And a bad landing in this airplane is really vicious. The airplane itself weighs better than 40,000 lbs and then you put about 2000 gals of gas at 6 lbs per gal and 150 gals oil at 8 lbs per gal plus about 3 tons bombs, 8 crew members, guns, ammunition, baggage and a few other things—the whole thing weighs between 60,000 & 70,000 lbs. It is really amazing how the thing flys. There are hundreds of switches, gauges, controls and things to keep track of. What with four engines you are really busy. Any one of the four engines on the B-17 are bigger (more horsepower) than any two engines I have ever flown. The AT-11 had only 2–450 hP engines and each of the B-17 engines are 1200 HP. You have to know quite a bit engineering to keep these power plants running. So that they will consume the minimum amount of gasoline and still get the results wanted. When you go on a long trip you set your engines at a certain RPM—(revolution per minute) and manifold pressure so that your speed won't be so great but your gasoline will last longer. When on a short trip you speed the engine up so that your speed will be greater but your gasoline will last no so long. This isn't a small airplane you don't have to sit in one place you can walk all over it. It has a toilet. We have a drinking water tank and paper cups if you get thirsty. The navigators & Bombadiers compartment is down in the nose and is as large as mothers kitchen.[50] But it is not quite tall enough for me to stand straight up in it. There are huge auxiliary gasoline tanks and fuel pumps to pump gasoline to any of the regular fuel tanks. There are 2 life rafts when released will fly out if you have to land on water. There are 6 radio sets in the plane and a portable one you can take out of the plane. There are emergency rations in the plane along with first aid kits. All of the newer planes have 14 guns and some have 16 guns on them.

I don't know anything else to tell you. If you have any questions you would like to ask, write me and I will try to answer them. We are only 5 miles from the Texas border.

It has been awfully hot down here in the daytime. I am wearing my khaki and I still sweat all the time. There are no trees on the post at all. There isn't much to do, but then I don't have much time to run around.

I have to get up at 5 AM in the morning so guess I'd better turn in. Please send this letter around so I won't have to write it all over again.

Don't look for any letters regularly from me but I will write when I can.

I hope you all have a very nice Easter and I send Easter greetings to you all.

Love
Ralph

★ ★ ★

May 7, 1943

Dear Mother & Dad,

I don't know if this letter will get to you by Mother's Day or not. I have been awfully busy and haven't been able to get into town to get you anything.

As I wrote you before I fly everyday now. I will have tomorrow afternoon off from 2:30 to 6:00 and that is the most time I've had off for over a week. I have to fly tomorrow night. I have over 60 hours in the B-17 now. The most of the time I get here now will be instrument time. When I get through here I will have an unlimited rating as a pilot. I will be qualified to fly every thing the Army has from a single engine, twin engine and 4 engine planes. In this course here I also get a special instrument course. I will take an instrument check and will have an unlimited instrument rating. In other words I will be qualified to fly in any kind of weather. The last few days I have been practising takeoffs and landings. We have a hood and curtains which we hang up around the windows so we can't see out. We take off—fly around the field and then land—not seeing the ground at any time. This is quite difficult and requires lots of practise. If you get off the least bit you will get into trouble. The other day I took off on instruments flew to Roswell—then to Carlsbad then to Wink[51] back to Hobbs and landed and never saw the ground from the time I took off until I returned.

The first part of this week we took a B-17 up to 32,000 ft and flew around for about 1 hr. Things look pretty small on the ground from up there. Wednesday this week I went to San Antonio, Tex (Randolph Field[52]) and took an altitude test to determine if I am fit to fly at high altitudes. They put us into a pressure chamber and by reducing the pressure in the chamber and sucking the Oxygen out of it, therefore making it a partial vacuum,—they are able to make the chamber equal to any altitude. They took us up to 40,000 ft and kept us there for 3 hrs. We breathed pure oxygen all the time. There were 16 started out and only 11 finished. Of the five that dropped out some stayed in only 20 min and the rest stayed for around 2 hrs before they had to take them out. Some of them would turn white and just keel over others would get the bends in their arms or legs. Some of the boys had stomach pains. At 40000 ft the gas in your stomach expands to 5 times its normal volume. When I got out I got a slip permitting me to fly at altitudes above 30,000 ft.

I wouldn't be surprised if I didn't take a X country to Columbus Ohio[53] some of these days.

Yes I have learned to land this plane without bouncing it. When it touches the ground it usually stays there because it is so heavy. This plane weighs between 25 & 30 tons depending on the amount of gasoline you have in the tanks. When all the tanks are full of gas we have about 2700 gals. gasoline weighs 6 lbs to a gallon.

I don't know much else to tell you. We will finish here around the 20th of May. Where we will go I don't know.

Have you got the roof as yet? Did you get any corn planted? It has been awfully hot down here and hasn't rained in a long time. It gets rather cool at night though.

I hope you have a nice Mothers Day Mother and I hope I will be with you when the next one rolls around—Best Wishes.

Love
Ralph

I still have my car but I think I will sell it some of these days.

★ ★ ★

May 16, 1943

Nazi forces crush the last remnants of Jewish resistance in the Warsaw Ghetto.

★ ★ ★

May 24, 1943[54]

Dear Mother & Dad

I suppose you wonder what has happened to me. Some how I just haven't had time or gotten around to writing letters. I have checked out at Hobbs and am on my way to Boise, Idaho. I don't know what my duties will be there. I am no longer in the West Coast Training Command. I am attached to the 2nd Air Force. While at Boise I will be in the 29th Bomb. Grp.[55]

I am stopping over here in Albuquerque visiting with Gloria[56] and her family. I will write you again from here before I leave.

I have sent home 2 suitcases. They have a lot of stuff in them that I didn't think I would need. I shipped them Railway Express and had them sent to Marcia's so they would be delivered right to the house. Only one of them is locked and I will mail her the key.

How is the flood?[57] I have been reading about it in the papers.

If I am not mistaken Juana's school is out soon so I will not write her at Richmond anymore.

I am going around to see Mrs. Wade[58] before I leave here.

I guess this is just about all for now. I will write you again from here.

Love,
Ralph

Lt. R.H. Schneck
29th Bomb. Grp.
AAB
Boise, Idaho

★ ★ ★

Image from the Hilton Hotel letterhead. At the time, the Hilton Hotel chain consisted of only nine properties.

May 24, 1943

Due to heavy losses, Karl Dönitz, commander-in-chief of the German Navy, withdraws submarines from the North Atlantic.

★ ★ ★

May 29, 1943

Outnumbered Japanese forces on Attu Island in the Aleutian Islands launch a suicide attack on US Army units sent to reclaim the island. The fighting is brutal as 1,800 American soldiers are killed or wounded. Of the 2,500 Japanese soldiers on the island, only twenty-eight survive the attack.

★ ★ ★

"You will never rule the world . . . because you are doomed. All of you, who have demoralized and corrupted a nation, are doomed. Tonight you will take a first step on a dark road from which there is no turning back. You will have to go on and on. From one madness to another . . . leaving behind you a wilderness of misery and hatred. And still you will have to go on . . . because you will find no horizon and see no doors . . . 'till at last you are lost and destroyed. You are doomed, Captain of murderers. One day, sooner or later, you will remember my words."[59]

★ ★ ★

NOTES

1. Closing lines of the 1942 State of the Union Address by President Franklin Delano Roosevelt, January 6, 1942.

2. Written on Hollywood Plaza Hotel stationery. The building is still standing but has been converted to apartments.

3. This is in reference to the Bachelors' Officers Quarters (BOQ). Ralph's room was located in building nine.

4. Harlow Wilcox (1900–1960) was a voice actor on the radio. He was most famous for his comedy routines on the *Fibber McGee and Molly* radio program.

5. Meredith Willson (1902–1984) was an American songwriter, conductor, composer, and playwright. He was best known for writing the Broadway hit *The Music Man.*

6. Harry James (1916–1983) was an American musician and bandleader. He was best known for his trumpet playing during the swing era. During his performance on this occasion, he played "He Wears a Pair of Silver Wings" and asked all US Army Air Corp pilots to stand. Later that evening, many people came by Ralph's table to congratulate them.

7. Grauman's Chinese Theatre, the Florentine Gardens, the Hollywood Palladium, and the Earl Carroll Theater are still in use today.

8. Buddy Clark (1911–1949) was a popular American singer. He died when the airplane he was traveling in ran out of gas and crashed on Beverly Boulevard in Los Angeles.

9. Lady Esther Cosmetics was a Chicago-based manufacturer of fine makeup. Their radio program featured Wayne King and His Orchestra. Today, the company is located in Bensheim, Germany.

10. This was actually Lewis Milestone, a notable director in the RKO stable. During this period, Milestone was not working on any project and was hanging around the studio when the boys showed up. The director of Buddy Clark's movie was Tim Whelan.

11. The movie was *Seven Days' Leave*, starring Victor Mature and Lucille Ball. It was not released until November 1942 after Mature had already enlisted in the US Coast Guard.

12. Victor Mature (1913–1999) was an American stage and film actor both before and after the war. In 1942, Mature joined the US Coast Guard after being rejected by the Navy because of color blindness. He remained in the service until November 1945, after which he resumed his acting career. Standing over six feet two inches tall, with a dark complexion, he was often cast in ethnic roles such as Samson in *Samson and Delilah* or as an American Indian.

13. Ariel Heath was appearing in only her second film. She went on to make twelve additional movies, playing mostly bit parts. When Mature found out Ralph was from Evansville and Swaggerty from Nashville, he said he was from Louisville, Kentucky (about 120 miles east of Evansville), and that one of the girls, Ariel, was from Lexington. He asked Ariel to pose with them for the photograph.

14. W. S. "Woody" Van Dyke (1889–1943) was a notable and well liked film director nicknamed "One Take Woody" for the speed of completing his movies. *Journey for Margaret* would be his last film. He died on February 5, 1943. Nelson Eddy and Jeanette MacDonald, two film superstars of the time, sang and officiated at his funeral.

15. Robert Young (1907–1998) was an American actor of radio, screen, and, later, television. He appeared in over one hundred movies but is best known for his work on television as the star of *Father Knows Best* and *Marcus Welby, M.D.*

16. Laraine Day (1920–2007) was an American movie and television actress. She was as popular in both areas and often starred opposite the top leading men of the day.

17. Dinah Shore (1916–1994) was an American singer and television personality. She is most noted as being the first singer of her era to find solo success, charting eighty hits in the 1940s and 1950s.

18. This is reference to Phoenix, Arizona.

19. Fearful that spies could be tracking troop movements, buses and some trains on the West Coast did not travel during daylight hours.

20. Ralph stayed at the Hotel Adams, located at Central Avenue and Adams Street. This letter is written on hotel stationery, which claims 350 rooms and "modern air conditioning." The hotel was replaced by a newer one, which later became the Wyndham Hotel. A portion of the old hotel was incorporated in the new construction.

21. This is in reference to Bob Saunders, Ralph's roommate, who drove him from Mather to Phoenix in his Ford Deluxe Convertible Coupe.

22. The trip was about 375 miles from Los Angeles to Phoenix. At one point, Ralph would later report, they drove at thirty-seven miles per hour to keep the car from overheating.

23. This refers to an "Immelmann turn," where the aircraft starts a loop, but at the top of the loop, it levels out and flips the plane right-side-up.

24. This refers to a "Cuban eight turn," where the aircraft starts a loop, but on the down side, the plane flips right-side-up and begins another loop, flipping again on the down side and leveling off at the original altitude and heading.

25. This is in reference to a twin engine Curtiss-Wright AT-9 advanced trainer, also known as a Jeep.

26. Ralph took out a life insurance policy before he left home. It would cover anything that happened, except in an act of war. Technically, they considered the training part separate from the actual fighting.

27. Before Ralph left home, he arranged for his account in the Wadesville Bank to be jointly held by him and his father. Ralph's plan was to leave the money there in case he needed it later. He told Rolla that he would let him know when he was going to take money out. It was from this account that Rolla would have paid the insurance premiums.

28. Rolla had been suffering from respiratory problems. Ralph was so concerned that he would call home just to hear Rolla's voice.

29. This is in reference to Captain Charles M. Opeil. He was eventually promoted to major.

30. The fact is that between the time Ralph received his orders to go to Roswell and the time he arrived, the twin engine school he was assigned to had been moved to Pyote, Texas, which is about one hundred miles east of El Paso. His options were to go to Pyote or stay in Roswell and go to a different assignment. Pyote Army Air Field was nicknamed "Rattlesnake Bomber Base." Ralph chose to stay in Roswell.

31. This is in reference to a Beechcraft AT-11 advanced trainer, also known as a Kansan.

32. This is in reference to a North American AT-6 advanced trainer, also known as a Texan.

33. In Ralph's case, he did not have much time off. When he was not flying instruction flights, he was busy checking out newly arriving pilot instructors in the AT-11.

34. This is in reference to the official "head shot" photo taken after graduation. Ralph sent several home for the family to enjoy.

35. This is in reference to a Douglas A-20 Havoc.

36. This is in reference to a Consolidate B-24 Liberator.

37. This is in reference to a Boeing B-17 Flying Fortress.

38. This was the first time that Ralph got to sit in the front of a B-17. He had dreamed of this day from the first time he saw the movie *I Wanted Wings*.

39. Williams Field was located in Mesa, Arizona, about thirty miles southeast of Phoenix. It was renamed Williams Air Force Base in 1948, but it closed in 1993.

40. A "Rat Race Formation" is where students fly in single file, following a single instructor/leader, duplicating every maneuver one after another.

41. Ralph eventually heard from the boy's father and was able to buy the car. It was an all-white 1937 Chevrolet Coupe with black interior.

42. The exact same letter was also sent to Juana.

43. This is in reference to the rank of 1st Lieutenant, a promotion from 2nd Lieutenant.

44. Jessie had just received some false teeth.

45. This is in reference to a North American B-25 Mitchell, named in honor of General Billy Mitchell.

46. Sugar rationing began in May 1942. A sugar ration coupon could be used to buy sugar, candy, or chewing gum. Ration levels and availability varied from region to region. For example, the same coupon could be good for a pound of candy, three packages of gum, or five pounds of sugar. The coupon only gave a person permission to buy the item; they still had to pay the retail price for it.

47. The boys at the training installations had access to a lot of things regular civilians could not get. It was normal for them to buy these items and send them home. Even then, their availability was often limited.

48. This is in reference to Hobbs Army Air Field, which opened in September 1942 and closed in May 1948.

49. The aircraft Ralph trained in was a B-17G, the last variant produced. It is this plane that he describes in the narrative.

50. Well, not quite. Ralph exaggerated some points so that everyone would think that the aircraft was safe to take into combat.

51. This is in reference to Wink, Texas.

52. Randolph Field, located near San Antonio, Texas, was one of the first Army airfields in the country, dedicated on June 20, 1930. Its primary purpose was to train pilots, and it was featured in the movie *I Wanted Wings*. It was renamed Randolph Air Force Base in 1948. The base is still in use today.

53. Columbus was home to Lockbourne Army Airfield and the Northeastern Training Center of the Army Air Corps. A cross-country flight to this field was part of completing the four engine training at Hobbs.

54. Written on Hilton Hotel stationery. At the time, Hilton Hotels consisted of nine properties in California, New Mexico, Texas, and Mexico. The hotel Ralph stayed in was only the fourth Hilton constructed, opening in 1939, at the corner of Second and Copper. It is listed in the National Register. The building has undergone complete renovation and restoration; it is now called the Hotel Andaluz.

55. This is in reference to the 29th Bombardment Group.

56. Gloria Fulcher lived with her mother and aunt in Albuquerque. Her father was a World War I veteran and lived at the VA hospital. One of the hotels in Albuquerque held a tea-dance every Sunday afternoon and invited all the local girls. Ralph met her at one of these dances, and a serious friendship developed. At some point, Ralph decided he was going to be in Roswell for the rest of the war, and it was safe enough to consider getting married. Ralph asked Gloria to marry him and presented her with a ring, which she happily accepted.

57. It had been raining for almost the entire month of May throughout all of the Midwest. This caused flooding along the Mississippi, Missouri, Arkansas, Illinois, Wabash, Osage, and White rivers, as well as many others. The Evansville area, especially along the Wabash River, did not escape the floods.

58. Mrs. Wade is Jim Wade's mother. She had relocated to Albuquerque because she suffered from respiratory problems, possibly tuberculosis. Jim Wade was Ralph's insurance agent in Wadesville.

59. Closing soliloquy of Professor Horatio Smith, played by Leslie Howard, addressing his captor, General von Graum, on the upcoming invasion of Poland. The character of General von Graum was based on Reich Marshal Hermann Goering. (*Pimpernel Smith*, British National Films, 1941. Released in the United States as *Mr. V* in 1942).

Chapter 5

A NEW NAVIGATOR

★ ★ ★

"The navigator's job is to direct your flight from departure to destination and return. He must know the exact position of the airplane at all times."[1]

Ralph had sold his car before leaving Hobbs, New Mexico, and he took a train to Boise. When he arrived, he went to headquarters to check in and get his room assignment. He had arrived later than expected, it was already starting to get dark, and he was eager to get settled. When he reported at headquarters there was a note saying that if he arrived before 4 p.m. he should report to the Operations Office. On the way to the barracks, he passed one of the boys he knew from Roswell, who stopped him for a chat. He asked if Ralph had heard the news. He said he had not, and the boy told him, "We're flying B-24s!"

"B-24s," Ralph wondered, "what happened to the B-17?"

Eager to confirm what he had just heard, he hurried to his barracks, found his room, and dumped all of his belongings on the empty bed without noticing numerous telephone messages that had been slid under the door. Room assignments were made in alphabetical order, by rank. Later, as units and crews were formed, things would be shuffled. Normally, he would have had a room with three other 1st lieutenants. Having only one roommate meant he was rooming with a captain or higher. He did not think anything of it at the time and hurried off to the Operations Office as instructed.

The Operations Office was located at one end of the main hangar. Ralph found the hangar and saw that a light was glowing. He opened the door and stepped in. The large room was dimly lit, but he could see the silhouette of a B-24 Liberator in the middle of the hangar. He walked all around it, running his hand on the metal surface, feeling the seams and the smoothness of the bright aluminum skin. When he got to the other side of the plane, he saw the Operations Office.

Ralph entered and found a sergeant standing behind a long counter. When Ralph told him who he was, the sergeant pointed to the corner of the hangar and said, "Out there."

There was a small library set up in the corner of the hangar, with walls formed by tall steel bookcases and lockers. Several lights were turned on, and it appeared that someone was there.

Ralph walked over to the area and saw one soldier with his face buried in a book. Other books were on the table in front of him. Some were open to specific pages, and others were stacked up on the corner of the table. The soldier looked up, his eyes rising just over the top of the book. Ralph said he was sorry to interrupt and started to leave. The soldier said he was not interrupting and that he was almost finished. He stood up and held out his hand, saying, "Hi, Ralph. Remember me?" Ralph shook his hand and said, "Of course I do." The soldier was Jimmy Stewart, whom Ralph had met earlier at Mather Field.

Stewart sized Ralph up, smiled, and said, "I think you and I are roommates." At that, Stewart pointed to a chair and invited Ralph to sit down. He told Ralph that he had looked over all the names of pilots coming to Boise, and Ralph's was the only one that he recognized.

They spent the next hour getting caught up on each other's travels. Like Ralph, Stewart had spent most of his time training other pilots. He told Ralph that so far, there were very few pilots in the group that were qualified to fly anything with wings, and he thought Ralph was going to be very busy. Ralph asked why he thought that, and Stewart replied that he was expecting to fly a B-17, the switch took him by surprise, and he could use some help in getting up to speed on the B-24. It seems that even though Stewart had a commercial pilot license, flying a DC-3 was a far cry from the complexity of flying a B-17. And the B-24 was that much more complicated. That is why he was studying up on the B-24. Before the evening was over, Ralph agreed to coach Stewart whenever he had a question, even though Ralph had never flown a B-24 before.

The two men walked back to their room. When they entered, Ralph finally noticed the telephone messages littering the floor. He pointed to them and said, "I think these are all for you." They shared a laugh, and Stewart headed for the pay phone down the hall.

This was the start of a professional friendship that would last throughout Ralph's military career.[2] They roomed together for only a couple of days, but over the next several weeks Stewart asked Ralph for some assistance. In later years, Ralph said that he was never sure that Stewart needed any help because they always ended up talking about more than just flying.

Stewart's prediction came true. Ralph was the busiest pilot in Boise. Because of his hours and the fact that he was certified to fly anything with wings, he was given the task of training all of the incoming pilots and their crews in flying the B-24.

★ ★ ★

June 1, 1943

The German Luftwaffe shoots down British Overseas Airways Corporation Flight 777 while it is en route from Lisbon, Portugal to London, England. The Luftwaffe explanation is that they thought British Prime Minister Winston Churchill was on board. Instead,

beloved British actor Leslie Howard was on board and was subsequently killed. Many believe that Hermann Goering, field marshal of the Luftwaffe, had targeted Howard and personally ordered the attack.

★ ★ ★

June 28, 1943[3]

Dear Mother, Dad & Juana,

I'm sorry I haven't answered sooner. But I have been real busy. I am just about finished up here[4] and I understand I will leave here about July 1st. I don't know where I will go. I have no idea. I have a whole crew now except a navigator & Co-Pilot. The Co-Pilot I have now will stay here and get a crew of his own. I will get a navigator & Co-Pilot in 2nd phase. Before I leave here I am going to get another Aerial Engineer. My assistant Engineer is just a Corporal now. I have already turned in the papers and he will get a buck Sargents stripes. Then I will make him my Aerial Engineer. Then I will just swap my present Aerial Engineer for an Asst. Engineer. I haven't got time to write you why I am changing these boys but will try to in my next letter.[5]

I think I will get to leave with one of the other boys who came up here with me. The rest of them aren't finished yet. They don't send out a whole bunch at a time. When a crew gets in enough time, bombs dropped and ammunition fired they ship them out.

I will let you know where I go as soon as I find out.

I had better get down to the flying line. I told all my crew to get down there early. You have to have a little pep talk every once in a while to keep every one on the ball. It is quite a job to keep 10 men in line. I had to go down and bail one of my men out of jail the past week-end. He was arrested for Jay walking—they do that up here.

Ralph

★ ★ ★

Image from Gowen Field letterhead.

July 28, 1943

Japanese forces on Kiska Island in the Aleutian Islands withdraw without being noticed by advancing American invasion forces.

★ ★ ★

Things were happening at lightning speed—at least for the Army. Boise was the first step in gearing up to go overseas. There, the pilots became familiar with the B-24 and started forming their crews. Ralph got most of his crew pulled together and was way ahead of the other pilots in preparing for the next step. When he left Boise, he still did not know what unit he was going to or, for that matter, where he was going to go.

★ ★ ★

Pocatello, Idaho, with a population of about 19,000, was about 200 miles from Boise at the southwest corner of the state. The city architecture, streets, and the people reminded Ralph of Evansville on a much smaller scale. Even though there was always something to do to occupy idle times, the four weeks flew by quickly.

Pocatello was similar to all the other training stations. The airfield was especially built for the war effort as a training facility for B-17s and B-24s. Until now, the object was to get as much time in an aircraft as possible and make sure it and the crew was in the best possible working condition before being sent to the front; however, Pocatello was all down time. There was no flying while the boys were there. Ralph had a full crew, except for two gunners, when he arrived from Boise. The gunners joined the crew, and they all sat around and talked . . . and talked . . . and got to know each other.

It was during this time that they decided on a name for their airplane, when they received one. They had all seen the nose art on the B-17s, and they wanted to have the same. They decided on the name *Sin Ship*[6] because they were all sinners. Additionally, they decided that it would carry an artful piece of nudity on the nose. But there was a very large glitch in their plans.

Charles Painter, the bombardier, had his wife and mother following him from point-to-point as he went through training. Also, John Decker, the copilot, had his wife, Gail, in tow. The women would stay in boarding houses in nearby cities, and the husbands would visit when they could. This was not that unusual, and occasionally, there would be so many women following their husbands that there were not enough boarding houses. In those instances, they would stay in a hotel and wait for the next assignment.

Painter and Decker told their wives of the plans for naming the aircraft, to which there was a female uprising as they all violently disapproved—so much so that they harassed Ralph about it whenever they saw him. Eventually, Ralph had no choice but to tell them they would select a new name. But he would wait until the ladies returned home before telling anyone.

★ ★ ★

While at Pocatello, Ralph met Margaret Christensen. She had been married to a navigator who was killed in a training accident several months earlier. Unfortunately, he died before he had finished filling out all of his Army paperwork, and the Army did not know he was married. As a result, Margaret did not receive any survivor compensation.

After Ralph learned of her situation, he volunteered to help her through the process so she could get her benefits. Over the course of time, she and Ralph developed a friendship that, without a raging war to fight, would have led to marriage. As Ralph left for England, he vowed to stay in touch with her.

Margaret was a nurse, which was a profession in high demand at the time. She moved to Salt Lake City to work at St. Mark's Hospital and continued to correspond with Ralph.

★ ★ ★

When Ralph arrived at Pocatello, he learned that he was going to be a replacement pilot to another unit. In fact, everyone he was training with would be replacements. This put a lot of pressure on the pilots and their crews, because they did not feel like developing any camaraderie; they felt as though they were in the war all alone, until they got to their final destination. Sometime during these last two phases the decision was made to form a new Bombardment Group. This was both a good thing and a bad thing. The good part was that friendships could be made, and every guy felt like helping everyone else. The bad portion would come much later in the form of loose operations. The leadership of the new group had been doing only training. Once crews finished their training, they were sent to another group for someone else to handle. The new Bombardment Group leadership was not fully attuned to managing all the men and equipment.

★ ★ ★

July 7, 1943

Dear Mother, Dad & Juana

Just a note to let you know where I am.[7] We finished up in Boise last Sat and they shipped us out today with 3 other crews. They were fellows I had known back in Hobbs. The First pilots I mean.

This is a 2nd phase base and we will get 2nd & 3rd phase here then we will be ready for overseas duty.

We will not be a new Squadron as this is a provisional group and we will be replacements. We will probably be here 6 wks or 2 months.[8]

I went out and had dinner with Uncle Clarence[9] and Aunt Cora Sun. They are all very anxious for you folks to come out here.

So you all can think it over. Pocatello is about 260 miles East & a little south of Boise or about 5 hrs ride on the train. I would like to see any or all of you who will come and I'm sure Uncle Clarence's would like to see you also.

I have to take my crew around tomorrow to the dispensary and see that they get their immunization shots. I am responsible for my crew at all times. They can't do anything unless they get my permission. If the Sqdn. Gives them a pass they still have to get my approval.

I don't know what kind of schedule I will maintain here but will write you as soon as I find out.

Love
Ralph.

Lt. R.H. Schneck
382 Bomb GRP
AAB, Pocatello, Idaho

★ ★ ★

Sioux City, Iowa was over 800 miles east of Pocatello. The airfield was another that had been built for the Army specifically for preparing B-17 and B-24 crews for war. Typical of airfields of the time, construction began in March 1942, and the field opened four months later on July 5.

With a population of about 83,000, Sioux City was also very much like Evansville. There were nice movie theaters, parks, and a nice river district near the Missouri River; however, time was short, and the boys almost never got a chance to relax.

The airfield did not have all the amenities Ralph had grown accustomed to at the other stations. For one thing, the PX was practically nonexistent, selling only the necessities. Consequently, there was no personalized stationery, and Ralph was forced to continue using the United States Army Air Forces stationery he brought with him.

★ ★ ★

August 2, 1943[10]

Dear Mother, Dad & Juana,

Well, at long last I am getting around to writing letters. I got off pass last week and there were 4 new crews in our Sqdn. So I had to fly every other 6 hrs for 3 days checking them out. I flew from 6 PM to 6 AM Tues nite and was just about dead. I was finished up and had gone to bed Wed morn. Had just got to sleep and they called and asked me to go to Casper Wyoming after an airplane. But when I got down there an hour later I had to go to Oklahoma City, Okla instead. So, I, my co-pilot, navigator, Engineer & Radio man caught the airliner here. We flew to Omaha, then on to Kansas City. Had a 5 hr. lay over in Kansas City. We went up and looked the town then had a big juicy Kansas City Steak. Then we caught the airliner and flew to Wichita, and got to Okla C. 7:30 the next morn. We got a hotel room and slept till noon then went out to Tinker Field[11] where I was to pick up the plane. We went out to the plane[12] and checked it over thoroughly. Found out it wasn't equiped with all the things I was to sign for. Also it had to have some work done on it before I would fly it. By the time I got everything straightened out and got headed home it was 6 PM. I was really disgusted with all the Civilians who were working on the plane. They didn't have any idea what was going on and they called them selves "specialists." It took 6 of them 2½ hrs to put air in the landing gear struts with an air compressor. I could do the job alone in 30 minutes.

All the planes are grounded now on this field, because of a defect in the landing gear.

Colonel Terrell,[13] our C.O., got a letter from the War Dept. last week to have this group ready to go overseas in 45 days. He wrote for an extension and it was granted. So we will be here during the month of Sept. Then we will move some other place in the states for the month of Oct. On top of this he asked for another extension but he hasn't heard from it yet.

As for the raids the bomber pilots participate in before they are sent home depends on the theatre of war, or combat zone they are in. Some places they get replacements regularily. Other places they come rather slow.

I don't know about my leave. I doubt if I get over 7 days at the most. Which isn't very long.

Guess I'd better close & get some sleep.

Love
Ralph.

★ ★ ★

August 9, 1943[14]

Dear Mother, Dad & Juana,

It sorta cooled off here[15] a few days but is getting hot again.

I hardly know what to tell you about coming up here. I only get one 24 hr pass a week and there is no other way of getting off the post. You could come out to the post to see me but I am usually pretty busy in the daytime. If you want to come be sure you come on my day off. Next Sunday is my day off. The next week it will be Monday. And each week it is stepped up a day.

We are supposed to get a leave when we finish third phase. But we are only authorized to get 6 days. We are supposed to get through second phase at the end of August. Then we are supposed to move to a satellite field probably in Nebraska or S. Dakota. We will then finish third phase. We probably won't be finished with third phase until the last of Sept or the first of October.

I have a Navigator now. A Lt. Fejes. This makes my crew complete. 4 of we officers & 6 enlisted men. I'm afraid I'm going to loose some of them though. One engineer is about to go to officers Engineering School, one is joining the Cadets and one of the gunners has bad eye sight. Both of my radio men are good so they are going to take one of them and give him to some one else. I sorta hate to see them do this because I have a good bunch of boys.

I am listening to the radio. I've never heard so many cowboy & cowgirl singing programs. Out west where you could expect things like that you never hear those kind of programs. I'm beginning to think the East is about 10 years behind the times.

Love
Ralph.

★ ★ ★

September 3, 1943

Operation Avalanche
The 15th Army Group, which includes the US 5th Army and the British 8th Army, invade Italy near Salerno. Two supporting invasions at Calabria and Taranto occur at the same time.

★ ★ ★

Watertown, South Dakota, was about 170 miles from Sioux City and was one of the smallest towns Ralph had been to since basic training. With only a population of about 11,000, there was little to do in town. The airfield was literally ripped out of the adjacent cornfields and featured the shortest runway Ralph had ever seen. He was assigned to a small barracks that was nothing more than a tar paper shack.

The crews' quarters at Watertown, South Dakota, could best be described as overly plain. The exterior was finished in tar paper, and the interior featured bare wooden slats and plywood. This was one of the last stops before going overseas, and it was a far cry from the "country club" Ralph started with at King City, California.

Watertown was one of the airfields used as the final staging location for forming groups to go overseas, and there was not much time to socialize. Crews that needed to complete specific training elements had to get those completed before they were ready to go. Everyone was busy.

Ralph spent much of his time making flights to manufacturing facilities and Air Corps depots to pick up parts. These trips were timely because he needed to break in a new navigator.

★ ★ ★

September 8, 1943

General Dwight Eisenhower announces that Italy has surrendered to the Allies. Surrender negotiations had been in progress for many weeks. The actual surrender was orchestrated to occur in conjunction with the September 3 invasion of Southern Italy.

★ ★ ★

September 30, 1943[16]

Dear Mother & Dad.

Well, it seems I am running into tough luck. I'll start from the beginning. We had been on a high altitude (23,000 ft) gunnery mission to Pierre, S.D. It was about dark and we were returning to the Watertown Bombing range and was going to do some nite bombing. It was to be high altitude also but there were low clouds over the target so we had to come down low. We missed the target and we searched for about ½ hr so finally I decided to fly back to the field about 50 miles away. I called the navigator for a compass heading home and he told me he was lost and didn't know where he was. So I immediately tuned in the Radio beam and flew us back into the field. This was about 8:30 PM. I called the tower and told them I was staying up till 10:30 PM. So we turned around and again headed for the Bomb Range. When we found it we had been up about 6 hrs. and since the planes are not filled to capacity with gas I knew we must be getting low. I called for the engineer to check the gas and he reported about 200 gals left. I said OK we will drop a couple of bombs. We were about ready to drop bombs when the engineer said that the guages read inaccurate and we had less than 100 gals left. Immediately I said we are going home knowing that it takes 30 min to get there and we had about 45 min. gas left. About that time #1 engine went out because of no gas. So we feathered it and about 2 min later #4 went out but we turned on all the fuel pumps and they pumped gas into #4 tank and we got it to running again. I had all the fellows put on their parachutes just in case. We made the field OK and landed. Just as we parked the plane and was in the process of cutting the engines the navigator runs out of the plane and right into one of the propellers. It cut the whole right side of his head open. They rushed him to the hospital but he died about 6 hrs. later. I don't know what will happen to us. I imagine we will get a new navigator.

We are scheduled to leave here about Oct 10. I don't know where we will go from here.

I have a hunch we will either end up in England or Italy.

We went hunting this morning. I didn't fly so my crew and the operations officer got in a jeep and started out. We got some automatic shot guns

& all the skeet shells we could get. We stayed out about 1 hr. but we didn't get anything.

I imagine you will get some more clothes of mine some of these days. I got the juices allright.

Will close for now,

Love,
Ralph.

Send this letter around and I won't write it over.

★ ★ ★

Wednesday[17]

Dearest folks,

I was sorry that I couldn't hear you or that you couldn't hear me. I called because I thought it might do you good to know that Ralph was O.K.

He left Watertown yesterday (Tues) about 6:00 AM and was due to arrive in Dayton at noon. He was one minute early. He said he flew over Joliet, Illinois and Lafayette, Ind. He missed Richmond. He was suppose to pick up parts and return to Sioux City by evening. As usual he said these Dam Civilians never have anything ready so he called back to Sioux City to ask them if he should stay and get the parts or what. They told him to stay and to go on to Cleveland Ohio and pick up some more parts and then go to Flint Michigan to get parts and then come on home today.

So when he found out that he was going to stay he called me. It was 7:15 when he called. Punch[18] and I had just sat down to eat—so we ate and were on our way by 8:00. We got there about 9:15 and visited with him until about 12: midnight. We took him back out to Patterson Field. We took our clothes and thought we would stay all night and eat breakfast with him. I had made arrangements for a substitute this morning but he wanted to go back to the field and stay as he had to be there early this morning. He said if they didn't get off and were there tonite he would call but he didn't call so guess he got off.

All of the crew were with him. I met the Bombadier. He is the one that is married and lived in town. He is the one Ralph took the rum to. He seemed like an awfully nice fellow. He said he would have his wife write to me when they left.

Since he is sqdn. Leader that calls for the rank of Major in the Army. His promotion as Captain he said he was looking for any day and it would come from the 2nd Air Force but his promotion to Major would have to come from Washington D.C. He didn't talk like he thought it would take so long to get them through after they once started. He expected his Captaincy any day.

They have their ship. He said they had less than 70 hours flying in it. They named it *Tasket, the 4 engine Casket.*[19] Isn't that some name?

He looks swell. I believe even better than he did when he was home.

He was wound up and talked just as hard as he could talk. We met him at the Biltmore Hotel so we just sat in the lobby and visited.

He said the usual custom was, when they left a satilite base that they went to a checking field. By that they check all the supplies, from airplanes to clothes. Then they went to a field and waited to get orders as to where to go. They think they are scheduled to go to Lincoln, Nebraska. If they do, that isn't a checking station—so they just don't know.

Also every sqdn. is supposed to have at least three water missions before leaving. One a gunnery mission, one a navigator's mission and one a bombing mission and they were to go to the Gulf for this but for some reason that has been cancelled.

His plane and 4 others are to carry the officials of the sqdn. when they go and he will lead all the other sqdns. across.[20]

They have been wanting them to get rid of their kaki uniforms. He said that meant one of 3 things. That they were going to the Aleutians, or too England where they wouldn't need them or they were bound for the Pacific and they wanted them to have new ones.

He is going to send some more clothes home and that was the reason he wanted the bag. Then he would have something to send them in.

He said not to send anymore fruit juices or canned stuff as he couldn't carry it around.

He wanted his Scout[21] and his razor that he wrote to Marcia about. I got the scout knife here and looked for a razor but no luck. Punch looked in Indianapolis but no luck.

This boy that was with him (Lt. Painter) wanted a candid camera.[22] He said that he had looked everywhere but no luck. I found one here for $4.98 so I'm going to send it with Ralph's knife.

He said there would be a time that we wouldn't hear from him. That would be when he went to this last Camp and got his APO etc because he couldn't write any letters until he got to the place that he was going.

He said he would liked to seen you folks too but you wouldn't have had time to get there after he found he was to stay before he would have been off again. He said to tell everyone hello.

As to the accident. He said this fellow was a very nervous sort of a fellow in the first place and somehow he got lost and couldn't find his way. He got all excited and when Ralph called the tower at the field to get on the beam they were further away than expected and too the gas meters read that they had more gas than they really did. They had their parachutes on all ready to jump but of course they landed all right. Just as soon as they landed he jumped out of the plane and some how walked in to the propeller. He said all they knew was that the plane shook and the fellow that was helping them to land with the lights and all yelled—call an ambulance someone has been hurt—so he did and when he got out he saw who it was. He said the boys tried to pick him up but he told them to let him lay until the ambulance got there.

They had a little trouble getting a doctor and finally the Army doctor got there and tied up all the veins and arteries that he could find and then they took him into town to an Xray machine. The fellow who read the Xray said there was no concussion or fracture and he was getting all right for about the first 3 or four hours and then he just went all at once. Ralph said he talked to the man afterwards that took the Xray. He said that there was a concussion.[23]

Ralph said his new navigator seemed to be very efficient.[24] This trip yesterday was their first trip out together.

I'm sending you some plums. These were much cheaper and Punch is coming straight home tomorrow so they out[25] to be in good shape. I hope that you will enjoy the stuff as much as I did the stuff you sent me. I have it all in the ice box. I am going to feast for a while.

If you have any more questions or if I haven't made anything clear just write and ask about it and I'll gladly answer if I can.

Will you let Marcia read this letter as I won't write all these details to her. I'm going to write her and Mrs. Beeler tomorrow evening as I know they will both be anxious to know about him.

Write when you have time.

Love,
Juana

★ ★ ★

On October 10, 1943, the flag at Watertown flew at half-mast in honor of Lieutenant Fejes. Fejes died the day before when he accidently walked into a turning propeller, an accident that happened all too often during training.

October 8, 1943[26]

Dear Mother & Dad,

Well, we are all restricted to the post now and we aren't going to do much flying till we leave here so I have a little more time.

I went to Patterson Field the other day. We had to lay over night so I called Juana. I guess you already know about it by now. From Dayton we went to Cleveland. Then we flew across Lake Erie to Flint Michigan. Then we flew across Lake Michigan to Chicago. We landed at all these places.

I am enclosing some snapshots we took at one of the parks in Watertown.

We are going to leave here pretty soon. I don't know when nor do I know where we will go. I do know that 5 of our planes are going to Sioux City and pick up all the Headquarters officials and they will fly with us to our next station. The Colonel (C.O.) and Col. Seashore[27] are going over in the boat.[28] It is my understanding that Major Schwartz the executive is going with us and as far as I know now I will lead the group in the overseas flight.

I don't know much else to tell you. The boys in my crew are

Whitfield G. Brooke, Biloxi, Miss.	Navigator	2nd Lts.
John R. Decker, Hollywood Calif.	Co-Pilot	
Charles C. Painter, Salem, Ore.	Bombadier	
Archie R. Sloman, Long Beach Calif	Engineer	
Sebastian Capobianco, New York	Engineer	
Albert J. Urbanik, Donora Pa	Radio	
Wilbur Pursel, Springfield Mo.	armorer gunner	
Joseph Flynn, New York	gunner	

and I have a new gunner named Robinson but I don't know where he is from

Love
Ralph

I will send home some more stuff some of these days.

★ ★ ★

The day before they were to leave Watertown, the leadership of Crew 59 posed in front of their barracks. With all the turmoil they had been through, none of them were sad to leave. Shown are Charles Painter (bombardier), Ralph, and John Decker (copilot). The different pants and uniform styles indicate that they did not get basic training at the same location; uniforms tended to be a local preference for post commanders.

At Boise, it was learned that Ralph and his crew would be part of the newly formed 445th Bombardment Group. Tentatively, the 445th Bomb Group was destined for England, but that could change many times before they finally got to their final destination. As squadrons completed their training, they were dispersed to various locations to wait for the entire Bomb Group to be completely assembled. Ralph and his crew were sent to Lincoln, Nebraska, to wait for final orders.

★ ★ ★

"From Berlin, Rome and Tokyo we have been described as a nation of weaklings—'playboys'—who would hire British soldiers, or Russian soldiers, or Chinese soldiers to do our fighting for us.
"Let them repeat that now!

"Let them tell that to General MacArthur and his men.
"Let them tell that to the sailors who today
are hitting hard in the far waters of the Pacific.
"Let them tell that to the boys in the Flying Fortresses.
"Let them tell that to the Marines!"[29]

★ ★ ★

NOTES

1. From "Pilot Training Manual for the Liberator," Burford Printing Company, 5-18-45, AAF Manual No. 50-12.

2. Ralph never called Stewart "Jimmy," only "Jim." The only time he used the Hollywood nickname was when people did not know who he was taking about or as a point of reference, as is shown in some of the later letters.

3. Written on Gowen Field stationery.

4. Gowen Field opened in 1926 as the Boise Municipal Airport. It became Gowen Field in 1941. Gowen Field is currently a US Air National Guard base and is located alongside the Boise Airport.

5. Ralph was a stickler for forming a team. Apparently, his current "aerial engineer" was not very happy with the Army or going off to war. He spent a lot of time berating the others on the crew and negatively discussing the Army in general. This was not something Ralph would tolerate, so he took matters in his own hands. Being a 1st Lieutenant and having the respect of the other officers certainly helped to expedite the process.

6. The one-word variation, *SinShip* or *Sinship*, is used interchangeably.

7. Pocatello Army Airfield was deactivated as an Army installation in 1945 and is now the Pocatello Regional Airport.

8. As time went on, the need for more and more aircrews became acute. Original training dates were cut, with the crews being asked to still get all of their flying done in the compressed timeframe. Ralph would not be there as long as he had thought.

9. This is in reference to Clarence and Cora Defur. Cora was actually Rolla's aunt (his mother's sister). Clarence was a preacher and had moved the family to Pocatello, and then later to Boise.

10. Mailed from Sioux City Army Air Base, which opened in 1942 as a training field. It closed in 1945, but reopened in 1946 as an Air Force reserve base. Today, it is a US Air National Guard base and shares runways with the Sioux City Gateway Airport.

11. Tinker Field was named in honor of Major General Clarence L. Tinker (1887–1942), who was from Pawhuska, Oklahoma and part Osage American Indian. Major General Tinker was a graduate of Wentworth Military Academy. He received his wings in 1921 and went on to become the first major general of American Indian descent in US Army

history. Although the base was not named in his honor until 1948, the field, which served the Army and a factory for the Douglas Aircraft Company (which made B-24s under a contract with the Consolidated Aircraft Company), carried his name almost immediately after his death in 1942.

12. This was a model B-24H, with serial number 42-7601.

13. Colonel Robert H. Terrell became the commanding officer of the 445 Bombardment Group on April 1, 1943, and he served until July 24, 1944.

14. Mailed from Sioux City, Iowa.

15. This is in reference to Sioux City Army Air Base.

16. Mailed from Watertown, South Dakota. Watertown Army Air Base was an auxiliary field used as a temporary location for units headed overseas. It is now the Watertown Regional Airport.

17. Written on school craft paper in pencil on October 6, 1943.

18. Punch travelled to Richmond on a regular basis to visit Juana. He wanted Juana to move back home, marry him, and start a family. At the time, Juana was not interested in that arrangement.

19. This is the name Ralph came up with after facing the wives of his bombardier and copilot. After Lieutenant Fejes died, Ralph began thinking of changing the name again. The plane had already claimed one life, and the name did not need to be a constant reminder. Additionally, as a lead pilot, his plane needed to reflect a better image than that of certain death. He eventually settled on going back to the original name, *Sin Ship*, but only after they arrived at wherever they were going.

20. Ralph's crew carried the designation of Crew 59. That would be their designation until they reached their final destination.

21. This is in reference to a Boy Scout pocket knife, which was very popular, even among non-Boy Scouts.

22. The Candid Camera Corporation of America (Chicago, Illinois) made the Perfex Fifty-Five. It had an aluminum body with a built-in exposure meter and a focal plane shutter.

23. For some reason, Ralph always had a very low opinion of the medical profession. He did not know how Fejes could have sustained the injuries he had without suffering a concussion or a fracture, so he asked around. He always believed that if they had treated Fejes for a concussion that he might have pulled through. It was situations like this one that made Ralph more and more skeptical of the medical profession.

24. Lieutenant Whitfield Brooke was selected by Ralph based on recommendations he received from some of his old instructor friends. Brooke had just come from navigator school and was the second highest rated student in the class.

25. Colloquial spelling for "ought."

26. Mailed from Watertown, South Dakota.

27. This is in reference to Lieutenant Colonel Malcolm D. Seashore.

28. On October 20, 1943, all of the headquarters personnel who were not flying moved to Camp Shanks in New York. They sailed for England on the *Queen Mary* on October 27, 1943.

29. Excerpt from President Franklin Delano Roosevelt's Fireside Chat 20, delivered on February 23, 1942.

Chapter 6

SHE WAS FULL-BLOODED PORTUGUESE

★ ★ ★

"As simple as a train-ride to the next town is a trip over the Pan American Airways System to one—or thirty-three—countries! For your convenience we have designated more than six thousand travel and ticket agencies throughout the United States and Canada."[1]

During World War I, the US Air Corps had been organized around the basic squadron as the smallest organizational unit, with multiple squadrons formed into groups. After World War I, the Air Corps demobilized and reshaped its core effort to the defense of the United States. During that period, very few groups were in existence with some squadrons reporting directly to US Air Corps Headquarters. But, believing that war was eminent, the Air Corps began to reorganize in 1939 and 1940. By December 7, 1941, the Air Corps had created ninety-four groups, each with multiple squadrons, with all squadrons reporting through a group.

Groups tended to be territorial in nature, meaning that a bombardment (shortened to "bomb"), fighter, or support group tended to occupy a specific facility all by themselves. This was especially true of bomb groups and fighter groups. To the military planner, groups provided the administrative services needed to handle a large number of people as well as providing a strong enough force to be used in executing a large-scale war.

A typical bomb group of B-24s was comprised of seventy-two aircraft and ninety-six air crews split into four bomb squadrons. The air crews amounted to about 1,000 men, but it would take another 1,200 to provide all of the maintenance and support of the group, for a total of over 2,200 men.

Even then, more coordination of activities was needed. In October 1940, the Air Corps created four air districts. Each air district was made up of a number of groups and assigned to defend a specific part of the United States. In March 1941, the Air Corps redesignated air districts as numbered air forces. The first four numbered air forces were obviously the 1st, 2nd, 3rd, and 4th. Other air forces were created as the need arose. For example, the 8th Air Force (originally established as VIII Bomber Command) was renamed in January 1942 when it was fully apparent that the United States would be doing its own mission planning and execution in England.

In creating units, only the numbered air forces had a reserved series of numbers. While the original plan was to have nice sequences of numbers, it eventually fell apart, and the numbers got mixed together. For example, the 93rd Bomb Group was comprised of four bomb squadrons: the 328th, the 329th, the 330th, and the 409th, with the 331st Bomb Squadron assigned to the 94th Bomb Group. During the course of the war and, in fact, the months during buildup, whole squadrons might be transferred from one group to another. Consequently, there really is no rhyme or reason for the numbering, other than to provide uniqueness.

The 8th Air Force became so big that it needed additional administrative levels for planning and executing the air war. Consequently, the 8th Air Force was further broken into three air divisions, with each division comprised of four combat bombardment wings. Each wing then had two, three, or four bombardment groups. The very first 8th Air Force unit in England was the 322nd Squadron, 91st Bombardment Group, 1st Combat Bombardment Wing, 1st Air Division.

★ ★ ★

Getting to war was not easy for the US Army Air Corps of 1941. There was the shortage of airplanes, the shortage of men to fly them, and the shortage of airfields. The airfield problem not only existed in the United States; it was a very serious problem all over the world. Up to this point in time, commercial aviation relied heavily on seaplane service, which did not need expensive runways and flight operation facilities. The United States could have had all the airpower in place but still would have nowhere to go to fight.

Once the United States entered the war, England had the problem of finding land and building enough airfields to handle the huge influx of aircraft, personnel, and matériel that would eventually be needed. Plus, they were still expanding their own forces and needed airfields for themselves.

All told, the British constructed sixty-six airfields[2] from which the United States could operate. This effort did not happen overnight. The availability of airfields in England had to match the availability of squadrons and groups coming from the United States. This was only compounded by the fact that the United States was at war all over the world, and sometimes, England had to take a backseat to operations elsewhere.

Getting to England was not just a matter of putting together numerous aircraft and flying over. There were considerable logistical nightmares that had to be overcome. Part of the problem was that no bomber or fighter aircraft in the arsenal had the capability to fly nonstop from the United States to England. Bombers could be outfitted with auxiliary fuel tanks in the bomb bay. This could give them an extended range that would allow them to fly directly from the United States to Ireland, where they could refuel and continue to England. Fighters did not have that luxury and needed to use as many stops as possible. Additionally, there was a growing need to get aircraft and personnel to other hotspots in the world, as England was not the only place the Army needed to go. To solve these logistical problems, four routes between the United States and England were utilized.

The North Atlantic Air Route originated at several Army airfields in New England. Bombers would fly to Newfoundland to refuel, then travel on to Ireland before arriving at their final destination. Fighters, on the other hand, would utilize bases in Newfoundland, Labrador, Greenland, and Iceland before finally arriving in England. The problem with this route was threefold. First, the skies were very congested with other aircraft patrolling the North Atlantic and providing air cover to vital shipping lanes. A second issue was the North Atlantic weather, which could potentially hamper aircraft movement. The third problem was that there were limited places for aircraft to park and wait, should their final destination airfield not be ready for their scheduled arrival. This was a bottleneck they needed to fix.

The Mid-Atlantic Air Route originated at Morrison Army Airfield near Palm Beach, Florida. From there, aircraft would fly to Kindley Field in Bermuda, then to one of two fields in the Azores before being shuttled to England. Occasionally, this route was used to supply aircraft to French Morocco in North Africa. This route was only used by multiengine aircraft fitted with auxiliary fuel tanks. This seemed like a good solution except for the limited facilities at the Azores. Again, should a final destination airfield not be ready on time, the facilities at the Azores would become a bottleneck. Additionally, this solution did very little in getting aircraft and personnel to other hotspots.

The Crimson Air Route was a route that allowed multiengine aircraft to be flown directly from manufacturers in southern California and the Midwest to Greenland, then Iceland, and finally England. This route utilized airfields in Montana, Québec, and Ontario, and flew a subarctic route over northern Canada. The route was abandoned when the South Atlantic Air Route was developed.

The South Atlantic Air Route was the last piece of the logistical puzzle put in place, and it solved the universal problem of getting aircraft to destinations all over the world. Pan American Airways (also called Pan Am) had been traveling in and out of many South American countries since the mid-1930s and had a great relationship with the various governments. By the time the war started, Pan Am was providing service throughout the Caribbean, Mexico, and up and down the coast of South America. Pan Am executives helped negotiate with various governments to permit the use of airfields and to build new ones that would later be turned over to the host country. In many cases the United States was able to utilize Pan Am's existing airfields and routes.[3]

The South Atlantic Air Route originated at one of three airfields in Florida: Morrison Army Airfield, Miami Army Airfield, and Homestead Army Airfield. From Florida, aircraft would be flown to San Juan, Puerto Rico, then to one of three other fields in Trinidad and British Guiana. Other locations in Bermuda, the Bahamas, Jamaica, Antigua, and St. Lucia were also used from time to time. From there they would proceed to Belém, in northern Brazil, before heading to Natal, on the east coast of Brazil. Natal was the primary jumping-off point for the transatlantic flight.

In July 1942, an airfield opened on Ascension Island, a prewar British cable station. The addition of this facility allowed multiengine aircraft to make the transatlantic crossing from Belém without the addition of auxiliary fuel tanks. Fighters could also make the crossing by using additional wing tanks.

Crossing the Atlantic was a trial-by-fire for every crew member. Practically no crew member had ever flown that far over water. They had made training flights over water, but no pilot had ever trusted his navigation skills to the point of leaving one continent for another. After leaving Brazil, bomber crews would fly to some spot on the western coast of Africa. In 1943, two engine aircraft usually went to Roberts Airfield near Monrovia, Liberia, while the B-17s and B-24s flew on to Dakar, Senegal.

From Dakar, there were a number of places a crew could go. Here, the South Atlantic Air Route linked up with several other air routes that provided aircraft for the 9th Air Force, operating in the Middle East; the 10th Air Force, operating in India and Burma; the 12th Air Force, operating in North Africa and the Mediterranean area; the 15th Air Force, also operating in the Mediterranean area; and the 8th Air Force, operating in England. It was even possible to get bombers into the south Pacific from there, but that route was not used very often.

At each location along the South Atlantic Air Route, crews and aircraft could be held for extended durations while they waited for their final destination to be fully operational. During these periods, orders could change several times before a true and real final destination was known. Even though Ralph reported to his folks that he was supposed to get rid of his summer uniforms, that was no guarantee he was going to a colder climate. Even though the lead echelon of the bomb group was going to England by boat, the air crews could be diverted to another location, and the headquarters staff would have to catch up when they could get there.

★ ★ ★

Getting a large number of aircraft from one place to another could have been a monumental task. Imagine a bomb group of seventy-two airplanes all trying to get to the same place individually. Not only would it have been a problem in the air, but trying to get all the planes lined up to land would have been a major issue. The Air Corps addressed the problem upfront by establishing lead crews.

Lead crews were made up of very highly qualified pilots, copilots, navigators, and bombardiers. The men who made up these crews usually had more training than others. They almost always exhibited a higher degree of organization, leadership, and discipline. And they were the men chosen to lead their bomb groups into war.

Initially every squadron had three lead crews that rotated the responsibility from mission to mission. For each mission, one squadron would be selected as the lead for the entire group. As time went on, some groups put all of the lead crews into the same squadron. This was not only good for morale, but it solved individual lead crew shortages within some squadrons.

In order to form up the massive bombing raids, each bomb group had a designated assembly area somewhere over England or the English Channel. After taking off from their airfield, planes would follow their lead crew to the assembly area. After all aircraft were airborne and had reached the proper altitude, they would move to their specified spot in the formation and continue on with the mission.

Once they had fought their way past the Luftwaffe fighters, they would enter the antiaircraft flack as they drew closer to their target. Even though a specific target had been designated, pinpoint accuracy was not the order of the day. One thousand planes bombing a single target would mean that they all had to line up one after another. That was not the case, as they tended to take up a vast amount of airspace. As a result, sometimes groups of bombers would splinter off from the main formation to bomb secondary targets, rejoining the main formation for the fight back to England. Should there be cloud cover or smoke over the target, the lead crews maintained a list of alternate targets.

Ralph and his crew were selected as one of the lead crews for the 445th Bomb Group. Ralph and one other pilot, Leo Cook, were selected as the "senior" lead crew pilots because of the amount of time they had in the air. As Ralph departed for the war, he had over 1,000 hours flying time. Other pilots following him had about 250 hours.

Just before leaving, Ralph got most of his crew together for a picture in front of a B-24. They are (standing) Archie Sloman (engineer), Ralph, Charles Painter (bombardier), John Decker (copilot), Whitfield Brooke (navigator), Albert Urbanik (radio operator), (kneeling) J. S. Robison (tail gunner), Joseph Flynn (ball turret gunner), and Sebastian Capobianco (engineer). Not pictured is Wilbur Pursel (armorer-gunner).

★ ★ ★

With their departure from the United States came the question of how to write home. Somewhere along the way everyone was given a crash course in the hows and wherefores of sending mail home. The two key elements to this were V-mail and censorship.

V-mail, short for Victory mail, was patterned after the British Airgraph mail system. Basically, soldiers would write a single-page letter on a V-mail form that measured about seven by nine inches. The letter would be addressed normally before it was folded along prescribed lines and sealed. Once mailed, it would go to a V-mail processing station, where it would be opened and photographed on microfilm, reducing it to the size of a thumbnail. An entire roll of microfilm would be flown to another processing station in the United States, where the microfilm would be enlarged to about 60 percent of the original size. The resulting letter would be folded, placed in a special envelope, and delivered through the regular US Postal Service.

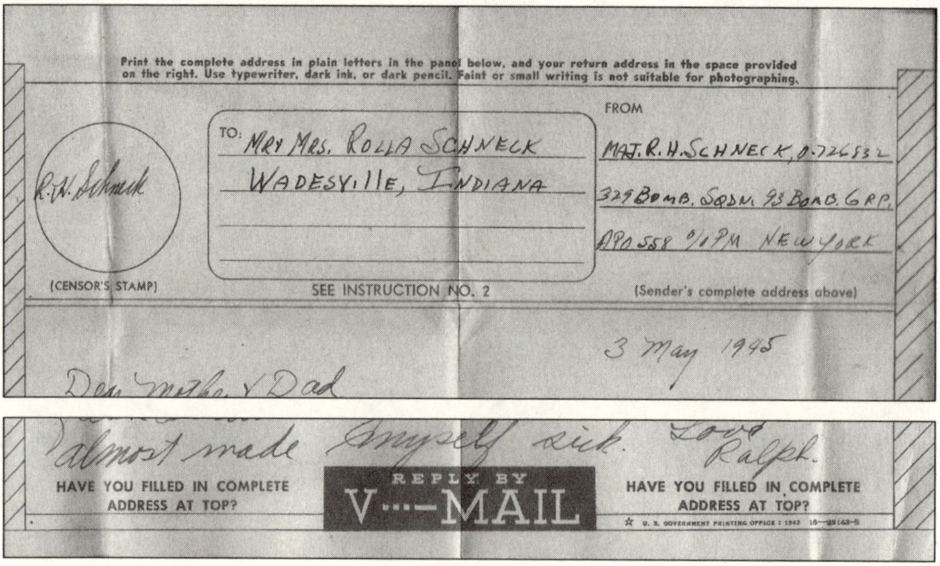
Print the complete address in plain letters in the panel below, and your return address in the space provided on the right. Use typewriter, dark ink, or dark pencil. Faint or small writing is not suitable for photographing.

R. H. Schneck
(CENSOR'S STAMP)

TO: Mr & Mrs. Rolla Schneck
Wadesville, Indiana

SEE INSTRUCTION NO. 2

FROM
Maj. R. H. Schneck, 0-726532
329 Bomb. Sqdn. 93 Bomb. Grp.
APO 558 c/o PM New York
(Sender's complete address above)

3 May 1945

Dear Mother & Dad

almost made myself sick. Love Ralph.

HAVE YOU FILLED IN COMPLETE ADDRESS AT TOP?

REPLY BY V---MAIL

HAVE YOU FILLED IN COMPLETE ADDRESS AT TOP?

U. S. GOVERNMENT PRINTING OFFICE 1943

There were two parts to V-mail. The first was filling out this form and mailing it at specially marked postal boxes. Shown here is the top and bottom of the form, which measured about seven inches wide by nine inches tall.

V-mail was not just for mailing from the war zone to home. Ordinary citizens could go to their local post office and obtain a V-mail form. There was no postage for them to mail V-mail, but the price was in the delay in getting the mail delivered at the other end.

This system freed up tons of cargo space. A single mail sack of microfilm weighed about forty-five pounds and contained about 150,000 one-page letters, which would have weighed over 2,500 pounds. In spite of the savings, air crews still had the option of buying US postage stamps and dropping a letter in specially marked mailboxes on their airfield.

Censorship was another issue. Every piece of mail that was sent by a soldier was read by a censor. Any references that the censor did not think should be there would be struck with a heavy black marker, which was particularly effective on V-mail. This included references to the soldier's location, most names of other soldiers, mission information of any kind, and almost anything else that related to fighting the war. It did not leave much to write home about, and sometimes it was a struggle to find something to say.

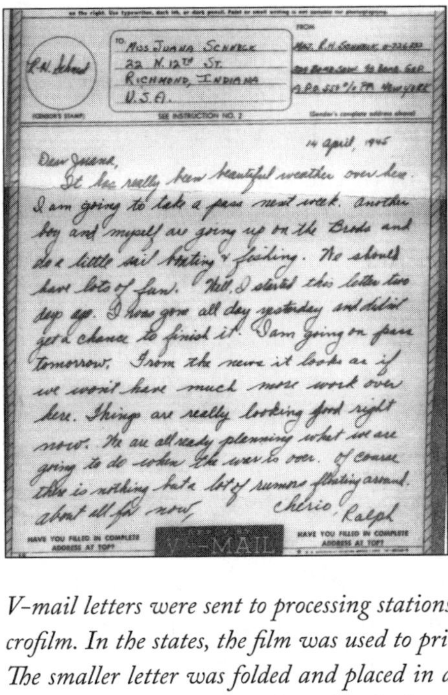
TO: Miss Juana Schneck
32 N. 12th St.
Richmond, Indiana
U.S.A.

14 April, 1945

Dear Juana,

It has really been beautiful weather over here. I am going to take a pass next week. Another boy and myself are going up on the Broads and do a little sail boating & fishing. We should have lots of fun. Well, I started this letter two days ago. I was gone all day yesterday and didn't get a chance to finish it. I am going on pass tomorrow. From the news it looks as if we won't have much more work over here. Things are really looking good right now. We are all ready planning what we are going to do when the war is over. Of course there is nothing but a lot of rumors floating around. About all for now,

Cheerio, Ralph

HAVE YOU FILLED IN COMPLETE ADDRESS AT TOP?

V-MAIL

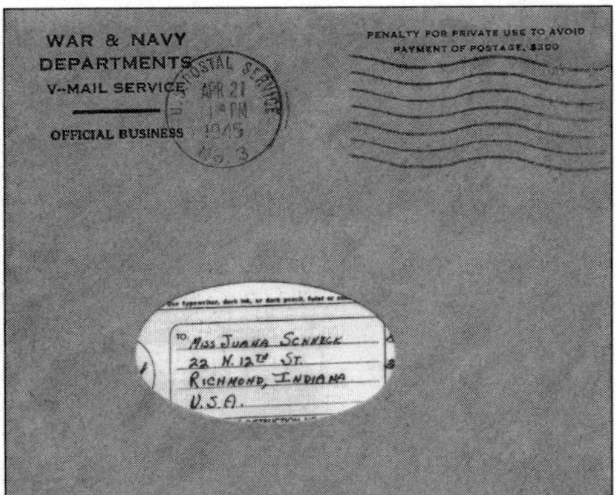

V-mail letters were sent to processing stations where they were opened and photographed on microfilm. In the states, the film was used to print a copy of the original letter, as shown on the left. The smaller letter was folded and placed in a very small envelope for delivery, as shown on the right. The letter measured about four by five inches, and the envelope measured about three and a half by five and a half inches.

The Air Corps had their own unofficial mail system, in that there was always someone who knew someone who was ferrying something or someone back to the Unites States. Often, this contact would be willing to take a pocketful of letters and drop them in the nearest mailbox when he arrived home. There was always debate on which method took the shortest amount of time, and everyone kept track.

★ ★ ★

The trip across the Atlantic and on to England started in Lincoln, Nebraska, where Ralph and a few other pilots waited for orders to form up and begin the arduous trek. When those orders arrived, they were instructed to proceed to Morrison Army Airfield.

At Morrison Army Airfield, Ralph's plane and crew became part of the complete bomb group as other aircraft flew in from airfields in the Midwest. After a brief layover, the crews were organized into flights[4] for the trip across the Atlantic. From there, they went to San Juan, Puerto Rico, then to British Guiana, and on to Belém in northern Brazil.

About an hour out of San Juan, Ralph noticed that his airspeed was continuously dropping. The tachometer and propeller pitch had not changed; nonetheless, the plane was going slower and slower. While all the possibilities ran through his mind, a call came from the aircraft directly behind and below. The pilot reported that Ralph's left landing gear appeared to be dropping. Ralph lowered the landing gear, and then raised them again. The following plane reported that the gear was up.

About a half hour later, another call came from the same plane, reporting that the gear had again fallen. For the remainder of the flight, Ralph had to continuously lower and raise the gear, while the flight engineer monitored the hydraulic fluid levels, looking for a leak.

They nursed the plane along until they could get to the next repair facility. In Belém, they found a representative from the Consolidate Aircraft Corporation. Ralph told him that he would not fly or attempt to fly the aircraft to Africa because he would run out of fuel before reaching land. The technician agreed and took charge of repairing the aircraft.

The next morning, the technician made repairs to the hydraulic system. That afternoon, Ralph and a basic crew took the plane up for a check ride. The problem persisted.

The following morning, the technician made additional repairs to the hydraulic system, and again, Ralph took the plane up for a check, but a solution had not yet been reached.

After landing, Ralph, the technician, and one of Ralph's two flight engineers began going over schematic drawings of the entire hydraulic system, looking for a possible cause. After a few minutes, another soldier joined them. Peering over the technician's shoulder, he asked, "What's going on?"

The soldier was an older sergeant, wearing a faded drab uniform with leggings and a well-worn campaign hat. The technician turned and told him what the problem was. The sergeant asked if they would mind if he took a look. They did not, and the he walked over to the plane while they continued to study the drawings. After a few minutes, the sergeant said he had found the problem. The rest of the group joined him under the left wing as he pointed to the wheel well. He said that the landing gear retaining latch was malfunctioning, and it needed to be replaced.

The retaining latch was a mechanical hook that held the landing gear in place so the hydraulic system did not need to maintain any pressure during flight. It was an electric latch that was triggered to open when the gear was lowered and to close after the gear was raised.

The sergeant pointed out that the latch was barely catching the landing gear, as was evidenced by the lack of scratches on the retainer.

That evening, the latch was replaced and tested on the ground. Early the following morning, Ralph took the plane up for a check, and the problem was solved. After landing, the technician told Ralph how lucky he was to have such a knowledgeable person on his flight crew. Ralph responded that he had never seen that sergeant before. The technician immediately left, saying that he needed to find him and see if he could stay behind.

★ ★ ★

The United States was at war throughout the world, and every element of the fighting machine had to be as fluid and flexible as possible. Lead crews, bomb groups, squadrons, and all the men had been fully prepared. There was nothing more for them to do except to continue their journey on the South Atlantic Air Route, which provided the boys with some experiences they never would have dreamed of—and that included a young, naïve, wide-eyed boy from southern Indiana.

★ ★ ★

November 26, 1943[5]

Dear Mother & Dad.

You will have to excuse this paper & writing. But it is all I can find at the present. I am now in British Guenia,[6] S. Amer. We spent one nite in Puerto Rico.

Our navigator is sick in the hospital but is getting along OK now. We have had a very beautiful trip so far. Have seen a lot of beautiful country, water and very educational places.

The natives down here are negros[7] with English accents.

Since the British system is in affect our dollar is worth 18¢ more. Most everything is cheaper. Cigarettes are tax free and cost 26¢ a carton or 2½¢ per pack. Liquor is $2.00 a qt. and mixed drinks are 15¢ each. You can get just about anything you want down here. People drive on the left side of the road in true English fashion and there are very few white people except the U.S. Army.

This is the rainy season down here. There are always clouds in the sky and it rains 2 & 3 times every day.

Write and let me know if you got my watch.[8]

Not much else I can tell you at the present. Please pass this around to everyone so I won't have to write it over anymore. You can write me at this APO number below and then my mail will be waiting when I get to my destination.

Use this address:
Lt. R. H. Schneck 0-726832
445 Bomb. GRP. 702 SQDN.
APO 4952
New York, New York

Love
Ralph.

★ ★ ★

November 28, 1943

President Franklin Delano Roosevelt meets with British Prime Minister Winston Churchill and Soviet Premier Joseph Stalin in Tehran, Iran. During the four-day conference, they discuss strategy for Europe and the Far East as well as the war fronts all across the world.

★ ★ ★

November 29, 1943[9]

Dear Mother Dad, & Everybody.

I have really been having a swell time the past few days. We were held up in British Guiana so I had a chance to see a little of the country.

One day we went into a native village close by. As I said once before in my letter these natives are negros with English accent. When I say English I mean they talk like the people in England. They live in small huts some of which are grass and some of boards. The English Landlord comes around every month and collects $3.00 from the house owner. In this one small village there is some 200 houses and they take up no more space than a 10 acre field. In the village I would say live about 2000 people. In the small houses, which are no larger than the largest room in our house, they sleep 10 to 20 people. In the larger house they have more. The owners of the houses charge the people who just sleep there a shilling per week. A Shilling is equal to 24¢ American money.

Most of the people work at the Air Base and the highest paid one gets 25¢ per hour but the average gets around 15¢ per hour. When the U.S. Army Engineers started building the Air Base they were going to pay them on the U.S. wage scale but the British objected so they had to cut it out. Even now though it is hard for the White British Folks to get servents, they say, because the negros would rather work for the Americans. We treat them better they say. There are a few white people who live up at the mouth of the river in a nice sized town, the name I cannot mention. Getting back to this native village. They kill meat once a week and it is just hung up in the store until sold. Most of the younger children wear clothes but some don't and they aren't particular about sanitation and there are very few toilets to be seen.

We stopped to talk to several of the natives and one shoe maker in particular was very interesting to talk to. He tried to trade us out of our wrist watches. Said he liked them very much. After every thing else failed he tried to swap us his wife for a watch. So here I am with out a watch and nothing to show for it but a big, black, fat gal who I have to keep in a cage. But she stinks too much and I think I'll try and sell her. Ha! Ha!

The large store in this village is run by a chinese, Ming Ha Chow, and he has quite a stock of canned goods. Rum is very cheap down here and sells for $1.00 to $1.25 per qt. at the chinese store. He also has four daughters who are 16 to 20 yrs of age and you can spend the evening with them in the parlor over the store if you buy 2 qts of rum and so desire. The natives say the chinaman is a rich man. We hired 3 native boys and their boat to row us up the river to an Indian village. These are East Indians. They are different then the negros. They are smaller and the women have fine features with long black hair. Some of them have hair down to their ankles. They care less about sanitation than the negros and very few of the children are clothed until they are 10 yrs old. To all American soldiers they say "Hi Joe" and aren't a bit bashful in talking except these are about the only American words they know. However, they are very expressive and after talking to them a while you can understand quite a bit of what they say. When the East Indians get married they hang up a red and a white flag and these flags stay up as long as they are married. After visiting the Indian village the boys then paddled us up a small stream into the jungle about 6 miles. Here we saw jungle like Frank Buck[10] talks about. Parrotts by the thousands, all colors, monkeys everywhere. We saw snakes 30 ft long and as big around as a 3 gal bucket. We had several native fruit including bananas and persimmons which grow as large as grapefruit. We saw wood that would burn even though it was soaked with water.

These negro boys told us that their books said the U.S. had never been in but one war and that was the one among ourselves. And that the British gave us the land in the U.S. because it was worthless. They seemed to know all of our movie stars and dance bands. They go to the town up the river and see 2 or 3 pictures a day they said.

The Air Base brought several girls from the large town and an orchestra so there was a dance the other nite. Having nothing to do naturally I went. I picket on one of the whitest girls[11] I could find and asked her to dance. She was very light complected, had brown hair and was very clean and neat in appearance. She told me she was full blooded Portugese. I don't believe I have ever spent a more interesting evening in my life. She told me lots of things about the people. The coal black negros are British. The Lighter ones with black hair are mixed. There were quite a few at the dance. The still lighter colored with lighter hair are portugese. Then there are a strain of

Indian girls in the town but they are refined people and very well educated. They also have beautiful long hair like the East Indian natives but they are of an altogeather different strain. Then there are some Dutch girls there with blonde hair. They are very light complexion and speak with a slight Dutch accent. There are also some Chinese girls in town and they are very pretty girls. They are from a different race than the ones who run the stores in the native villages and are rather tall and slender. The British people in town do not like the American soldiers and charge them high prices for anything they buy. At the same time the other people do not like the British either and this girl did not speak of them as British only in the phrase "British Subjects" all other times as Limeys and frequently Damned Limeys. She said most people in town were in hopes that the Americans would take over B. Guiana when the war was over but said she knew they wouldn't. She also said the people in town hardly knew what Divorce was until the Americans came. All the girls that could got jobs at the Air Base and they lived in a Barracks next to the Nurse quarters as it is quite a distance to town with the only means of transportation being a boat. It was just like Christmas to these girls to get to come to this dance. They had been planning on it for weeks she said.

She also said it was the ambition of most of the girls to marry an American so they could go to the U.S. She said a few had been lucky but not many. She had been to the U.S. herself. New York, Chicago and Los Angeles. Most of the natives are diseased but the Limeys won't do anything about it except the ones who work in the tobacco factorys and that is because the tobacco is shipped to England. Henry Ford tried to build a railroad from the town down to his rubber plantation in Brazil but the British wouldn't let him because "the people weren't ready for those modern conveniences."

She said you could take a tube of lipstick and a compact and walk down the street and probably the richest girl in town would be following you around. Tubes of lipstick like you buy in the dime stores at home coast about $3.00 down here and they have very little powder. It is all British product and they cost too much.

After talking to these girls[12] and to various other people my opinion of the British isn't very high. I tell you this now because I may not be able to express my opinion of them later on.

I am in the best health and hope that you all are enjoying the same. I hope that this letter has been interesting and wish that you will pass it around so that every one will get a chance to read it. Please don't any of you feel hurt if you don't get a letter personally, but it is such an ordeal to write one and I have to be careful what I say, I'm afraid one would just be a repetition of the other. But I write the letters to all of you and I hope that they are enjoyed by all.

Love,
Ralph.

★ ★ ★

December 3, 1943[13]

Dear Juana,

Just a line to let you know I am OK. I am in Brazil[14] S.A. now. We aren't doing anything much. Just waiting around. The weather down here is fine. About like you will find in Fla. this time of year. There is a nice beach and we can go swimming here. The water is very nice.

I have written Mother & Dad a couple of letters before. I have tried to make them as interesting as possible. So have them mail them to you as you might like to read them.

Most of the people down here speak Portuguese. I can understand them sometimes if they talk slow. And have learned enough words so that I don't starve. I don't want you to feel slighted if I don't write you every time. But I am rather limited in my letters and I would just be writing the same to everyone.

I hope this finds you in good health and everything.

Ralph

Please note my change in APO from 4952 to 4949

★ ★ ★

December 7, 1943

Two years to the day after the Japanese attack on Pearl Harbor, President Franklin Delano Roosevelt informs General Dwight D. Eisenhower that he will become the Supreme Commander Allied Expeditionary Force and command *Operation Overlord*.

★ ★ ★

The war started for England on September 3, 1939. At that time, the Royal Air Force (RAF) looked nothing like their American counterpart, the US Army Air Corps. After the conclusion of World War I, the RAF continued to grow their airpower and technology. In 1939, the RAF already had about forty facilities, airfields, training bases, radar installations, and headquarters facilities scattered around England, Northern Ireland, Scotland, and Wales. In the two years that followed, the RAF would only add about a dozen more facilities for their use. While they may have seemed to be fully prepared, what they had in place was nothing compared to what they would need for the Americans following December 7, 1941.

After the United States declared war against Germany, negotiations on placing American aircraft in England began. The main fighting element of the war at that time and for the foreseeable future (until an invasion could be mounted) were the bomber forces of what was then called VIII Bomber Command and RAF Bomber Command. Early on, there were a number of plans developed for deploying American bombers, and all were rejected for one reason or another. The first realistic plan was submitted on March 24, 1942. That plan called for a specific number of light, medium, and heavy bombardment groups, fighter groups, and other support operations. That plan became the blueprint for the presence of American airpower. Although the actual mix of aircraft type changed, the total number of groups remained roughly the same. The plan called for a total of seventy-two bombardment groups and twenty-six fighter groups.

In May 1942, East Anglia was chosen as the area for American aircraft to be located. In short, most of the American airfields would be located between London and Norwich,[15] with the heavier concentration north toward Norwich. A list of existing facilities was prepared that showed which RAF airfields would be transferred to what was VIII Bomber Command, now called the 8th Air Force. By July, new airfield procurement plans were drawn up, and the construction process began.

The very first airfields to be occupied by the 8th Air Force were existing airfields located around London. These fields were originally designed for the British-made aircraft, but they proved suitable for the B-17 Flying Fortresses. As the B-24 Liberators started rolling off the assembly lines, new bases were needed, and these would be located closer to Norwich.

The location of B-17s eventually became a point of contention. News correspondents usually set up their offices in London, and when they wanted to visit American aircrews, they were taken to the closest airfields, which all had B-17s. It was not until late in the war that correspondents began venturing outside of London and covering the B-24 aircrews. Hence, the perception that the B-17 Flying Fortress was more prevalent and more important than the B-24 Liberator, when in fact, there were more B-24s manufactured than B-17s.[16]

The area around Norwich was ideally suited for modern airfields. There were few tall obstacles, lots of flat land that drained well, and relatively good weather. Construction crews again began clearing the way for the massive runways and campuses that would be needed. Before they were finished, the 8th Air Force would occupy a total of seventy-seven stations, including about sixty-six airfields, for eighty-two operational units.[17]

★ ★ ★

The airfields were carved out of the rich English farmland. It was not uncommon for large Tudor homes and estates to become part of an airfield complex. In some cases, the buildings and grounds were fenced off, and the residents stayed in their homes. In other cases, the owners turned their homes over to the RAF to be used as they saw fit.

A typical airfield was comprised of three runways forming a triangle. Because there were so many airfields in such close proximity, it was a necessity that each base's runways used slightly different runway headings. Otherwise, an aircraft taking off could fly directly into other aircraft trying to take off on the same heading from a different airfield.

New for the US Army Air Corps was the wide use of hardstands. The British had a lot of experience defending their aircraft on the ground. Parking aircraft wingtip-to-wingtip was good for maintenance and armament crews because all of the planes were in one place. That concept was also good for the foot soldiers who guarded the aircraft because they could cover every angle with very few guards. However, the British learned early on that wingtip-to-wingtip parking also made it extremely easy for a solitary enemy fighter to make a pass, following the line of parked aircraft, and dish out severe damage in a single strafing run—a lesson the United States learned at Pearl Harbor.

The solution was to park aircraft all over the airfield using hardstands. An enemy fighter would have to single out one target at a time and make repeated passes, thus decreasing the odds of catastrophic damage. Additionally, if an aircraft caught fire and exploded, there was very little chance that adjacent aircraft would also be damaged. Hardstands had another advantage in that they provided an all-weather concrete surface from which maintenance and ordnance crews could work. Plus, concrete was seemingly impervious to gasoline and oil spills, unlike the tarmac used for taxiways and other parking areas.

Hardstands were placed along the perimeter taxiway that surrounded the three runways. There was one hardstand for each aircraft. They were about 150 feet in diameter, big enough for an aircraft to turn around under its own power. Some hardstands sat all alone, with a single ramp connecting it to the taxiway. These were called "frying pans" or "pans" because they resembled a frying pan from the air. Other hardstands were situated in a diamond formation, accommodating two or three aircraft. These were called "loops" because all of the hardstands were connected. In the late stages of the war, the risk of air attacks diminished, and loops became the norm because they could accommodate more aircraft by joining several loops in a row.

Each hardstand had a tent located nearby for tool and parts storage. Maintenance crews sometimes erected huts using scrap wood from bomb crates or pallets. Sometimes, especially in good weather, maintenance crews would even sleep or nap in the tent or hut. This was a lot more convenient

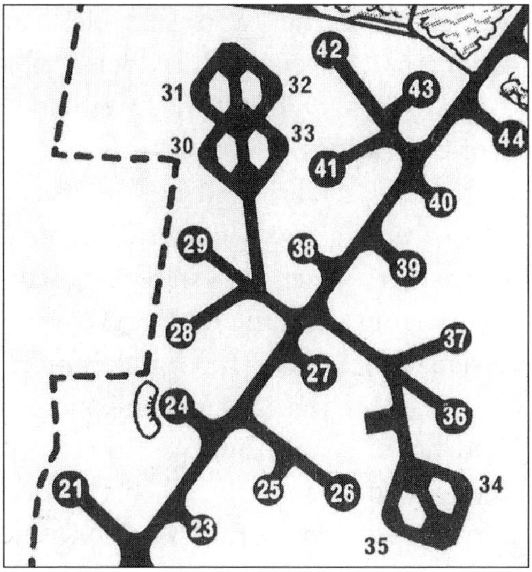

Shown here are the two types of hardstands, loops and pans, as they appear on an airfield drawing. Notice how two loops are joined together. Seeing this configuration, it is not difficult to image the traffic congestion when a large mission was trying to get off the ground.

than going back to their barracks, which could be two or three miles away, especially if they were waiting on parts or bombs to be delivered.

Every airfield had offices, maintenance facilities, hangars, fuel, bomb and ammunition storage, living quarters for about 3,000 men, a single mess hall that served officers and enlisted men, a medical unit, separate "clubs" for officers and enlisted men, recreational facilities, and a post office for mailing letters back to the United States.

The RAF also had a presence at each location. As owners, it was their responsibility to maintain the airfields when necessary and to provide coordinated security with the US Army Military Police. The US Army was responsible for mowing the grounds and maintaining the rest of the facilities. If an aircraft ran off the runway or taxiway and damaged the turf, the RAF supposedly did the repair and sent a bill to the bomb group; however, it did not always happen that way.

The mainstay of all new construction was the Nissen hut and other prefabricated buildings, all of which were simply referred to as huts. The Nissen hut was invented by Major Peter Norman Nissen of the Corps of Royal Engineers during World War I. It was manufactured by bending corrugated steel sheets in an arc such that when three sheets were bolted together, they formed half of a circle, with a radius of about eight feet. By adding additional half circles, the structure could be as long as needed. The American version of the Nissen hut was the Quonset hut. They were very close in design, except that the Quonset hut had a ten-foot ceiling. This allowed for taller objects to be placed next to the outer walls. Quonset huts were used most extensively in the Pacific Theater of Operations.

There were six different manufacturers of prefabricated huts in England, producing thirteen different types in four sizes. The most common huts were 576 square feet and 1,110 square feet. Nissen huts were originally designed to have an earthen or wooden floor, but all of the huts at the newly constructed airfields had a concrete slab, which made them much more comfortable than the World War I predecessor. Even though the concrete floor was an improvement, the huts had little or no insulation, were very drafty, and sometimes were not completely weather tight.

Large huts were usually divided into two sections with a common wall in the middle. Each room in a hut was heated by a single coke stove situated on a raised concrete base in the middle of the room. Fitting windows and doors in the middle of a Nissen hut was not impossible, but doing so was difficult and not always weather tight. Consequently, the ends generally served as the entrances and the place where a window could be fitted.

The interior of the huts varied widely depending on its intended use. Office buildings usually had a common work area at the entrance with small, private offices in the back. A high-ranking officer might have one office in the back with his own private entrance. In some cases, in larger buildings there might even be a door so someone could go from one end to the other without walking outside.

An enlisted man might share a hut with as many as twenty to twenty-five other men. As many as eight low-grade officers might also share a single hut, with a common area and four very small bedrooms. As an officer increased in rank, the accommodations increased in comfort. A major, for example, could expect to have a private bedroom.

Electrical service to all of the buildings was limited. Most of the buildings or individual rooms were lighted with bare bulbs hanging from the ceiling, with a pull chain. If the occupants were lucky, there might be one electrical outlet in the common area that everyone had to share.

In most cases, the huts had cold running water and toilet facilities. There was usually one hut that had bathing facilities and another that had toilets and wash basins. Hot water was usually only available in the bathhouse for a few hours a day. Everyone was issued a canteen, which they kept in their living area. They used that water for a spit bath, shaving, and doing a very small amount of laundry by using their metal helmet to heat water over the stove.

★ ★ ★

The largest part of a bomber complex was the airfield, which was fenced in with the bomb storage, two hangars, and the technical site. The technical site included facilities for the repair, maintenance, and storage of aircraft and crew equipment. The buildings used for briefings, crew rooms, and group administration were generally also within the technical site. Other facilities included bulk storage of all fuels, lubricants, and other flammable liquids, parking for all of the airfield trucks and other vehicles, a fire department, storage for wood, coal, and coke, bombsight storage and repair, training facilities, and the flight offices.

Outside of the airfield fence, everything was organized into individual sites. About a quarter mile from the technical site was the headquarters site, which provided facilities for group operations and the headquarters function. These buildings were generally windowless and highly guarded. The group operations building was usually brick with an airlock to guard against chemical or gas attack.

Nearby, was the communal site, which provided for the morale and well-being of the men stationed at the airfield. This site had the mess halls, food storage, ration storage (for distributing individual packaged rations), a PX, barber shop, tailor, shoemaker, library, gymnasium, and the two clubs for officers and enlisted men. The mess halls could seat about two hundred men each and shared a central kitchen. At some airfields, there may have been more than one communal site, depending on the availability of land.

Medical facilities were located at the sick quarters site. There was usually a large Nissen hut that could accommodate about twenty beds, another hut for isolation and quarantine, huts for medical staff offices, living quarters, and an ambulance garage. The sick quarters site was usually centrally located within a quarter mile of all other sites.

Bomb and fuel storage were almost always on the opposite side of the airfield, away from the rest of the sites. The bomb storage site provided partial subterranean brick and concrete structures. For the most part, the only thing that could be seen was the rooftop. Fuel storage was also buried and provided about 14,400 gallons[18] of aviation gas.

Living sites provided housing for all of the aircrews and ground crews. Each site consisted of between ten and twenty-five Nissen huts. Each hut slept between four and forty-two men, with each site housing between two hundred fifty and three hundred. All electricity, water, and sewer were obtained from the local communities. One site was usually designated to locate all of the bathing facilities. Depending on the availability of water and sewer, each site could have a latrine, or the latrine would be situated near the bathing facilities.

Security was straightforward. The runways and taxiways were fenced off and guarded around the clock. Normally, there were two or three gates for automobile, truck, bus, pedestrian, and bicycle traffic. Each of the other sites were also fenced and guarded. Everyone knew everyone else, and a stranger, such as a Nazi spy, would probably have been singled out fairly quickly.

Since air raids were commonplace at the beginning, every site provided air raid shelters, which sometimes were nothing more than ditches or trenches, some of which were always full of water and affectionately were known as ponds or lakes. All of the sites were connected to a central speaker system for broadcasting special announcements and other news.

★ ★ ★

Every bomb group and fighter group had a budget. Some things like food staples, bombs, fuel, and ammunition were provided for the asking. Other things had to be purchased by the group's quartermaster on the open market. These included fresh vegetables, canned goods, coal, and other rationed items.

Bomber and fighter crews did not fly missions every day, at least not at first. Weather, holidays, and flight rotations meant that a pilot and his crew would spend a lot of their time sitting around, if there was not something else to do. To help deal with this situation, each group had an officer in charge of keeping everyone busy and, thus, keeping morale high. These individuals had a lot of input in the furnishings and offerings of the officers' and enlisted men's clubs as well as planning special events. A good morale officer was constantly looking for a reason to throw a party, have a parade, or just to blow off steam. Some groups were very good at this and devoted part of their budget to make sure there was plenty to occupy the flight crews. Other groups spent all of their money on food and on the two clubs. As a result, their group's morale tended to suffer, a fact that did not go unnoticed by the upper echelons.

The morale officer was also in charge of arranging special activities to occupy everyone. These usually came in the form of educational classes, discussion groups, and contests. At some airfields, attendance at these activities was mandatory, but most of the crews needed little coaxing.

★ ★ ★

The build-up of the 8th Air Force was very slow. The US Department of War had designated the 8th Air Force as the operational command on April 7, 1942, but the first headquarters personnel did not arrive until May 11 and it took until the end of June for the headquarters operations to finally be at full strength. The first B-17 arrived on July 1.

The 8th Air Force consisted of the VIII Air Service Command, the VIII Ground Air Support Command, the VIII Fighter Command, and the VIII Bomber Command.

The VIII Bomber Command was further divided into five air divisions. Each air division had five combat wings. Each wing was comprised of three bombardment groups. Each bombardment group incorporated three or four squadrons of ten to twelve aircraft.

Bombing operations and mission planning generally originated from the very top at VIII Bomber Command, dictating what was needed from the next level in the chain of command, the air division. They, in turn, would then dictate what they needed from the various combat wings, and so on, until a mission was put together.

★ ★ ★

Ralph and the others arrived from South America and parked their aircraft at Dakar Airport on the outskirts of Dakar, Senegal. They planned to stay one night while their aircraft were refueled and repairs completed. Unfortunately, bad weather in England had caused a backup, and there was no place to park any additional aircraft, so the group waited for weather to clear up in England.

After two days and no sign of good weather in England, orders came for them to move their aircraft to Menara Airport near Marrakech, French Morocco.

On the first day at Menara, Ralph was walking around the airport and saw a familiar figure: a boy he had played basketball against from Princeton, Indiana, which was about thirty miles north of Wadesville. Ralph approached him and started a conversation. It turned out that the lad had joined the Army and was now driving a bus from the airport to Marrakesh, shuttling native workers. Ralph asked if there was any way he could catch a ride into town to see the sights. His friend got clearance from his commander, and the next day, Ralph and some buddies were walking through the streets.

★ ★ ★

After three days, the order came in to ready the aircraft for departure. Ralph and his navigator received final instructions and headed the group toward England.

From Marrakesh, they flew northwest over the Atlantic, staying about two hundred miles off the coast of Europe, well out of range of any roaming Luftwaffe fighters. After clearing the northernmost point of Spain, they turned due north, entering the Celtic Sea and headed for the English coast.

England had just come into view when, out of nowhere, British fighters appeared alongside. They took a good look at all the aircraft, and then, just as suddenly as they appeared, they vanished into the clouds.

Early in the war, the United States had agreed to utilize the RAF's flight control system, which included their radio system. This system called for each airfield to operate their own radio stations, called bunchers, which were essential to getting aircraft back home. When aircraft first arrived in England, they did not have the proper radio equipment, call signs, frequencies, and homing instructions. Without this information, it was impossible to navigate through the huge number of airfields and find their way home. As a result, every airplane made one stop, an overnight layover, at one of the airfields on the extreme southwest coast of England.

Ralph took his group to RAF Lands End near the town of St. Just in Cornwall. Everyone was transported to a hotel, where they were fed and stayed the night. Their aircraft was serviced and made ready to leave in the early morning.

The next day, Ralph was introduced to an RAF pilot, who was going to fly a Bristol Blenheim, which was a much smaller aircraft, for them to follow to their final destination: RAF Tibenham, designated Station 124.

★★★

"Good old Watson. The one fixed point in a changing age. But there's an east wind coming all the same. Such a wind as never blew on England yet. It will be cold and bitter, Watson, and a good many of us may wither before its blast. But it's God's own wind none the less. And a greener, better, stronger land will be in the sunshine when the wind is cleared."[19]

★★★

NOTES

1. From "Wings Over the Americas," a 1933 Pan American Airways brochure.

2. The actual number of airfields varies from one historian to another because some airfields shifted back and forth between United States and British usage. Records show that the British prepared seventy-seven stations that included sixty-six airfields and eleven depots and support facilities.

3. In an odd twist of fate, Pan American Airways was formed in 1927 by Henry Arnold (1886–1950), John Jouett (1892–1950), and Carl "Tooey" Spaatz (1891–1974) to compete against SCADTA (Colombian-German Air Transport Society), a German carrier operating out of Colombia. SCADTA attempted to gain access to the Panama Canal and obtain contracts for mail service from the United States. Concerned that SCADTA was an intelligence operation for Germany and posed a threat to US interests, the three men founded Pan American Airways. Pan Am was able to get a mail contract to serve Cuba but

had no planes or landing rights. To solve this problem, Pan Am merged with the fledging Aviation Corporation of the Americas (ACA). The resulting company retained the Pan Am name, and the original founders took a backseat in the management of the company. By the time the war started, Henry "Hap" Arnold was commanding general of the US Army Air Forces, and Spaatz was his chief of staff and later would become commander of the 8th Air Force in England. John Jouett, a retired colonel in the Air Corps, became the president of the Aeronautical Chamber of Commerce of America. At the outbreak of war, Jouett was asked by the US Army to be their liaison with Pan American Airways.

4. The flights consisted of a small number of aircraft ranging from approximately five to ten.

5. In the lower left corner of the envelope was written, "Censored, R. H. Schneck, 1st Lt. A. C." in Ralph's handwriting. In this era, a great deal of trust was placed on Air Corps leadership. When no censorship office was available, squadron leaders and others provided the censorship duties for their men, including the censoring of their own letters, something Ralph took advantage of whenever he could. This was written the day after American Thanksgiving. Apparently, in all the excitement, Ralph lost track of time as he makes no mention of it.

6. They were located at Atkinson Field, about twenty miles from Georgetown. Atkinson Field opened in June 1941 as a weather station and later as a staging point for aircraft traveling the South Atlantic Air Route. The base took on the additional role of providing protection to the east coast of South America against Axis attacks. Atkinson Field was renamed Atkinson Air Force Base in 1948, but was closed in 1949 and turned over to the British. Today the facility has become Cheddi Jagan International Airport. British Guiana is now the independent nation of Guyana.

7. Up to this point, Ralph could count the number of black people he had seen face-to-face on one hand, and he had never had a conversation with a black person.

8. The Army issued Ralph a new watch, so he sent his personal watch home for safekeeping.

9. Written on Officers' Club—Army Air Base—Lincoln, Nebraska stationery and mailed from Belém, Brazil. The envelope indicates the letter is self-censored.

10. Frank Buck (1884–1950) was a noted big-game hunter, actor, director, and author. He occasionally provided jungle story narratives for radio.

11. Ralph had to be very careful about describing the evening. His parents and almost anyone who might have read this letter would have had a conniption if they thought he spent any time with a black woman. Unfortunate as this is, that is the way things were in 1943.

12. Here the truth comes out. Ralph spent the entire evening going from one girl to another and back again. This was his first exposure to people from different races and cultures, and he was very curious.

13. Written on United States Army Air Forces Meatball & Wings stationery. The letter was "Passed by Base Army Examiner," a polite way of saying it was censored. Ralph

probably mailed the letter while he was still in Brazil, but it did not get posted until he arrived in England. From this point forward, all of Ralph's mail was censored.

14. He was at Belém Airfield, located inland on a waterway in the northern part of the country.

15. Pronounced "nor•ich."

16. 12,731 B-17 Flying Fortresses and 18,842 B-24 Liberators were manufactured.

17. As previously mentioned, the actual number of facilities provided by the British varies from one historian to another.

18. Actual storage was about 12,000 imperial gallons.

19. From the last exchange between Dr. John Watson and Sherlock Holmes. *Sherlock Holmes and the Voice of Terror*, Universal Pictures, 1942. This is an exact quote from "His Last Bow" by Sir Arthur Conan Doyle.

Chapter 7

V-MAIL, CRACKERS, AND WASHING SOCKS

"Yea, though I walk through the valley of the shadow of death, I will fear no evil."[1]

After Ralph's group took off from Lands End, they circled until every plane was in a formation. The only communication with the guide plane was through Morse code by way of flashing lights, as German listening posts monitored every frequency used by the British and Americans. Their guide plane turned and headed in a northeasterly direction. Their course took them across England, north of London, and toward Norwich. The countryside was littered with airfields and it was impossible to avoid flying over them and through their airspace.

Barrage balloons had been deployed in all of the large cities as a means of protecting them. The balloons, floating as high as 5,000 feet, were tethered to the ground with steel cables. The idea was that low-flying aircraft would snag their wings on the cable, become disabled, and be unable to continue their attack. Alternatively, an aircraft could try to avoid the balloons but would end up flying directly into antiaircraft fire.

As they flew past London, all necks craned toward the starboard side to get a look. From the cockpit, the barrage balloons were clearly visible. From Ralph's seat, he could see smoke rising from smoldering fires, causing a pall over the entire city. It looked dark, foreboding, and ominous.

Within minutes they were beyond London, listening to some radio chatter bark coordinates and instructions, which at the time they did not comprehend. Ralph stayed close to the guide plane for fear of getting lost. Finally, they were ordered to circle a particular airfield and begin their final approach. Ralph gave all the others orders and procedures to follow, and then he pointed his plane at the end of the runway.

Once they landed, each pilot was directed to his assigned hardstand. After they parked, transport trucks and Jeeps raced out to collect the crews and take them to the Mess Hall for processing. At the Mess Hall, they got their hut assignments, a brief orientation of the complex, and were released to find their new homes.

Ralph was told to settle-in and then immediately report to squadron headquarters. He had arrived. All of the planning and training he and the others had been through now would be put to the ultimate test. They were going to war.

★ ★ ★

RAF Tibenham was located thirteen miles southwest of Norwich and about twenty-five miles from the coast and the English Channel, just south of the village of Tibenham.

The village is located near the intersection of three roads: Church Road, Hill Road, and The Street (outside of the village, this road becomes Black Barn Road). The Street, originally called Churchgate Street, is the main thoroughfare and center of commerce. In 1943, the main focal point in the village was All Saint's Church, a medieval structure dating to the thirteenth century. The bell tower rose high above the small, modest homes and shops.

There were several shops, the most popular being Tommy English's Shop and the Post Office Stores. Most anything that one needed, and that was not severely rationed, could be found between these two shops. There were also two pubs: the Boot of the Long Row and the Greyhound. The Greyhound was the most popular, although both pubs had plenty of business in 1942.

The end of the nearest runway was about 2,000 feet from the center of Tibenham. After the airfield was turned over to the 8th Air Force, it was designated as Station 124.

Aside from the three runways, the airfield included thirty-six frying-pans and fourteen loops. Bomb, ammunition, and fuel storage was on the east side of the airfield, just south of the village. There were two hangars, one south of the runways and one near the main gate, on the east.

Outside of the fenced airfield, there were seven residential sites, two communal sites, and separate sites for headquarters, sick quarters, and for the RAF offices.[2] The residential sites were located just north of Sneath Common and were the furthest points from the airfield. There were enough Nissen huts to accommodate about 2,900 men.

Within the two communal sites were the two clubs, toilet and bath facilities, the mess hall, post office, and recreational facilities. Headquarters and the sick quarters were between the communal sites and the main gate to the airfields.

Located next to Hangar 2 but outside the security fence was one of the more interesting structures in the area, Channoz Hall. Channoz Hall was originally constructed around 1478[3] as a moated fortification. Over the years it had undergone several reconstructions and transformations. It was not used by the RAF or the 8th Air Force and, in fact, very few of the men stationed at Tibenham ventured over to take a look. Out of respect to the people of England and especially those in the immediate area, Air Corps personnel typically kept to themselves and tried not to bother the local residents; they were bothered enough by the constant roar of engines.

★ ★ ★

Norwich was the closest city in the area and one of the largest cities in all of England, with a population of around 120,000. It was situated

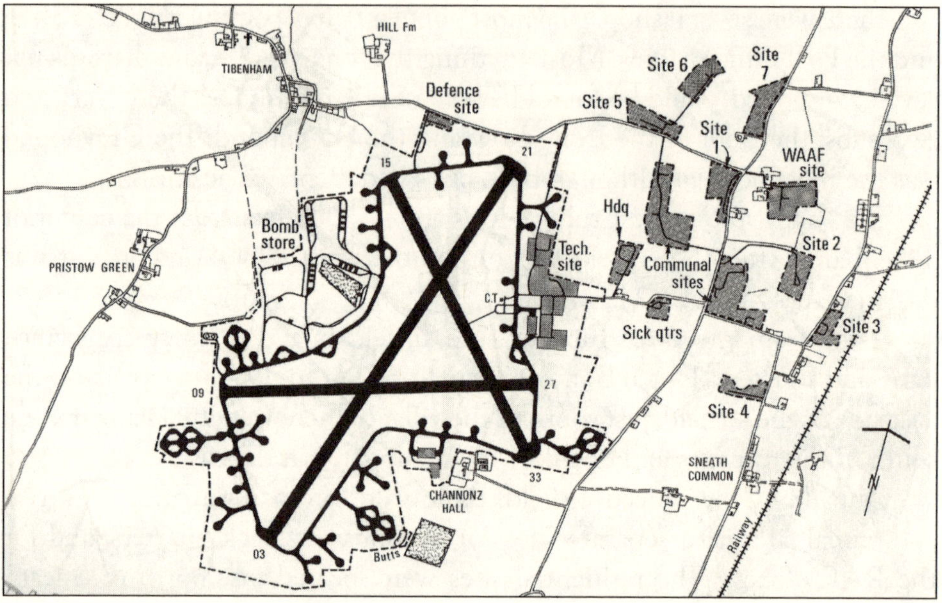

Official RAF "as built" drawing provided to the 8th Air Force of RAF Tibenham, Station 124. Of special note are the fifty-one hardstands and the location of all of the various sites. The village of Tibenham is about 2,000 feet northeast of the bomb storage site. Channonz Hall is located in the lower middle. The short runway 09/27, which runs mostly east-west, is about 4,180 feet long or about .8 miles.

in the heart of all the 8th Air Force airfields. There were over sixty airfields within twenty miles of Norwich. It may have been sheer coincidence or brilliant planning, but the location of the airfields resembled the location of the training bases the Americans had just come from—isolated, with nothing to do but fly. And a large nearby city, in this case Norwich, provided a place to go for brief rest and relaxation. As a result, the boys had little trouble settling in and adapting to their new surroundings.

Norwich offered many sightseeing opportunities with its museums, parks, churches, and cathedral. There was also the Electric Cinema and the Regent movie house on Wales Road near the train station. Norwich also had a significant number of theaters, which were very popular. There was the Haymarket Theater on Theater Street, the Carlton Theater on All Saints Green, and the Odeon Theater on Botolph Street, plus a number of smaller ones sprinkled around the city.

An Officers' Red Cross Club, run by the American Red Cross, was located on Tombland, which was close to the Erpingham Gate entrance to Cathedral Close. Among other things, they provided travel assistance to and from other parts of England (especially London), food, beverages, and a kind ear for the boys to talk to. Near the Officer's Red Cross Club on Tombland was the Samson and Hercules Dance Hall, which featured wooden pillars carved with the images of Samson and Hercules supporting the entrance portico. With the shortage of English men in the community, the dance hall was taken over by the Americans, mostly enlisted men. The local girls flocked to the dance hall every chance they got, which made it perhaps the absolute most popular place in the city.

There was limited bus service between the airfields and Norwich, and most of the airfields provided a troop transport in the evenings, leaving the airfields at 6 p.m. and returning at 9 p.m. Travel to Norwich was restricted to nonmission days. On mission days and the day before, everyone was restricted to the airfield. In some cases, before big missions, the restriction could last for a week or longer.

In addition to bus service and the troop transport, bicycles were a mainstay. Almost every officer and many enlisted men had access to a bicycle to assist them in getting around the airfield complex. On their days off, they could take their bicycle and venture throughout the countryside. If they did not have one at their disposal, they could find one in Norwich. A popular place to go was Dodger's Bicycle Shop on Chapel Street. There they could find a wide variety of machines for rent at the modest price of one shilling per hour. Indeed, anyone in Norwich who wanted a good laugh went for a walk down Chapel Street to watch American boys trying to ride a bicycle for the very first time.

The citizens of Norwich were no strangers to the Blitz, which caused so much damage in London; however, since London is where the press set up shop, almost all of the attention was given to Londoners. Between 1939 and 1943, Norwich was bombed 44 times, killing 340 citizens and injuring another 1,092. The low death toll is a testament to Britain's air raid preparations. In the first four years of the war, 30,354 homes were damaged or destroyed in Norwich. At the start of the war, Norwich had a total of 35,569 homes.

★ ★ ★

★ V-Mail ★
December 18, 1943

Dear Mother & Dad,

Well it is getting close to Christmas but it hardly seems like it.

I am now somewhere in England. You probably already know this if you read in the paper where Jim Stewart is.

The people talk rather funny here at first but I don't mind it at all now. The money situation also gave me a little trouble but what with all the Florin, shillings pounds and pence[4] but it isn't bad at all. So far we have had very good food and the people over here are very friendly.

I haven't received any of your mail at all. I haven't had a letter in over a month. From now on if you will send my mail V-Mail I will get it a lot quicker.

Merry Xmas to you all.

Love,
Ralph

★ ★ ★

★ V-Mail ★
December 19, 1943

Dear Mother & Dad

I had nothing to do so I thought I would write a letter when I could. Did I tell you that I saw ____________[5] There isn't much to do over here on Sunday. Most everything is closed. The people over here get 2oz of butter a week per person. Meat twice a week and about 1 egg a month per person. Everything is rationed. They still have silk hose, clothes, shoes and about anything you want to buy. But it takes so many ration stamps that they can't afford them. It is against the law to make ice cream and English cigarettes cost about 50¢ for ten. Most of the pubs or Bars will not allow music or __________________[6] singing. I haven't heard from Gloria[7] for a long time. I guess she has some one else on the string by now.

Love,
Ralph

★ ★ ★

★ V-Mail ★
December 19, 1943

Dear Juana,

I don't imagine you will get this until after the Holidays if you go home. I don't know what I will do to celebrate the Holidays but don't imagine it will be too exciting. So far the food has been very good and the people real friendly. The money system gave me a little trouble at first but with the shillings, pence & pounds I get along with it OK by now. Over here instead of hamburger stands they have Fish & Chip places. They are really fish and French fried potatoes but are very good. All bars or Pubs and cafés close by 10 PM. While in Africa I had the good fortune to go thru a Medina. This is a Sultans place. I will tell of my experiences there in another letter later on. I will be glad to answer any questions you may have so you can tell the kiddes.

Best Wishes
Ralph

★ ★ ★

December 21, 1943
#1

Dear Mother & Dad, Juana

Well, I am at last at my final destination. I wrote some V Mail letters from England but I was not at my home base. We live in these corrugated, Niessen Huts.[8] Ours is divided into 4 small rooms. With 2 men to a room. We have a small stove in each room. But coal is rationed and we can only have a fire after 5 PM. Most of the huts have just one large room, but they saved this one for Lt. Bussing & myself & the officers on our crews. The toilets are in an another building but there is no hot water. So to shave we heat our canteen full of water then use our steel helmet as a wash basin. To take a bath we go about a mile to a building which has several tubs & hot water.[9]

Myself and Lt. Bussing are leader crews. So to help us perform our extra duties easier, They have given us each a brand new English bicycle. I never did learn to ride one but I have it now and it has only taken me 2 days. It is a good thing that I have one because I have a lot of running around to do and some places on the field are 2 & 3 miles apart. I haven't got my electric razor working yet as this is 220 volt current over here. I also am wearing my long handled wool drawers. I never thot I would ever wear them but they feel darn good. I also bought some thick English pure wool socks. They cost 2 shillings 6 pence or about 50 cents. In the states they would cost at least $1.50 if you could buy them at all. We have to wear overshoes all the time as it is very muddy all the time.

I was among the last crews to arrive and was surprised that some of the boys had already been on a raid.[10] I have lots to learn so I am going to school for a while. Me being a leader crew I am supposed to get a little extra school. I am also getting some extra equipment on my plane. I wish I could tell you of the really interesting things. Such as our school. The wonderful radio equipment on the plane, how we lead a formation & lots of things that people could never realize. But I can't put them in a letter.

I would have written this V. Mail but I wanted to send these francs.[11] These are from French Africa. The people are French but there are also a lot of natives who are coal black & speak a mixture of French & Arab called,

Morol, I think. You can see it printed on the 10 franc note. Notice that the new money is made in the U.S. These niggers[12] pray 3 times a day & believe in Allah. They only wash their feet to the ankles. Hands to the wrist & behind the ears. Then they pray and when finished they rub dirt on their hands, face & feet. They eat stuff called chop. It is like cornmeal. It is cooked in a barrel then poured in large bowls. Several squat around the bowls on the ground & eat only with their right hand. It was in Dakar,[13] Africa I saw Pres. Roosevelt. I also saw the largest boat in the French navy their. I forgot to tell you that 1 franc is worth 2¢ American. In Marrakech,[14] Africa I got to go thru the Medina or the Sultans City. They had a snake charmer there who would get the snake out of the basket then get its head flattened out. Then he would put a coin on its head then pick it off with his own lips. We saw the Sultans own riding horses. They were really beautiful. The Sultans son had some of the wives dance for us and we saw the market place where all girls are sold at the age of about 12. If they don't like the woman they have they just sell her & buy another. Then we went to the slums where all the Arabs live. In the town of Marrakech the Jews run the Arabs & the French run the Jews. I also ran into Jew boys[15] who could talk good English. Most of them have relatives in the U.S. They have horse-drawn taxis & instead of saying Gaddap or Get Up they say eeeeh or a long e.

I was very happy yesterday, I got some mail. I had one letter from each of you. It really made me feel good as it is the first I've had for over a month. I am starting to number my letters[16] so you can tell if you get them all. I wish you would do the same.

These Englishmen over here eat funny. They turn their fork upside down in their left hand. Then they take the knife & push everything on the prongs of the fork. And no matter how fast you eat they always beat you thru. They never lay down the fork until they finish – even when you pass them something. And you have heard of afternoon tea. It really means the evening meal.

We hear good radio programs – From Germany. They are all American recordings. They play about 20 min then some man gets up & gives England Hell for being in the war. Then a girl with a sexy voice announces the next piece. Then we listen to Harry James, Tommy Dorsey, Glenn Miller & all the rest.

We get 7 pkgs of cigarettes per week (which I don't use[17]) 1 pkg of gum per week. 2 candy bars & 1 small pkg of cookies & 1 bar of soap per week.

Note my change of APO # to 634. I guess this is about all for now. I'll be glad to answer any questions you have if I can. And I hope I get some more mail soon.

Love,
Ralph.

★ ★ ★

The Nissen hut was the standard home-away-from-home for the boys in England. Here Ralph stands in front of the hut he shared with his bombardier and copilot. The hut was almost brand new but already had the appearance of being quite used.

★ V-Mail ★
December 24, 1943

Dear Juana,

I really haven't got much news to tell about. I just didn't have anything better to do. You will have to get hold of the letter which I sent air mail and I wrote to the folks. I sent some French francs in it.

I have just finished shaving and have my laundry on the stove now.[18] I think tomorrow I will ride my bicycle thru some of the countryside. I visited one of the oldest churches in Norwich last week. You can see a lot just riding around and you don't have to ride far either.

I got one of your letters today. You wrote it on Dec. 9. But I think Vmail is lots faster.

If there is any questions you would like to ask I will be glad to answer them if I can.

Ralph

★ ★ ★

December 31, 1943
<u>Mission 1</u>

8th Air Force Mission 171 targets various locations in France. 418 B-17s and 154 B-24s participate in the raid, escorted by 548 fighters; 25 bombers and four fighters are lost; 264 men are killed or missing.

For Ralph's first mission, he followed other aircraft in the 445th Bomb Group to their target at the Saint Jean d'Angely Airfield.

★ ★ ★

January 1, 1944
Letter #7

Dear Folks,

Not much to write about. It being New Years day we sorta took it easy today. I got paid today and am going to send some more money home. I have already sent $400.00 to the bank and tomorrow I am going to send $200.00 more. Now if you folks want to use this you are perfectly welcome to do it.

We had a fairly good meal today for a change. Roast turkey, whipped potatoes, corn, peas, dressing, apricot pudding and hot cocoa. Something else I have learned to eat is coffee. It is so darned cold up here that a cup of hot coffee really tastes good.

We bomb from such high altitudes that the temperature reaches from 40 to 50 degrees below zero[19] and that is really cold. The windows all frost up the controls freeze, we have trouble with the Engines and that really makes the going tough.

I wish I could tell you about the missions I go on but about all I could write is what you would read in the newspaper & you would know about it before I could write you. Some of the missions are pretty tough with lots of flak and enemy fighters. Other missions are pretty easy. So far we have lost only 1 crew & 1 plane from our squadron.

The planes like they make in Evansville[20] are quite the thing over here. And I'm telling you we love the boys who fly those planes[21] because enemy fighters don't hang around when they are along. When we go on a big raid with several hundred planes taking part in it is one of the greatest air shows ever seen in the world. But we don't look at it as a form of entertainment.

We are having picture shows this week. "It Happened One Night"[22] is going to show.

Please check with the bank to see if all my money gets there. There should be $600.00 in all besides the monthly allotment of $150.00

Ralph

★ ★ ★

January 5, 1944
Mission 2

8th Air Force Mission 176 targets the industrial complex and shipyard on the Kiel Canal in Germany as well as the Bordeaux/Merignac and the Tours airfields both in France. 405 B-17s and 114 B-24s participate in the raid, escorted by 714 fighters; 24 bombers and 12 fighters are lost; 287 men are either killed or missing.

Ralph flew as lead pilot for the 445th Bomb Group and led the 2nd Combat Wing to their target over the Kiel Canal.

★ ★ ★

★ V-Mail ★
January 6, 1944

Dear Juana,

The new year is getting off to a good start over here. We have had putrid weather lately. I just returned from a pass and I rode thru the country side a bit. You can still see the houses with the grass roofs like you used to see in pictures etc. If I get a chance I want to go to Scotland.

I think the folks are cutting out of the paper all accounts of the 8th Air Force bombing Europe. Later on I may be able to tell them on which ones I was on.

How is everything at school? We have school every day we don't fly[23] or go on pass.

I guess this is about all for now.

Ralph.

★ ★ ★

January 11, 1944
Mission 3

8th Air Force Mission 182 bombs three aviation industry targets at Oschersleben, Halberstadt and Brunswick. German opposition is estimated at 500 Luftwaffe fighters. 525 B-17s and 138 B-24s participate in the mission, escorted by 592 fighters; 60 bombers and five fighters are lost; 626 men are killed or missing.

Ralph led his squadron, but they did not hit the primary target. Instead, they hit secondary targets at Meppen and other targets of opportunity.

★ ★ ★

A noteworthy aspect of this mission was the actions of Major James H. Howard, a P-51 pilot who shot down a Bf 110 and then found himself the lone escort for a B-17 group being attacked by thirty Luftwaffe aircraft. For the next half hour, he repeatedly turned into the enemy fighters, firing until he had only one gun left. He was credited with shooting down two Luftwaffe aircraft and saved the B-17s. Major Howard was awarded the Congressional Medal of Honor.

★ ★ ★

January 12, 1944

Dear Mother, Dad & Everybody

I received your first V Mail letters today. I also got one from Marcia. In the same mail I got one from Mr. & Mrs. Beeler.

I haven't been doing much lately. I got the Dec. 6 Sunday paper the other day and have read it clear through.

We had fresh eggs this morning for breakfast. That is quite a treat for us because we very seldom see an egg over here. They have these powdered eggs but they don't taste like fresh ones. I was sleeping so late I almost missed breakfast all together.

I had to get up awfully early yesterday as we went on a mission. I was really tired when we came back. Wearing all the equipment we do is enough to make you tired. We have electric heated flying suits because of the extreme low temperatures at which we fly. We wear white silk gloves[24] and over them we wear the leather electric heated gloves. We also have electric heated shoes which we wear under our sheep skin lined flying boots. If your electric suit goes out in flight you sometimes get frost bite. It is so bad some loose their hands & feet. On top of this electric suit we usually wear some kind of a light pair of coveralls. Then we have our flak suit. These are made of heavy mail. But will stop a .45 caliber bullet. But they are very heavy. They cover our chest and back and are the shape of a baseball catchers breast protector.[25] After wearing them for a few hours they really weight you down. We always fly high so we have to wear an Oxygen Mask and they get awful tiresome after 4 or 5 hours.

Well, I guess this is about all for now.

Ralph.

★ ★ ★

January 12, 1944

Dear Juana,

I wrote Mother & Dad today about my flying equipment, Marcia & Herb about the flying & Mr. & Mrs. Beeler about the ground school so I will write to you about England.[26]

I was on a mission yesterday. It was long and hard. It seems funny to listen to the news propaganda after a raid.

Juana, I have taken up the study of geography and I study maps look at photographs and read about German and French cities & industries. So you think and make notes on what you would like to know and I will try to answer them. I also study first aid. How to treat wounds, fractures & frost bite. We have men who loose whole hands & feet because of frost bite. So when I come home we can compare notes on first aid.

This country of England is really amazing. When you get on a train they put your baggage in a separate car but they never give you a check. When you get where you are going your bag will be put off. If you happen to forget a small bag or parcel and can't get back to your station for it for a few days it will still be there. If you get tired carrying a large bundle or something you can set it down on a sidewalk somewhere. Then go back a few hours later and it will still be there.

The English prepared food is real good. Of course in our G.I. mess hall we have our C rations.[27] All the bread over here is dark. I haven't seen a piece of American light bread since I have been here.

The roads are rather narrow and are hard surface. Most every one has a bicycle. It is the national mode of travel I think. You notice very few of the people wearing gloves. Most of the English are very friendly. There are only two classes the upper or rich and the working class or lower class. When a man once gets down they keep him down and he has to work for the rich class for just about anything they want to give him. The term "tea" when they say "come over for tea" means the evening meal. They don't have ice cream and right now we have a hot argument on as to which is the better city, New

York, Chicago or Los Angeles. When we aren't working or studying we sit around and argue or tell all the tales we know.[28]

About all for now.

Ralph

★ ★ ★

★ V-Mail ★
January 12, 1944

Dear Mother & Dad,

This is just a letter to you and you don't have to pass it around. Before I left the States I talked to Gloria over the phone and we decided to call things off for lots of different reasons. It seems one of her old boyfriends came home and I met another girl in Pocatello – so that's the way it is. I received a Xmas card from Mrs. Fulcher today and she said she had mailed the ring to you. It should be there by now. While I am on the subject If anything ever happens to me I wish you would advise this person of what happened. Miss Margaret Christensen, St. Marks Hospital, Salt Lake City, 3, Utah. She is a nurse and I met her in Pocatello.

I received word that my promotion had been accepted so I should get it back soon.

I hope you are all in the best of health. I am also writing another letter to you tonight.

Ralph.

★ ★ ★

★ V-Mail ★
January 19, 1944

Dear Mother & Dad,

I got Dad's letter today but it still had my old A.P.O. number on it. I hadn't received any mail for almost a week but today I got 6 letters so I didn't do so bad. I got an Xmas card from Mr. & Mrs. Wade, Patsy Ruth Miller and Ed Rutledge. Will you please thank all these people when you see them.

I hope you are all over the flu.

I didn't get to see any of the S. Amer. cattle[29] and I didn't eat much beef. The thing that impressed me was the native Bananas and pineapple. They were delicious.

I have just been over to the War room. They are planning a mission.

These British radio programs get me. A radio is a wireless, auto tire is tyre, picture show is electric cinema, flash light a torch, gasoline is petrol, airplane is aircraft or Machine. Hardware dealer is Ironmongers, beer hall or bar is a Pub.

I am taking a short course in German. A lot of their words are like ours but the pronunciation is difficult. I go two nights a week.

About all for now.

Ralph

★ ★ ★

★ V-Mail ★
January 19, 1944

Dear Juana,

I received your first Vmail letter today. Yesterday, I also received a box from Mrs. Gay. I want you to thank her very much. I always enjoy her boxes they always seem to hit the spot. I also got a box the other day from you or Marcia I couldn't make it out. I really enjoy the eats. Fruit cakes, candy, cookies and the like. You see all of that is rationed over here.

Nothing (Xmas) was decorated over here. I went into Norwich the other day and had two pkgs of gum with me. I soon had quite a following. The kids go crazy over gum.

I am taking a short course in German. I am after the pronunsiation mostly. The vocabulary isn't too hard. You see we can get most any language over the radio and you get so you can tell about what they are talking about.

I have to go to the War room now. There is a mission working and I want to start preparing my information and do a little studying.[30]

All for now.

Ralph.

★ ★ ★

January 21, 1944
Mission 4

8th Air Force Mission 187 targets 36 V-weapon sites[31] in the Pas de Calais and the Cherbourg areas of France. 597 B-17s and 198 B-24s fly the mission and are escorted by 628 fighters; six bombers and one fighter are lost; 78 men are killed or missing.

Ralph led the 702nd Bomb Squadron to their target at Bonnières, France, 25 miles southwest of Pas de Calais.

★ ★ ★

★ V-Mail ★
January 22, 1944

Dear Juana,

I received two boxes from you today. Only one of them was from an address I had never heard before. The candy, gum, juice and all of it is delicious. I have received so much lately that I have quite a reserve now.

In your letter #2 of Jan. 11 you asked if I was in the raid over Germany which you heard described over the radio. I was in that raid. There is no use of me telling you about it because you probably heard more about it over the radio than I could tell you.

I still haven't received my trunk[32] so I have only the clothes I brought with me. I am getting my mail regularily now except when we have bad weather. We don't have any snow here. In fact most everything is green and it hardly gets cold enough to freeze.

Thanks again for the boxes.

Ralph.

★ ★ ★

January 23, 1944

Dear Juana,

I just returned from a pass, on which, I visited the City of Norwich and especially the Castle Museum.[33] Do you still teach history? Any way I thought maybe you might like to read parts of this letter to your kiddies.

This castle was built in 1000 and the City of Norwich was built around it.[34] The Castle was built by William Osborne[35] to impress the people. All the materials were shipped from France and there was a moat around it with a draw bridge to protect it against invaders. The walls are about 3 ft thick and are the original walls. They are in good condition to be 800 or 900 years old. We went up on top to the battlements where the soldiers warded off invaders. This offers a very good view of the City. One thing notable was the church spire 385 ft high and is the second oldest church in England. Then we went down to the dungeons where they kept prisiners. This Castle was captured in the 12 Century by the French and was in their hands exactly 1month. After that it was used after a fashion, as a prison. The prisiners were put there because of religious beliefs and not because of any wrong doing. You can still see pictures and drawings scratched into the walls by the prisiners. They show crusificition of Christ. The diciples, the betrayal and several inscriptions. They also have several forms of punishment. One was straps of iron which fit around a persons head and a piece with sharp spikes on it which fit in the persons mouth. They put this on people and lead them thru town for everyone to see. It was designed for people who talk about other people. There is a well in one of the dungeons which is 115 ft deep. There are several rooms in the Castle and several of them are now devoted to the museum. They have stuffed birds & animals from all parts of the world. There are several rooms devoted to art and paintings. There is a real Egyptian Mummy and they have costumes of the Indians of America. The furniture, pottery and furnishings are of the Elizabethian period and they are quite a collection. When they elected a Commissioner (or Mayor) of the town they put him in a chair covered with red silk and paraded him thru the town in it. Every few steps they would toss the Commissioner high in the air and catch him when he came down. This is so the ones who liked him could cheer and the ones who didn't could throw brickbats at him. They have the chair there in the museum. There is a copy of the Declaration of Independence and there is also an original deed to some ground which was signed by some relative of Pres. George Washington. They seem to be very proud of the fact that Washington was the descendent of an Englishman. There are several other things which I couldn't begin to describe. So this is about all for that.

Right now I am listening to a German news broadcast by William Joyce.[36] As you know he is an American citizen serving the Axis. He sure is putting out propaganda. For a while he was trying to seperate Russia from the U.S. & England. Now he is trying to tell the English that the U.S. & Russia will kick England out of the Allies. I really have to laugh every time I hear him.

If there is anything or question you would like to ask I would be glad to answer them if I can –

Ralph

★ ★ ★

★ V-Mail ★
January 23, 1944

Dear Mother & Dad,

I have just returned from a 48 hour pass. I visited in Norwich the old castle museum built in 1000. You can read about this in the letter I wrote to Juana.

Do the packages you send me have to be with in a certain size. I would like to have some soda crackers or better yet some Ritz Crackers. Every once in a while I get some K rations[37] that have a small can of American cream cheese. Boy it really is good. The only kind of cheese you can get over here is a pale yellow or lemon color is rather hard and stinks a little more than cream cheese. But I would like a box of crackers if you can get them. The only thing these British have is Soda Crackers with no salt and you might send me some Air Mail stationery as you can hardly get paper of any kind. I also drank some Limey beer but you can read about that in Marcias letter.

The people over here are getting ready to plant spring crops. It hasn't been cold enough to freeze the ground but twice since I have been here but it is the dampness that hurts.

About all for now. Did you check with the bank to see if my allotment came in.

Love
Ralph

★ ★ ★

★ V-Mail ★
January 25, 1944

Dear Juana,

I received the box today with the candy and nuts in it. They were both in fine shape and the nuts were especially fresh. Thank you an awfully lot for the box. We can't get things like candy and such over here. Another thing I miss is reading material. I was wondering if I was still suppose to get Esquire and Life & Time? I still receive them and wondered if I was supposed to. If my subscription has run out have the folks give you some of my money and send in my subscription please. If a person doesn't have things to read he has lots of time to do nothing. Thanks again for the candy and nuts.

Ralph

★ ★ ★

★ V-Mail ★
January 29, 1944

Dear Juana,

Received your letters of Jan 13 & 16 both today. My mail has been coming thru pretty good lately and I want to thank you again for the packages. My clothes as yet haven't caught up with me. All I have is what I brought along. You asked about the Sultan's wives. The *wall* around the Medina where the Sultan and his people live was built in 1150 A.D. The Sultan who lives there now[38] is 34 years old is 6 ft 8 in tall but has only 8 wives. However, he has 350 dancing girls. But they told us the Sultan before this one[39] had over 600 wives. The Medina & Sultan I am talking about is at the Capital of French Morocco[40] in Africa.

The food here is just so so. I would give anything for some good milk. All we have is canned stuff. All our food is regular Army C ration which is furnished by the Quartermaster. I guess this is about all for now.

Ralph

★ ★ ★

January 30, 1944
Mission 5

8th Air Force Mission 200 again targets aircraft factories in the Brunswick area of Germany. Cloud cover over the primary target forces the group to move on to secondary targets in the area. 623 B-17s and 154 B-24s are escorted by 644 fighters; 20 bombers and four fighters are lost; 214 men are either killed or missing.

Ralph led the 702nd Bomb Squadron to secondary targets in the Hannover area.

★ ★ ★

★ V-Mail ★
February 1, 1944

Dear Mother & Dad,

We are just brewing some tea. It has been rather cold today and a "spot of tea" doesn't taste bad. We have some nice music on the radio from Germany. About all the British play is classical and that gets tirisome after so long a time. I am getting to be a real seamstress. The seams in my trousers are always ripping open so I get out the sewing kit and start to work. And buttons they are really a job. But if it weren't for sticking my fingers it would be alright. I haven't learned to wear a thimble yet – just give me time though.

I wrote you in an Air Mail letter yesterday that I was getting the "Air Medal"[41] for my raids over Germany. And now today I learned I am getting another medal[42] for one particular raid on which we did a very good job. Well I must close now as I may have to get up early in the morning.

Ralph.

★★★

February 5, 1944
Sat. nite

Dear Mother & Dad,

Writing letters isn't much to be doing on a Sat. nite but I can't think of much else to be doing. I have been pretty busy the last few days as your papers no doubt have indicated. I had very little to do today so I started building. I now have a new wash stand attached to the wall. A new clothes rack with a shelf over it. Book ends, and a few other little things. I'm getting to be quite handy by now.

I have also borrowed a set of tools and am making plans for a house and garage. I am making rough drawings now and will transfer them later to some good paper. A person has to have something to keep his mind occupied. It doesn't do any good to just sit around and think about the raids we go on and the things we see and do. But now with my foreign language and everything I keep my spare time pretty well filled up.

My mail comes in spells. I'll get a whole lot of it for 2 or 3 days then I won't get any for a long time.

This poem[43] I am sending you is from the Stars & Stripes. You never have said if you were keeping the news paper clippings. I wish you would keep all this I am sending home.

Next time you write tell me how much money I now have in the bank. You said you got the $150.00 allotment but you haven't said anything about the $200.00 or the $400.00. I sent these 2 amounts in January and they should be coming to the bank soon. Please let me know about this the next time you write.

All for now,

Love
Ralph.

★ ★ ★

★ V-Mail ★
February 6, 1944

Dear Mother & Dad,

I just mailed an Air Mail letter to you today but I received your Air Mail letter of Jan. 16 so thought I would answer it.

Guess you noticed I have received a promotion.[44] I just got word of it today. This will mean a little more pay. Approximately $50.00 a month more. But it will also mean more work and a few more extra duties and responsibilities. I guess it is worth it.

How did the county tournament[45] turn out? Is Bob W in England? You said in a recent letter you hadn't quite figured out where I was stationed. I am in England but I can't tell you exactly the location of our field. We are rationed I bar of soap per week but I have enough. I can't think of anything I need at present. Don't forget to make the change in my address.

Love
Ralph.

★ ★ ★

★ V-Mail ★
February 7, 1944

Dear Juana,

Today has been a rather quite day for me. I got to sleep in until 10 AM. Usually someone wakes me up sometime between 2 AM and 8 AM. I got the crew together and we shot a round of skeet.

I guess you noticed my change of title! It became effective Jan 31. It will mean more money but will also mean more work and responsibility. But I guess it is worth it.

I want to make my bed over tonight. I haven't had time to do it right lately and it is a bit lumpy. So I guess I'd better get it done so I will get some sleep.

Ralph

★ ★ ★

February 10, 1944

Dear Juana,

I am writing this Air Mail because I don't think I could get it all on a V Mail. You will have to excuse the paper but it is all I can find.

I just returned from visiting several of the historical places in London. The place that impressed me the most, I guess, was Westminster Abbey. As you know all of the Kings are buried there except the last King George who was buried in Windsor Castle. The Abbey is very high and the windows with the stained glass are beautiful. Many other famous people are also buried there and they have marble statues of most of them. Some of the statues are Black Marble and cost as much as £2000 or $8000.

I forgot to tell you that the Red Cross fixed me up a date with a girl who works at the American Embassy. She more or less "took me in tow." She was a rather pretty girl and was awfully nice about showing me the town and answering all my questions. Having lived there all her life she knew about all the most interesting places.

After leaving the Abbey we went to the House of Parliament. That is the building where Big Ben is. It is a very beautiful building. We drove past Downing street and then to Buckingham Palace. If the king is there they fly the Kings flag and they take it down when he is away. In front of the Palace is Queen Victoria's statue.[46] Then we drove by another Palace, of which I do not know the name.[47] It is larger than Buckingham and was occupied by the Duke of Windsor before his marriage to Mrs. Simpson. People in London have a very low opinion of her and do not like her.

As you know there are no tall buildings or sky scrapers in London. Most of the buildings aren't as tall as in Evansville. But it isn't unusual to see a hotel that covers a whole block. We drove out thru some of the most bombed parts and you remember the song "London Bridge is Falling Down." Well there actually is such a bridge. Then thru Oxford Square and on to Piccadilly Circus which is the heart of the theatre section. We drove down Park Lane which is the same as Park Ave in New York City. And we stopped for Tea at the Grovenor House.[48] It is one of the swankiest hotels in town. There was an Orchestra, dancing and all. We had 2 cups of tea each, Some small sandwiches and cookies which all cost 6's[49] or about $1.20. I had tickets to the theatre down at Leichester Square which they pronounce – Leister. The play was a musical comedy entitled "Strike a New Note."[50] It was very funny although I did have a bit if trouble understanding some of the players as first. The Highlight of the play was a skit showing the difference between the British & American officer. A British officer was telling another that the Americans were coming over and that they would have to relax a bit more and make the Americans feel at home. The whole conversation was all yes sir & no sir. Then two men dressed in American officers clothes walked out. They had hands in pockets, hats pushed back on their heads a big cigar in their hands and a wad of gum in their mouth. As a whole the show was very good. Then we went to a place called Pastorias for dinner. It was a very exclusive place and the Red Cross made the reservations for me. We had Roast chicken which was very good. One thing I have noticed you will never get water with your meal unless you ask for it. But they do serve wine with your meal. After that we danced a while and most of the places close at 11 PM.

There are lots of theatres around Picadilly Circus, Movies & plays. The next time I go there is one play I want to see in particular. The people in London are a bit different than other parts of England and I can see that in peace time it would be a lot different than it is now. But it is like all other foreign cities, when they see the Americans coming they start multiplying their prices by two. I guess they think we are all millionaires. Well, so much for this trip, maybe I can write about someplace else next time.

Ralph

★ ★ ★

Ralph left out a few details in this letter. His first trip to London did not go as he had planned. He took the train to Charing Cross Station and checked in at the Allied Officers' Billet across the street. This facility provided a place to sleep for officers from all of the Allied forces who wanted to come to London. The sleeping was dormitory-style bunk beds and did not amount to much more than an upscale flophouse. There were people of all nationalities wandering in and out, with parties and gambling going on all night. Ralph was afraid that someone would steal his uniform, so he put it under his mattress while he tried to sleep.

The next day, he checked out and tried to move into the Normandy Hotel. Most of the officers stationed in London were living in the Normandy Hotel, which had an American-style bar, a free Mess Hall, and nightly entertainment. Unfortunately, it was a very popular place, and they had no vacancies. The desk clerk told him to try the Kensington Palace Hotel.

The Kensington Palace Hotel was operated by two older ladies. It had five floors, but the top two floors had bomb damage and could not be used. Ralph got a room on the second floor for $9.40 a night. The room was heated by a coin-operated fireplace and cost one shilling an hour.

Ralph made many trips to London and always stayed at the Kensington Palace Hotel. All he had to do was call ahead and let one of the ladies know he was coming. They always put him in the exact same room and provided him with a reserved, private table for breakfast.

One of Ralph's favorite places to go was the Windmill Theater,[51] which advertised the motto "We Never Close." No matter when Ralph arrived in London, he knew he could get good entertainment at a reasonable price. Each show featured a nude sequence put on by the "Windmill Girls." It was a favorite of all the soldiers.

★ ★ ★

February 11, 1944
Mission 6

8th Air Force Mission 218 sends 201 B-24s to bomb the V-weapon site located near Siracourt, France, and 223 B-17s to bomb the marshalling yards at Frankfort, Germany, over 280 miles further on. The B-24s are escorted by 126 fighters; one bomber is lost, with 11 men killed or missing.

Ralph led the 702nd Bomb Squadron to their target at Bonnières. While they experienced a low casualty rate, the flak was the worst Ralph had seen. One flak burst sent a fragment through the side window next to him, causing a hole about the size of a quarter. The flak fragment landed in his lap.

★ ★ ★

February 15, 1944
Mission 7

8th Air Force Mission 223 sends 54 B-24s to bomb V-weapon sites in the Siracourt region of France. They are unescorted and sustain no losses.

Ralph was lead pilot for the 445th Bomb Group.

★ ★ ★

February 16, 1944[52]

Dear Mother, Dad and Everybody

I haven't written for a few days so will try to catch up on everything tonight. I received your letter of Feb. 7 today which isn't bad time.

Was sorry to hear that Wadesville didn't win a game in the county tournament. What grade is Betty Ann in? I doubt if I would know her if I were to see her. There was something about a basket ball team being organized here but I haven't heard any more about it lately. You mentioned about sending a box. It usually takes a month or more for it to get here. I hope you included a box of crackers or Ritz. Every once in a while we get some American cream cheese and it would taste good with crackers. We can buy one can of orange juice a week now. I never did like canned orange juice very well but it sure tastes good now. I have been on seven raids over enemy territory. The dates are Dec. 30, 1943, Jan 5, 1944 Jan 11, Jan 21, Jan 30, Feb 11, Feb 15. The one on Feb. 11 was the roughest one we have been on. The Flak was very bad and we had several holes in my plane one about the size of a quarter in the window next to me. Its just like a big fireworks to watch that stuff burst all around you. When a shell goes off near you all you hear is a loud whop! then a little black puff appears. The ones you see don't hurt you, it is the ones you don't see that do the damage. Capt. Blanchard a boy who I flew with back in New Mexico was killed on this raid. There were enough black puffs in the sky that you could almost walk on it. But it is part of the game over here. I may get a chance to go to school shortly to study this new type of bombing thru clouds[53] like you read about in the papers.

When Jim Stewart goes on a mission he usually sits in the Co-Pilots seat. He assists the pilot in flying.

It seems I never get any rest anymore. When I fly a mission I usually get up between 2 and 3 AM so that we can get everything planned. When I don't fly they usually start coming in my room from 6 AM on. To tell me this, or ask me that or I'm supposed to be some place at a certain time. Of course, actually I get plenty of rest but I would like to lay in bed till noon, undisturbed, just one day to see how it feels. It must be wonderful.

I am glad to hear that all my money is in now. I was sorta worried for awhile. With my promotion I get about $50.00 more a month. If I were married I would get about $100.00 more than that. Do you think it is worth it?

Base pay	$200.00	
10%	20.00	(for overseas)
flying pay	110.00	(50% of 220.00)
Rations	21.00	
Total	351.00	

Yes, Dad when I was in Africa I did see some of those women who wear veils. But not very many as they are in a different part of Africa. I must say however, that they wear veils for custom only. No matter what you read or hear, when there is an American soldier around you can bet he has figured out a way to get around custom. But I know you hear all kinds of things.

I learned about hot water and wool a long time ago. I washed a pair of socks one night and the next morning I couldn't even get my thumb in them. You learn fast, don't you?

We don't get to town very often. There is a bus goes on 3 times a day but I am usually so busy that I never get a chance to go over once a week. But I look forward to the 48 hr. pass and try to go someplace where I can see something. I have one other letter to write tonight so I guess I had better get started on it.

Love
Ralph.

We have re-named our plane to SINSHIP[54]

★ ★ ★

★ V-Mail ★
February 16, 1944

Dear Juana,

I received a letter just a few days ago from you but I have lost it so I don't remember exactly what it said. But I remember you asked how many raids I have been on. I have been on seven raids at this time. I don't seem to get them in very fast as I am a lead crew and don't fly as often as the other fellows. I was on a raid yesterday Feb. 15. I was also on one on the 11th. Now I probably won't go on another for a week or so. Yes I have received a lot of boxes. I thought I wrote you before. I got one from an address in Richmond which I didn't know. Well this is about all I have room for now.

Ralph.

★ ★ ★

This was the last letter Ralph would send from Tibenham. Much to his surprise, after only two months, he and his crew were transferred.

★ ★ ★

"There are a lot of people who say that bombing cannot win the war. My reply to that is that it has never been tried . . . and we shall see."[55]

★ ★ ★

NOTES

1. From Psalm 23.
2. The RAF offices at most American airfields were located in an area originally set aside for the Women's Auxiliary Air Force (WAAF). WAAF pilots and crews were part of the RAF and provided noncombat transport services within England.
3. There is a cornerstone carrying the date of 1659, which may have been for an addition to the original structure.
4. There were twelve pence to the shilling and twenty shillings to the pound. A florin, also called a cupronickel, was a coin equal to two shillings or one-tenth of a pound. One pound equaled $2.80 US.
5. Censored or redacted text. Ralph saw President Roosevelt while in Africa. This is mentioned in a later letter, but it was not censored.
6. Censored or redacted text.
7. This is in reference to Gloria Fulcher, Ralph's fiancée.
8. Ralph's Nissen hut was located in Site 2, next to the southernmost communal site.
9. There were bathtubs for bathing and laundry tubs for washing clothes located in Site 7, which was only about one-third of a mile from Ralph's hut, although on the first day it probably seemed like a further walk. The bathhouse had five private rooms with bathtubs, and there was hot water from about nine in the morning to three in the afternoon, or until the hot water ran out.
10. Crews from the 445th Bomb Group began flying missions on December 3, 1943.
11. Enclosed in this letter were several bank notes from different countries.
12. This is a word that Ralph would never have heard at home. He no doubt picked it up from some of his crew. At that point, Ralph was struggling to figure out what was proper and acceptable. He later noted that his mother wrote and told him to stop using the word.
13. This is in reference to Dakar, Senegal.
14. This is in reference to Marrakech, Morocco.
15. Ralph did not consider this a derogatory term. It was just the way people talked.

16. There were a couple of reasons Ralph wanted to number his letters. First, he was concerned that the censors would lose his mail. Second, as mail from home crisscrossed with his, he did not want to answer questions that he had already answered in undelivered mail. Lastly, he wanted to make sure he and they received every letter. Unfortunately, he failed to devise a method to know what the next number should be, and his numbering eventually trailed off. This is the first letter he numbered.

17. Ralph did not smoke. However, he took his ration and used it to trade for other things he wanted.

18. In a previous letter, Ralph explained what they had to do to get hot water for shaving. Doing the laundry was about the same process. There was not much to wash: socks, underwear, and T-shirts. All of the trousers, shirts, and blouses were sent out.

19. As a rule of thumb, temperature drops 3.5°F for every 1,000 feet of altitude. For example, the average temperature in England for January is about 37°F. If a B-24 flew at its maximum service ceiling of 28,000 feet, the temperature would be about 61°F below zero.

20. Republic Aviation Corporation constructed an aircraft manufacturing facility in Evansville to manufacture P-47 Thunderbolts. Construction began in April 1942, and the first P-47, named *Hoosier Spirit*, rolled off the assembly line on September 20, 1942. The facility leased the runways from the adjacent airport and added an aircraft gunnery testing range. At peak production nearly 5,000 employees worked at the facility. The Evansville plant was the second largest P-47 facility, producing nearly 39 percent of all P-47s. After the war, the plant was sold to International Harvester, which later sold it to Whirlpool, where it remained in production until 2010. What remains of the runway is now part of the Evansville Regional Airport.

21. The P-47 Thunderbolt, also known as the "Jug" (because its shape resembled a milk jug), was the largest, heaviest, and most expensive fighter aircraft to be powered by a single reciprocating engine. It provided bomber escort from England to the German border, and then could attack ground targets on its way back to refuel. Eventually, with external tanks, the range was extended to cover much of Germany.

22. *It Happened One Night* starred Clark Gable, Claudette Colbert, and Walter Connolly.

23. This is in reference to the special programs put on by the morale officer.

24. The silk gloves helped wick away any sweat, thus keeping the hands dry. Even with electrically heated flight suits, wet hands, fingers, feet, and toes were all susceptible to frostbite in the extreme temperatures. From a technical standpoint, the suit Ralph describes is an F-3 heated flight suit, as the F-2 type did not provide silk gloves.

25. By December 1943, over 13,000 mail flak suits had been delivered to American flight crews. They protected crew members from machine gun fire, flak fragments, and shell splinters. Over the course of the war, crews wearing the mail armor suffered 58 percent fewer causalities than crews that did not have them. The armored flak suits were manufactured by Fashion Frocks, Inc., of Cincinnati, Ohio, and consisted of a number of two-inch square steel-magnesium alloy plates, linked together to provide complete coverage. The

piece was then encased in a padded garment. There were three individual parts to the entire garment: front vest, back vest, and front apron. A pilot or someone who sat in a certain position may not have worn the back vest. Overall, the entire flak suit weighed twenty-five pounds, ten ounces.

26. Ralph counted on everyone circulating his letters. To keep them "entertaining," he would often tell different people different things. This technique was probably therapeutic as it gave Ralph some extra time to get his mind off the war.

27. The Type C Rations (C-Rations or commercial rations) were commercially prepared, individually canned food products. They were typically packaged in a small, square cardboard box. A typical box contained meat, fruit, crackers, peanut butter, candy, and an accessory pack. The accessory pack typically contained sugar tablets, a flat wooden spoon, a piece of candy-coated chewing gum, nine cigarettes, a book of matches, a P-38 can opener, and in some cases, salt, pepper, a paper napkin, and four small sheets of toilet paper.

28. This rambling is typical of someone who has been on a long, hard mission. Ralph was just glad to be back on the ground, and one of the ways he decompressed was to write home. In all likelihood, he did not read what he had written before he mailed the letter.

29. Rolla was very curious about the cattle in South America. Even in 1944, South America, especially Argentina, was famous for its beef.

30. Most pilots did little preparation for an upcoming mission. This was not the case for lead pilots. They were expected to know every aspect of a mission, from forming up over the English Channel to knowing all of the target information, then regrouping for the return trip. In some cases, lead pilots provided input to the mission planners on issues that would make the mission more successful or more comprehensive.

31. V-weapon sites were commonly known to all Allied pilots as "skee sites."

32. Before leaving the United States, every officer was issued a footlocker. They were to pack all of their personal belongings in it and take only what they could carry on the plane. The footlockers traveled by ship and sometimes took a long time to find their way to the owner.

33. This is in reference to Norwich Castle Museum.

34. Actually, the city existed long before the castle was constructed between 1066 and 1075.

35. This probably is in reference to William Fitz Osbern, who played a principle role in the preparations for the Norman invasion of England and the Battle of Hastings (1066). He became 1st Earl of Hereford and was a prolific Norman castle builder. While there is no evidence of him participating in the actual construction of Norwich Castle, he may have been consulted during its design. Depending on who gave Ralph the tour of the castle, what was actually said, and what he thought he heard, some actual facts may have been obscured.

36. William Joyce (1906–1946) was born in Brooklyn, New York, in 1906. A few years after his birth, the Joyce family moved back to their native Ireland. At the age of fifteen, Joyce moved to London in search of higher education. In 1932, he joined the British Union of Fascists and quickly became a major spokesperson. For a few years, he was in and out of

politics and owned a radio shop. In late August 1939, he and his wife were tipped off that the police were going to detain him under Defence Regulation 18B. To avoid detainment, they escaped to Germany, where he became a propagandist for the Nazis. While listening to Joyce's broadcasts was discouraged (but not illegal), they became very popular with the British public. In 1940, Joyce had an estimated twenty-four million listeners in England. The British press nicknamed him Lord Haw-Haw, and he occasionally would introduce himself as "William Joyce, otherwise known as Lord Haw-Haw." All of his broadcasts began with a voice speaking with a thick German drawl, saying, "Germany Calling. Germany Calling. Germany Calling." The broadcasts urged the British people to surrender and always berated them for being in the war. After the war, he was arrested by British soldiers and returned to London to stand trial for treason. His trial was compounded by the fact that he was an American citizen, had obtained a British passport by lying about his citizenship, then had never disavowed his British citizenship that came with the passport, and had become a naturalized German citizen. William Joyce lost his court battles and was hanged for treason on January 3, 1946, in Wandsworth Prison.

37. The K-ration was an individual daily food ration used by the Army during World War II. It was originally intended as an individually packaged daily ration for mobile forces for short durations. The K-ration came in three courses: breakfast, lunch, and supper. The breakfast course consisted of canned chopped ham and eggs or veal loaf, biscuits, a dried fruit bar or cereal bar, halazone water purification tablets, a four-pack of cigarettes, chewing gum, instant coffee, and sugar. The lunch course included canned processed cheese, ham or ham and cheese, biscuits, fifteen malted milk tablets or five caramels, sugar, salt, a four-pack of cigarettes, a box of matches, chewing gum, and a powdered beverage packet. The supper course contained canned meat (either chicken pâté, pork luncheon meat with carrots and apples, beef and pork loaf, or sausages), biscuits, a two-ounce chocolate bar or tropical bar, a very small packet of toilet paper tissues, a four-pack of cigarettes, chewing gum, and bouillon soup (cube or powder packet). The K-ration reportedly got its name because the letter K was phonetically different than other letters already in use. However, unofficial reports say that the letter K stood for cracker. The K-rations were produced by the Cracker Jack Company of Chicago, Illinois, and were packaged in a wax-lined box similar in size to the original Cracker Jack snack food. K-rations were made available to air crews before they took off and were intended as survival food in the event the aircraft was shot down. Many times the rations were not reclaimed from returning air crews, so they had them to enjoy at their leisure.

38. This is in reference to Mohammed V, sultan of Morocco (1909–1961). Mohammed V International Airport, located in Casablanca, is named after him.

39. This is in reference to Yusef ben Hassan, sultan of Morocco (1882–1927).

40. Rabat was the provisional capital at the time.

41. In most bomb groups, including the 445th, the Air Medal was awarded to crews after they had completed their first five missions. In some bomb groups, an Air Medal was awarded to crews for every five missions completed.

42. This is in reference to Ralph's first Distinguished Flying Cross (DFC).

43. Included with this letter was a poem, "Ground Crew Baby," from the *Stars and Stripes* newspaper, which is shown in Appendix A.

44. Ralph's long-awaited promotion to captain had come through on January 31.

45. This is in reference to the Indiana High School Basketball Tournament. In the days before there were leagues and conferences, the tournament was organized around individual counties. The winner of the county tournaments would advance to the next level of the statewide tournament.

46. This is in reference to the Queen Victoria Memorial, completed in 1911. It includes a large statue of Queen Victoria facing northeast toward the Mall.

47. This is in reference to Kensington Palace, the residence of many members of the royal family. After King Edward VIII's abdication, Edward and Wallis became the Duke and Duchess of Windsor and relocated to Europe, finally settling in France. During the war years, he was briefly brought back to England before being sent to the Bahamas as governor. After the war, he and the duchess returned to France, where they lived until their deaths. After each of their deaths, they were finally allowed to return to England for burial.

48. The Grosvenor House is a large and luxurious hotel located in London's Mayfair district. It was built in the 1920s and opened in 1929 on the site of the former London residence of the Duke of Westminster. The hotel underwent a four-year remodeling, which was completed in 2008. There are 494 rooms and a ballroom that can seat 2,000 for a meal. The property is now managed by Marriott International.

49. Six shillings.

50. *Strike a New Note,* directed by George Black, appeared at the Prince of Wales Theatre and starred Sid Field, Jerry Desmond, and Evelyn Barr. It was a comedy review that featured nineteen skits, several musical arrangements, and many young people from around England who were trying to break into theatre, called the "Rising Generation." Every performance concluded with the cast and audience singing "God Save the King."

51. The Windmill Theater opened in 1931 and provided a review that included motionless nude ladies or *tableaux vivants*. The theater was extremely popular with soldiers. Now known as the Windmill International, the theater presents adult entertainment. The story of the original Windmill Theater is artfully depicted in the movie *Mrs. Henderson Presents* (Pathé Pictures/BBC Films, 2005).

52. This is the first letter with the return address with Ralph's rank of captain.

53. This is in reference to Gee-H radio navigation.

54. The plane was renamed much earlier, but Ralph forgot to tell his parents. They apparently asked about it.

55. Marshal of the Royal Air Force Sir Arthur "Bomber" Harris, from an early 1942 newsreel.

Chapter 8

THE BIG SHOW

★ ★ ★

"Almighty God: Our sons, pride of our nation, this day have set upon a mighty endeavor, a struggle to preserve our Republic, our religion, and our civilization, and to set free a suffering humanity. . . . For these men are lately drawn from the ways of peace. They fight not for the lust of conquest. They fight to end conquest. They fight to liberate. They fight to let justice arise, and tolerance and goodwill among all Thy people. They yearn but for the end of battle, for their return to the haven of home. Some will never return. Embrace these, Father, and receive them, Thy heroic servants, into Thy kingdom."[1]

The 93rd Bomb Group was known as "Ted's Flying Circus," in honor of Colonel Edward J. Timberlake (affectionately known as "Ted"), who was the 93rd's first commander. Timberlake was promoted to the rank of brigadier general in May 1943 and, later that year, assumed command of the 20th Bombardment Wing. Wing headquarters was coincidentally located at Hardwick, alongside the 93rd Bomb Group.

Ralph was previously stationed with the 445th Bomb Group at Tibenham, commanded by Colonel Robert H. Terrill. Terrill and Timberlake had known each other since their days at West Point and flying school at Kelly Field near San Antonio. For some reason, the two did not get along very well, and during the early stages of the war, Timberlake had very few good things to say about Colonel Terrill and the 445th Bomb Group. After Timberlake was promoted to brigadier general, Terrill, who now reported to him, made a conscious effort to get on the general's good side.

★ ★ ★

Gee-H navigational bombing was a technique developed and used by the British that proved very effective in bombing targets at night or on days when the target was obscured by clouds or smoke. The technique used a single radio beam for the planes to follow. A second beam intersected the first beam at a point directly over the intended target. The navigator would hear a tone that indicated the beams had intersected, and he would release the bomb load. One key advantage was that planes with Gee-H did not carry a bombsight or a bombardier, instead utilizing the navigator for that function; however, one drawback was that Gee-H had a range of about 400 miles, which could only target points in eastern Germany. This became an obstacle late in the war.

In late 1943, the 8th Air Force decided to outfit one squadron with Gee-H navigational bombing equipment. That squadron would provide lead crews for many other bomb groups.[2] The unit they choose was the 329th Bomb Squadron of the 93rd Bomb Group, under the watchful eye of General Timberlake.

Timberlake hung his career on making sure he had the best pilots in the right position for every situation. So he put out a call for the best and brightest pilots to join the retooled 329th Bomb Squadron. Before anyone was chosen, Timberlake had a short list of pilots nominated by unit commanders, and he knew who he wanted. Colonel Terrill, eager to get on Timberlake's good side, nominated Ralph as a "possibility." Timberlake jumped at the opportunity, and Ralph and his entire crew, except the bombardier, were transferred overnight. They started back to school to learn the new system.

★ ★ ★

The 93rd Bomb Group was the oldest B-24 group in the 8th Air Force, flying their first mission on October 9, 1942. Later that year, most of the 93rd was loaned to the newly formed 12th Air Force, operating in North Africa. They were supposed to be there for ten weeks, but ten months later, in February 1943, they finally returned to England. Instead of going back to their original base, they were sent to RAF Hardwick.

RAF Hardwick was much different than RAF Tibenham. The most noticeable difference was that there was no nearby town as the airfield was truly carved out of the English countryside. The town of Hardwick was about two miles to the west and was the only village of any size in the area. There were no nearby landmarks, although there were three patches of woods that were locally historic: Long Wood, Bush Wood, and Spring Wood.

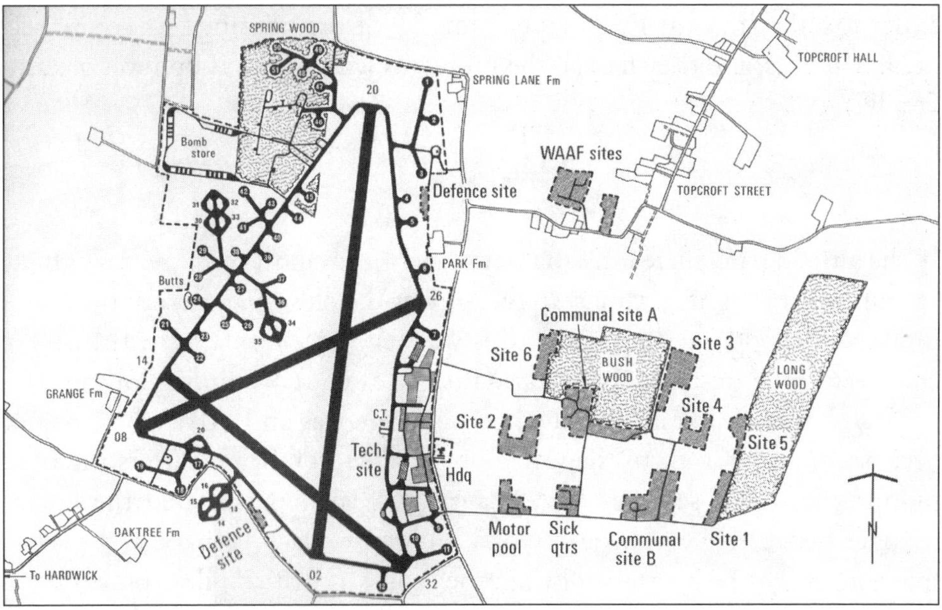

Official RAF "as built" drawing provided to the 8th Air Force of RAF Hardwick, Station 104. Ralph's Nissen hut was originally located in Site 3, but he was moved to other locations later on. Runway 08/26, which runs in a general east-west direction, is about 4,180 feet long or about .8 miles.

As with all of the airfields, Hardwick had three runways that intersected to form a triangle. The airfield featured a total of fifty-one hardstands (forty-one pans and the rest in loops). The main runway ran in a basic north-south direction, but departing aircraft almost always took off heading south. One reason was the direction of the prevailing winds, but the main reason was that about twelve miles north, off the end of the runway, was RAF Horsham St Faith. Any aircraft taking off that experienced handling problems or could not get proper altitude in that distance would interfere with the flight operations at the other airfield. Consequently, most of the time, Hardwick took off heading south and Horsham St Faith took off heading north.

All of the residential and common sites were on the east side of the field. A road, Barondole Lane, separated the business end of the airfield from the residential sites. The residential sites were much more compact and closer together than at RAF Tibenham. All of the housing was comprised of Nissen huts, and they had all the problems with which Ralph was already familiar.

★ ★ ★

The airfield had one feature that set it apart from most of the rest: a lighted runway for night landings. In fact, it was the closest airfield to the English Channel with landing lights. This was very important to the British air crews returning from a mission in a damaged aircraft or running low on fuel.

Ralph was always intrigued whenever there was an RAF night mission, because when he went to the war room or squadron headquarters the next morning he could see that British aircraft of all types littered the grassy triangle between the runways. Not having any place to park and fearful that they might be overtaken by another aircraft, British pilots pulled their planes off the runway and into the grass as soon as they could. These pilots could be transported to their bases immediately, but most waited until after they finished breakfast, admitting that they liked the American breakfast better than their own.

★ ★ ★

Landing at night was a tricky adventure and not one for an apprehensive rookie pilot. First, the radio operator had to tune into the right radio station, called a buncher, which was operated by the local airfield, and request permission to land. The airfield would turn on a set of lights that formed a circle around the airfield. The pilot would follow the lights until he saw a specific set of colored lights. Then he would turn his aircraft in the general direction of the runway and begin his final descent, without actually seeing the airfield. The runway lights would be turned on at the very last moment. While all of this was going on, the aircraft would be continuously challenged and sometimes would be directed to send out a specific colored flare.

Part of Ralph's responsibilities at Hardwick was to test the night landing lights and procedures. About every ten days he would take off after dark, fly out over the English Channel, and return. Keeping the lights operational was extremely important, and if they did not work, Ralph had to land as best he could, then wait for repairs to be made and try it all over again.

★ ★ ★

The headquarters for the 20th Combat Bombardment Wing was officially located at RAF Hardwick. However, the actual location was about two miles to the north, near Topcroft Hall, in a manor house that had been loaned to the RAF for the war effort. General Timberlake and his staff worked and lived in the mansion.

Ralph had a friend, Major Glenn Martin, who was on Timberlake's staff. On nonmission days the two would get together for lunch, taking turns at each other's location. Martin was in charge of Timberlake's operations center, where the general monitored mission progress. On Ralph's first visit to see Martin, Timberlake saw them in the dining room and asked if he could join them. After that, Timberlake joined them quite frequently, and Ralph struck up a casual friendship with the general.

★ ★ ★

All of the aircraft stationed at Hardwick were B-24 Liberators, except for one. The sole exception was a Russian-built Ilyushin Il-2 Sturmovik.

This fighter-type aircraft was part of the Lend-Lease program with Russia. The plane was at Hardwick for General Timberlake's use. Reportedly, Timberlake would follow the bombers as they formed up and kept notes on any stragglers. Ralph never saw the aircraft being flown by the general and doubted that he ever flew it, except for an occasional joyride. Timberlake could monitor everything from the comfort of his own operations center.

The Sturmovik was a curiosity for the bomber pilots. Most had not flown a small fighter-type aircraft since leaving basic training, and on occasion, the bomber pilots were allowed to take the plane up for a check ride. Ralph was as curious as anyone and took his turn at trying to figure out all of the Russian markings. Fortunately, someone had taped some notes on the instrument panel for reference.

★ ★ ★

Moving to Hardwick added a large number of responsibilities to Ralph's schedule. It did not take him very long to figure out that he could not do everything the 93rd asked of him and keep up with all of his own housekeeping chores, specifically, doing his laundry. Laundry facilities were small and sparsely furnished. In 1942, automatic washers were nonexistent; the manual ringer-washer was the norm. The facilities at the 93rd only provided a few ringers but had many washbasins and washboards. Doing laundry was a long and involved process, assuming that facilities were available when you arrived and you did not have to wait.

Ralph began asking around and found that some of the senior officers were taking their laundry to a farmer's wife just outside the main gate. The farmhouse was located across the fence from Ralph's Nissen hut, and one quiet day he wondered over to the farm and introduced himself. He and the farmer hit it off right away. The farmer told him that no Yank who knew anything about farming had come to see him until Ralph walked up the lane.

Every Sunday when Ralph did not fly he would bundle up his laundry and take it to the farmer's wife, picking up his clean laundry before leaving. Afterward, the farmer would invite Ralph into their parlor and the two would drink a glass of homemade Brandywine, a distilled spirit made from wine.

Ralph got a small bottle of Kentucky bourbon from the Officers' Club and took it to the farmer for him to try. After one sip, he screwed up his face, puckered his lips, blew some air out to clear his mouth, and told Ralph how great it was and how much he liked it. Ralph made it a point to keep the farmer stocked with the liquor.

★ ★ ★

The Officers' Club at Hardwick was located in a converted Nissen hut and provided officers with a place to unwind. When it was open, officers could get a scotch, gin, or ale. Periodically, they had Kentucky bourbon from the United States. Majors and above could purchase small bottles of spirits for their own use, although, on occasion, other ranks could be afforded the privilege. The club also provided games and music (either from a record player or from the radio). This photo was taken by the 93rd Bomb Group photographer on November 19, 1944.

Ralph was very busy at the 93rd, but he tended to dramatically understate his schedule in his letters. In addition to being a lead pilot, flying Gee-H-equipped aircraft, he eventually became the operations officer of the 329th Bomb Squadron. This meant that when a mission was planned and the orders came down from the 20th Bomb Wing for a specific number of planes and bomb loads, he worked with the group operations officers to figure out how many aircraft the squadron could provide. Then it was up to Ralph to find crews to put in those aircraft, make sure the planes were mechanically ready, get them loaded, fueled, and off on their mission. All of this was complicated, of course, because Ralph was still flying combat missions as a lead pilot.

★ ★ ★

★ V-Mail ★
February 18, 1944

Dear Mother & Dad,

Just a line to let you know my new address. 93rd Bomb Grp. 329th Sqdn. everything else is just the same. I have been transferred over here to study this new kind of bombing they do thru clouds. I feel very honored as we were one of a very few crews in England selected to go to this school. We probably won't fly any missions for a couple of weeks. This new group is a pretty old group—one of the oldest over here. We have to wear our blouse to the evening meal. I also have another medal—Citation Medal to wear. I'll get a string of them yet. Will write more later.

Love
Ralph.

★ ★ ★

February 21, 1944

Dear Mother & Dad,

As you can see my address has changed. It is a permanent change of station for me and my crew. However, it isn't far from my old station and I will get to see some of my old friends once in a while.

The first navigator, Lt. Howice, I had in Boise is here in this Group. I have also run across a few other fellows I knew back in the states.

The barracks here are the same but the weather is colder as we are closer to the coast. You wouldn't think a 20 min drive would make very much difference in temperature. This is a much older group here and things run pretty smooth. It isn't quite as muddy and everything is a little easier. When we officers moved into our barracks there were already 4 other officers in there.[3] Two of them finished their tour of duty today. They hope they will go home right away but they keep them over here for an extra 3 months duty but not as combat personell.

My radio was out of order for awhile but I took it to the radio shop yesterday and it is OK again now. We can get tubes for American radios in some places but they are rather hard to find.

We had fresh oranges from Spain. Boy they were really good. We very seldom have fresh fruit.

I was all set to take a few snap shots today but the sun didn't shine. I'll catch a good day some time and take a few.

How did the cold wave strike you? I heard the radio say there was lots of snow in the U.S. It hasn't snowed very much here. They say it usually doesn't come until March or April. I will write more later in the week.

Ralph

★ ★ ★

★ V-Mail ★
February 21, 1944

Dear Juana,

It was real pleasant here today until tonight when it started getting cold.

I have my radio fixed so we are enjoying some good music.

We had some fresh oranges from Spain today. We don't have fresh fruit very often.

I guess you know by now my address has changed. Me and the crew are permanently transferred. Charlie Painter didn't come with me they kept him[4] in the 445th. I now have Jack Fiengold as a Bombardier.[5] I have known him since Boise and he is a pretty good fellow. We will be in school for awhile. We are allowed to discuss our work with anyone as it is very secret.[6]

Write Later

Ralph.

★ ★ ★

★ V-Mail ★
February 29, 1944

Dear Juana,

Not much doing for me today so I am taking it kinda easy. I have taken a few pictures in England but haven't had them censored[7] yet. Lt. Painter isn't on my crew any more. We left him at the old Group. I don't think he has ever taken any pictures.[8] As yet I haven't received the magazines but it will take a little time for them to come thru. Well it is about dinner time and that is one thing I can't afford to miss so guess I'd better get going. Will write later on.

Ralph.

★ ★ ★

★ V-Mail ★
March 2, 1944

Dear Juana,

We have been pretty busy the last few days but haven't been on any missions.

We don't get any broadcasts directly from the States only command performance[9] but most of the better programs are re-broadcast to us. We have a movie on the post but they are pretty old. Then there is the electric cinema in town, about 4 of them also two theatres which have plays.

Was it you who asked about my going with the girls over here? I have had a few dates, but you spend most of the time waiting on a street corner or someplace. It is ill mannered to invite a man to your house so you meet them some place. It seems a very silly custom.[10]

Ralph.

★ ★ ★

March 3, 1944

8th Air Force Mission 246 sends 748 bombers deep into Germany. This marks the first mission to targets in Berlin.

★ ★ ★

Lieutenant Colonel George S. Brown was the commander of the 329th Bomb Squadron for a brief period. While there, he was awarded the Silver Star by General Timberlake. Shown here after the ceremony are General Timberlake, Lieutenant Colonel Brown, and Colonel William Robertson, commander of the 93rd Bomb Group. Brown had a storybook career in the Air Corps and the Air Force, eventually serving as the Chairman of the Joint Chiefs of Staff from 1974 to 1978. Note the different styles and colors of the uniforms.

★ V-Mail ★
March 10, 1944

Dear Mother & Dad,

There isn't much to do over here for us today. I took a few snap shots this afternoon. I have bought a developing outfit so I do my own pictures now.[11] All I have to do is have them printed. They turned out real good.

So Ken Strauss is a Major? Is he overseas or still in the U.S?

How did the sectional[12] turn out? I doubt if Wadesville got very far.

We took a bicycle ride around the country side this afternoon and I think it is just about put us all under the weather.

We have a nice warm fire tonight since we got our coal ration[13, 14] yesterday. It sure feels good to have the place nice and warm for a change. I guess this is about all for now.

Love
Ralph.

★ ★ ★

March 12, 1944
Mission 8

8th Air Force Mission 256 sends 52 B-24s to hit V-weapon sites in the Siracourt area of France. One plane is lost.

Ralph led a squadron from the 445th Bomb Group using Gee-H navigational bombing equipment.

★ ★ ★

★ V-Mail ★
March 14, 1944

Dear Juana,

I hardly think I'll be able to speak German as I had to give up the class when I moved over here. But about these art classes of yours. Who do you use as models?

Richmond did about as well as Wadesville in the tournament didn't they.

I think I told you Lt. Painter isn't on my crew anymore? We left him back at the other place.

"Thank your Lucky Stars"[15] is playing in town this week and I think I will go and see it some night. Thanks for the Reader's Digest. About all for now.

Ralph.

★ ★ ★

When Ralph knew he was going on leave, he would plan his itinerary in advance. Here, he is waiting for transport to Norwich to catch a train to London. While waiting, he is perusing a guidebook of sorts.

March 21, 1944
<u>Mission 9</u>

8th Air Force Mission 270 sends 65 B-24s to V-weapon targets at Watten, France. They are escorted by 48 P-47s. There are no losses or casualties.

Ralph was lead pilot for the 382nd Bomb Group and lead the 2nd Air Division for the mission.

★ ★ ★

March 23, 1944

After three months of fierce fighting, attacks and counterattacks, American forces finally break out at Anzio, Italy.

★ ★ ★

March 28, 1944[16]

Dear Mother & Dad,

I just returned from a 3 day pass to London. I went to see a couple of stage plays and took a few snap shots. I hope they turn out good. I am developing my own film now but I have to get the negatives printed in town and they don't get much supplies so it takes a long time.

Next week we get our 7 day leave. I am going to Scotland. You may not get any letters from me during that time. There are just certain places we are allowed to post our letters. We can't mail them thru the British Postal System.

I received your box today with the crackers and stationery. I want to thank you an awfully lot. It is exactly what I wanted. I also had a couple of letters. I also read in the "Stars & Stripes" where Bosse won the state this year.[17] I guess they really celebrated. I also read about the Detroit Tigers training in E'ville.

I'm glad to hear your steers are doing good this year. The weather is really good over here. It has turned a lot warmer. I guess Summer is about here.

Are any of my letters censored? I seem to be getting all of yours. I guess you have noted that my A.P.O. is changed. Every thing else is the same though. I must go to bed now as tomorrow may be a big day.

Love
Ralph.

★ ★ ★

March 30, 1944

Dear Juana,

I received your very nice package today. The crackers are very good—fresh too. The candy is awfully good. I want to thank you a lot. But please—don't send any more chewing gum. I brought over 6 cartons with me and I have more than I know what to do with.

I am developing film tonight. I can't print it though because I can't get the paper. Thanks a lot for the writing paper. We can get Stamped envelopes & Stamps but it is the paper we cant buy.

I just returned from 3 days in London. About all I did was sight see and go to the theatre. I took a few snap shots also. I saw Alfred Lundt & Lynn Fountaine[18] in "There Shall be no Night."[19] It was a rather of a tear Jerker but pretty good. Then I saw Bebe Daniels[20] in "Panama Hattie."[21]

Our 7 day leave starts next week and I want to go to Scotland.

I am getting Time Magazine and I will get the rest in due time I'm sure. I read in our paper over here about the State Finals basket ball games. I guess you noticed my APO is changed to 558 but the rest of the address is the same. Have any of my letters to you been censored?

We haven't been doing much work lately in fact we haven't been doing much of anything. But there isn't much I can write about. Our Sqdn. had a party last night. Fried Chicken, potatoes, peas, coffee, apple pie & ice cream. The pie & ice cream were really a treat. It was the best meal I have had since I have been in England. About all for now.

Ralph

★ ★ ★

March 30, 1944

British Bomber Command sends 795 aircraft to targets at Nuremburg, Germany. About 200 Luftwaffe fighters shoot down 95 RAF bombers, killing 540 men. This becomes the highest single air raid loss in history.

★ ★ ★

April 10, 1944
Mission 10

8th Air Force Mission 295 sends 729 bombers, escorted by 496 fighters to targets in Belgium and France; three bombers and two fighters are lost; 30 men are listed as missing.

Ralph led a squadron of the 467th Bomb Group to hit V-weapon sites at Wizernes, France.

★ ★ ★

April 11, 1944

8th Air Force Mission 298 sends 917 bombers and 819 fighters to production facility targets in northern Germany; 64 bombers are lost. One of the casualties is Ralph's original aircraft, *Sin Ship*, which is shot down over Belgium. Of the ten crew members, four are listed as deceased and six as prisoners of war.[22]

★ ★ ★

Dear Friends,[23]

We received this fine letter from Ralph yesterday.[24] I read it to Marcia and she thought it would be nice to send directly to you. (She & Sandra are feeling all right this morning). Doesn't Ralph write a fine letter? And isn't he good to remember as many of us? We think and talk of him many times daily. Dear Boy May God watch over him. I know he will.

This typed letter is a copy Lula made of his interesting letter to Juana. Thought maybe you would like a copy. We enjoyed Juana's visit so much. All of you come see us. We are all well & love this weather. I wrote Ralph yesterday and sent clippings.

Hope you are all well.

As ever sincerely
Stella Beeler

★ ★ ★

April 12, 1944

Dear Juana,

I have written everyone else and told them something of my trip. In this letter I will try to give a full account and I want you to send it around so every one can read it. So here is my trip—The other three officers on my crew were with me, so when I say we, that is who I mean.

We left on the train to London then we rushed over to another station[25] where we just barely caught our train. It rained most of the way but the train runs close to the coast and we got several good views of the coast line and ocean.

The country is rather hilly and everything was green. We saw lots of sheep and a few cattle, but mostly sheep.

When we arrived in Edinburgh, pronounced Edinborough, it was dark. They have black-outs up there same as England. I had already wired for reservations, so we went straight to the hotel. We were hungry but all we could get was tea and sandwiches, but it helped.

Edinburgh is a beautiful city. It is very old and I guess you would say the architecture is 17th century. The town is very clean and there are many parks and monuments, each dedicated to some famous person.

Princess street is the main street. The observatory is at one end and the Caledonia hotel,[26] where we stayed, is at the other end. On one side of the street is a large park.[27] All the streets leading into Princess street are dead ends. At the end of each street is a monument. There is a very large one dedicated to Sir Walter Scott.

At the end of the street there is a large hill and on top of this hill is the observatory.[28] The only thing unique about this is the decorations. On top is a large cross (H) and on top of the cross rests a ball about the size of a basket ball and every day at 1 PM this ball lifts into the air about 1 ft then comes to rest again.[29] A short ways away there are six stone pillars, the start of a new building. It seems as though when the other observatory was built a local man wanted to build the city an observatory but he ran out of money and all that was built is the six pillars. So now it is the disgrace of Edinburgh, say the natives.

Across the park from Princess St is the Edinburgh Castle. It was built in the 15th century. It is on one of the highest hills in Edinburgh and was built this way so as to defend the city from invaders. Parts of the building are being used as a hospital; the rest has been turned into a museum. The walls are very thick and some of the original cannons are still there.

Several weapons and armor suits are on display there and from the looks of the suits, the men were not very large. From the castle you can see most all the city. When Mary Queen of Scots was in exile she spent a lot of time here.

I don't know if you are up on your history or not but Queen Mary[30] and Queen Elizabeth were cousins. Lord Dudley, Earl of Leicester, was a favorite of Elizabeth but Q. Mary stole him away, as she did most of Elizabeths friends, and married him.[31] Queen Elizabeth and Mary both were equally entitled to the throne. But Q. Elizabeth was very jealous of Mary's good looks, and her way with the men. So she had Mary put in Exile and finally be headed. I read the original letter, in French, that Queen Mary wrote to her brother, King Francis of France, the night before she was be headed. Q. Mary and Lord Dudley had two children one of whom was Charles I,[32] first of the Stuart line kings.[33]

Not far from the castle is another tall hill and an old lady lives in the house at the top. It is called the "Mirror Obscure."[34] There is a mirror on top of a large round table[35] and is lying flat down on the table. By looking in this mirror you can see a reflection of the city and by turning the table you can see the different parts of the city. It is magnified and on a clear day it is uncanny what can be seen. It is almost a wonder of the world.

Another famous place is Holyroodhouse Palace.[36] It is the home of the previous Kings & Queens of Scotland. The present King & Queen of England still live there when they come to Scotland. There are several old paintings in the Palace. The walls are about 7 ft. thick. Q. Mary's bedroom & Lord Dudley's bed rooms are about as they where when they lived there. Lord Dudley[37] lived on the second floor and Q. Mary on the floor above. She had her private stair way from the celler to the roof and a few years ago they discovered a loose stone in the wall of the stairway and upon removing it they found it looked right in to Lord Dudley's bedroom. Trusting soul wasn't she?!!

In one of the rooms is an original tapestry on the wall. It is of two children playing in the street and you are looking down the street. You get squarely in front of the tapestry and you are looking straight down the street. Get to one side and it looks as though you were off to one side. No matter where you get in the room you still look down the street. It is a wonderful piece of work.

I visited several other minor places. Edinburgh University, several monuments and things. As I said before, Edinburgh is a very clean place. I think the people dress a little better up here than they do in England.

They are far more friendly and easier to get along with. The Scots speak more like Americans than anyone I have talked to. The English who speak with an Oxford accent are easy to understand but I think the Scots are also easy to understand.

I saw a lot of the "Ladies from Hell" or the Scots who wear the tartans.[38] Maybe you know that all Scots belong to a clan and each clan has their own tartan and they are very proud of these. Especially the Scots in the Highlands.

We took a bus trip out in the country to a small town at the edge of the highlands. It is very pretty country and next time I want to spend more time in the Highlands. They speak English with a different accent also.

We caught the train back to London and spent the night there. I saw the show "Something for the boys."[39] It was very good.

We were gone 8 days. And I thoroughly enjoyed myself and I want to visit up there some more if I have to opportunity.

I guess I have done all the damage I can today so guess I'll close.

If you have any questions I would be glad to answer them.

Best Wishes
Ralph.

P.S. You won't forget to send this on will you?

I guess I must have over looked this page[40] but here is something of interest.

One evening in Edinburgh we all got dates went to the theatre and then to dinner and dancing.

During the evening June, the girl I was with, and I some how got to the subject of marriage. I asked her why she had never been married and she said that, now, she new so many boys she couldn't make up her mind. So she would wait a few years until all but two of them gave up and then she would marry the first of them who asked her. That way she said she wouldn't have to worry about getting the right one.

She really had it figured out, didn't she?!!!

★ ★ ★

April 14, 1944
Bombay, India

The SS *Fort Stikine*, an American cargo ship, explodes while being unloaded in the harbor. It was carrying 1,395 tons of explosives and gold for the Indian treasury. The explosion destroys ten other ships, killing 500 people and injuring 8,000 more.

★ ★ ★

April 19, 1944
Mission 11

8th Air Force Mission 308 sends bombers to three locations in Germany and one in France. Combined, 799 bombers, escorted by 744 fighters fly the mission; six bombers and two fighters are lost; 114 men are killed or missing.

Ralph led a squadron of the 448th Bomb Group to V-weapon targets at Watten, France.

★ ★ ★

April 21, 1944

Dear Juana,

Well, I am getting my magazines now. I am getting Time. But the rest hasn't started yet. I did get Readers Digest so that makes two that I am getting. I am wondering if you will write and tell them to change my address from 445 Gp. 792 Sqd. APO 634 to 329 SQDN 93rd Grp. APO. 558 (my new address). I hope you have received my letter telling of my trip to Scotland. If you haven't please tell me and I will write another.

It won't be long before School will be over for this year. Will it.

What are you going to do this Summer? Why don't you take a trip some where? Why don't you go to some lake in Minnesota or something like that?[41]

It has been bad weather all day. I have in another two missions. Which I collected last week and can now wear an Oak leaf cluster to my Air Medal.[42]

How do you like working at the USO? Please don't send me any more candy for a while at least. I have quite a bit of it and get a regular ration. We also get juice now. And we most always get some kind of juice for breakfast. Tonight we had steak for supper of course it wasn't the best or largest but it was steak.

About all for now

Ralph.

★ ★ ★

★ V-Mail ★
April 22, 1944

Dear Mother & Dad,

It is raining outside and is a pretty nasty day. I have just returned from a three day pass. I really had a good time. We went up on the Broads[43] which is the same as a lake. We rented a sail boat and tried to sail. I liked it. I also got a sun tan. It was sore for a couple of days then it was OK. Did you get all your garden planted? I sure would like to have a nice dish of straw berries. Have you had any Morels yet? These Vmail letters are making pretty good time over here. Better than I thought. I guess I'd better go eat now

Love
Ralph.

★ ★ ★

April 22, 1944
Norwich

B-24s returning from a mission approach their airfields after dark. Unfamiliar with night landing procedures, the bombers turn on their navigation lights. Unbeknownst to them, Luftwaffe fighters had followed the aircraft back to England and had mixed into the formations. The B-24s became illuminated targets for the Luftwaffe. Local reports estimate that 14 B-24s are shot down or damaged. One crashes in the middle of Daniels Road in Tuckswood. A second attack around 2 a.m. is the result of similar Luftwaffe activity by following returning RAF bombers. Unable to find any RAF aircraft to attack, they turn their attention to other targets of opportunity.

★ ★ ★

April 24, 1944

Dear Mother & Dad,

Not much doing these days in the way of work but there is lots of excitement.

The other night I went into town to see a picture show. Just as I came out it was about dark. It doesn't get dark until about 10 PM. The Air Raid Sirens were blowing. People were running every where trying to get in the Air Raid Shelters. About 2 min later the planes came over. They were rather low and you could see them clearly. The guns started firing at them and the search lights were playing all over the sky. There were a few bombs dropped but not too close to me. But you could feel the ground tremble and see window lights break, etc. By this time the people, especially civilians, were about crazy. Everybody trying to get in cover. People were screaming, crying and carrying on about right. Most all the Yank soldiers, including myself, were out in the middle of the street enjoying the show.

I caught the truck home and just as I stepped out a German plane started strafing our air field. I jumped in the ditch and he made several passes at the field and finally went away. Then about two o'clock that night the raiders came over and started dropping bombs not too far away. Of course I got up to see it. I saw about 2 planes go down. One while I was in town and one later on. There were quite a few crashed around here though. I learned the next day. It was really quite a night but I wouldn't want to experience it every night.

People who have never been in an Air Raid have no idea what it is like. And I must say it isn't exactly safe.[44]

Well, Dad I'm real proud of you. I guess they recognize a good Basket ball coach[45] when they see one. You will have to let me know what kind of a team they intend to build and what tactics they are planning on.

There is more distraction to a fellow writing a letter in this barracks. There are three fellows playing craps. Two more arguing over some silly thing one boy practising on a flute and one reading. I'm trying to write a letter and listening to the radio at the same time. When it gets too bad I just go to bed.

I hope you are all well and feeling good now that summer is almost here.
About all for now.
Sitting ducks

Love
Ralph.

★ ★ ★

April 25, 1944
Mission 12

8th Air Force Mission 317 sends 572 bombers to three locations in France and one in Germany. They are escorted by 759 fighters; seven bombers and two fighters are lost; 75 men are listed as killed or missing.

Ralph led 28 aircraft from the 392nd Bomb Group and led the mission for the 2nd Air Division to hit V-weapon sites at Wizernes, France.

★ ★ ★

April 24, 1944

Dear Juana,

I am getting about all my magazines now. I get the Time & Readers Digest regularily. Then a couple of days ago I got Esquire. Will you please have my address changed on them?

There hasn't been much doing in the way of work.

We go cycling and play volley ball quite a bit.

Summer is practically here. It stays light till about 10 PM and gets light about 5 in the morning.

There isn't much to write about these days so will try and get some more off later.

Ralph

★ ★ ★

April 27, 1944
English Coastal Area

During practice for the invasion of the European Continent called *Operation Tiger*, German *Schnellbootes* sink two landing ships and damage six others, killing over 700 men. As a result of this incident, Hitler orders the reinforcement of defenses in lower Normandy.

★ ★ ★

May 2, 1944

Dear Juana,

Received your letter of Apr 25 today. It made exceptionally good time.

I am glad you could get some of the paper. We can't get it over here. I don't know what size to tell you to send as I want to do some enlarging and I don't know what kind of set up I can work out for that. My negatives are very small and it doesn't do much good to print them unless they are enlarged. I can use the dark room here on the field so I can cut it to size.[46]

You must be mixed up in your geography of England. You were about right where I am. Even so I saw the coast on my way to Edinburgh and Eding'h is on the East coast. I had to go down to London & catch the train. I back tracked a little but was still faster as the fast train from London to Edinburgh makes very few stops & I couldn't make connections any where else.

Just in case you want to send something I will say "Please send me a box of candy." You don't have to send this and please don't send candy as I have plenty but in case you want to send something you will have the request.[47]

All for now

Ralph

Did you hear about the moron who cut a hole in the rug to see the floor show & then sewed it up again because he didn't want to see the whole show.

★ ★ ★

Siracourt, France was a favorite spot for the Germans to hide their V-weapon sites (called "skee sites" by American pilots). It also became the favorite target of the Allies. This picture shows the bomb damage in the Siracourt area (circled) from about 21,000 feet. It was taken on April 30, 1944. Each white dot in the photograph represents a spot where a bomb exploded (8th Air Force reconnaissance photograph).

May 2, 1944
Mission 13

8th Air Force Mission 335 bombs V-weapon sites at Siracourt, France, with 50 B-24s. They were escorted by 102 fighters. There are no losses.

Ralph led a squadron from the 389th Bomb Group.

★ ★ ★

May 3, 1944
<u>Mission 14</u>

8th Air Force Mission 336 returns to V-weapon sites at Wizernes, France, with 51 B-24s and 101 fighters. There are no losses.

Flying his second mission in as many days, Ralph led the 2nd Air Division as lead pilot for the 44th Bomb Group.

★ ★ ★

May 4, 1944[48]

Dear Juana,

I received the developing paper yesterday. It is just fine. Thank you very much. I haven't printed any pictures with it yet because I haven't had time. I have tested it though and believe it will be OK. But I will let you know soon and if it works OK I would like to have you mail me some more but I will let you know.

The size is just fine and I think it will be OK.

Things are rather slow today not much doing. The weather is kinda bad.

Right now I am listening to a British variety show. It is pretty good but I'll take Command Performance any old day of the week.

Your school will be out pretty soon won't it. What are you going to do on your vacation? I would take a trip if I were you.

I will let you know about the paper

Ralph

★ ★ ★

May 5, 1944
Mission 15

8th Air Force Mission 339 sends 46 B-24s, escorted by 52 fighters, to V-weapon sites at Sottevast, France. No aircraft are lost, but four airmen are killed.

Ralph led the mission as lead pilot for the 466th Bomb Group.

★ ★ ★

May 6, 1944
Mission 16

8th Air Force Mission 340 sends 168 bombers and 185 fighters to bomb V-weapon targets in France. All of the B-17s return with their bombs because of cloud cover. There are no losses.

Ralph, as lead pilot for the 93rd Bomb Group, led the B-24s and successfully bombed their target at Siracourt.

★ ★ ★

In the weeks before the invasion, Allied bombers focused on targets in the French coastal area. Here, B-24s from the 330th Bomb Squadron, 93rd Bomb Group hit targets from a low altitude. The English Channel and the coast of England are visible in the background.

May 9, 1944

8th Air Force Mission 347 sends 823 bombers and 668 fighters to targets in France, Belgium and Luxembourg. This marks the beginning of pre-invasion bombing of enemy installations.

★ ★ ★

Mid-May 1944

Supreme Commander of *Operation Overlord*, General Dwight D. Eisenhower, sets June 5, 1944, as D-Day.[49]

★ ★ ★

May 12, 1944

Dear Juana,

Just received your letter of May 4. Reading of all your bad luck I should say you should be glad this isn't Friday the 13th.

I also received a package from you today with the nuts and candy. They were very good. The nuts were real fresh too. More so than I expected.

I have tried the printing paper. It is OK. and the size is just fine. But it is for contact printing. I would like some I could use for enlarging. With the paper like you sent it takes too long in the developer to use it as an enlarging paper. Will you please see if you can get me some Bromide paper suitable for enlarging? If you can will you send me some? It doesn't have to be any certain size and can even be in larger sheets. Just so I can get some that I can use for enlarging.

Now to answer some of your questions—

I don't know off hand what the Wellington Boots[50] are. But I will find out. As near as I can figure out it is some kind of nut or candy.

The Republic Houses[51] are Pubs or Bars,—saloons. It is the drinking place of the common people. Of course you know there are only two classes of people in England. Most everybody but the rich people go to the Pubs. It is not unusual for the children to talk about them because the parents take them in with them while they have a glass of "Mild & Bitters" (beer)—a favorite drink. Pubs are open in most places from 12 noon to 2 PM & from 6—10 PM. It is in these places that the famous game of darts is played. Only they don't play darts like we play them.[52]

Their school system is quite a bit different. They go so long to the County school. Which is the same as our public school. But for each advance they have to take an exam for entrance and so it goes for each successive step on up thru graduation from college.

I don't know what stamp you are talking about. But I am sending a used 10 pence stamp. It cost 10 pence or about 15¢ in out money. The way they write their money signs over here is much different. To write 5 pounds is £5 and they say pound 5. Pence is written D like 10^D pronounced 10 pence. shillings are s like 5^s and pronounced 5 shilling. For the different pieces of money they have a 1 pence piece or penny. It is usually called a "copper." There is a 3 penny piece. Called 3 pence or Thrupenny or Thrupennybit. Then there is the 6 pence or 6 penny piece. It is about the size and equal in value to our dime. Then the shilling equal to about 20¢ and is equal to 2 six pence. Then the two shilling piece or florin. Then the half-crown or two shilling and a sixpence piece. There is also a half penny piece two of which is equal to a penny. They are called Haypenny.

1 shilling is called a "Bob" and 1 pound or 20 shillings is called a "Quid."

21 shillings is a "Guinea." But there is no paper or silver worth this amount.

They have a 10 shilling note or piece of paper. The 1 pound note & the 5 pound note.

Prices are written thus £1-4-7 1 pound, 4 shillings, 7 pence 6-4½ 6 shillings, 4 pence, 1 half pence. Maybe this will straighten you out.[53, 54]

It has been a beautiful day here. The sun was out all day and it was so warm you didn't need a coat. That is pretty warm for over here.

Well, I can't think much to write about so will close,

Cherio & Best Wishes
Ralph

★ ★ ★

May 16, 1944

Dear Mother & Dad,

The weather has been kinda bad the last few days. Last Sat. though it was warm enough for us to take a sun bath and I spent about an hour in my shorts. But today it is cold again and my sweater and my jacket feel pretty good.

We have had steak and ice cream twice this week. Then Sunday I went into town to go to a movie which don't open until 4PM. As I got in about 2 PM I went around to the Officers Red Cross Club to spend the 2 hrs. In between meals they serve grilled cheese and real coca colas. It really tasted good. Now if I could just find a place that had Chocolate Malted Milks I would be alright.

I am sorry to disappoint Bob J. but Jimmy Stewart doesn't have a Bombardier.[55] Stewart may have ridden in the same plane as the boy, on a mission. But Stewart doesn't have a crew of his own.

We get pork to eat most of the time. We get pork chops quite often which don't make me mad. For breakfast we have fresh eggs about twice a week. About twice a week we have hot cakes and the rest of the time we have powdered eggs. There is usually bacon but it is too salty to eat much. We most always have some kind of juice and some kind of cereal, either hot or cold. So we usually have a pretty good breakfast. Our noon meal usually doesn't amount to much but the evening meal is pretty good. Sometimes before supb[56] and get a small glass of beer. Of course this "Mild & Bitter" doesn't taste much like U.S. Beer but the Pale Ale over here is pretty good.

I don't know why but there is no static on the radio over here. It is perfectly clear and the only interference are electric razors which are being used close by.

I see by the paper that both the St Louis teams are doing real well this year.[57] That is something that hasn't happened for a long time.

Well I guess this is about all for now so

Best Wishes & Cherio

Love
Ralph.

★ ★ ★

May 21, 1944

Dear Juana,

You wouldn't know it was Sunday around here. I worked today and I missed my dinner so I wasn't very happy. But tonight we had baked chicken, peas, dressing and all the trimmings.

I wouldn't know where Mrs. Gays daughter is. If you could give me the Hospital no. or something more than A.P.O. I could find out very easily where she is at and could be she is close by here.

The mission number is 30 now to complete a tour of duty instead of 25.

I am getting most of the letters from the U.S. in about 10 to 12 days. They are coming in pretty good time.

The Germans are broadcasting radio programs to us now telling us how nice it is to be back in the states. They play us Bing Crosby[58] records and all the popular recordings. They are trying to play on our nerves but we just enjoy the music but laugh at the rest.

About all for now.

Cherio & Best Wishes

Ralph.

★ ★ ★

May 21, 1944
Mission 17

8th Air Force Mission 360 sends 150 bombers to V-weapon sites in France. They are escorted by 48 fighters. There are no losses.

Ralph led the 467th Bomb Group and the other B-24s to their target at Siracourt.

This mission also sends 617 fighters to strafe targets in Germany. One P-51 pilot reports killing 25 cows.

★ ★ ★

May 22, 1944
Mission 18

8th Air Force Mission 361 bombs targets in Germany and France, using 438 bombers escorted by 568 fighters. Five bombers and seven fighters are lost; 88 men are listed as killed or missing.

Ralph led the 2nd Air Division as lead pilot of the 453rd Bomb Group. They bombed V-weapon facilities at Siracourt and had no losses.

★ ★ ★

June 1, 1944

Dear Juana

There isn't much to write about. Just a few lines to let you know I'm OK.[59]

I guess by the time you get this letter you will be getting ready to leave Richmond. So I won't write anymore letters to Richmond.

We have had a few bright sunny days lately so I managed to get in a couple of sun baths.

I don't get into town much anymore because I don't have much spare time.

There isn't much to write about anymore.

About all I get done anymore is work and a volley ball game now & then. I usually listen to the news over the radio before I go to bed. We get news from the U.S.A. It is re-broadcast over the B.B.C. I always listen to that.

I guess that is about all for now.

Cherio
Ralph.

★ ★ ★

June 2, 1944
Mission 19

8th Air Force Mission 384, in preparation for the invasion, sends 926 bombers to hit V-weapon sites in the Pas de Calais area of France, unescorted. No aircraft are lost, but one airman is killed and another listed as missing.

Ralph led a squadron of the 448th Bomb Group to their target at Beauvoir-Wavans.

★ ★ ★

June 4, 1944

At 0600 hrs (6 a.m.), General Dwight Eisenhower orders that D-Day be postponed until June 6 to allow bad weather to clear.

Allied forces capture Rome.

★ ★ ★

June 6, 1944

The invasion of the European continent begins. Using 6,939 ships, Allied forces land about 160,000 men in one day. This is the largest armada ever assembled.

Mission 20

8th Air Force Mission 395 puts 1,729 bombers in the air, attacking coastal targets and enemy transportation chokepoints in support of the invasion. There is no fighter escort because all available fighters are busy attacking

enemy troop movements. One bomber is lost; 25 men are listed as killed or missing.

Ralph was lead pilot for the 93rd Bomb Group. He was scheduled for a second mission on the same day, but it was cancelled.

★ ★ ★

On the morning of June 6, 1944, nearly 7,000 Allied ships appeared in the mist just off a fifty-mile stretch of the French coastline and began an assault on the European continent. By the end of the day, over 160,000 Allied soldiers had gained a foothold and were prepared to march toward Germany.

The combined air forces of the 8th Air Force, 9th Air Force, and the British RAF placed about 30,000 additional troops on French soil far to the east of the beachhead. These were accomplished by paratroop drops and glider landings. Additionally, all Allied aircraft, almost 11,000, were placed at the disposal of SHAEF[60] to respond to any threat that might arise.

Bomber crews started practicing for the invasion on May 9. In every crossing of the English Channel, pilots, navigators, and bombardiers paid specific attention to the coastline and the first few miles of the interior. None of them knew when, where, or the size of the invasion.[61] During this pre-invasion period, the 8th Air Force flew 46 missions with a total of almost 30,000 sorties.[62] They lost over 400 aircraft and about 3,000 men. In the week before, lead crews flew very light missions or stood down altogether so they could practice new assembly instructions and flying at lower altitudes.

For Ralph and the other bomber crews, June 6 was somewhat of a surprise. At 11 a.m. on June 5, they were briefed on the mission but were also told that there was bad weather holding things up. Because of this, most of the crews did not expect to fly the next day. Ralph was awakened at midnight and told to get to the Mess Hall as fast as possible and get something to eat. He then rushed through getting dressed and ready to fly before attending an abbreviated pilot briefing.

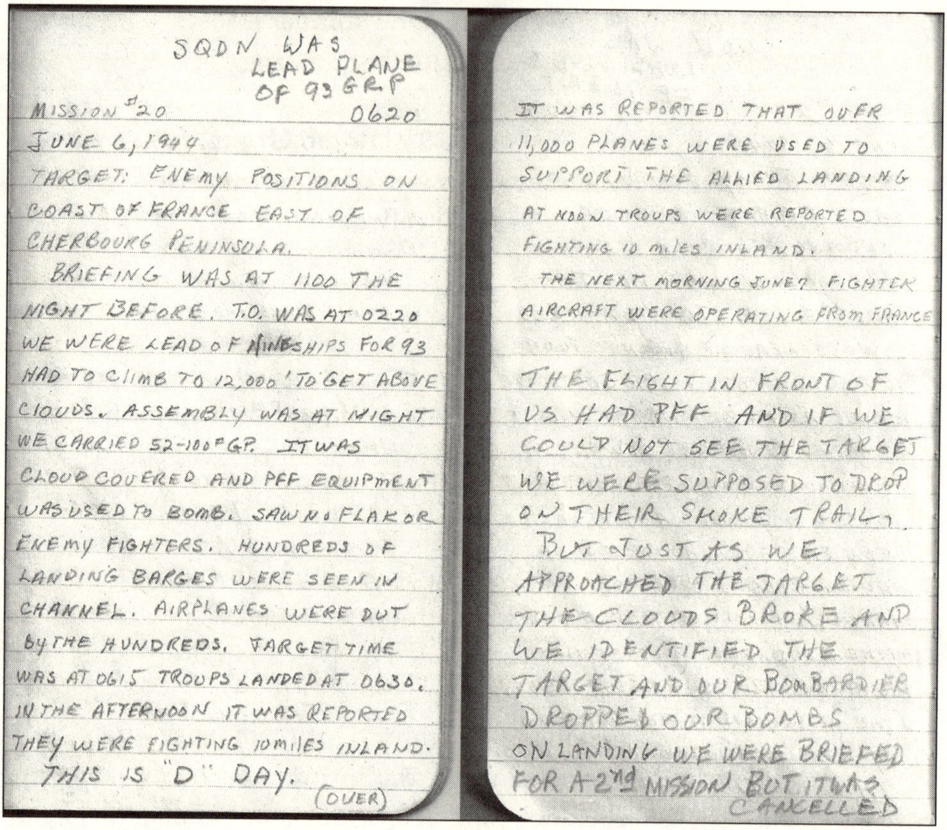

SQDN WAS LEAD PLANE OF 93 GRP

MISSION #20 0620
JUNE 6, 1944
TARGET: ENEMY POSITIONS ON COAST OF FRANCE EAST OF CHERBOURG PENINSULA.
BRIEFING WAS AT 1100 THE NIGHT BEFORE. T.O. WAS AT 0220 WE WERE LEAD OF NINE SHIPS FOR 93 HAD TO CLIMB TO 12,000' TO GET ABOVE CLOUDS. ASSEMBLY WAS AT NIGHT WE CARRIED 52-100# GP. IT WAS CLOUD COVERED AND PFF EQUIPMENT WAS USED TO BOMB. SAW NO FLAK OR ENEMY FIGHTERS. HUNDREDS OF LANDING BARGES WERE SEEN IN CHANNEL. AIRPLANES WERE OUT BY THE HUNDREDS. TARGET TIME WAS AT 0615 TROUPS LANDED AT 0630. IN THE AFTERNOON IT WAS REPORTED THEY WERE FIGHTING 10 MILES INLAND.
THIS IS "D" DAY. (OVER)

IT WAS REPORTED THAT OVER 11,000 PLANES WERE USED TO SUPPORT THE ALLIED LANDING AT NOON TROUPS WERE REPORTED FIGHTING 10 MILES INLAND.
THE NEXT MORNING JUNE 7 FIGHTER AIRCRAFT WERE OPERATING FROM FRANCE

THE FLIGHT IN FRONT OF US HAD PFF AND IF WE COULD NOT SEE THE TARGET WE WERE SUPPOSED TO DROP ON THEIR SMOKE TRAIL.
BUT JUST AS WE APPROACHED THE TARGET THE CLOUDS BROKE AND WE IDENTIFIED THE TARGET AND OUR BOMBARDIER DROPPED OUR BOMBS
ON LANDING WE WERE BRIEFED FOR A 2nd MISSION BUT IT WAS CANCELLED

Ralph kept a personal pilot logbook, which became a diary, where he documented all of his flights. Here he describes his mission on D-Day. At the top of the page, he writes he was lead pilot and the flight took six hours and twenty minutes (0620). Logbook entries were always made after the mission, and sometimes it took several days to recall everything.

Their targets were transportation chokepoints east of the Cherbourg peninsula. They would have two opportunities—one in the early morning and one immediately after that. Timing was crucial; they had to be directly over the English Channel, approaching the coastline at dawn, and instead of flying at over 20,000 feet, Ralph would lead his group at 9,000 feet. The last words of the briefing were that they would have two chances at their target, but everyone was counting on them hitting it in the first pass.[63]

They took off at 2:20 a.m. and met up with the larger formation as scheduled. There were many miracles that occurred during the Invasion of Normandy, and one of them was during the assembly of the 1,729 aircraft.

The 8th Air Force almost always flew during daylight hours, so forming up at night was an extreme challenge. In the chaos over the English Channel, it was indeed a miracle that no aircraft collided during this phase of the invasion.[64]

In the early morning light, Ralph could see the ships waiting to begin their assault.[65] He could see the troop landing ships[66] circling around their transports, waiting for the signal.

Ralph's targets were a railroad switching yard and a nearby highway and bridge. Cloud cover forced him to take his group to 12,000 feet, where the targets still looked so close that he could almost hand deliver the bombs one at a time. They did not have Gee-H for this mission and had to rely on another aircraft equipped with Pathfinder equipment (PFF). The bombardier found the target and dropped his plane's load. All of the other aircraft in his group followed his cue.

As Ralph turned to head home, he was surprised to see Allied reconnaissance aircraft following them. The smoke had not yet cleared, and they were already taking pictures for bomb damage assessment. Within minutes, those aircraft passed his group on their way back to England. Another minute passed before he saw C-47 Gooney Birds[67] taking paratroops into the area they had just bombed. Ralph knew that if they did not get their target the first time, then they needed to get back as fast as possible.

At RAF Hardwick, they were briefed for the next mission and instructed to remain with their aircraft while it was refueled and armed with more bombs. When that was done, everyone climbed back into their aircraft and waited for the signal to start their engines. There they sat . . . waiting. Finally, the word came to stand down and return to the Mess Hall. The reconnaissance photos showed that the railroad interchange was completely disabled, the highway was badly damaged, and the bridge was destroyed. There was no necessity to return; however, they were required to remain on alert in case they were needed later in the day.

When all was said and done, all Ralph could say was that it was a very Big Show.[68]

★ ★ ★

"The best way I can describe this vast armada and the frantic urgency of the traffic is to suggest that you visualize New York city on its busiest day of the year and then just enlarge that scene until it takes in all the ocean the human eye can reach clear around the horizon and over the horizon. There are dozens of times that many."[69]

★ ★ ★

NOTES

1. Beginning of the prayer "Let Our Hearts Be Stout," written by President Franklin Delano Roosevelt and delivered by him on the radio on the evening of D-Day, June 6, 1944.

2. When Gee-H-equipped planes led a mission for another bomb group, the lead pilot sat in the left seat (pilot's seat), and the bomb group's senior pilot for that mission would sit in the right seat as copilot.

3. There were eight men assigned to the hut, two to a room, with a single shared "living room."

4. Lieutenant Charles Painter was widely considered as the best bombardier in the 445th Bomb Group. His departure would have left a big void in their capabilities. Ralph was told that he would not need a bombardier with the new equipment, and there was no reason for Painter to go. Consequently, Painter went to the next most senior lead crew.

5. Even though Gee-H did not require a bombardier, Ralph was given one just in case he needed to lead a mission beyond the 400-mile limit.

6. This was a misstatement. He probably meant to say that he could *not* discuss his work. Surprisingly, this line should have been redacted by the censor.

7. Photographs that were not censored prior to mailing could be confiscated and destroyed during the censoring process. It was best to have them censored beforehand; therefore, any photographs that were deemed unacceptable could be saved until after the war. However, there were some subjects that could cause a photograph to be confiscated during the preapproval.

8. Apparently, Lieutenant Painter had corresponded with Juana, perhaps providing her with some information she could share with her students. She must have asked Ralph for a picture of him.

9. *Command Performance* was a radio program that was broadcast between 1942 and 1949 on the Armed Forces Radio Network. A shortwave transmission was provided for the troops without commercial radios. It was never broadcast in the United States over domestic radio stations. The format allowed troops to send requests for particular performers or programs, and they could also suggested unusual ideas for music and sketches, such as Ann Miller tap dancing in military boots. All of the top performers of the day appeared,

including Fred Allen, the Andrews Sisters, Jack Benny, Judy Garland, Bob Hope, Ginger Rogers, and Frank Sinatra.

10. In some cases, living conditions and other hardships were embarrassing for the British. As a result, it was not unusual for a social outing to start at a meeting place rather than at someone's home.

11. Getting film developed was a problem for the American military in England. Film was hard to obtain. Rolls were usually packaged for only eight pictures, and it could take a long time to get them developed because of the shortage of chemicals and paper. By developing his own film, he could get prints just for the pictures he wanted. In most cases, he could only get "mini" prints, which measured about one inch square.

12. This is in reference to the Sectional Playoffs, part of the Indiana High School Basketball Tournament.

13. Coal was rationed in England to everyone, including the US military, starting in July 1941, not because of any shortage, but because so many miners had been called up and there were fewer to work in the mines.

14. By 1944, England was rationing gasoline, electricity, eggs, meat, butter, margarine, sugar, tea, jam, cheese, clothing, coal, rice, dried fruit, soap, canned tomatoes and peas, sweets, chocolate, and biscuits. Presenting a ration coupon only allowed one to make a purchase; he or she still had to pay the retail price.

15. *Thank Your Lucks Stars* was a comedy about two producers trying to put together a wartime charity show. It starred Eddie Cantor, Dennis Morgan, and Humphrey Bogart, with appearances by most of what was left of Hollywood, including Bette Davis, Olivia de Havilland, and Errol Flynn. All of the actors played themselves.

16. Included in this letter was a poem, "A Toast to 'Little Friends,'" from the *Stars and Stripes*, which is shown in Appendix B.

17. Evansville Bosse (pronounced "bossy"), coached by Herm Keller, completed a 19-7 season, by beating Kokomo, coached by Ralph King, for the state championship, with a score of 39-35. The game was played in the New Coliseum at the Indiana State Fairgrounds in Indianapolis.

18. Alfred Lunt (1892–1977) was an American actor and stage director who appeared in film, television, and over twenty Broadway plays in the course of his distinguished career. Lynn Fontaine (1887–1983) was a British actress and major stage star in the United States for over forty years. They were husband and wife and often appeared together. In 1964, they were presented with the Presidential Medal of Freedom. The Lunt-Fontaine Theater on Broadway is named in their honor.

19. *There Shall Be No Night* played at the Aldwych Theatre. Written by American playwright Robert E. Sherwood and set in Finland between 1938 and 1940, the play tells the story of a scientist and his American-born wife as they deal with the impending Russian invasion. The play was awarded a Pulitzer Prize for Drama in 1941. Lunt and Fontaine were in the original cast when it opened at the Alvin Theatre (now the Neil Simon Theater) on Broadway on August 29, 1940.

20. Bebe Daniels (1901–1971) was an American actress. She began her career as a child doing silent films. She went on to star in musicals like *42nd Street* and gained fame as a radio and television personality in Britain.

21. *Panama Hattie* at the Piccadilly Theatre was a musical comedy, with songs by Cole Porter. It starred Bebe Daniels, Max Wall, Ivan Brandt, Claude Hulbert, and Richard Hearne. In a previous letter, Ralph mentioned that he wanted to see one play in particular the next time he was in London. No doubt, this was the play he had in mind because he loved Porter's music, and more importantly, Cole Porter was from Indiana.

22. Missing Aircrew Report #3828, which documents the incident, is dated April 12. On April 12, Mission 300 dispatched bombers to central Germany, and no B-24s were shot down. The report is dated the day after the raid.

23. This was sent to Rolla and Jessie.

24. This is in reference to the following letter, dated April 12, 1944.

25. This was probably St. Pancras and King's Cross stations.

26. The Caledonian Hotel was built in 1903 by the Caledonian Railway Company and is made out of red sandstone from western Scotland. It was originally built above the main entrance to the Caledonian Railway Station, which is now closed. The hotel underwent a multimillion dollar renovation and is now part of the Hilton Hotel chain.

27. This is in reference to the Princess Street Gardens.

28. The City Observatory has a long and colorful history dating back to 1736. The main purpose of the observatory was to provide accurate time for watchmakers and mariners.

29. In 1854, a "time ball" was installed on Nelson's Monument, which is adjacent to the City Observatory. The time ball was originally controlled by electrical pulses from the observatory clock. Today the time ball has become a tourist attraction and is manually operated.

30. This is in reference to Mary, Queen of Scots.

31. Actually, Robert Dudley refused to marry her. Instead, Mary was married to Lord Henry Stewart Darnley.

32. This was actually James I.

33. This is a very short explanation and somewhat inaccurate. The actual story is very complicated, and it is easy to become confused with all the names. However, the folks back home probably did not know the difference, and Ralph came across as a very intelligent person.

34. The camera obscura was established by Maria Short in the early 1850s. Maria was the daughter of Thomas Short, who established the City Observatory.

35. This may have been a mirror in 1944, or it may have looked like a mirror to Ralph. In any event, it was a light surface that reflected the images of the camera obscura.

36. The actual name is the Palace of Holyroodhouse or Holyrood Palace.

37. This should have referred to Lord Darnley.

38. Ralph is using the "Ladies from Hell" to describe any man wearing a kilt. The actual Ladies from Hell is the Black Watch, 3rd Battalion, Royal Regiment of Scotland. Their tartan is the Black Watch (plaid).

39. *Something for the Boys* played at the Coliseum at Charing Cross. It was a musical comedy starring Evelyn Dall, with music and lyrics by Cole Porter. This musical was strictly for the American audience, with scenes at locations like the "Alamo Plaza," Kelly Field, and an "Army Plane."

40. Ralph's letters were almost always written on both sides of the paper. He forgot to do so on this page until after he had finished the letter.

41. In the course of the winter, Juana and Punch decided to go their separate ways. The upcoming summer would be the first in a long time that Juana would spend alone. Living most of the year in Richmond, Juana did not have very many friends left in Wadesville or Evansville. Ralph wanted to encourage her to travel and see the country.

42. Instead of continuing to award the entire Air Medal for every five missions, recipients would add an oak leaf cluster to the original ribbon, thus signifying multiple awards.

43. The Broads is a group of rivers, lakes, and recreation facilities located in Norfolk and Suffolk counties not far from Hardwick. Some portions of the Broads were as close as fifteen miles from the airfield.

44. This is in reference to the raid of April 22. As no bombs were dropped, what Ralph felt was either the antiaircraft guns firing into the sky or a B-24 that crashed in the middle of Daniels Road in Tuckswood.

45. With the shortage of men in the United States, older men and women were asked to fill in wherever they could. Rolla was asked to be a "volunteer" basketball coach for Wadesville High School. There were several men in the community who helped out until the war was over.

46. The 93rd Bomb Group maintained a darkroom with developing and enlarging equipment. It was intended to provide General Timberlake and the 93rd's war planners with photo reconnaissance, but Ralph got permission to use the equipment during off-hours.

47. D-Day was about a month away, and the US Department of War knew how difficult it would be to get mail to the troops. At this point, the number of troops in England already made mail delivery very difficult, and all of the packages made things even worse. As part of the planning process, they started to crack down on the number of packages sent to England. Post offices and parcel post stations in the United States were asked to discourage folks from sending parcels to England unless the individual had specifically asked for something. No proof was necessary. Here Ralph provides the request.

48. Enclosed with this letter was a copy of *Warweek Newspaper*, dated May 4, 1944.

49. To military planners, D-Day is a future point in time when something is scheduled to happen. It is from this point that all backdating and scheduling occurs. H-Hour is a similar point in time used for the same scheduling.

50. Wellington boots are rubber boots that are designed to look like a leather boot of the nineteenth century. Field Marshal Arthur Wellesley, the 1st Duke of Wellington,

popularized them among British aristocracy. More common names for these boots are muckboots, gummies, gumboots, sheepboots, barnboots, and rainboots.

51. This should have referenced public houses.

52. Ralph was not a pub crawler. In later years, he would recall that he only went to the local pub two or three times while he was in England. He much preferred the theater and movies, so any reference to what went on in the pubs came from his roommates.

53. In 1971, the British decimalized their currency so that one pound equals one hundred new pennies. All other coinage was discarded.

54. This is a playful jab at Juana. He knew she would have a hard time following this explanation. You can almost see the smile on his face as he wrote the words.

55. Finally, Ralph learned to spell "bombardier."

56. This is the Officers' Club located in one of the communal sites, which is not to be confused with the Red Cross Officers' Club in Norwich.

57. It is very early in the baseball season, but by the end of September, the St. Louis Browns had the best record in the American League at 89 wins and 65 losses. The St. Louis Cardinals had the best record in the National League with 105 wins and 49 losses. They played each other in the World Series, with the Cardinals besting the Browns for the title, four games to two. Had the war not started and Ralph not joined the US Air Corps, he may have been playing for the Cardinals—something he would comment on in his later years.

58. Bing Crosby (1903–1977) was an American recording star and actor, whose bass-baritone voice made him one of the most popular artists of his time. During the war, he recorded his biggest hit ever, Irving Berlin's "White Christmas", which he introduced in a radio broadcast during the 1942 Christmas season and again in the movie *Holiday Inn*.

59. As a lead crew pilot, Ralph would have seen the upcoming mission schedule. Because of the number of scheduled missions and the obvious troop movements that had been going on within England, Ralph must have known something big was about to happen. This letter could have possibly been his last, and he may have wanted to say hello to his family. Repeated references to his work were a way of letting them know.

60. This is reference to the Supreme Headquarters Allied Expeditionary Force, the office of the commander of all Allied forces in northwest Europe.

61. The actual location was so closely held that many of the soldiers landing on the beaches had no idea where they were.

62. As used in the military, a sortie refers to an individual aircraft taking off specifically to engage the enemy. For example, thirty B-24s taking off to fly a mission represents thirty sorties. Sorties only count take-offs and an aircraft does not need to return for its sortie to be counted.

63. This was typical 93rd Bombardment Group bravado.

64. In later years, Ralph recalled that pilots got confused as to where they were. There were planes all over the place, flying at every altitude and in every direction. Things were so chaotic that some squadrons could not find their lead aircraft and failed to attack any target.

Records indicate that only four aircraft from the 9th Air Force were involved in midair collisions in two separate incidents.

65. Ralph would later say that all the ships looked like stepping stones in a brook, as though one could hop on them from one shore to the other.

66. Many of the LSTs (*Landing Ship, Tank*) used in the invasion were manufactured in Evansville, Indiana, and floated to New Orleans. The LST was so important to the war effort that Evansville has established an LST memorial on its waterfront.

67. The Douglas C-47 is the military version of the DC-3 airliner. Originally named "Skytrain," it was also known as "Dakota." But to the enlisted men who rode in them and the men who flew them, they were more affectionately known as "Gooney Birds." The C-47/DC-3 is the fourth most produced aircraft in the world (behind the Polikarpov Po-2 Mule, the Ilyushin Il-2 Sturmovik, and the Messerschmitt Bf 109), with over 28,000 being produced. This aircraft has appeared in every war between World War II and the Vietnam War, has been flown by almost every country in the world, and many are still in service today.

68. The "Big Show" was what everyone in England called the invasion before the press latched onto the phrase "D-Day."

69. Ernie Pyle on preparations to invade Normandy.

Chapter 9

FRENCH FOLLIES AND THE BROADS

★ ★ ★

"Now, that's the thing we have got to avoid in this country. The war isn't over by any means. This operation isn't over. You don't just land on a beach and walk through—if you land successfully without breaking your leg—walk through to Berlin. And the quicker this country understands it the better. Again, a question of learning a little geography."[1]

Early in the war, the 9th Air Force had been operating in the eastern Mediterranean and later was a dominating force in the invasion of Sicily. Because they had almost all of the expertise in airborne assaults and invasions, they were the most likely organization to lead the airborne operations during *Operation Overlord*, under General Eisenhower's purview. They began arriving in England in October 1943, with headquarters officially established on November 1, at Sunninghill.[2] When they arrived in England, all of their B-17s and B-24s were transferred to the 8th Air Force in return for the 8th's B-26 Marauders,[3] C-46 Commandos,[4] and C-47 Gooney Birds.

By June 6, 1944, the 9th Air Force had become the largest tactical Air Force ever assembled. Including the additional aircraft transferred from the 8th Air Force, the 9th Air Force was comprised of about 1,500 operational units with around 3,500 aircraft and a force of 250,000 men. Their major components included medium bombers, fighters for ground support, and aircraft to deliver airborne troops and equipment, as well as their own command infrastructure.

★ ★ ★

For the 8th Air Force and the 9th Air Force, the war had two distinct and separate directions. The 8th Air Force continued to support the invasion until it became clear that the mission had shifted from the invasion phase to the ground-war phase. After that, the 8th resumed bombing the Nazi war infrastructure to slow down the production of war matériel and hamper their ability to resupply and wage war. The 9th Air Force supported only the troops on the ground, providing them with air cover and keeping them in full supply of everything and anything they needed. On occasion, however, the two organizations helped the other, depending on the necessity.

On a daily basis, the 9th Air Force was bombing targets just in front of the ground troops, and then providing fighter support to suppress enemy advances. These tactical missions were flown at lower altitudes. Above them was the 8th Air Force and British Bomber Command, flying to strategic targets deep into Germany or over France at twenty thousand feet or more. It would be an understatement to say that coordination was all-important.[5]

★ ★ ★

While the 8th Air Force's mission had not changed, there was a new degree of urgency. Now that the Allies had troops on the ground, it was imperative that the war draw to a close as fast as possible. The longer it took, the more lives would be lost.

For Ralph and the 93rd Bomb Group, there was no time to waste. Missions were scheduled at every available opportunity. Some missions were scheduled even if weather would have previously kept them on the ground.

With Gee-H, as long as a plane could get airborne, they could be scheduled for a mission . . . and somehow, they would be able to see the ground when they returned home.

★ ★ ★

June 8, 1944
Mission 21

8th Air Force Mission 400 sends 1,178 bombers and 1,353 fighters to hit targets in France in an effort to isolate forward German positions and to prevent Luftwaffe support. Three bombers and two fighters are lost; 58 men are killed or missing.

As lead pilot for the 458th Bomb Group, Ralph led the 2nd Air Division to bomb the railroad yard at Pontaubault in western France.

★ ★ ★

June 11, 1944
Mission 22

8th Air Force Mission 405 puts 1,055 bombers and 914 fighters in the air to bomb targets in Germany. Bad weather, at the last minute, forces the mission to move to secondary targets in France. Three bombers and eight fighters are lost; 25 men are killed or missing.

Ralph was lead pilot for the 389th Bomb Group and lead the 20th Combat Wing to bomb eight airfields near Paris.

★ ★ ★

June 12, 1944
<u>Mission 23</u>

8th Air Force Mission 407 dispatches 1,442 bombers to airfields and landing grounds in northeastern France and bridges on the Brest Peninsula. They are escorted by 515 fighters. Eight bombers and seven fighters were lost; 72 men are killed or missing.

As lead pilot for the 445th Bomb Group, Ralph led the 20th Combat Wing to hit railroad bridges at Rennes.

★ ★ ★

June 13, 1944
<u>Mission 24</u>

8th Air Force Mission 410 sends 372 bombers, escorted by 233 fighters, to several targets in northern France. Two bombers and one fighter are lost; 11 men are listed as killed or missing.

Ralph was lead pilot for the 445th Bomb Group leading the 20th Combat Wing to hit the railroad bridge at Dinan.

★ ★ ★

June 14, 1944

Dear Mother, Dad & Juana,

I hope by now you are getting my letters.

What probably happened is they held all letters up until after the "big show."

I got a letter from Marcia & Juana today also. I got your Vmail of June 5 today.

There isn't much to tell except that I have been working like the very devil.

I think I have had about 10 hrs sleep the last 5 days. But last night I got back from our mission about 1030 PM and haven't had anything to do all day. So I had a good nights rest.

It never gets very dark here now. At 1230 past midnight the sky is still light and about 2 AM the sun starts coming up.

How are the crops doing this year?

I was standing in our equipment room a couple of mornings ago about 3 AM getting my clothes on for a mission and a fellow came up to me and inquired if I knew where a certain airplane was parked. I had to look twice to believe my eyes—it was Ken Strauss.[6] He is stationed just a few miles from me. We had a nice little chat after the mission. One of our planes was leading his group on the mission and he had come over here to ride in that plane. I was really surprised.

Ralph.

★ ★ ★

June 15, 1944

American B-29 Superfortresses bomb Japan for the first time since the Doolittle Raid of April 18, 1942.

★ ★ ★

June 16, 1944
Mission 25

8th Air Force Mission 416 sends 370 bombers, escorted by 425 fighters, to airfields and V-weapon supply sites in France. One bomber is lost; seven men are listed as killed or missing.

Ralph was lead pilot for the 448th Bomb Group and led the 2nd Air Division to bomb a storage area at Renescure.

★ ★ ★

June 17, 1944
Mission 26

8th Air Force Mission 418 dispatches 332 bombers to airfields in France. They are escorted by 429 fighters. Two bombers and one fighter are lost; 23 men are listed as missing.

As lead pilot for the 445th Bomb Group, Ralph led the 20th Combat Wing to bomb the Bretigny Airfield near Paris.

★ ★ ★

June 18, 1944
Mission 27

8th Air Force Mission 421 puts 1,378 bombers in the air to hit targets in northern Germany and France. They are escorted by 585 fighters. Eleven bombers are lost; 110 men are killed or missing.

Ralph was lead pilot for the 467th Bomb Group and led the 20th Combat Wing to hit V-weapon sites at Watten, France.

★ ★ ★

Ralph was flying this plane while on a mission to bomb German positions with incendiary bombs. All of the 329th Bomb Squadron lead planes had red noses. Clearly visible here is the extra armor plate added to help protect the pilot. Also visible is a radome that replaced the ball turret. It housed radar equipment for H2X, a self-contained radar bombing system, often called Pathfinder or PFF. This aircraft is equipped with both Gee-H and Pathfinder.

June 19, 1944

The US Navy prevails in the Battle of the Philippine Sea, sinking three Japanese aircraft carriers and damaging two others. In two days of fighting, US Navy fliers destroy 426 of Japan's 473 aircraft.

Missions 28 and 29

8th Air Force Mission 424 sends crews flying back-to-back missions on the same day to the same targets. In the morning, 703 bombers hit V-weapon sites in the Pas de Calais region. After landing, airworthy aircraft are serviced and then returned to hit the same target as in the morning. 366 fighters provide escort in the morning, and surviving aircraft fly escort in the afternoon. One B-24 is lost with its crew of ten listed as missing.

In both missions, Ralph was lead pilot for the 44th Bomb Group and led the 20th Combat Wing to their target at Autheux.

★ ★ ★

June 20, 1944
Mission 30

8th Air Force Mission 425 dispatches 1,548 bombers and 762 fighters to 14 targets in northern Germany and V-weapon sites in France. Forty-nine bombers and seven fighters are lost; 457 men were listed as killed or missing.

Fittingly, for his thirtieth mission, Ralph was lead pilot for his original group, the 445th Bomb Group, leading the 20th Combat Wing to the V-weapons target at the St. Martin Airfield near Bernay.

★ ★ ★

June 20, 1944

Dear Mother, Dad & Juana,

I guess by this time you are getting my letters. At least I hope so. Your mail is coming thru pretty good. I received a package from Juana today with the cheese & Ritz. It was mailed May 20. I want to thank you a lot. It really comes in handy when the food at the mess hall isn't so good.

Today I finished my thirtieth (30) mission today. It is all I have to do I hope. I can be relieved if they can get a crew to take my place. We really had it tough today. Lots of flak. And it was very accurate. We had 2 engines knocked out and lots of holes in the plane. However no one was hurt. You talk about "sweating it out." I was really worried. I just hope we don't have more to do. I have flown 12 missions this month and one day I flew 2 missions. I haven't had enough sleep to keep a dog alive. We are just walking around groggy. But I got in some sleep this afternoon and I feel pretty good right now. I will get some more sleep tonight.

I wish you folks could get some of the rain we have been having. It hasn't rained a lot but it drizzeles most of the day. The farmer who lives right back of our hut here cut some hay about 2 weeks ago but it hasn't been dry enough to take up. They don't raise corn in this section but they do have some kind of wheat.

Well I guess this about all for now. I will write more in a couple of days and let you know all the news.

Love
Ralph

Thanks again for the package.

★ ★ ★

Flak (anti-aircraft bursts) was considered the worst weapon the Germans employed against Allied bombers. This was after Ralph's thirtieth mission, where flak had severely damaged the right rear tail. As a tribute to the maintenance crews who would work all night on damaged aircraft, this plane was repaired and ready to fly the next morning. Notice that the rear of this plane is supported by a sawhorse, a normal situation for empty B-24s.

June 1944

During the month of June, Germany launches 2,452 V-1 Buzz Bombs toward England. The first V-1 bomb lands in Norwich on June 26, with no casualties or damage reported.

★ ★ ★

July 5, 1944

Dear Mother, Dad & Juana,

Well another day has passed. It was real pretty over here today. The sun shined all day and it was pretty warm. The farmer is cutting the hay in the field right back of our hut and it really smells good.

I guess by now my money has gotten there. At least it should be. I suppose my monthly allotment is in also.

Well. How did the wedding go? How long were you in T.H.?[7]

So Margie Dean's husband is still a private? That doesn't give her much money to live on does it?

I finished the pictures myself. But they have taken our enlarger away so I have no way to enlarge any more of my pictures. But I'll try to get some more made.

Is my mail coming thru all OK now? I get mail from the states in about 12 days. It is a little slower that it was.

Just listening to the Bob Hope[8] show—re-broadcast by B.B.C. I really enjoy it.

I still get the Evansville Courier, Life, Readers Digest, Sat. Eve. Post and Esquire. The magazines over here aren't any too sharp. Some of their books are OK but most of them are about murder mysteries.

I have moved up to a new barracks now and I have a small room all of my own. I have a bed, an easy chair, bureau and table. Also a small stove to keep it warm. It is a corner room with 3 windows. I am quite proud of it too.

Every body went out and shot flares yesterday.[9] Most everybody shot a clip of bullets in their pistol too. The English didn't appreciate our celebration but we liked it.

Love
Ralph.

★ ★ ★

Keeping morale high was a serious problem, especially after the invasion. To assist in this area, the 93rd Bomb Group formed a post band, shown here. As the war wound down, they performed almost daily, taking requests from the audience. They had a lot of musicians but not enough instruments for everyone. At every concert more musicians showed up than they could accommodate, hence the spare musician sitting next to the piano in front of the drums.

July 16, 1944
Norwich

Because of V-weapon activity in London, plans are introduced to evacuate 2,500 women and children to Norwich. The first group of 400 arrives.

★ ★ ★

July 21, 1944

Japanese Prime Minister Hideki Tōjō resigns and the United States Marines land on Guam.

★ ★ ★

August 12, 1944[10]

Dear Mother, Dad & Juana,

Well this won't be much of a letter because there is nothing much to write. When I do nothing but work it makes it very difficult to write because I can't write about my work.

I'm sorry to hear about Bob Wendworth. Some people just seem to have tough luck. Who was his wife? I remember you writing he was married but I forgot to who.

What do you hear from Maurice? Has he been made a Commanding General yet?

I sure wish I was there to help you eat some of that Watermelon. They don't have melon over here. You can get most any other fruit over here though. The apples are pretty good. The oranges come from Spain and most of them are Blood Oranges. They have red meat just like "pink" Grapefruit. Then we get lots of tangerines from Africa. The only trouble is fruit is rationed and we don't get it very much.

About all for now.

Love
Ralph.

★ ★ ★

September 2, 1944

Dear Mother, Dad & Juana,

Another quite Saturday evening with nothing much to do but listen to the radio. So will try to get caught up on my letters. I guess you are wondering why I haven't written for a few days. The fact is I have just returned from France after a brief stay.[11] I can't tell you much about by trip. Except you can't beat those French people. We landed at this airport just a few miles behind the lines. Heavy shelling was going on just a little ways from us. The French came to look at our plane and seemed to pay no attention to the heavy explosions at all. I enjoyed the trip a lot and only wish I could have stayed longer.

It has turned cold here and I guess winter is ready to set in.

I don't want you folks to send me a lot off stuff because it will be just that much more for me to carry around and I promise I won't feel hurt if I don't get any presents.

I guess this is about all I can think of and please don't worry if you don't hear from me as I may be moving some of these days.[12] At least I hope so.

Well Cherio for now

Love
Ralph.

★ ★ ★

September 8, 1944

The first German V-2 rocket, launched from Walcheren Island, Holland, lands in London, killing three and injuring 20. The crater is 40 feet across and 20 feet deep.

The British government cancels further evacuation from London to Norwich. During the year, 3,557 women and children were evacuated.

★ ★ ★

September 11, 1944

Allied ground forces cross into Germany.

★ ★ ★

September 16, 1944

Dear Juana,

I'm afraid this will just be a short note but I wanted to get a letter off to you before I went on leave. I am getting five days.[13] I don't know where I will go as yet but I imagine I will go to London for a couple of days then to the West Coast some where.

I can't imagine George Ann Moye[14] Married. The last time I saw her she wasn't even in High School. You asked if School had started in England. School has been going on all the time. It never stops. It is different than we have back home. It's rather hard to explain but I will tell you all about it some time.

By the way,—*please don't send* me any more boxes. I don't want anything more of any kind, clothes food or anything. It will be just that much more to carry around.

Now as to the magazines. I get the Sat. Eve Post but I signed for 5 yrs. when I was home—so I still get it. As for the ones you signed me for. I get the Time, Esquire, Life but that is OK. I like the Newsweek also but I guess you had better wait a couple of months as I will probably have a new address by then so if they won't run out by then just wait on them.

As to my flying. I am not flying any more missions over enemy territory but I have been to France a few time. I only wish I could speak French.

I don't know about my piano playing. I am learning to play popular music only. But I will be able to teach you a few things.

Ralph.

★ ★ ★

September 21, 1944[15]

Dear Mother & Dad,

At last I got my 5 days leave. I came down here[16] Tues. Morn. I haven't done much except eat and sleep. I have been to a couple of plays which I thought were pretty fair. Nothing to brag about.

The bombs[17] are still coming over. They have alerts most all night. I'll tell you about them later.

I went down to see if I could buy some china but the dealers here don't have much to sell. Most all the good china is going to U.S. on lend lease.

Did you folks get my letter saying not to send any more boxes? I have plenty of stuff to last a couple of months and by then I won't need it. So please tell everyone not to send me anymore boxes. I don't want anything about all for now

Love
Ralph.

★ ★ ★

September 24, 1944

Dear Juana

Well I have just returned from a 5 day leave. I really had a swell time.

How is school by now? I guess things are in full swing.

We have the Charlie McCarthy[18] program on—straight from the states. It is rather good to hear a program from home.

The buzz bombs were not too bad. There were a few that came over but not too many.

I saw a few good plays and pictures while I was in London. The weather isn't too good right now. It is raining and cold.

I have received some of the boxes. I got the soap. The candy. The jelly peanut butter popcorn, taffy and everything. Thanks an awfully lot.

I guess Mother has written you but I'll tell you any way. Please don't send me any more boxes. I don't want anything else right now.

I expect a few changes to be made in the next two months so don't send anything more.[19]

I hope everything is going all right with you.

I guess this is about all for now.

Love
Ralph.

★ ★ ★

October 5, 1944

Dear Juana,

It certainly has turned cold over here. It has been raining for the last couple of days. I guess winter has really started.

The buzz bombs are coming over pretty thick now and some are hitting too close for comfort.

You asked about the French people. They are much different than the English.

What do you this milk weed stuff for? I have never heard of it before.

Well have you started your course in Indiana history yet? Have you learned all the governors yet?

I have a fire going in my small stove tonight and it sure feels good.

I don't want you to send me any more boxes I have lots of everything and I'm afraid it will be just that much more for me to worry about.

I hope everything is all right with you,

All for now

Ralph

★ ★ ★

October 20, 1944

200,000 American troops, led by General Douglas MacArthur, begin amphibious landings on Leyte in the central Philippines.

★ ★ ★

October 23–26, 1944

During the Battle of Leyte Gulf, the first Japanese kamikaze aircraft attack and sink the aircraft carrier *St. Lo*. At the conclusion of the naval engagement, the Japanese Navy lost four carriers, three battleships, ten cruisers, eleven destroyers, and about 10,500 men. The United States lost six ships and about 3,000 men. This remains the greatest naval battle in history.

★ ★ ★

October 31, 1944

Dear Juana,

Well I guess school is in full swing by now. Everyone must be looking forward to the Xmas holiday.

I thought I would be home for Xmas. But I don't know. They promised me I could go home as soon as they could get some one to take my place. But they seem to have difficulty getting some one.

I made another "trip" last week[20] and I got to stop over in London for two nights. I saw two plays. One was "Lisbon Story"[21] which had some of the most beautiful music I have ever heard. The other was "Sweeter & Lower."[22] It was good too.

I am working tonight and it looks as if I will be up all night. But I really intend to sleep tomorrow.

I have sorta let my letter writing slip lately so maybe I'll catch up on it. It has started turning cold and the weather is very bad. We seldom have a pretty day any more. It has started getting dark early and light late in the mornings. Pretty soon we will be going around all day in the dark.

Well there doesn't seem to be much else to write about. Everything is about as normal now that the buzz bombs are not so frequent.

I guess this is all for now,

Love
Ralph.

★ ★ ★

November 19, 1944[23]

Dear Mom & Dad,

Well, this will be a short note just to let you know that I am now a Major.[24] It sure feels good to be wearing those gold leafs.

The weather over hear is pretty bad right now.

I'm glad to hear Wadesville won a basket ball game from Poseyville.[25] That should be a big event.

I don't guess the election[26] went to suit dad but then everyone can't be pleased.

Well, I guess this is about all for now.

So—Cherio Ta & all the best

Love
Ralph

★ ★ ★

November 19, 1944

Dear Juana,

Just a line to let you know that I am now a Major. It sure feels good to be wearing those gold leaves.

There isn't much doing over here now everything is pretty quiet.

Did the election go to suit you? I guess you can't please everyone.

Well, how does it feel to be an old engaged person right now? Doesn't that ring make your finger tired?

I guess I'd better close now & get some sleep.

Cherio, Ta & all the best,

Love
Ralph

★ ★ ★

Promotion day always led to a celebration. Here, some of Ralph's friends gather to help him pin on his new major's gold oak leaf. Shown above are Bill Hartness, "Doc" Burnett, Ralph, Tom Slack, and Floyd Langford.

November 24, 1944
Norwich

A B-24 from the 458th Bomb Group, returning from a practice mission, attempts to make an instrument approach at Horsham St Faith. Due to a very low ceiling and bad visibility, it clips the tower of St. Philip's Church, damaging the right wing and a portion of the tail. The plane crashes in an open area a short distance away, near Barker Street. The pilot, Ralph Dooley, is credited with sacrificing his own life to keep the plane aloft and crashing away from the main part of town.

★ ★ ★

December 10, 1944[27]

Dear Mother & Dad,

Well how is everything this fine winter evening. It is pretty cold here for a change.

I have a nice fire going so I am pretty comfortable. They have some pretty good music over the radio on Sunday nite now. I sure do enjoy my radio & record player.[28]

I just returned from a fighter base. Myself & two other fellows were visiting some friends of ours down there. We flew down there last evening and spent the night and came back today. We were shown all over the base. Last nite we had to go to the Sat. nite party. They had a good orchestra and lots of the local girls came in. Every one seemed to have a wonderful time.

So now I am back on the job. I don't have much to do anymore. Most everything is supervisory on my part. I am going to draw a very handsome pay check this week. Did I ever write you how much I made each month now?

250.00	Base pay
12.50	Fogy pay for 3 yrs service, 5% of 250.00[29]
262.50	
26.25	overseas pay 10% of 262.50
288.75	
144.37	Flying Pay 50% of Base, fogy & overseas pay.
433.12	Total Monthly pay.

I get about $21.00 per month for food but I pay that right out again. And I don't get any rental allowance because the Army furnishes me my quarters. But if I were married I would receive $63 per month more for food and $105.00 per month for rental allowance. Do you think it would pay me to get married? ha! ha!

The mail is pretty slow now but that is to be expected I guess. I will close now and will get some sleep

Love
Ralph

★ ★ ★

January 2, 1945

Dear Juana,

Just a line to let you know I'm OK. There was a lot of celebrating going on over the holidays.

Did you have a nice vacation? I think the folks wrote me you were to come home on the 19th.

I was rather hoping I could be home for Xmas but I guess it just wasn't in the cards.

Did you enjoy your visit to Miami University?

The weather here isn't too bad but it isn't very pleasant either. There isn't much doing anymore. Seems as if I never get anything done at all.

I don't know when I will get home. Sometimes they talk like they will and other times they won't. But I am ready to go any time they will send me.

Well, I guess this is about all for now. But I will try to write more later.

Love
Ralph.

★ ★ ★

January 9, 1945

Dear Mother & Dad,

Well there isn't much doing over here right now. We had our first big snow last night—about 3 inches. It is pretty cold but mostly a still cold there isn't very much wind.

I'm sure glad to hear Wadesville is doing so good in basketball. I guess Coach Saunders knows something about the game after all. Or have the cracker box players already decided that?

You asked about my working nights. I only work every once in a while all night. But about every 3 or 4 nights I get up around 2 in the morning and help get the mission off and the days work started. It certainly is a fine feeling to be a Major. It has its advantages. I get my own transportation. A jeep and driver when I want it. I have more privacy. Also it has its draw backs—I have more responsibility. Every one takes you more seriously. I have to be careful what I say and do. I have to do a lot of undesirable details. Such as inspections, etc. I have 32 crews under me which is about 350 men. Of which 180 are officers and the rest are enlisted men. I had a meeting the other day and gave a little talk. And when you start to telling that many men what to do you run into all sorts of situations. But it is good experience and I like it a lot. So much for now.

Love
Ralph.

★ ★ ★

Ralph's actual schedule was more grueling than he let on. As operations officer and later as squadron commander, he was heavily involved with any mission that included the 329th Bomb Squadron. Since it was made up entirely of lead pilots, he was busy almost every day. His schedule for missions went something like this:

The day before a mission:

1700 hrs. (5 p.m.)	Review maintenance reports on all participating aircraft.
1800 hrs. (6 p.m.)	Bomb and fuel load information arrives from 20th Bomb Wing Headquarters for his review.
1900 hrs. (7 p.m.)	Bedtime (hopefully).

Day of the mission:

0200 hrs. (2 a.m.)	Wake up and go to the war room to review current target and route information provided by 20th Bomb Wing.
0300 hrs. (3 a.m.)	Check routes, departure information, and flight plan check points, comparing them to the original orders to make sure there are no mistakes.
0500 hrs. (5 a.m.)	Mark route and target on the big map in the briefing hall.
0600 hrs. (6 a.m.)	Start briefing.
0700 hrs. (7 a.m.)	Have breakfast with pilots and crews.
0800 hrs. (8 a.m.)	Go to the control tower to watch take offs.
0900 hrs. (9 a.m.)	Go to the office to do paperwork, prepare the next day's crew alert list, and take a nap (if possible).
1500 hrs. (3 p.m.)	Go to the control tower and watch landings.
1600 hrs. (4 p.m.)	Monitor the debriefing while eating dinner.
1700 hrs. (5 p.m.)	Start the entire process all over again.

★ ★ ★

Each squadron had their own offices. Shown here is the entrance to the 329th Bomb Squadron while Ralph was the commander. The bomb casing over the door says "329th Lead Crew Squadron RE." "RE" is the squadron designation painted on the side of all their planes.

January 13, 1945

Dear Juana,

Well the new year is well under way so I guess you are back at work again. Our lights have been out here for the last two days. The main cable was broken and it takes these Limeys forever to fix anything.

It snowed about 6 inches here the other day and it has been awfully cold. But it isn't so bad right now. I seem to do pretty good on the coal, of course me being a Major wouldn't have anything to do with it.

Punch didn't last long at the janitor's job did he?[30] I guess he didn't feel like going to school again.

The war news sounds pretty good tonight for a change.

Boy the mail is really a mess I have received letters mailed at Xmas and I am still getting letters written way back in Nov.

I received several nice Xmas cards including one from Earl & Ely Cox. Well I've about run down

Love
Ralph.

★ ★ ★

January 16, 1945

Dear Mr & Mrs Schneck,[31]

I arrived home only yesterday from England on a 30 day recuperation leave. I've served with Ralph for the last eight months and during this time we've become very close friends. He asked me before I left if I'd be willing to drop his folks a note when I got back and I quickly assured him it would be a privilege. It is a privilege because I can pass on to you to whom it means the most my respect and admiration for Ralph. I can honestly say that I have never served under a finer officer or man and he not once, even under some mighty trying circumstances and in making some difficult decisions, has ever lost my respect and admiration. By his fairness and sense of justice he has made only friends. I know of no one who feels ill-disposed towards Ralph. To me, he has certainly been a "pillar of strength" and he has more than once helped me over some pretty tough fences to hurdle. There's nothing I wouldn't do for Ralph and I sincerely mean that.

It sure seems good to be back in the States once more. Ralph should be home for good before long. While I don't want you to build up your hopes too much (just in case plans fall through) I look for Ralph to be on his way home inside of 60 days.

I should be very happy if you care to write me. I'll be going back to England in 30 days and will be more than happy to carry back any message you wish to Ralph.

Yours sincerely,
Bill Hartness

Capt W[m] M. Hartness
616½ No. Kenmore
Los Angeles, Calif.

★ ★ ★

January 17, 1945[32]

Dear Mother & Dad

Just a few lines to let you know I'm OK. It hasn't been so cold here the last couple of days. In fact the weather has been pretty nice.

I received lots of nice Xmas cards including one from Earl & Ely Cox. I was rather surprised when I got it.

Dad asked if we got good Whisky over here. About all we get is Scotch. I bought a bottle of special stuff and I want to bring it home with me. We also get Gin, Rum, Rye & Irish. We get some Bourbon once in a while. There is also some very good wine. But most of it is Scotch. Any officer from the grade of Major & above can buy Whisky from the officers club for their own personal use.

There is some good music on the radio. I just finished listening to the Jack Benny[33] show. Over here they don't say Bob Hope. They call him Robert Hope.

We seem to do pretty good on the coal and coke this winter. Of course it hasn't been very very cold so much.

Our food is pretty good too. The field recently bought an ice cream plant.[34] So we have ice cream about 2 times a week. We also get steak about once a week. Officers go to the movies on Sat, Sun, Tue & Thur. nights so everything is a little better than it was last year.

Well about all for now

Love
Ralph.

★ ★ ★

February 11, 1945

Dear Juana,

There isn't much to write about now. The weather hasn't been too cold. But is awful nasty—raining and the like.

I am just wondering how all the tournaments have turned out. I was in hopes of Wadesville winning something. But I don't know.

I just returned from London.[35] I went down to buy some shoes but the PX was closed so I couldn't buy anything. I did buy some new records. There are some real nice ones too. But they are rather expensive over here. About 75¢ apiece.

In regards to my promotion. Anything that is Major & above is called Field Order grade. In this case "gr̩ade" is the same as rank. So you could say I was Field Order rank. It has nothing to do with what you do or where you work.

I guess this is about all for right now.

Love
Ralph.

★ ★ ★

February 27, 1945[36]

Dear Juana,

I have decided to get caught up with my letter writing so everyone will get one at the same time. Mail seems to come in spurts over here. I will get a lot one day then I wont get any for a couple of weeks.

It is very pleasant over here now. You can wear a light jacket in the day time. At night you need a little fire but not much.

Jim Stewart is still over here. He has a nice quiet job with very little to do.[37]

I am planning on taking a pass sometime soon. I am thinking of going to Cambridge. I want to visit the University there. It is supposed to be one of the most famous in the world. I have flown over it and it is a very beautiful place. I get tired of going to London all the time.

How did Richmond come out in the State Tourney?[38] I was sure sorry to hear that Wadesville lost in the County Tourney.

It won't be long before school will be over for another year,—will it? Boy! the months sure do slip by especially over here. I will be over here 1½ yrs pretty soon—guess I'll have to add another "Hershey" bar[39] to my sleeve—ha! ha!

Love
Ralph

★ ★ ★

March 3, 1945
Norwich

About one hundred Luftwaffe night fighters attack 27 RAF airfields, destroying 22 aircraft and damaging many more. This raid marked the last Luftwaffe intrusion into England for the duration of the war.

★ ★ ★

March 6, 1945

Dear Mother & Dad,

Well not much doing in the old camp tonight. Things are rather quiet now. I guess you read where the Luftwafe was over last night.[40] They really stirred up some trouble. One of the planes was shot down near here. Some excitement.

You asked if I knew where Wilford Becker is. I looked it up and did find out where his camp is but I cannot write it in this letter.

Sure was sorry to hear that Wadesville lost the Co Tourney I was hoping they would win it.

I don't think they have anything over here that corresponds to our ground hog. At least I don't know of it.

Just had a phone call from Capt. Hartness. He is back over here now. I haven't had a chance to see him yet. But will tomorrow. Guess I'll find out how everything is back in the States. He will probably have all kinds of tales to tell. He is a pretty good talker anyway.

It is getting warmer over here and before long the farmers will begin to plant their crops. Seems funny doesn't it. The grass has been green all winter over here. You wouldn't believe it if you didn't see it.

About all for now

Love
Ralph.

Am enclosing a wedding invitation I got from one of the fellows in my Sqdn. He is marrying a girl from over here.[41]

★ ★ ★

March 10, 1945

279 B-29 Superfortresses from the 20th Air Force target Tokyo with incendiary bombs, destroying over 267,000 buildings, killing over 83,700 people, and leaving over one million homeless. This is the largest single-day casualty rate in the history of modern warfare. Fourteen B-29s are lost.

★ ★ ★

March 14, 1945

Dear Mother Dad & Everyone,

I have just returned from a trip to Paris.[42] I really had a swell time. We flew over and I stayed in the Hotel Louvre[43] which is taken over by the ARC.[44] You have to eat where you stay on account of the food shortage. However you can buy Wine, Champagene or any of the native drinks. Most of the water isn't good to drink that is why French people drink so much wine. The women dress very smart there. Their hats are very colorful & unique. They seem to have a knack for wearing the right colors of everything. Clothes, Perfume & everything is very high. Hats cost up to $200. apiece. However I didn't see over a dozen women without stockings. I saw a couple of Revue's[45] and I enjoyed them immensely—especially the Follies.[46] Most everything was in French but I could understand enough of it to be interesting. They made lots of fun at the Yanks but nobody seemed to mind—least of all the Yanks. I saw the Eiffel tower, Notre Dame, arc de Triumph where the unknown Soldier is buried, Champs 'Eliase where the fashionable shops are. I walked up and down the Seine river. It is very green & very clean. There are lots of parks in Paris and lots of trees. You don't see many dirty little kids playing around in the streets like you do in London. The streets are rather wide with lots of sidewalks. The transportation is rather poor. You either walk or ride the Metro. The Metro is the Sub way or Underground. There was a big buss which took us to town from the airport, it had a French driver. These Frenchmen are really wild with an automobile. They get one hand on the wheel, one on the horn and the food feed clear to the floor. That's how you go thru town. They would make the drivers on the Indianapolis speedway look like amateurs.

I didn't have too much trouble with the French language. I believe in a month I could learn it pretty well.

When we went back to the airport to go home I was sitting in the lounge waiting for the time to go. A big transport plane taxied up to the ramp and they announced over the loud speaker "All aboard for New York and all points in the United States" I would have got on that plane if I could.

Please keep these programs, papers and things[47, 48] to put in my Scrap book. The programs have my tickets in them.

Well I guess I've rambled on enough so will close, ask me anything about Paris I'll be glad to tell you. I took some pictures will send you some when I get them

Love
Ralph

★ ★ ★

In Paris, Ralph stayed at the American Red Cross Hotel. Because of the shortage of photo paper and chemicals, Ralph usually could only get what was called "mini print" or "minis," which measured about one and a half inches by two inches. Often, the minis showed more detail than larger prints, as shown above.

★ V-Mail ★
March 20, 1945

Dear Juana,

Just waiting around for the mission to return.[49] It has been a beautiful day today. I went out and played some volley ball. I decided I better loose a little weight or I would have to buy some new clothes. I don't know if I have the right address on this letter. But you will probably get it anyway. Our Coke stand started up again now so we have to take time out to have our Coke and cookies.[50] Well, it won't be long before you will be thru school again, will it. I guess you will be happy. Have you decided what you are going to do this summer? I wish I knew what I was going to be doing. The planes are back so I will have to go

Best Wishes
Ralph.

★ ★ ★

March 27, 1945

The last V-2 rocket lands in England, near Orpington in Kent. A total of 1,054 rockets landed in England during the seven months of the V-2 attacks, killing 2,754 and injuring another 6,523.

★ ★ ★

★ V-Mail ★
March 30, 1945

Dear Juana,

There sure isn't much doing around here today. Seems as if our work runs in shifts. Sometimes we are busy all the time, other times we have practically nothing to do. The school season is out over here and come to think of it yours will be out pretty soon. I guess you will be glad, eh?. It has been pretty warm over here the last few days. We have been playing volley ball almost every evening. The war news really sounds good today. The boys over on the Continent are really doing a swell job. Well guess this is about all for now

Love
Ralph

★ ★ ★

April 1, 1945

Ralph is promoted to commanding officer of the 329th Bomb Squadron, 93rd Bombardment Group.

★ ★ ★

(Images on right page.) These two pages came from Ralph's personal photo album that he put together after the war. It is normal for command centers to post pictures of the unit's leadership so that everyone will know what they look like. The photos and typed name tags came off the 329th Bomb Squadron's command board. Ralph took them down while he was packing things up. Shown above are (top row) Ralph, (second row) Major Bullock, Captain Everrett, Lieutenant Meadors, (third row) Captain Hammock, Lieutenant Blailock, Lieutenant Schultz, (fourth row) Lieutenant Lange, Lieutenant Justen, and Lieutenant Buffington. Ralph considered Lieutenant Justen to be one of the better lead pilots. Ralph always tried to get him as a wingman whenever he flew, because Justen was always where he was suppose to be no matter how bad the flak, the fighters, or the weather. This is not the entire staff; it only represents the leadership for lead bomb crews.

WHEN I WAS C.O.
OF THE
329TH SQUADRON
MAJ. SCHNECK
MAJ. BULLOCK
CAPT. EVERRETT
LT. MEADORS
OPERATIONS STAFF

CAPT. HAMMOCK
BOMBING
Lt. Blaileck
GUNNERY
LT. SCHULTZ
NAVIGATION
LT. LANGE
LT. JUSTEN
LT. BUFFINGTON
OUR HOT-ROCK PILOTS

April 8, 1945

Dear Mother & Dad,

It has been beautiful all day. But it is pretty darn cold. I hope it is nice out tomorrow for I want to fly some fellows down to Southern England. You wouldn't believe it but it is nice and warm all the year round on the South Coast.[51] They even have palm trees growing down there.

The war news really looks good tonight. Maybe this thing won't last so very much longer. I least I hope not. I guess that's one sure way of me getting home.

Have you got your garden planted yet? People over here have already planted some things such as onions etc.

Things have been pretty quiet for us around here the last few days.

The movie "Wilson"[52] is going to show in town this week. I want to get in to see it if I can possibly do it.

When I went to the Finance office to get paid this last month I talked to a fellow from Evansville. He said there were about 12 fellows stationed at the 93rd who are from Evansville. However, I don't know any of them.

Well, I guess I'd better get some sleep as I have to get up early in the morn. I hope you all had an enjoyable Easter. Did any of you go to church? Well I'll close now

Love
Ralph

★ ★ ★

April 12, 1945

While sitting for a portrait in Warm Springs, Georgia, President Franklin Delano Roosevelt suffers a stroke and dies. Harry S. Truman becomes the thirty-third president.

★ ★ ★

★ V-Mail ★
April 14, 1945

Dear Juana,

It has really been beautiful weather over here. I am going to take a pass next week. Another boy and myself are going to the Brods and do a little sail boating & fishing. We should have lots of fun. Well I started this letter two days ago. I was gone all day yesterday and didn't get a chance to finish it. I am going on pass tomorrow. From the news it looks as if we won't have much more work over here. Things are really looking good right now. We are all ready planning what we are going to do when the war is over. Of course there is nothing but a lot of rumors floating around. About all for now,

Cherio,
Ralph

★ ★ ★

April 15, 1945
Mission 31[53]

8th Air Force Mission 951 sends 1,348 bombers, unescorted, to targets along the French Atlantic Coast. Targets include tank trenches, gunpits, pillboxes, and heavy gun emplacements. There are no losses

Ralph was lead pilot for the 93rd Bomb Group and led all bombers as command pilot for the mission.

★ ★ ★

April 16, 1945[54]

Dear Mr & Mrs Beeler,

I don't get to write you as much any more. I confine most of my correspondence to Vmail. But its not because I don't want to write, its just that I'm too busy.

This Squadron Commander job really keeps one busy. You see in a bombing squadron a great number of your men are officers on Combat Crews. A Bomber Crew has 5 officers and 5 enlisted men. Then the ground men, maintenance men, etc are all enlisted men except for the officer in charge of the section. So you have to be "on the Ball" in order to keep everything going smoothly. There is always some one with a problem.

Well, enough of my problem. However I do enjoy Commanding a Squadron and to know that it is a great responsibility and that you had the final word in regards to the men of your command.

Another boy and I are going on pass tomorrow. We are going up to the brods and go boating and fishing. They have lots of sail boats up there. I'm sure we will have a good time if it doesn't rain all the time.

I enjoyed the clippings about the Bosse Bulldogs. But you needn't send me the Ernie Pyle[55] articles. They are published in the Stars & Stripes.

It has been beautiful weather here. I have never seen it so pretty over here. This is by far the nicest time f year.

I read the article you sent me on Tom Black. It is in error a little bit. I looked up his job in our records over here. I don't know where the newspapers get their information but quite a bit of it, concerning men overseas, is untrue. Has Keese left for overseas yet? I imagine he will be pretty soon.

You certainly had lots of company around Easter holidays. So Frances is Engaged? What does her folks think of that.

I am still waiting for the letter from A.G.[56] Maybe he could get one of these post cards where you just check the phrases you want to say. Well, I have just about run out of news. I hope you are all enjoying this good weather and maybe all this mess will be over soon.

Cherio & Best Wishes,
Ralph.

★ ★ ★

April 16, 1945

8th Air Force Mission 954 sends 1,252 bombers and 913 fighters to hit railroad targets and other targets of opportunity in Germany and Czechoslovakia. Running low on fuel and ammunition, with badly damaged runways, sinking morale, and crumbling leadership, the Luftwaffe does not fully respond to the attacks. Fighters escorting the bombers attack Luftwaffe bases, destroying over 700 aircraft on the ground. Some dismayed ground crews and pilots watch the destruction from a safe distance.

★ ★ ★

★ V-Mail ★
April 22, 1945

Dear Juana,

Well there isn't much to do this Sunday. It is raining outside and it has turned a little cold. I had three beautiful days up on the Broads. It was pretty weather and we had a nice time sailing and boating. I didn't think sailing would be much fun but I really enjoyed it. The war news sounds good all over this morning. I don't think it will be long now. But you never can tell. I guess you will be glad when school is over. Are you planning on taking a vacation this year? About all for now,

Cherio,
Ralph

★ ★ ★

When time permitted and officers were looking for a leisurely weekend, they went to the Norfolk Broads. Here, Ralph learned to sail a boat from Glenn Meadors, who was on his staff.

April 30, 1945[57]

Dear Mr & Mrs Beeler,

I thought we were going to have lots of nice weather but last night we got 2 in. of snow. So it just goes to show you can't depend on this English weather.

We aren't doing much these days. Things are pretty quiet and have been for quite a while. We are starting schools of all sorts to keep the men occupied. About all I get done is go to meetings. When you have several hundred men under you there is always plenty to keep you busy.

I guess Keese is pretty well fed up with the States from what you say. Several of the fellows coming over now say it is a relief to get away because of the many unnecessary things they have you do. Over here we do only essential things that will benefit us and pro long our life. We keep the men busy but they realize if they don't do as we say they will be missing something they should know, something their life might depend on sometime.

I expect to visit some parts of Germany next month. I don't know when or how long I will be allowed to stay but I am looking forward to it. I only wish I could speak foreign languages more fluently. I have made up my mind that if ever I have any children they will speak some foreign language.[58]

I thought I would be able to go home some time ago but they have "frozen" most all personnel over here. In other words you have to keep the job you now have. So I guess I'll wait until the war is over. The Air Force will be the first to leave this theatre of war,—I think.

Tell all the neighbors hello for[59] also all the rest of my friends and maybe I'll have more to write next time.

Cherio
Ralph

★ ★ ★

April 30, 1945

At 3:30 p.m., while Ralph composes this letter, Adolph Hitler commits suicide.

★ ★ ★

Ralph wanted letterhead stationery for his squadron but couldn't get it approved because the 93rd Bomb Group did not have the money. Someone at General Timberlake's office suggested having a rubber stamp made. Because the 8th Air Force used a lot of rubber stamps, no one ever looked closely at what was being ordered.

May 3, 1945[60]

Dear Mother & Dad,

Finally I am able to write letters again. We haven't been doing very much hard work but it has kept everyone busy. Everybody is wondering what will happen to us. Some say we will go home others say we will go to the Pacific. Actually I don't think anybody knows what will happen.

We had about 2 in. snow day before yesterday. And it has been awfully cold and raining since then. But today the sun has been shining today and it may warm up a little later on.

You asked how much I weighed. I don't actually know but I have been going to athletics lately and have lost some fat.

I am enclosing 3 money orders in the amount of $275.00. Will you please put them in the bank for me and buy me two $100 dollar bonds. Please write me when the money arrives and when you get the 2 bonds. If you don't let me know I will think you haven't gotten the money. You had better write it in a couple of letters just in case I don't get all the mail. Thanks a lot.

I am going to make a trip over in Germany at the end of this week or first of next week.

I went into town last night to see a play "Pink String & Ceiling wax."[61] It was pretty good. I enjoy the plays a lot and they have been rather good lately.

I guess I had better get some work done now. I will write more later

Love
Ralph

★ ★ ★

★ V-Mail ★
May 3, 1945

Dear Mother & Dad,

This will just be a short note as I have written you an air mail letter today. I have enclosed 3 money orders in the amount of $275.00. Please write me when you receive the letter. Be sure & let me know when you get all this done.

I thought today would be pretty but it looks as if it might rain right now. I hope you have your garden planted. We had fresh radishes yesterday. I ate so many I almost made myself sick.

Love
Ralph.

★ ★ ★

May 8, 1945

Mission 986 sends 12 B-17s to drop leaflets over Germany, marking the last mission of the 8th Air Force as the Allies accepted Nazi Germany's unconditional surrender. Forever more, this day is known as "Victory in Europe Day."

★ ★ ★

"It is not given to us to peer into the mysteries of the future. Still, I avow my hope and faith, sure and inviolate, that in the days to come the British and American peoples will for their own safety and for the good of all walk together side by side in majesty, in justice and in peace."[62]

★ ★ ★

NOTES

1. During the afternoon of June 6, 1944, 181 journalists crowded into the Oval Office to interview President Franklin Delano Roosevelt about the events of the invasion. This is in response to a question about the mood of the home front and was preceded by a story of a man who quit his job after the invasion of Sicily because he thought the war was over.

2. The newly formed 15th Air Force took over eastern Mediterranean operations.

3. The Martin B-26 Marauder was a two-engine medium bomber that featured twelve fifty-caliber machine guns, four of which were mounted on the exterior of the plane and fixed facing forward. This allowed the aircraft to strafe enemy ground facilities.

4. The Curtiss C-46 Commando was a large transport originally designed as an airliner. It combined a spacious storage compartment with a long range and a good cruising speed.

5. Coordination was provided by the office of the US Army Air Forces in the United Kingdom (USAAFUK), which was opened specifically for the task.

6. This is the same Ken Strauss who played trombone in the Wadesville High School Orchestra with Ralph.

7. This is in reference to Terre Haute, Indiana.

8. Bob Hope (1903-–2003) was an American comedian entertainer of radio, stage, screen, and television. He made several movies with Bing Crosby and was a favorite of all the troops. During and after the war, he toured with the USO many times, hosting a total

of 199 shows in the course of his lifetime. In 1996, Congress named him the "first and only honorary veteran of the U.S. armed forces."

9. This is in reference to Independence Day celebrations.

10. Included in this letter was a program for the 93rd Bomb Group's 200th Mission Celebration, which was held on July 25 and 26, 1944. The dignitaries in attendance included Lieutenant General James H. Doolittle, who led the raid on Tokyo on April 18, 1942.

11. Supreme Headquarters Allied Expeditionary Force (SHAEF) was located at Bushy Park, on the outskirts of London. Prior to D-Day, Eisenhower's staff began making plans to establish a forward headquarters in France. On August 28, 1944, elements of the Bushy Park staff began relocating to a temporary facility at La Colonie Scolaire de St. Ouen, a school on the outskirts of Jullouville, France. Ralph was seen as one of the most experienced pilots still remaining in England, with over 1,500 hours of flying time. Since he was not assigned to combat missions, he was selected (along with other pilots) to assist in moving headquarters personnel to the forward location.

12. At this point Ralph is thinking that any day he is going home or to a different unit someplace else in the world. He believes he is waiting for a replacement crew.

13. Ralph had been asking his squadron commander when he would be going home, but he always got the same answer: "I don't know." Then he started asking about getting some time off, and the reply was always, "We'll see." One day, Ralph approached the group commander and asked about being going back to the United States. The next day he was told he was to receive a five-day pass, and he was to leave almost immediately.

14. George Ann Moye was related to Punch, Juana's boyfriend.

15. Written on American Red Cross stationery.

16. He wrote this letter in London and mailed it from the Red Cross.

17. This is in reference to the V-2 bombs.

18. *Edgar Bergen and Charlie McCarthy Show* was a very popular radio show. Edgar Bergen (1903–1978) was an American actor and radio performer who was best known as a ventriloquist. Charlie McCarthy was his most well-known "dummy" and lifelong sidekick. Bergen was also actress Candice Bergen's father.

19. The rumor has surfaced that the entire unit may be going home "soon." The longer it persisted, the more convinced Ralph became, thus his insistence on "no more boxes" and the talk about magazine subscriptions.

20. Almost as soon as Eisenhower arrived at Jullouville, it was clear that the facility was no longer adequate. Eisenhower directed that another, more permanent facility be established in Versailles. During the middle of September, the new facility opened and all of the personnel located at Jullouville began relocating. The remaining staff in England began moving from Bushy Park to Versailles around October 10. Ralph assisted in that move, making several flights.

21. The *Lisbon Story*, at the Stoll Theatre, was a musical drama starring Maria Elsner, with lyrics by Harry Purcell. The story takes place during World War II, as Parisian singing star, Gabrielle, is separated from the man she loves, David, of the British Foreign Office,

when he is sent to Washington. Entirely by chance, they meet again in Lisbon, a neutral center of wartime intrigue.

22. *Sweeter and Lower*, at the Ambassadors Theatre, was a musical revue starring Hermione Gingold and Henry Kendall. The revue included twenty-seven musical numbers and skits. This revue was the middle of two other revues: *Sweet and Low* (1943) and *Sweetest and Lowest* (1946). Gingold starred in all three.

23. Included in this letter, but not referred to, was a program for *Mrs. Warren's Profession*, which played at the Theatre Royal in Norwich, the week of November 13, 1944. *Mrs. Warren's Profession*, written by George Bernard Shaw, centers on the relationship between a mother, who owns a brothel, and her daughter, who has just discovered the source of the family's money. The Theatre Royal barely survived World War II, as buildings all around it were destroyed in German bombing raids. On June 27, 1942, two incendiary bombs landed on the roof, but the fires were extinguished before they could damage the building. The theatre is still in operation today.

24. Along with becoming a major, Ralph now has become the 329th Bomb Squadron Operations Officer. It has now become clear why he got the single room, the five-day pass, and the special assignments. It is also starting to set in that he will not be going home until the entire unit returns. In later years, it would be noted that General Timberlake interrupted a meeting to congratulate Ralph on his promotion.

25. Wadesville and Poseyville were archrivals in baseball and basketball. The two schools were only about five miles apart.

26. In 1944, President Roosevelt easily won reelection over Thomas E. Dewey, then governor of New York. Rolla was never a Roosevelt fan and had often criticized him for taking America to war.

27. Included in this letter was a program for the "November Banquet for the Lead Crews," held on November 20, 1944. Very little information about this banquet exists today. Since Brigadier General Timberlake was in attendance, it is likely that this was a one-time event.

28. Record players were a rare item. Ralph purchased his from someone who was returning to the US, along with a few records. He managed to pick up some more records as others left for home.

29. "Foggy pay" is pay received for being in a war zone. The name comes from Foggy Bottom, a neighborhood in Washington, DC, which was the location of the Department of War when the war started. The department was often referred to as Foggy Bottom.

30. Juana had told Punch that he needed to find a full-time job and stick with it before she would marry him. He got a job with the Evansville schools, but he quit after a few months.

31. Jessie transcribed this letter so she could pass it around to the rest of the family. She kept the original for safekeeping.

32. Included in this letter was an invitation to the "Sud Guzzler's Steak Fry," held on January 30, 1945. This is another event for which little is known. It was held in honor

of the armament section of the 329th Bomb Squadron. All of the honorees were privates, corporals, and sergeants. Ralph was "invited" because he headed up the waitstaff, which was made up of captains and lieutenants.

33. *The Jack Benny Program* starred Jack Benny (1894–1974) and a host of other people playing characters in a radio situational comedy. Benny was perhaps one of the single-most popular radio entertainers of all time. A master of the carefully timed pregnant pause, Benny would later apply his talents to television and movies, always playing a penny-pinching miser who was forever thirty-nine years old, no matter how old he really was.

34. This was not a factory, but the equipment to make bulk ice cream. It was located in a walk-in freezer at the Mess Hall. Typically, it ran about eighteen hours a day. Ice cream was served to both officers and enlisted men when enough had been made so everyone could be served at the same time. Schoolchildren touring the field were also treated to ice cream before they left.

35. Enclosed with this letter was a program for *Happy and Glorious*, a musical revue playing at the Palladium. *Happy and Glorious*, by George Black, starred Zoe Gail and Tommy Trinder and is heralded as one of Black's best musicals.

36. Included in this letter was a program for the "Enlisted Men's Funfest," which was held on February 24 and 27, 1945, for enlisted men of the 329th Bomb Squadron. A dance was held on February 24, featuring "W/O Nicholas and the Musical Crew" and "Peggy Carr and the Variety Crew." On February 27, the main order of business was drinking beer from 2000 to 2300 hours (8 p.m. to 11 p.m.). The invitation says the "Gas Load" is 180 gallons.

37. Jimmy Stewart completed his twentieth mission in July 1944. He was then made Chief of Staff of the 2nd Combat Bombardment Wing of the 8th Air Force. What Ralph and others did not know at the time, was that Stewart continued to fly some combat missions, even though he was not required to do so. Before the war ended, Stewart was promoted to colonel and became one of the few Americans to rise from private to colonel in four years.

38. In 1945, Evansville Bosse, coached by Herm Keller, again won the Indiana State Basketball Championship by beating South Bend Riley, coached by Wayne Wakefield, 46–36. Bosse finished the season with an overall record of twenty-five wins against only two losses.

39. This is in reference to the overseas service bars that are worn on the right sleeve of the Class A and service uniforms, indicating the number of years of overseas service. One bar is awarded for each six-month period.

40. This is in reference to the raid on March 3.

41. The wedding was between Olive Ashwell and Lieutenant Edward Gochey. They were married at Our Lady of Dolours Servite Church on Fulham Road on March 10, 1945.

42. A number of officers from the 93rd Bomb Group were flown to Paris for three days directly from Hardwick.

43. Hotel du Louvre is located at Place André Malraux, in the heart of Paris. Its architecture is from the Second Empire style. The interior is grand, featuring marble walls and dark wood. The hotel is located near the Louvre Museum.

44. This is in reference to the American Red Cross.

45. Casino de Paris featured a large production called *Charming Paris*. The program was in French, but Ralph was given a printed English translation of the musical numbers. This was a favorite of American soldiers, because it included numbers like *Naked Bath at Midnight* and *Undress Throughout the Ages*.

46. The Folies Bergère was a little more upscale, featuring sixteen skits and musical numbers. Some of the skits were in three parts, featuring additional musical numbers.

47. Ralph sent the programs from the revues and a newspaper clipping with the letter.

48. Enclosed in the envelope, but not referenced in the letter, was a program from the Theatre Royal in Norwich for *Gather No Moss*, a little-known comedy by Max Catto. This play starred Winifred Shotter, a popular London comedienne who was best known for her stage performances in many farces presented at the Aldwych Theatre.

49. Mission 898 consisted of 451 bombers and 355 fighters. There were four segments to the mission. The 93rd Bomb Group was part of the third segment of 129 B-24s attacking the oil refinery at Hemmingstedt. One B-24 is lost and nine others are damaged. Twelve crewmembers are missing in action.

50. This is a playful jab at the English tradition of tea and crumpets. Ralph was probably the only one who got the joke, and he probably wrote it with a smile.

51. This is in reference to the beaches and resorts in Cornwall, located at the extreme southwestern end of England.

52. *Wilson* is a biographical film about President Woodrow Wilson. Filmed in 1944, it starred Charles Coburn, Alexander Knox, Geraldine Fitzgerald, Thomas Mitchell, and Sir Cedric Hardwicke.

53. One day, while visiting Glen Martin at 20th Air Wing Headquarters, General Timberlake joined them for lunch. After a little small talk, Ralph asked Timberlake what it would take to get promoted to lieutenant colonel. Timberlake thought for a moment and said, "Fly me five more missions, and I'll see to it you are promoted." After thinking about it for a few days, Ralph put his name on the roster. He was able to fly this one mission before the war ended.

54. Written on 329th Bomb Squadron stationery.

55. Ernie Pyle (1900–1945) was an American journalist who wrote for the Scripps-Howard newspaper chain. He wrote in a folksy style about out-of-the-way-places and the people he met. He won a Pulitzer Prize in 1944. Pyle was born near Dana, Indiana, and attended Indiana University. He is one of a very few American civilians to receive a Purple Heart. Pyle was killed two days after this letter was written, on April 18, 1945, by a Japanese sniper on the island of Shima off Okinawa.

56. This is a tongue-in-cheek jab at Add Beeler, who would obviously read this letter.

57. Written on 329th Bomb Squadron letterhead.

58. True to his word, Ralph's oldest son learned to speak German, Turkish, and Spanish. Unfortunately, his youngest son only learned to speak Mexican slang, which he picked up from the barrios of Dallas.

59. me: This word was left out of the letter. Ralph probably got distracted while he was writing.

60. Written on 329th Bomb Squadron stationery.

61. *Pink String and Sealing Wax* was a British drama set in 1880. It played in theaters from 1943 to 1945, and then it was released as a movie.

62. From a speech by Sir Winston Churchill to a joint session of Congress, December 26, 1941.

Chapter 10

BOMBED TO PIECES

★ ★ ★

"One day sooner or later you will remember my words."[1]

Ralph may have flown his thirtieth mission on June 20, 1944, but that did not mean that he was finished flying. In most cases, pilots and crews that completed the required number of missions were reassigned to other duties until they could be sent home. Sometimes the reassignment was within their current unit, and other times it was at a different location. Sometimes it was even stateside. The US Army needed leadership in every part of the world, and a non-flying, combat-experienced veteran was in high demand. Ralph's case was no different, and the Army planned to use him to the best of his ability.

Returning from a parachute drop to Holland, planes from the 93rd Bomb Group flew over these ships anchored in the English Channel. These ships were probably involved in the invasion and now were waiting to take the boys back home. This picture was taken from the right waist gunner's position.

★ ★ ★

Since Hardwick was equipped with night landing equipment, it was only natural that they had at least one plane that could take advantage of the capability. That plane was a specially converted B-24, which had been painted all black and nicknamed *Black Beauty*.[2] The bomb racks had been removed and a plywood floor put in place. Bench seats were installed and windows were added so that passengers could see outside. In the back of the plane, the waist gunner's positions were removed and the area could be used for more passengers or for hauling a modest amount of freight. The plane was designed for one specific purpose.

Sweden was a neutral country that enjoyed the position of being able to stay neutral for the entire war. They provided assistance and conducted business with both the Allies and the Nazis. One thing they were able to provide the Allies was a safe haven for disabled aircraft. Damaged planes that could not make it back to England, but could make it to Sweden, were allowed to land or crash-land. Surviving crews were interred in a prison camp for some period before they were allowed to return to England and rejoin their unit. Aircraft that had crashed were kept by the Swedish government and converted to scrap metal. Other planes were inspected by the Swedish aircraft industry, some even being dismantled, before being given back to the Allies.

The dilemma that faced the 8th Air Force was how to get their men and equipment back to England without being shot at by the Luftwaffe. This is where *Black Beauty* came in. About every ten days or so, a mission would be scheduled for *Black Beauty* to fly to Sweden to pick up returning aircrews. If a plane could be flown back, repair teams were brought in to make the repairs, and a crew would be shuttled in for the return flight.

Black Beauty, with a basic crew, would leave Hardwick as soon as it was completely dark and fly a precarious route to an airfield at Bulltofta, Sweden. Bulltofta is in the extreme southern end of Sweden, framed between Germany, Denmark, and Norway, all Nazi strongholds. The flight was considered to be very dangerous, and the 93rd only used crews with around five missions to make the flight, as crews with more missions were considered too valuable.

On one returning flight, Ralph was assigned to greet the passengers and see to it that they got what they needed before being sent on their way to their unit. Ralph recognized one passenger as someone he knew from Roswell. The pilot was from Texas, and when he disembarked he was wearing a huge cowboy hat and boots, which he said he got in Sweden. Ralph wanted to talk to him and get more information about what was going on in Sweden, but time ran out and his friend was sent back to his unit.

Ralph was intrigued about Sweden and wanted to make the flight. Every time he saw that a flight was coming up, he would volunteer. When he served as operations officer for the 329th Bomb Squadron and later as commander, he penciled his name on the roster. Every request and every other attempt was denied. The reason was that it was far too dangerous a mission for group and squadron leadership.

★ ★ ★

After D-Day, when the Germans began pulling back, they pilfered almost everything that was not nailed down. Anything of value was taken and sent to Germany. Food, including stored crops, was sent to feed the German people or the retreating German soldiers. This was devastating to France, as the French people faced enormous food shortages. As a result, humanitarian flights began bringing food into the country.[3] Holland faced the same dilemma when it was liberated; again, food was flown in to designated supply depots.

Ralph was called upon to lead some of these flights. He would fly to London for the aircraft to be loaded, and then fly to some designated airfield in France for them to be unloaded, never staying very long on the ground. Sometimes he would make two trips a day to different locations. In Holland, most of his flights involved air dropping supplies by parachute.

The Germans took almost everything when they vacated Holland, forcing a huge effort by the Allies to provide food and other supplies. Here, planes from the 93rd Bomb Group make a low pass over Holland for a parachute drop during Operation Chowhound. Note the makeshift bridge and bomb damage along the shore.

Some of the airfields were grass bases and others were paved airports—both kinds had formerly been used by the Luftwaffe. One such location, which Ralph visited late in the war, was an airfield at Orlèans, France. Ralph was scheduled to make two trips in the same day. After delivering flour and sugar, he and his group of planes prepared to take off. A sergeant approached him as he was about to board his plane to tell him that there were a lot of German troops about five miles directly off the end of the runway. He went on to say that American forces had them surrounded, but they had not yet surrendered, and it would be best if Ralph did not fly directly over them. Ralph told the other pilots, and after takeoff, he took up the landing gear and made a hard bank toward England to avoid the troops. When he returned for the second trip, he made sure that all the planes were lined up to take off in the opposite direction.

★ ★ ★

Delivering food to France was not the only duty he drew. At first, Ralph was asked to use *Black Beauty* on night missions to take war planners to and from meetings. Some of the meetings were held at Bushy Park, some in London, and some at grassy airfields in France. In later years, Ralph would say that almost every general he had ever heard of, and some he had not, were passengers on *Black Beauty* at one time or another. As the warfront advanced out of France, Eisenhower began moving the meeting site for Supreme Headquarters Allied Expeditionary Force (SHAFE) from Bushy Park to France. First, they moved to Jullouville, and then to Versailles. Ralph again was asked to provide transport.

★ ★ ★

After each bomb mission there were always aircraft that had fallen behind in their return flight. These stragglers usually had some sort of damage or failure that made it impossible to keep up with the main formation. Noncombat pilots and crews were sent up to look for these aircraft and assist them in returning to England. Assistance ranged from guiding them to the nearest airfield to circling a ditched aircraft until everyone was accounted for, then arranging for their rescue.

Here is another example of the difference between an enlarged print and the mini print. Ralph is shown with Black Beauty in Paris. Note that the front wheel is off the ground, while the tail is resting on the ground. This was a normal phenomenon for the B-24, especially Black Beauty, because all of its front-end weight had been removed (bomb racks, guns, etc.).

On many occasions, Ralph was called upon to greet the main formations and stay until all aircraft were accounted for.

★ ★ ★

As hostilities wound down, bomb groups began making plans to take non-combatants on a tour of Germany. Ralph was part of the planning at the 93rd Bomb Group and made a vague reference that he would be going to Germany in his letter to the Beeler family on April 30, even though at that point there was still a lot of fighting going on.

Some bomb groups called these "Trolley Missions," others called them "Bus Tours." The 93rd called them "Lib Tours." Whatever they were called, the idea was simple: load a B-24 with passengers and fly them over former German targets, low and slow, so the passengers could see what they had accomplished. Most bomb groups only flew these tours for a couple of days, making it a round-trip over and back in one day. The 93rd took it to the extreme.

First, the S-2 Section (Security Office) of the 93rd prepared a travelogue of Europe to familiarize the non-combatants with the entire region. The "Libs Tour of Europe" was an eight-page document that went into great detail and was intended to be given as a souvenir of the flight. They intended to have the document bound with an artsy front cover, but they did not have time to get that done.

Second, they took the men to Paris for a day. The men would have an evening and part of a day in Paris on the front end of the tour. Then they would fly a specified route over Germany, low and slow. After completing the flight, they would return to Hardwick. Ralph and some of the other pilots who flew these missions had already been to Paris, and they acted as tour guides to make sure the boys did not stray into the seedier parts of the city.

Lastly, they had *Black Beauty*.

Ralph made one of the first trips. He had a basic crew that consisted of a copilot, navigator, and radio operator, and *Black Beauty* carried about a dozen passengers, all from the headquarters staff, who sat in the main cabin, the waist gunner's area, and the nose of the aircraft.

★ ★ ★

May 13, 1945[4]

Dear Mother & Dad,

I'll write just a few more lines this bright Sunday. I went on this trip into Germany last week. I flew low so we could see as much as possible on the ground. We flew to southern Germany then flew up the Rhine river and saw such cities as Frankfort on M. Bonn, Coblenz, Weisbaden, Cologne, Dusseldorf and many others. It is hard to realize that whole cities of almost a million population are completely destroyed. But it is the truth. Practically no buildings standing at all. Huge factories that cover acres of ground are bombed to pieces just blown apart. I saw the Ford plant blown apart and the great A.G. Farben-Industrie,[5] the largest chemical plant in the world. I would hate to say how many acres the plant covered. But it is practically worthless. But Germany is a beautiful country. There are lots of woods and the fields are well kept. The rhine river is a beautiful river and I don't believe the German people have sacrificed much until the Allies got on German territory.

Well so much for that. I hope your garden is doing fine. I sure would like to have fresh radishes. Well about all for now

Love
Ralph

★ ★ ★

The Lib Tour took ground crews low and slow over Germany for a close look at what they had accomplished. Flying at about 2,000 feet, Ralph took this picture of a bombed-out bridge over the Rhine at Koblenz, Germany.

On May 14, a Monday morning, Ralph went to his office and started going through files and cleaning things up. A messenger arrived and handed him a note from Lieutenant Colonel Therman Brown, group commander, asking him to report to the War Room. When Ralph arrived, he joined the other squadron commanders and headquarters staff. Brown announced that they had received orders to proceed to the United States. They were going home.

But it was not as easy as packing a few bags and getting on a plane. The 8th Air Force had been working on the plan for months. They faced many of the same challenges getting men and planes back home that they faced during the war in getting those same men and planes to England. The only thing they did not have to worry about was getting shot down.

While there was no shortage of airfields in the United States, there were only a few that were of sufficient size to handle the huge numbers. The men would need someplace to eat and sleep, and the Army needed facilities to

Shortly after Ralph learned that the 93rd Bomb Group was going home, he gathered his staff to tell them the good news. This picture was taken about fifteen minutes after he returned from headquarters.

process paperwork. There were not enough aircraft for everyone to be able to fly back, so some would have to take a ship home. Personal belongings created the same type of problem—some of it could go on a plane, most would go by ship, and some would simply stay in England. Last was the entire process of closing an airfield and turning it back over to the RAF; what to take home, what to leave behind, and what to destroy were questions that stirred debate.

Some of the final plans and processes were shared in order to get feedback, but most of it was kept secret until the very last moment. On this day, the 93rd received a package that had specific details on what needed to be done. All aircraft were grounded while an evaluation was completed on their airworthiness. Then necessary repairs needed to be completed as soon as possible. Since there were multiple copies of everything, only specific documents were to be packed; the rest was to be destroyed. Some officers did not like that idea, so they took some documents with them in case someone looked for them later.

Before Ralph left for home, he made a tour of all the planes on the field, having his picture taken with several of them. Here he poses with Tom Slack in front of Solid Comfort, aircraft 42-50501.

Personal belongings created the worst problem. There was only so much room on the planes, and the ships would fill up quickly with all of the equipment that had to come back to the United States, so limits had to be imposed. Men, like Ralph, who had been stationed for a long time had acquired a lot of items that made their quarters more like home. Ralph had a radio, a record player with a collection of records, and some photographic developing equipment. Because of the different plugs and voltages, electric appliances purchased in England would not work in the United States, and items like the photographic equipment had to stay in England or take the place of something else. The instructions were very clear: each man was allowed a small duffle bag (or some travel bag) that would stay with them all the time and one footlocker, which would go by ship and someday catch up with the men; most ship-bound passengers would carry everything with them in a duffle bag of some sort. In some cases, the boys left clothing and uniform parts so they could take home some valued souvenir. There were also instances where the footlocker was packed so tight that the bottom fell out when they tried to move it.

The last problem each bomb group faced, especially those returning first, was that they were given very little notice to get everything done. In the 93rd's case, they had barely eight days to get everything accomplished. Because of the need to service the aircraft, some groups did not know how many planes they would have available until the last moment, so some men were bumped from plane to ship, which did not sit well with mothers who were expecting their sons to come home sooner rather than later. The 93rd fared well in this department as they maintained their aircraft after the armistice, and they had a very good feel for how many planes they would be using. Then it was up to the group and squadron commanders to decide who went on which plane. The squadron commanders placed the crews on the planes and selected a plane for themselves. After that, they were filled in order of rank. For the most part, only officers flew home; enlisted men were placed on ships. Some men were needed in the Pacific, and they went directly to their new assignment without going back to the United States.

Ralph packed almost everything he owned. He gave the record player and radio away but packed the records.[6] Anything that he could not get into the footlocker was left behind, and that included all the developing equipment. Presumably, after the boys were gone, the huts were opened and the locals had their pick of anything left behind.

And so it was that on the morning of May 22, 1945,[7] the Liberators of the 93rd Bomb Group were made ready. Crews and passengers had been taking belongings to their aircraft throughout the night so there was little delay. The engines were started, and just as they had done 396 times[8] in the last 31 months, they taxied into takeoff position. Only this time, they were not facing the guns of the Luftwaffe or flak over a target. This time, they were going home.

★ ★ ★

Ralph flew as a passenger with Joe Clemmens and his crew. Clemmens' plane took off and formed up with the others as they headed for their first stop at RAF Valley on the Isle of Anglesey, Wales. It was a short 200-mile hop, where they unloaded everything so that British inspectors could make sure they had not taken anything they were not supposed to. After a night's stay, they loaded up again and flew 850 miles to Reykjavik, Iceland, experiencing another one-night layover with almost everything staying on the planes. The next morning, they flew to Goose Bay, Labrador, 1,300 miles east, for their last stop. Finally, on May 25, they flew the final leg: 850 miles to Bradley Field at Windsor Locks, Connecticut. When Ralph arrived on American soil, he had been gone eighteen months to the day.

Finally back home on May 25, 1945, he stands next to Joe Clemmens' aircraft at Bradley Field.

Ralph spent three days at Bradley Field. His barracks was next to the officers' Mess Hall, which was open all day and night. They could eat as often as they wanted, anytime they wanted, and they could have as much as they could hold. The number-one item at the top of most everyone's menu was white bread, served with butter or gravy or eaten plain.

They were all given a thirty-day pass, but first they had to turn in all their government equipment. Ralph did that on the first day and went to the Transportation Office to see about getting back to Indiana. It turned out that the boy he was talking to was from Princeton, Indiana,[9] and he was eager to help. He told Ralph there was a troop train heading west in two days, and it would be stopping in Indianapolis. Ralph got his travel orders before he left the Transportation Office, and that evening he called home with the news.

Ralph arrived at Indianapolis' Union Station on May 30 at two in the afternoon and was transported to Camp Atterbury, about 140 miles to the

Over the course of the war, Ralph, like all of the boys, grew up. Here is an interesting before and after comparison. The photo on the left is Ralph's official Army commissioning photo, taken in July, 1942. The photo on the right is another Army photo, taken in November, 1944, after his promotion to major. The youth and innocence may have vanished, but the passion remained.

south. After a short delay, he was granted his thirty-day pass and told to report to central processing at Sioux Falls, South Dakota, by July 7. Ralph took a bus to Evansville and was greeted by the entire family. He had not seen his mother or father for over two years, and he was very glad to be home.

★ ★ ★

When he left Hardwick, Ralph had flown thirty-one combat missions and many other sorties. He always said that he was just doing his job, and the most important thing was that he was responsible for the lives of the men in his crew. With all of his other accomplishments, he is most proud of the fact that none of his crew was ever injured or killed in combat.

★ ★ ★

There were almost 350,000 men that served with the 8th Air Force during World War II. Each of them has a story. Most will never be told. This was just one account, but similar to all the others, it is a story about a boy from the heartland of America, who had a dream to fly and went to war carrying his most important belongings in a sturdy cardboard box tied together with fishing line.

★ ★ ★

NOTES

1. Last line of Professor Horatio Smith, played by Leslie Howard, addressing his captor, General von Graum, on the upcoming invasion of Poland (*Pimpernel Smith*, British National Films, 1941).

2. There is some confusion about the name. In Ralph's papers there are two different names attributed to the same aircraft. *Black Beauty* is used more than the other, *Black Mariah*.

3. Holland faced the same shortages when the Germans pulled out. This time the British took the lead on April 29, 1945, with *Operation Manna*, dropping food in four preapproved drop zones. By the end of the first day, 239 Lancaster bombers dropped over 500 tons of food. The operation continued for ten days, delivering 7,000 tons of food. The 8th Air Force joined in, with *Operation Chowhound* delivering over 4,000 tons of food and supplies.

4. Written on 329th Bomb Squadron stationery.

5. I. G. Farbenindustrie AG was a chemical company formed in 1925 from a number of major companies that had been closely working together since World War I. At its peak, I. G. Farben was the fourth-largest company in the world, behind General Motors, US Steel, and Standard Oil. During the planning of the invasion of Czechoslovakia and Poland, I. G. Farben worked closely with Nazi officials and directed which chemical plants should be secured and delivered to I. G. Farben. After the war, due to war crimes they committed, I. G. Farben was broken up in to a number of smaller companies. Of the original founding companies, only BASF, Agfa, and Bayer still exist.

6. Only three or four of the records broke in transit.

7. The airfield was not completely vacated and returned to the RAF until June 12, 1945.

8. This was the most number of missions (396) flown by any bomb group in the 8th Air Force. They lost one hundred aircraft during the war. By contrast, the 445th Bomb Group at Tibenham flew only 282 missions and lost ninety-five aircraft.

9. Princeton is about thirty miles north of Wadesville.

Chapter 11

FRIENDS AND FAMILY

"In three words I can sum up everything I've learned about life: it goes on."[1]

At the height of the war, boys and girls of all ages would play hooky from school to watch the American bombers take off and form up in the skies over England. With so many planes, the air would vibrate, causing some to cover their ears. In the afternoon, the children would line the fences or get as close as they could to the airfields to watch the bombers return—many trailing smoke, with damage clearly visible, and some shooting off flares to signify they had wounded aboard or were running low on fuel. Those were given first priority to land. The schoolchildren would watch in complete silence, holding their breath for each landing.

For the war effort, there were 18,482 B-24 Liberators manufactured by five different companies. At the end of the war, some of these aircraft were sold, given, or leased to other countries, but most returned to the United States. Considered obsolete, these aircraft were placed in "mothballs" and parked in the southwest desert to await their final demise. Some of these aircraft were sold to collectors and museums. Some were sold to flight service operators and became transport and fire-fighting planes. Almost all of the others were chopped up and sold for scrap metal.

Today there are less than twenty remaining in the world. Museums in six different countries have twelve on display. Three others are airworthy and make special appearances at various air shows in the United States, Canada, and the United Kingdom. Two others are being restored.

★ ★ ★

Station 124, RAF Tibenham, home to the 445th Bomb Group, was vacated by the United States in May 1945. It was turned back over to the British Air Ministry in July. Having no use for the facility, it was closed in 1959 and later sold around 1964. All three original runways still exist, but the perimeter taxiway and hardstands have been removed.

Today the facility is home to the Norfolk Gliding Club. Originally, the organization utilized the old control tower for their clubhouse; however, the building was rumored to be haunted, and several members refused to enter. In 1975, a new clubhouse was built, and four years later the control tower was torn down.

★ ★ ★

Station 104, RAF Hardwick, was home to the 93rd Bomb Group until the unit returned to the United States in May 1945. The following month, the airfield was returned to the British Air Ministry. Having no use for the facility, it was closed in 1962 and subsequently sold. For several years in the 1970s, the field was used by an aerial agricultural spraying business.

Today there is practically nothing left. All of the major buildings, runways, perimeter taxiway, and hardstands have been removed and the ground returned to farmland. Some smaller buildings, mostly to the east, are still in existence and used by a local farmer. Some of the Nissen hut concrete pads and connecting walkways can still be found, and there is a privately owned museum occupying one of the old Nissen huts.

★ ★ ★

Before Ralph left for the United States, one of his last stops was to visit the farmer next door and retrieve his laundry. Ralph took him a bottle of Kentucky bourbon, shared a taste with him, and picked up his laundry. He knew that the farmer's wife was expecting a child, and he congratulated her.

When he returned home he asked his sister, Marcia, to help him put together a baby box to send over. They filled a box with clothes and toys and took it to the post office. A few weeks later, the box was returned with a note that said they could not accept it because the duty[2] was more than

While Ralph was on leave in the late spring of 1943, family and friends gathered at Marcia and Herb's house in Evansville for a visit. Pictured are (left to right) Juana, Marcia, Stella Beeler, Rolla, Jessie, Add Beeler, and Margaret Rose Becker (a high school friend Ralph dated from time to time).

the value of the items in the box. Ralph wrote back how sorry he was and wished them well.

★ ★ ★

Upon Ralph's return to Wadesville, he visited with Add Beeler, his long-time friend and mentor. Add was in poor health and died on September 19, 1945, at the age of seventy-nine. His wife, Stella, stayed in the area. She passed away in 1956 at the age of eighty-six.

★ ★ ★

After Lewis Parker died in 1944, L. A. Parker and Company was run by his son, Lewis, Jr. Over the years, more emphasis was placed on warehousing than on selling coffee or distributing groceries. Lewis Parker, Jr. died in 1979. The warehousing part of the business continued operations until 1993, under the name Terminal Warehouse Company.

★ ★ ★

In 1941, the Army contracted with the Raymond-Richardson Aviation School to provide primary ground and flight training for the 63rd Army Air Force Flight Training Detachment located in Douglas, Georgia. The school asked Paul Schlundt, the man who gave Ralph flying lessons, to be a flight instructor and squadron commander. His vast experience as a pilot and flight instructor helped to establish Douglas as one of the most efficient and safest flight schools in the program. Over nine thousand cadets who learned to fly at Douglas went on to fly every type of aircraft in every theatre of operations with the United States Army Air Force. While in Douglas, Paul met and married Tannie Hancock of Alma, Georgia. They had one son, Wayne. When the war ended, the school was closed, and the Schlundts moved to Indiana where Paul resumed his flying career. He served as pilot for Roscoe Turner of Nichols Construction Company, and eventually, he retired as chief pilot of Huber, Hunt, and Nichols Construction (now Hunt Construction Group). Paul died in Indianapolis in 1999, at the age of ninety.

★ ★ ★

Ralph was not the only boy from southern Indiana who had a dream to fly. During the first refresher course, Ralph met Carl Beggs from Princeton, Indiana. Carl lived at home and worked as a clerk at the Princeton Rexall Drug Store. The two boys became fast friends and began corresponding with each other. Carl passed the first examination and entered the Air Corps in September 1941. He trained to be a fighter pilot in Florida, South Carolina, and Alabama. Upon graduation he was assigned to the 33rd Fighter Group of the 12th Air Force, flying the P-40 Warhawk. He completed his required seventy missions during the Allied campaign in North Africa prior to the invasion of Sicily. He was then reassigned as a gunnery instructor, flying the P-47 Thunderbolt at Millville Army Airfield in New Jersey. While there, he won the Thunderbolt Gunnery Contest. When the war ended, the trophy was retired while it was in his possession. After the war, he graduated from Harvard College and resumed working for Rexall before starting a chain of coin-operated laundries in the Boston area. Carl died in 1983, at the age of sixty-two. The Thunderbolt Gunnery Contest trophy was donated to the Millville Army Airfield Museum by his family.

★ ★ ★

After the war, Rolla and Jessie continued working the farm near Wadesville. In the summer of 1946, they finally got electricity and were able to put an electric pump on the well off the summer porch. This allowed them to at least have cold running water in the kitchen, but they still utilized the outhouse and the wood-burning stove. They also added lights to the main floor, but the second floor was still lit by lantern, which was fine with them because it was rarely used.

Sometime around 1952, the crank telephone mounted on the wall in the dining room was replaced with a "modern" telephone with a handset and a cradle. The new telephone was located in the living room. It did not have a dial as they were still on a party line controlled by the local operator. Around this same time, they traded in their wood-burning stove for a propane gas variety.

On August 14, 1958, Rolla and Jessie sold the farm and moved to a small home in nearby Poseyville. Rolla never bought a tractor and worked the farm with a horse team up to the day the farm sold. Ironically, the backyard of their new home opened up to the local farm implement dealer's sales lot, where he could see the new tractors coming and going.

In 1965, Rolla developed dementia. Jessie, who had her own health problems, could not take care of him, so he was placed in a nursing home in nearby Mount Vernon. Later, he was moved to a home that was closer, located in Cynthiana. He died on September 16, 1968.

Jessie lived alone until her failing health made that impractical. She first moved in with Herb and Marcia, but as her health declined, she was placed in a nursing home where she died on November 19, 1971.

When the war ended, she removed the "sweetheart wings" that Ralph had given her and put them back in the original box. After she died, the box was given to Ralph along with the letters.

★ ★ ★

Juana, Ralph's oldest sister, was teaching school in Richmond, Indiana, when the war ended. After she ended her engagement with Punch, they drifted apart. Punch continued to live in Posey County, becoming a model citizen. In 1980, the Posey County Council on Aging honored him as the "Most Outstanding Senior Citizen" in the county, noting his lifelong contributions and the past year's involvement in county activities. He died in June 1982, at the age of ninety.

At the end of the war, Juana bought a new Chevrolet and got $800 as trade-in value on the car she bought from Ralph for $400.

She continued to work in the Richmond School District as a teacher and administrator. She retired in 1968 and moved back to Poseyville, into her parents' home.

She never married but had several serious "boyfriends." One in particular of whom she was very fond had entered the US Foreign Service and was killed in South America.

Juana was the primary influence in making sure that Ralph's letters were saved. Not only did she make sure the letters lent out to friends were returned to Jessie, but she also had her own collection. When Jessie died, Juana made sure the letters were kept in a safe place until she could give them to Ralph.

In 1984, Juana was diagnosed with advanced breast cancer. She died on July 7, 1985.

★ ★ ★

Marcia and Herb eventually moved to the west side of Evansville. Herb continued to work in the oil business, distributing and delivering heating oil and other bulk products.

Marcia was a very good cook, but she did not want anyone in her kitchen asking her questions. She was also a very private person, and it was sometimes difficult for outsiders to befriend her. Although Ralph says in his letters that he wrote separately to Marcia, none of those letters exist today. It is entirely possible that she did not pass them on to friends and relatives beyond showing them in person and taking the letter back. These letters are probably the only ones missing from the collection.

Shortly after Juana's cancer diagnosis, Marcia visited her own doctor and was diagnosed with breast cancer as well. She died on December 28, 1985, about five months after Juana.

In retirement, Herb continued to live in their home on the west side of Evansville. He kept busy with church and friends until his death on April 20, 1999.

Sandra,[3] Ralph's niece and Marcia's daughter, went on to graduate from Indiana University. After graduation, she became a schoolteacher in the Evansville Vanderburgh School Corporation. One of her first assignments was cutting edge for its time. "Miss Sandy" helped write and taught on the educational television program *Ride the Reading Rocket*. The program was distributed throughout Indiana and made available to other television stations across the country. She continued as a teacher and administrator until she retired in 2005. She still lives in the Evansville area.

★ ★ ★

Captain William Hartness, who sent a very nice letter to Jessie and Rolla, stayed in the Army. He was stationed at Kirtland Field near Albuquerque immediately after the war. He eventually attained the rank of lieutenant colonel before he retired.

During the course of his career, he became a noted authority on counterinsurgency and published many papers on the subject. He became Chief of the Counterinsurgency Committee at the US Army Intelligence School at Fort Holabird, Maryland. In 1963, he was honored by the Central Intelligence Agency for his research in counterinsurgency. He later became a consultant to the US Army Combat Developments Command Special Warfare Agency at Fort Bragg, North Carolina.

He passed away in September 1993, at the age of seventy-three. He is buried at Arlington National Cemetery.

★ ★ ★

When the war ended, Jimmy Stewart resumed his acting career in Hollywood. He remained active in the Army reserves and later in the Air Force reserves. He was a strong advocate for the Air Force and often used his stature and notoriety in Hollywood to lobby for stronger air power. In 1955, he starred in the movie *Strategic Air Command*, a film aimed at promoting the US Air Force. In 1959, he was promoted to brigadier general.

Over the years, he and Ralph maintained a strong professional friendship. They would spend time together whenever their paths crossed, usually at formal Air Force events and annual reunions.

Stewart died in 1997 after making ninety-two films. He received five Academy Award nominations for best actor and won one for his performance in the *Philadelphia Story.*[4] While he had many memorable roles, he will always be best known for his role in the timeless classic *It's a Wonderful Life.*[5]

★ ★ ★

General Edward Timberlake had a storied and much-traveled career in the US Air Force. He served in the Far East Air Force at Tokyo and Korea, and the US Air Force in Europe at Wiesbaden, Germany. In 1962, he became commander of the US Continental Air Command. Three years later, in 1965, he retired. He died in 1990. Ralph and Ted's paths never crossed again.

★ ★ ★

Ralph reported to central processing at Sioux Falls, South Dakota, on July 7, 1945. The Army had devised a point system to determine who they had to keep and who was eligible to be released. Ralph found that he could get out in December, but instead, he reenlisted for another year.

The placement office maintained a list of openings across the United States. They posted the openings on a large bulletin board for everyone to see. If a person was interested in a posted job, he would jot down the posting number, get in line, and talk to a desk clerk to obtain the details. If the job was still open, the person could submit his name and wait for evaluation. There were almost 30,000 airmen waiting to be reassigned, so this was a tedious process.

After weeks of waiting, Ralph finally saw a posting for a training operations officer for Kirtland Air Force Base near Albuquerque, New Mexico. He remembered how much he liked the southwest when he was stationed at Roswell, in spite of the neighbors and the heat. He was not sure what a training operations officer did, but he had been a squadron operations officer and figured the position was similar. He ripped the posting off the board and walked over to the first available clerk. Handing him the paper, he said, "I want that job."

The clerk made a couple of calls and told Ralph he was exactly the type of person needed. After he got his travel orders, he headed for Albuquerque.

Upon his arrival, he was told that his job would be twofold. First, Ralph would be responsible for all flight operations for the entire airfield. Second, Ralph would become the pilot for a group of scientists located at a place called Los Alamos about fifty-five miles away. His primary contact would be a chap named Robert Oppenheimer.[6] Ralph had never heard of the place or the name, but that did not bother him.

Just after he got settled in, he called his old fiancée, Gloria Fulcher, to see how she was doing. He talked to her mother and learned that Gloria had married and moved away from the area. A day or so later, he ran across

Captain William Hartness, who was stationed there. During the war, Hartness' wife, Maxine,[7] had moved to Albuquerque to work in a government job. She and another girl had moved in with another woman who owned a home in town. Hartness told Ralph that if he ever got to Albuquerque, there was someone he should meet. Now that they were both stationed there, Hartness set up a double date.

The woman Ralph met was Norma Bowman,[8] originally from Rector, Arkansas. Her husband had died before the war and had left her a small home at 436 North Maple Street in Albuquerque. She was known as the quintessential party hostess—normally hosting a party at her house, with the help of her two roommates, almost every weekend. Ralph and Norma developed a fast relationship, and on January 15, 1946, they were married.

At first, Ralph thought he would be doing a lot of flying, but Kirtland was undergoing a series of changes that would eventually reduce the need for flight operations. The last B-24s stationed at Kirtland were relocated in October 1945 as other bomb groups prepared to switch over to new aircraft like the Boeing B-29 Superfortress and the Consolidated B-36 Peacemaker.

Around this time, about 2,200 aircraft of all sorts were shuttled to Kirtland pending their sale. Included in these aircraft were many of the planes from the 93rd Bomb Group. A photo journalist from *Life* magazine came to the airfield to take pictures and asked Ralph to pose with some the 93rd's aircraft that he had piloted.

Lastly, the school portion of the airfield was transforming from flight training to ground school training and then to no training at all. Finally, with no aircraft left, the airfield was placed on the inactive list on December 31, 1945.

At this point, Ralph's flying was limited to taking the scientists, including Oppenheimer, anywhere they wanted to go. He developed an unusual friendship with Oppenheimer and some of the others because none of them had ever been on a bomber, let alone on one that was actually dropping bombs. They were all curious about how the plane handled and the differences in flying with a full load versus no load. Wherever he took them there was always another group of scientists waiting to grill him.

In February 1946, the base was reopened, and a resurgence of activity began just as the scientists' notoriety was wearing off. Ralph found himself back in flight operations but not flying very much at all. As time went on, he longed for the days of getting in a plane taking off. Instead, he had a job that required him to be in the office almost all of the time. This was not what he wanted to do for the rest of his life; he was bored. He mapped out a plan, which he posed to Norma, and in October 1946, he got out of the Army. In another odd twist of fate, the man who signed Ralph's discharge papers was Colonel Perry M. Hoisington III, the same man who, as a 1st Lieutenant, greeted Ralph when he first arrived at King City in 1942.

They decided to sell Norma's house and move to Portland, Oregon. Ralph had friends there who told him that the area had the best weather, lots of opportunity, and a strong German community. That was everything Ralph was looking for; they packed the car and headed out.

Along the way, they stopped to visit some of Ralph's friends. Their first stop was in San Diego, and then they continued north to Los Angeles. Ralph had many acquaintances in Los Angeles, including Jimmy Stewart, so there were numerous parties to attend. One night, Norma complained to their hostess that she had not been feeling well. She was obviously pregnant, and the hostess suggested that she see a doctor as soon as possible. The next day the lady took Norma to see her doctor, who told Norma that she was having complications and should not travel any further.

Ralph was disappointed but decided that the Los Angeles area could be a great place to live. They bought a house at 825 Lacy Street in Santa Ana, and Ralph began looking for work. Ever since his days at L. A. Parker and Company, Ralph had dreamed of owning his own business. While looking for a job, he ran across an advertisement for a dry cleaning business in Santa Monica that was for sale. He made an inquiry, and a few days later he bought the business.

On March 1, 1947, with many complications, Norma gave birth to a baby boy, and that was when reality set in. Norma was a party girl and knew nothing about cooking, housekeeping, or raising a child. Worse yet, Ralph was no better; however, with the help of friends, neighbors, and employees, they survived.

By September, everything seemed to be going smoothly. The business was turning a handsome profit, Norma was finally in good health, and their baby was growing like a weed. Ralph had taken a Monday off for a long weekend in San Diego. They were returning when they noticed a telegram message on the front door. The message said that Western Union had tried to deliver a telegram, and since no one was home, they would be back on Tuesday.

They both panicked. Ralph tried calling home to Wadesville but could not get a circuit. Norma tried to call with the same result. They spent a sleepless night thinking of all the possibilities. The next morning, Western Union delivered the telegram, which read: "Proceed September twenty nine Stewart Field Newburg New York report commanding officer two naught naught two Air Force Base unit. TPA[9] not authorized. Appointment letter and orders to follow."

Ralph read the telegram again and again. Then he looked at the calendar. It was September 16. He had less than two weeks to wrap up his affairs, travel nearly 2,500 miles, and report to the base commander at Stewart Field, New York. And he had to do it all alone, without any assistance from the Army.

That evening he and Norma discussed their options. Both of them knew that it would not be a good idea for him to report alone and leave her in California to tend to all the business and take care of a baby at the same time. They would have to make the trip together.

The next day, he gathered his employees together and told them he had been recalled to active duty and would be selling the business. That afternoon, they put their house on the market. Miraculously, everything happened quickly.

The following day, Ralph's most trusted employee approached him to say that she and her husband wanted to buy the business. They had wanted to buy it before, but they did not have the money. They still did not have the money, and they wondered if Ralph would take an IOU. They agreed to some terms, and the business was sold.

Two days later, a couple came to look at the house. They had gotten married before he went in the Army. Now he was out, and they needed someplace to live. They liked what they saw and made an offer.[10] Only five days had passed since receipt of the telegram, and all Ralph and Norma needed to do was load the car and leave.

They drove east and made a pass through Rector, Arkansas, to visit Norma's mother, staying one night. Then they headed north to Wadesville and stayed two nights on the farm. Norma had never been on a farm before, and she was scared of the chickens that guarded the outhouse. And she never got use to the idea that someone had to pump the water. It simply was not her style, but she put up with it while everyone else got a good laugh.

Stewart Field was about sixteen miles from the US Military Academy at West Point. The primary responsibility was to provide flight training to any cadets who wanted to learn. Upon reporting to the commander, Ralph was told to get settled in and make arrangements to meet the superintendent of West Point, Major General Bryant E. Moore.

No one expected Ralph to show up with a wife and baby, so they had to make do with temporary quarters until something more suitable could be arranged. First, they stayed in a hotel in Newburgh, New York, for a couple of days, and then moved into a converted Bachelor Officers' Quarters (BOQ) at Stewart Field. The converted BOQ was great for Ralph. It was close to work and across the street from the Officers' Club, but it was not a good environment for a family. After a short stay there, they moved into a small house at West Point. Just as Norma became comfortable, the young family moved again, this time into a house that was nearly 150 years old, called the Shoemaker's House, located on Silver Springs Road just south of Stewart Field.

When Ralph met Major General Moore, he was told that he had two responsibilities. First was to provide flight training to any cadet that was enrolled in the flight training program. Second, when not doing training, he was to be available to fly faculty and staff anywhere they needed to go, and that included shuttling dignitaries to and from West Point. He went on to say that he did not expect very many cadets to sign up for flight training because there was not the demand that had existed prior to the war. On the way back to Stewart Field, Ralph knew his career of flying for the Army had just been jump-started.

As for the duties, Major General Moore was right—very few Cadets reported for flight training. But when they did, Ralph and his copilot gave them their money's worth as they received first-class treatment. When they were not training, they did a little traveling, taking faculty and staff to and from meetings and occasionally picking up a congressman for a ride to The Point.[11] One highlight of this duty was that they also provided the football coach transportation whenever he wanted to go on a recruiting trip. The coach was Earl H. "Red" Blaik, perhaps the most famous coach at West Point.[12]

Ralph spent only eighteen months at Stewart Field before he was transferred to Hunter Air Force Base near Savannah, Georgia. While he was there, the couple had another son, and Ralph was assigned to several temporary duty (TDY) tours to England before being sent to Okinawa to fly combat missions over Korea. When he came back, he was transferred to Second Air Force Headquarters at Barksdale Air Force Base outside of Shreveport, Louisiana. Three years later, he was transferred to Little Rock Air Force Base, and then to Inçirlik Air Base in Turkey. His return to the United States put him at Wright-Patterson Air Force Base near Dayton, Ohio. After an extended stay there, he was sent to Vietnam as material advisor to the Vietnam Air Force (VNAF).

Upon his return, he was offered a prestigious spot in the Pentagon. But Ralph had had enough. No longer flying combat missions and having to constantly master one new computer system after another had taken its toll on him. His oldest son had grown up without him, and his youngest son needed more of his attention. He was ready to get out of the Air Force and resume pursuing the dream of owning his own business. He and Norma settled in North Little Rock, Arkansas.

Before leaving Vietnam in January 1971, Ralph was honored by the Vietnamese Air Force for his service, dedication, and loyalty. This official Air Force photograph was taken at a military review in his honor. Here, Ralph is congratulated by General Tran Van Minh, who had just presented Ralph with two medals. General Minh was the last commander of the Vietnamese Air Force.

Over the next several years, Ralph embarked on a business start-up binge. He first opened Ralph's Reliable Tax Service, which was a huge success. Reinforced by that, he partnered with two friends and opened several mini-storages around the area, followed by a chain of self-serve car washes and another chain of coin-operated gas stations. He also dabbled in real estate and land development. He owned a liquor store and interest in a franchise restaurant, both located outside the main gate to Little Rock Air Force Base. Everything he touched turned to gold, and he was on a roll.

Unfortunately, while his business ventures succeeded, Norma's health began to decline. In 1989, he decided that it was time to fully retire and spend the rest of his time traveling the world with Norma. They sold their house and moved to the Air Force Village at San Antonio, Texas. They did quite a bit of traveling, including some cruises and trips across the United States, but Norma's health continued to worsen, and she died on October 25, 1999.

Ralph stayed in their small duplex, living alone until the summer of 2010, when he asked his oldest son to help him move into an apartment in the adjacent high-rise tower. It was through this move that these letters were discovered.

★ ★ ★

"Life is what we make of it."[13]

★ ★ ★

NOTES

1. Robert Frost.
2. After the war, England imposed a tax on goods coming in from other countries as a way of supporting their own industries.
3. As she grew up, she preferred to be called Sandra, rather than Sandra Jane.
4. Metro-Goldwyn-Mayer (MGM), 1940.
5. Liberty Films (II), 1946.
6. Robert Oppenheimer (1904–1967) is credited as the father of the atomic bomb. He was lead scientist for the Manhattan Project, which developed and built the two atomic bombs dropped on Japan on August 6 and August 9, 1945. When Ralph reported to Kirtland, these two events had not yet occurred.

7. Bob and Maxine got married after the war.

8. Born Norma Beatrice Purcell.

9. Transient Personnel Assistance would have included assistance in moving household goods and transportation.

10. After the war, there was an acute housing shortage caused by the huge number of veterans looking for housing. It was not unusual for veterans to quickly purchase the first house they visited.

11. West Point is affectionately known as "The Point."

12. Earl Blaik (1897–1989) was head coach at West Point for seventeen years. During that time, he coached three Heisman trophy winners and eleven Hall of Fame players. Twenty of his former assistant coaches became head coaches in college and in professional football. Among them was Vince Lombardi, who coached the Green Bay Packers to five NFL titles and won the first two Super Bowls. Lombardi was an assistant coach at West Point for part of the time Ralph was stationed at Stewart Field.

13. Motto of the 1937 Wadesville High School graduating class.

APPENDICES

Appendix A

★ ★ ★

Ground Crew Baby[1,2]

There's something akin to a human bond,
As men watch a ship take off in the dawn.
It's a love you'd never understand;
What a Flying Fort can mean to a man.

To them, you see, she's a rhapsody,
A powerful thunderous symphony
Of craft and speed and sweat and skill,
An aery creation of human will;
A thousand years of kings and courts
And the minds of men in a Flying Fort.

Her voice is her bombs and spattering guns
Her heritage, victories up by the sun,
Her spirit, American, pioneering anew,
Her mission, destruction, her soul is the crew.

That's why, to the ground crew, she's something more
Than "just a Fort" as they watch her soar
Away toward a fighter-and-flak-filled hell,
That pilots and gunners know so well.

It's personal pride when they hear what she did
Like a father's, whose son licks the neighbor's kid,
She's a Dempsey, a Gerhig, a champ of champs,
She's pennies the kids put in war saving stamps.

She fights her load through and comes back for more.
Take a look at her side, at her bombing score.
To the ground crew guys they mean battle scars,
Campaign ribbons pinned there by Mars.
When she battles home from a long, tough ride,
With a shell-torn wing, or a hole in her side.

You can understand the reason why
There's pride in the heart of a ground crew guy.
They're proud of the way she out-rode the flak,
Out-gunned and out distanced a fighter pack.

Like the mother whose ever-loving son
Played in the ball game and knocked a home run
And her voice, the bombs and the cannons too,
The pilot, the gunners, the whole damn crew
Know that ground crews are guys that cook,
And there's more to a "Fort" than you read in a book.

- Cpl. Ellsworth B. Lawrence

★ ★ ★

Appendix B

★ ★ ★

A Toast to "Little Friends"[3, 4]

If ever I mount up to heaven
And enter those high "pearly gates,"
My first word of thanks
To the Lord from us "Yanks"
Will be for the P-38s.

High in the blue, like angels,
Winging their way to the aid
Of the bombers that soar,
And lessen the price to be paid.

In the very next sentence I utter
Before I have scarcely begun
With awe in my voice
I shall humbly rejoice
For the gift of the P51.

Ask the lad who goes up in a Fortress;
If he must he will swap off his gun,
For a dear "little friend,"
To protect him no end
He will trade for a P51.

Though now I should be rather breathless
As I give out thanks up in heaven,
'Tis a fool I would be
If I didn't agree
To give thanks for the P47.

Up where the con trails linger,
Five miles up and more,
He's a demon from hell
The "Huns" know well
And a sight the "Forts" adore.

Say, here's to our fighters;
A toast to their crews of one.
And a word of thanks
From a crew of "Yanks"
Who make the bomber run.

- Clement L. Lockwood

★ ★ ★

Appendix C

★ ★ ★

The chronology presented below describes Ralph's major events and travels from December 7, 1941 to June 1, 1945. This timeline is presented to help the reader navigate through the events.

1941

December 7	Evansville, Indiana
December 12	The Schneck farmstead near Wadesville, Indiana
December 13	Fort Benjamin Harrison, Indianapolis, Indiana
December 19	King City Army Airfield, King City, California. Traveled by train through St. Louis, Kansas City, Denver, Ogden, Reno, and San Francisco.

1942

January 8	Soloed after only six hours and forty minutes of instruction while at King City Army Airfield.
March 1	Lemoore Army Air Field,[5] Lemoore, California
April 25	Stockton Army Airfield, Stockton, California
June 23	Graduated from flight school with the commission of 2nd Lieutenant
June 26	Mather Field, Sacramento, California
July 30	Roswell Army Air Field, Roswell, New Mexico. Traveled by car from Mather Field through Los Angeles to Phoenix, then by bus to Roswell, passing through El Paso.

1943

February 2	Promoted to 1st Lieutenant while at Roswell Army Air Field
April 17	Hobbs Army Air Field, Hobbs, New Mexico
June 4	Gowen Field, Boise, Idaho
July 8	Pocatello Army Airfield, Pocatello, Idaho
July 22	Sioux City Army Air Base, Sioux City, Iowa
Mid-September	Watertown Army Air Base, Watertown, South Dakota
November 7	Lincoln Army Airfield, Lincoln, Nebraska
November 20	Morrison Army Airfield, Palm Beach, Florida
November 24	Mercedita Airport, San Juan, Puerto Rico
November 26	Atkinson Field, Georgetown, British Guiana
November 29	Val de Cans Airport, Belém, Brazil
December 10	Dakar Airport, Dakar, Senegal, via Parnamirim Airport, Natal, Brazil
December 13	Marrakech-Menara Airport, Marrakech, Morocco
December 20	RAF Lands End, St. Just, Cornwall, England
December 21	RAF Tibenham, Station 124, Norfolk, England
December 31	Flew first mission over Europe

1944

January 31	Promoted to Captain while at RAF Tibenham
February 18	RAF Hardwick, Station 104, Norfolk, England

June 6	D-Day (also called the "Big Show"), flew one mission
June 20	Completed thirty combat missions
June 24	Became Operations Officer for the 329th Bomb Squadron
November 16	Promoted to Major while at RAF Hardwick

1945

April 2	Promoted to Commanding Officer of the 329th Bomb Squadron
April 15	Completed his thirty-first combat mission over the French Atlantic coast
May 12	Flew *Libs Tour* over Germany
May 23	RAF Valley, Anglesey, Wales
May 24	Refueled at Reykjavik Airport, Reykjavik, Iceland, then flew to Goose Air Base, Goose Bay, Labrador
May 25	Bradley Airfield, Windsor Locks, Connecticut
May 30	Camp Atterbury, Edinburgh, Indiana
June 1	The Schneck farmstead near Wadesville, Indiana

★ ★ ★

NOTES

1. This poem was included in Ralph's letter dated February 5, 1944.
2. Used with permission from *Stars and Stripes*. © 1944, 2011 *Stars and Stripes*.
3. This poem was included in Ralph's letter dated March 28, 1944.
4. Used with permission from *Stars and Stripes*. © 1944, 2011 *Stars and Stripes*.
5. At this point the US Army had not yet standardized the spelling of "airfield," so it appears as both one word and two words.

REFERENCES AND RESOURCES

No book depicting historical events could ever be written without the sincere help of a few very fine people. *Cheerio and Best Wishes: Letters from a World War II Hoosier Pilot* is no exception. While there is always a risk of forgetting someone, it is important to recognize those who took the time to remember the past and help preserve it for the future. I owe them a sincere debt of gratitude.

Betty Alexander, Posey County, Indiana
Sandra Altheide, Evansville, Indiana
Jack Beggs, Novi, Michigan

Brad Hall, Phoenix, Arizona
Jack Hayes, King City, California
Ralph H. Schneck, San Antonio, Texas
Kenneth Frank Yaxley, Norwich, Norfolk, England

★ ★ ★

World War II is perhaps the most documented and studied event in modern times. I wish there was one single source for all of the background information presented here, but that is not the case. For as much information that is available, there are still discrepancies from one source to the other. As a result, it was necessary to cross-check referenced material with additional sources. The following is a list of sources that were invaluable during research and preparation.

★ ★ ★

BOOKS AND OTHER PUBLICATIONS

Actual Shadow, The. A3 Section, 2nd Bombardment Division, 8th Air Force, n.d., ca. 1944.

Army Air Forces West Coast Training Center. *Aviation Cadet Regulations (2132-Santa Ana-5-6-43).* Santa Ana, CA: Santa Ana Army Air Base, 1943.

Banger, Joan. *Norwich at War.* Cromer, Norfolk: Poppyland Publishing, 2002.

Baylis, Charles D., Capt., USMC (Ret.), ed. *Roswell Army Flying School Yearbook.* Baton Rouge, LA: Army and Navy Publishing Co., Inc., 1942.

Class 43B. *Passing Light*, Lemoore, CA: Lemoore Army Flying School, ca. 1943.

Eisenhower Communiqués, The, Harold B. Lee Library, Brigham Young University, Provo, UT. http://www.lib.byu.edu/digital/eisenhower/

Freeman, Roger A. *The Mighty Eighth War Manual.* London: Cassell & Company, 2002.

Mesa Del Rey. *Army Pilots in the Making.* King City, CA: Palo Alto Airport, Inc., n.d., ca. 1942.

US Army. *Aviation Cadet Training for the Army Air Forces (LX-110-RPB-6-3-43)*, Washington, DC: US Army, 1943.

US Army Center of Military History. *United States Army in World War II (Green Books).* 80 vols. Washington, DC: US Army Center of Military History. 1953–.

Schneck, Ralph H. *The Flyer* (private collection), video.

Stars and Stripes, Washington, DC.

The WWII Flight Training Museum. *The Cadet Flyer: The Official Newsletter of the 63rd Preservation Society and the WWII Flight Training Museum*, Spring 2008.

★ ★ ★

CHAMBERS OF COMMERCE

Greater Stockton Chamber of Commerce, Stockton, California; http://www.stocktonchamber.org

King City Chamber of Commerce, King City, California; http://www.kingcitychamber.com

Lemoore Chamber of Commerce, Lemoore, California; http://www.lemoorechamberofcommerce.com

Roswell Chamber of Commerce, Roswell, New Mexico; http://www.roswellnm.org

★ ★ ★

LIBRARIES

King City Branch, Monterey County Library, King City, California; http://www.co.monterey.ca.us/library

Monterey County Library, Marina, California; http://www.co.monterey.ca.us/library

San Joaquin County Library, Stockton, California; http://www.stockton.lib.ca.us

Second Air Division Memorial Library, Norwich, Norfolk, England; http://www.2ndair.org.uk

★ ★ ★

HISTORICAL SOCIETIES AND ASSOCIATIONS

Ames Historical Society, Ames, Iowa; http://www.ameshistoricalsociety.org

Army Air Forces Historical Association, Oradell, New Jersey; http://www.aafha.org

Eighth Air Force Historical Society, Pooler, Georgia; http://www.8thafhs.org

The Heritage League of the 2nd Air Division of WWII, Pacifica, California; http://www.heritageleague.org

Historical Society for Southeast New Mexico, Roswell, New Mexico; http://www.hssnm.net

Independence Hall Association, Philadelphia, Pennsylvania; http://www.ushistory.org

The Wartime Memories Project, Stockton on Tees, England; http://www.wartimememories.co.uk

★ ★ ★

MUSEUMS

The California State Military Museum, Sacramento, California; http://www.militarymuseum.org

The Mighty Eighth Air Force Museum, Pooler, Georgia; http://www.mightyeighth.org

Monterey County Agricultural & Rural Life Museum, King City, California; http://www.mcarlm.org

National Museum of the US Air Force, Wright-Patterson Air Force Base, Dayton, Ohio; http://www.nationalmuseum.af.mil

Stockton Field Aviation Museum, Stockton, California; http://www.twinbeech.com/stockton_field_page.htm http://www

Walker Aviation Museum, Roswell, New Mexico; http://www.wafbmuseum.org

★ ★ ★

GOVERNMENT ORGANIZATIONS

British Royal Air Force Historical Society, Wotton-under-Edge, England; http://www.raf.mod.uk

National Archives, Washington, DC; http://www.archives.gov

US Air Force Historical Research Agency, Maxwell Air Force Base, Montgomery, Alabama; http://www.afhra.af.mil

US Army Center of Military History, Fort McNair, Washington, DC; http://www.history.army.mil

US Army Corps of Engineers—Formerly Used Defense Sites (FUDS) Program, Sacramento District, Sacramento, California; http://www.corpsfuds.com

★ ★ ★

INTERNET WEBSITES

"American D-Day." American D-Day, last modified 2012. http://www.americandday.org.

Aragon, Mark. "U.S. Army Air Forces in World War II." *Military History Group & Antique Militaria Network*, last modified 2010. http://www.usaaf.com.

Brooks, David W. "Military Airfields in WW2" *Open and Closed Listing of Airports/Airfields*, last modified 2011. http://www.airfieldsdatabase.com/WW2/WW2.htm.

Chen, C. Peter. "The World War II Database." *Lava Development, LLC*, last modified 2012. http://www.ww2db.com.

Clancy, Patrick. "A Hypertext History of the Second World War." *HyperWar Foundation*, last modified 2011. http://www.ibiblio.org/hyperwar/.

Conrad, Tim. "Tim's 445th Bomb Group Page." *Tim Conrad's Home Page*. http://home.ptd.net/~tconrad1/b24.html.

Cotton, Mark. "HobbsHistory.com." Last modified 2012. http://www.hobbshistory.com.

Engler, Joseph. "Historic Evansville." http://www.historicevansville.com.

"Evansville, Indiana Area Obituary Search." *Browning Genealogy Database*. http:browning.evpl.org.

"EVV History." *Evansville Regional Airport*, last modified 2010. http://www.evvairport.com/About_EVV/evvhistory.html.

"Exploring the Japanese American Internment through Film and the Internet." *National Asian American Telecommunications Association*, last modified 2002. http://www.caamedia.org/jainternment.

Freeman, Paul. "Abandoned & Little-Known Airfields." Last modified 2012. http://www.members.tripod.com/airfields_freeman/.

Grüschow, Peter and Grüschow, Ulrich. "Globemaster US Military Aviation." Last modified 2010. http://www.globemaster.de.

"History of War On-line." Last modified 2006. http://www.historyofwaronline.com.

"The History Place." *The History Place™*, last modified 2012. http://www.historyplace.com.

"Official Site of the U.S. Air Force." Last modified 2012. http://www.af.mil.

Plunkett, Jonathan. "George Plunkett's Photographs of Old Norwich." *George Plunkett's Photographs of Old Norwich and Norfolk*. http://www.georgeplunkett.co.uk.

Polsson, Ken. "Chronology of World War II." Last modified 2011. http://www.ww2timeline.info.

Stowe, Michael. "Accident-Report.com: Military Aviation Incident Reports." Last modified 2012. http://www.accident-report.com

"Tibenham - A Norfolk Village." Last modified 2010. http://www.tibenham.fsnet.co.uk.

Tollan, John. "The Postal History Website." *Postalhistory.org*, last modified 2010. http://www.postalhistory.org.

Truman, Robert. "Control Towers." http://www.controltowers.co.uk.

"The United States Army Air Forces in World War II." Last modified 2006. http://www.usaaf.net.

Voisin, Mike. "Army Air Forces Collection." Last modified 2011. http://www.aafcollection.info.

"A WW2 Timeline." Worldwar-2.net, last modified 2006. http://www.worldwar-2.net.

Yaxley, Ken. "Messengers Remembered WW2 Norwich." *History of PA Charity Trust*, last modified 2009. http://www.ww2messengerboys.co.uk.

★ ★ ★

INDEX

Italicized page numbers refer to appearances in photographs. Occurrences in letter salutations or closings are not included.